Organizational Design and Research

Approaches to Organizational Design

EDITED BY JAMES D. THOMPSON

Methods of Organizational Research

EDITED BY VICTOR H. VROOM

UNIVERSITY OF PITTSBURGH PRESS

Library of Congress Catalog Card Number 70–137859
ISBN 0–8229–5222–X

Henry M. Snyder & Co., Inc., London

Manufactured in the United States of America

Approaches to Organizational Design and *Methods of Organizational Research* are products of the 1963 and 1964 Seminars in the Social Science of Organizations, sponsored by the Graduate School of Business, The University of Pittsburgh, with the support of The Ford Foundation.

Approaches to
Organizational Design

EDITED BY JAMES D. THOMPSON

VERNON E. BUCK

WILLIAM M. EVAN

RALPH M. STOGDILL

HARRY C. TRIANDIS

JAMES Q. WILSON

UNIVERSITY OF PITTSBURGH PRESS

Participants

1963 SEMINAR ON THE SOCIAL SCIENCE OF ORGANIZATIONS

THE UNIVERSITY OF PITTSBURGH

IRVING ABRAMOWITZ, Graduate School of Business, The Ohio State University

BERNARD BASS, Graduate School of Business, University of Pittsburgh

VERNON BUCK, Department of Industrial Administration, Yale University

WILLIAM EVAN, School of Industrial Management, Massachusetts Institute of Technology

FRED FIEDLER, Department of Psychology, University of Illinois

MYRON GORDON, School of Business, University of Rochester

JOHN GULLAHORN, Department of Sociology and Anthropology, Michigan State University

DEAN H. HARPER, Department of Sociology, University of Rochester

MURRAY HORWITZ, Graduate Department of Psychology, New York University

RAYMOND KATZELL, Department of Psychology, New York University

HERBERT KAUFMAN, Department of Political Science, Yale University

PAUL LAWRENCE, Graduate School of Business, Harvard University

HAROLD J. LEAVITT, Graduate School of Industrial Administration, Carnegie Institute of Technology

NATHAN MACCOBY, Department of Psychology, Stanford University

JACK MINER, School of Business, University of Oregon

DALTON McFARLAND, Department of Management, Michigan State University

ROLAND PELLEGRIN, Department of Sociology, University of Oregon

KIMBALL ROMNEY, Department of Anthropology, Stanford University

RALPH STOGDILL, Bureau of Business Research, The Ohio State University

SHELDON STRYKER, Department of Sociology, Indiana University

HARRY C. TRIANDIS, Department of Psychology, University of Illinois

JAMES D. THOMPSON, Graduate School of Business, Indiana University

ALBERT WESSEN, Department of Sociology, Washington University

THOMAS L. WHISLER, Graduate School of Business, University of Chicago

JAMES Q. WILSON, Department of Government, Harvard University

Contents

Figures

Tables

Preface

This book is a product of the second seminar in the Social Science of Organizations, held at Chatham College, Pittsburgh, in June, 1963. Like the book that followed the first seminar in 1962,[1] it is distinctly a result of the seminar, rather than a collection of papers prepared for the seminar. The papers offered here were written after the authors had spent ten days of intensive discussion with small groups of their colleagues assessing the state of the art in organization theory. In this second seminar the art being assessed was the art of *organizational design*. Right now designing organizations does indeed seem to be almost exclusively an art, and great artists are scarce. One purpose of our seminar, and of this book, is to help to move the field toward better artistry and, hopefully, toward better science.

A word on the origins and structure of these seminars on the Social Science of Organizations: They have been supported by the Ford Foundation through a grant to the University of Pittsburgh. They have taken place for a ten-day period each June in Pittsburgh. The invited participants have come from American universities. Generally two faculty members from different disciplines have come from each university. All participants were asked to prepare short papers in advance, this year on the theme of organizational design. During the seminar we spent most of our time in small groups with others of similar interests and backgrounds. One member of each of these groups was charged with the preparation—after the seminar—of one of the papers for this

---

1. Latane, Henry A.; Mechanic, David; Strauss, George; Strother, George B. (ed. H. J. Leavitt), *The Social Science of Organizations* (Englewood Cliffs: Prentice-Hall, 1963).

book. The paper is his own, mellowed and enriched by his interactions with his colleagues. Under the watchful eye of James Thompson, these five papers were edited and collated into one volume. The authors are solely responsible for its content, although the book is, in a real sense, the product of all twenty-seven participants.

All of us who worked in this seminar express our thanks to the Ford Foundation for sponsoring it, to the University of Pittsburgh for administering it, and to Chatham College for hosting it. The editor and authors of this book deserve special commendation for their efforts. All of us associated with this project are indebted to them.

HAROLD J. LEAVITT
Carnegie Institute of Technology
Pittsburgh, Pennsylvania
August, 1965

Approaches to
Organizational Design

1

Dimensions of Organization Theory

Ralph M. Stogdill

Professor of Business Organization, Bureau of Business Research, The Ohio State University. The author is deeply indebted to Bernard M. Bass, Murray Horwitz, Paul Lawrence, and Harold Leavitt for the stimulation and integrative impetus provided by their germinal and wide ranging speculations regarding organization. John Gullahorn, Raymond Katzell, Dalton McFarland, James Thompson, and Harry Triandis also made valuable contributions.

It is the purpose of this paper to examine the scope and dimensions of organization theory. This is not an exciting task compared to that of developing the structure of a theory; but it is a potentially useful undertaking. Hemphill (1956) and Rapoport (1961) have addressed themselves to the task of identifying quantifiable parameters of groups. Due to the pioneering work of Rashevsky (1951) and Rapoport (1947), the development of systems is coming to be recognized in the social sciences as a respectable scientific activity. Publications by Luce, Bush, and Galanter (1963), Willner (1962), Guetzkow (1962), Flament (1963), Crisswell, Solomon, and Suppes (1962), and Suppes and Atkinson (1960) demonstrate the range and intensity of activity concerned with the development of models of groups and organizations.

Students of organization are at present confronted with a situation in which numerous fragments of theory are presented as complete theories. It is often difficult to find any overlap between two different systems of variables. The systems developed by business organization theorists, behavior scientists, and operations researchers are likely to consist of widely different variables. Each developer is likely to insist that his system includes the variables that are really important to a theory of organization. The value systems and theoretical allegiances of different schools of thought tend to make each distrustful of the concepts and problems regarded as important by the others. It is not our purpose to referee the contest among different schools of thought. We shall be content if we can arrive at some basis for consensus regarding the variables that should be included in an adequate theory of organization. The proposed solution indicates that organization is far more complex than is assumed in many theoretical systems.

The unsatisfactory condition of organization theory is evidenced by the great variety of theories available. In Table 1 eighteen different conceptualizations of groups and organizations are listed, and this is not an exhaustive list. In some theories two or more of the different points of view are combined. But one of the frequently observed features of recent writings on group theory and organization theory is an introductory section that rejects as invalid one or another of the points of view in Table 1.

Which concepts and problems are regarded as important in the study of organization are determined in part by the view or combination of views held by the theorist, in part by the philosophical and professional

TABLE 1

BASIC PREMISES AND ORIENTATIONS IN THEORIES OF ORGANIZATION

1. Organization as a cultural product
2. Organization as an exchange agent with its environment
3. Organization as an independent agency
4. Organization as a system of structures and functions
5. Organization as a structure in action over time
6. Organization as a system of dynamic functions
7. Organization as a processing system
8. Organization as an input-output system
9. Organization as a structure of subgroups
10. Subgroups in interaction with the organization
11. Subgroups in interaction with each other
12. Groups as biological-social necessities
13. Groups as cultural products
14. Groups as independent entities
15. Groups as interaction systems
16. Groups as interaction-expectation systems
17. Groups as collections of individual members
18. Groups as summations of member characteristics

schools to which he subscribes, and in part by the individual conceptualizations he wishes to advance. The present writer does not differ from his contemporaries in these respects; but he sees something that is useful, valid, and important in each of the views outlined in Table 1. The concepts, problems, and research methods connected with each of the different theoretical orientations had their origins in a concern with realities of organization that cannot safely be ignored in the development of an adequate theory.

The structure of a theory can be stated in the form of a system of interrelated propositions (hypotheses) or in the form of a system of mathematical equations. It is not possible at present to formulate a complete theory of organization either as a system of propositions or as a system of equations; but numerous subsets of propositions and equations, well supported by research findings, are available. These subsets specify the relationships found between variables in widely different segments of organization theory. It should be noted, however, that as far as research evidence is concerned the subsets of hypotheses usually apply to limited classes of organizations and to limited ranges of variance in the variables involved in the hypotheses. A serious disadvantage resulting from the tendency to regard small subsets as complete theories is the attenuation of inquiry. Attenuation may be noted not only in the design of research, but also in the growth of theory. An associated disadvantage in regard to practice and application is the tendency to promulgate research findings with limited ranges of validity as general solutions to management problems.

A complete theory tends to stimulate systematic and exhaustive research. It would therefore seem desirable to strive for completeness in theory development. It seems likely that various subsets of hypotheses that now stand in isolation could be shown to be logically interrelated. The contemporary trend in scholarship, however, appears to be oriented toward examining such hypotheses chiefly for their implications for management practice rather than for the development of an integrated theory.

There is a need not only for synthesis but also for an examination of the scope and dimensions of organization theory as a basis for synthesis. What should be included in a complete theory of organization? An answer to this question is the concern of the present paper. The author's proposal is only one of several possible answers to the question.

An organization can be represented as a system of interrelated variables. In order to determine relationship it is necessary to isolate and define the component variables in the relationship as a basis for their independent observation and measurement. This is not an easy task, because the major conceptual dimensions of organization theory have to be defined in terms of sets of component variables. Some of the variables within a given set are certain to be interrelated. In addition, some of the variables in any one set are likely to be related in varying degrees to variables in other sets. The overlap of variables within sets and between sets complicates the problem of clearly conceptualizing and defining the variables.

The present paper is concerned not with the problem of determining relationships between variables, but with the problem of identifying major dimensions of organization. It is possible to isolate and identify several panels of concepts that have been used by theorists and researchers in the study of groups and organizations. The major concepts in these panels are listed in Figures 1 to 6. Since only three-dimensional representations can be easily accommodated by the printed page, the panels of variables will be discussed in sets of three; this division is for convenience only. Only the strongest and closest connections between panels will be represented in Figures 1 to 6. All the panels in the six figures are considered to be part of a single coherent system and to be interrelated in varying degrees. Each set of three panels will be referred to as a segment. In the following chart (Figure A) the different segments are represented as an input-output system with feedback effects. The variables in each segment can be influenced by those in the other segments. The classical theory and the interbehavioral segment are combined in this figure. Except for departmentation, the two theories attempt to explain the same sets of variables, which can be regarded as mediators between inputs and outputs.

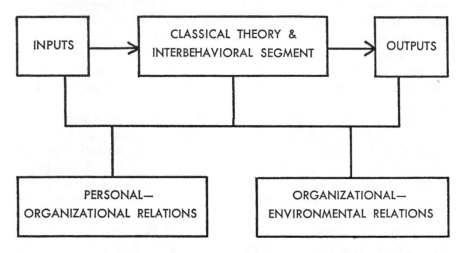

FIGURE A

Urwick (1956) has shown that the classical theory began to take shape almost a half century before behavioral theories and input-output models were developed. It will be convenient, therefore, to consider the classical theory first, and then to consider later theoretical developments in relation to the classical theory.

THE CLASSICAL THEORY

Classical organization theory, as represented by the writing of Fayol (1949), Koontz and O'Donnell (1955), Petersen, Plowman, and Trickett (1962), and others, is concerned with three panels of variables. One panel is concerned with departmentation, or the subdivision of activities into units, each with a more or less clearly differentiated function and with a separate supervisor. A second panel is concerned with the formal structuring of the organization that differentiates positions in relation to status and function (duties). The third panel is concerned with operations, or the activities carried out by the various departments. The three panels of variables representing *Departmentation, Structure,* and *Operations* are shown in Figure 1.

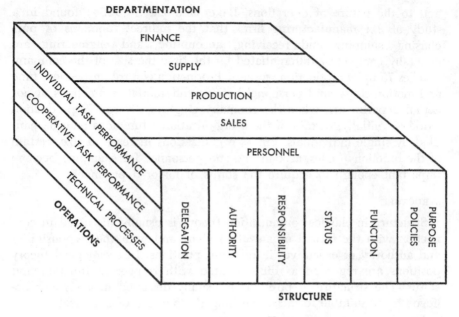

FIGURE 1
The Classical Theory

DEPARTMENTATION

Departmentation is a characteristic of large organizations. When organizations become so large that all activities cannot be supervised directly by the owner or manager, the supervisory task can be eased by making different executives responsible for different phases of activity. Koontz and O'Donnell (1955) outline eleven criteria or principles for assigning activities to different departments. Dale (1952) and others have shown that organizations differ greatly in the number, structure, and names of their departments. The departments shown in Figure 1 are frequently found in organizations, but many other departments are also encountered.

Davis (1951) observes that three functions concerned with the creation and distribution of utilities are found in all manufacturing organizations: production, distribution, and finance. Other supporting functions become differentiated as the need for them is perceived. Departmentation may be based on considerations such as function performed, product or service, location, process sequence, equipment, time or coordinative convenience.

Departmentation is directly related to the size of the organization and to the nature of operations. Baker and Davis (1954) found in a study of 211 manufacturing firms that the indirect functions of purchasing, shipping and receiving, accounting, and engineering are generally completely differentiated by the time the size of the company reaches 75 to 99 production workers. Production control, inspection, time and motion study, and personnel become differentiated functions, if not actual departments, when the company employs 100 to 499 production workers. Initially, certain of these organizational functions may be handled by single individuals. But as organizations increase in size, certain of the functions (sales, accounting, and personnel, for example) become important enough to acquire the status of major departments.

STRUCTURE

Structure in classical organization theory is usually discussed in connection with the formal organization chart and with the responsibility and authority of executives in different positions. In sociological theory positions are regarded as differentiated with respect to function and status. The structure of positions is usually designed in a manner believed to be suitable for accomplishing the purpose of organization.

Purpose.   One of the most stable and enduring characteristics of organization, purpose serves as a criterion or anchorage in terms of which a structure of positions is differentiated and a program of operations is designed. Because of its highly normative character and stabilizing function, it belongs in the panel of structural variables. It is not necessary to assume a "group mind" in order to speak of organization purpose or goal. If an organization characteristically carries out operations that are instrumental to the attainment of a given class of outcomes rather than other possible outcomes, the given class of outcomes may be regarded as an objective of organization. The class of outcomes for which two football teams compete includes *win, lose,* and *tie.* The operations of both teams are designed as instrumentalities for winning. The fact that one team suffers a loss does not invalidate the assumption that it played with the objective of winning. Any organization that sets out to succeed in a mission thereby undertakes all the other possible outcomes in the same class of outcomes, including the possibility of failing.

Many large organizations compile organization manuals that are prefaced with statements of purpose and policy. But policy does not reside in organization manuals. It resides in the decisions and actions of the members of the organization. The policies of an organization are, in the last analysis, defined by the characteristic practices of its members. These may or may not conform to written statements of policy.

Function and status. It is possible to draw a chart that specifies the function and status of each position in an organization. In practice, individual operative members are usually excluded from such charts. Many companies use organization charts to define the status structure of the organization, while the functions of each position are fully outlined in an organization manual.

The *status* of a position defines its place in the vertical hierarchy of the organization. In military organization this structure defines the "chain of command." *Function* is defined by the job specifications for a given position. Function and status specify the general nature and scope of the role to be performed by the occupant of a position. Function and status may remain unchanged as different members, one after another, occupy the same position. Barnard (1938, 1948) has presented penetrating and scholarly analyses of function and status in formal organizations.

Responsibility, authority and delegation. In the writings of the classical theorists it is often difficult to differentiate between authority and status as well as between responsibility and function. The functions of a position are often called the responsibilities of a position. Although authority is seldom identified with status, a direct equation is implied. The authority residing in high-level positions is regarded as being wider in scope and as having greater directive power than that in lower-level positions.

Petersen, Plowman, and Trickett (1962) identify three different definitions of authority. The *traditional* conception of authority as defined by Fayol (1949) is "the right to command or the power to make oneself obeyed." The *behaviorist* school tends to follow Barnard (1938) in maintaining that "authority is another name for the willingness and capacity of individuals to submit to the necessities of cooperative systems." According to this view, authority is a relationship between individuals and becomes operative only if the expectations of a superior are recognized and acted upon by his subordinates. The *functional* view of authority is represented by Follett (1949). According to this view, "authority belongs to the job and always stays with the job." Petersen, Plowman, and Trickett define authority as "freedom to act or decide."

The concept of authority has served as a locus of contention among different schools of thought. There is merit in viewing authority as the area of freedom for decision and action exhibited by an organization member. This area of freedom can be reduced or enlarged by the actions of peers and subordinates as well as by those of superiors. It can be restricted or expanded by the personality, inclinations, perceptions, and expectations of the member himself. This view permits the student of organization to direct his attention to the event being defined and to the conditions that modify it in one way or another.

Delegation. This variable is concerned with complex relationships between responsibility and authority involving a superior and a subordinate. In the classical theory this is a highly rationalized system of relationships. Brown (1945) has reduced the system to a set of "principles of organization." It is generally maintained that a superior cannot divest himself of a responsibility by delegation. He can delegate authority to a subordinate to act in his behalf, but he remains responsible for the performance of the act.

Delegation is the primary organizational means by which a member can enlarge his assistants' areas of freedom. Failure to delegate tends to restrict the area of freedom and to be associated with frustration and job dissatisfaction on the part of the assistants. Research conducted by the writer has shown that over-delegation and over-permissiveness cause subordinates to feel overburdened and resentful and to complain that superiors are "dumping off their work loads on people who already have enough to do." These findings suggest that the "job enlargement" recommended by various behavior scientists is not a universal solution to problems of job dissatisfaction.

Members of higher-level positions tend to rate themselves higher in responsibility, authority, and delegation than do members in lower-level positions. Stogdill and Scott (1957) studied the responsibility and authority relationships between juniors (subordinates) and seniors (superiors) in twenty-five naval organizations. It was found that "when seniors feel more highly burdened with responsibilities, their immediate juniors attempt to cope with the situation by assuming more responsibility and authority and by delegating less to their assistants. If seniors perceive themselves as having a high degree of authority, their juniors feel a reduction in their responsibilities and delegate still less to their assistants. However, if seniors delegate more, then their assistants feel an increase in their own responsibility and authority and delegate more to their assistants." These findings suggest that there is a complex relationship among responsibility, authority, and delegation and that the three variables exert differential effects down the line.

OPERATIONS

In classical theory the operations of organizations are usually discussed in terms of time and motion study, work flow, and production charts. This approach is particularly applicable to the manufacturing organization. In operations research and various automated approaches operations are treated as process-flow systems. The reports edited by

Shultz and Whisler (1960) indicate that the introduction of the systems approach exerts a marked effect upon the structure of an organization. For purposes of a general theory of organization, it would seem desirable to analyze operations in terms of basic concepts that apply to all organizations. Whether an organization is a manufacturing plant, a government agency, a public school, a bridge club, or a discussion group, the basic factor in its operations is described by the performances of its members. Whisler and Harper (1962) describe methods for evaluating performance. Some aspects of task performance may be executed by individuals working independently of other members. Other aspects may be performed by two or more interacting members. Thus, *individual task performance* can be distinguished from *cooperative task performance*. A third aspect of operations is the *technical nature of the process* that describes the activity of the organization. A bridge game, for example, involves a complex and highly differentiated kind of process or technology. Manufacturing operations usually involve mechanical, chemical, or electrical technologies or combinations of complex technologies.

The technical nature and magnitude of the operations being carried out by an organization will determine to a high degree the structure and departmentation designed for the operation. Thus, structure, departmentation, and operations are highly interdetermined panels of variables.

* * *

The classical theory is concerned primarily with the subdivision of work and with the differentiation of responsibility and authority. It constitutes an empirical and logical analysis of these aspects of organizations. As such it can be utilized as a model or set of principles for developing the structure of new organizations. It has proved to be a highly effective instrument for the accomplishment of this task. Knowing the nature, technology, size, and complexity of a task to be achieved, it is possible to design a structure of positions, assign functions to the positions, specify the status relationships among the positions, outline communication channels, and determine the flow of operations necessary for the achievement of the task. Given adequate time and resources, it is generally possible to recruit or train persons qualified for assignment to the positions.

Classical organization theory represents penetrating and realistic analysis of practical problems that confront the manager in his daily work. The operations of an organization describe the activities that it carries out in order to accomplish its objectives. The differentiation of positions in relation to status and function is a basic characteristic of all mammalian social groupings (Allee, 1951). The division of work into departments with related functions is a practical necessity in large organizations.

The analysis presented above necessarily constitutes an oversimplification of the classical theory. Various writers deal with different sets of variables, and they differ in their definitions of the variables. The closely reasoned system developed by Davis (1951) represents a highly sophisticated statement of the classical theory and incorporates variables such as leadership and morale that the social scientist regards as important in a theory of organization.

THE INTERBEHAVIORAL SEGMENT

The classical theory describes the skeletal structure of organization, but it does not explain the basic processes from which structure develops in originally undifferentiated social aggregations. Sociologists such as Simmel (1950), Cooley (1909), and Mead (1934), among others, must be given credit for the origination of insights into the basic processes that account for the differentiations of social structure. Utilizing the insights generated by these theorists, it is now recognized that structure becomes differentiated in the process of social interaction; based on the insights of workers such as Mead (1934), Mayo (1933), Barnard (1938), and Parsons and Shils (1952), students of group behavior have discovered that the structure of organization is based upon, and is a function of, interpersonal expectations that become differentiated in the course of interaction.

Both the theoretical and the experimental accomplishments of the behavioral sciences suggest that the three panels of variables treated in classical systems do not constitute a basic theory of organization because they do not account for the origination of structure (Homans, 1950). The departmentation panel of variables does not belong in a basic theory because it is characteristic only of large organizations; but the structural and operations panels of variables belong in a basic theory because they are characteristic of all organizations. Recent theorical developments suggest that a basic theory of organization should include a new panel of variables, which the present author has identified as *interpersonnel*. The concepts used by the social scientist to describe *structure* differ from those used by the classical theorists. In describing *operations* the behavioral scientist differs from the classical theorists and operations researcher in being more deeply concerned with cooperative task performance than with individual task performance or technical processes. The social scientist tends to regard organization as an interbehavioral system. We shall discuss this system in terms of three panels of variables, *Interpersonnel, Structure,* and *Operations,* as outlined in Figure 2.

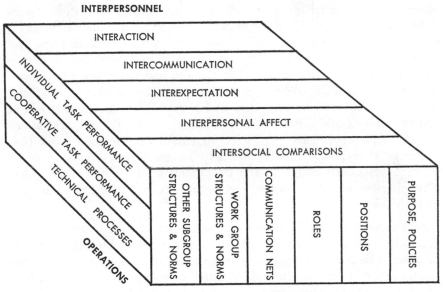

FIGURE 2
The Interbehavioral Segment
(Input and Output Panels Omitted)

INTERPERSONNEL

Interpersonnel seems to be an appropriate title for this panel since all the variables define aspects of relationships between the members of an organization. Interaction, intercommunication, interexpectation, interpersonal affect, and intersocial comparisons are basic processes that account for the differentiation of structure in newly formed groups. Two of the variables—interaction and interexpectation—provide a basis for defining the concepts *group* and *organization.*

For purposes of theory we may define a group as a *social interaction system with minimum structure.* We shall regard an organization as a *social interaction system in which the differentiation of expectations defines the structure of positions and roles in the system.* Most of the groups and subgroups with which we shall be concerned will exhibit characteristics of organization. The differentiation of positions and roles implies the differentiation of member expectations regarding the contributions each is to make to the organization. Structure continues to be maintained in the expectations of the members during periods when they are not in direct interaction.

Interaction. A social group is defined as an interaction system. Interaction is a process in which the performance of one member serves as a stimulus to the response of another member, who responds in turn. The behaviors that serve as stimuli to response in an interaction sequence may be overt and easily observed or obscure and based upon inference. Interpersonal actions, communications, expectations, feelings, and social comparisons may all be perceived and responded to in the interaction process. Bales (1950), Bales and Strodtbeck (1951), Borgatta and Bales (1953), and others have conducted extensive experimental work that indicates that newly formed, initially unstructured groups progress through systematic stages in the development of positions and roles. This progressive differentiation of structure grows out of the interaction process itself.

Intercommunication. This merits attention as a special form of interaction because of the critical role it plays in formally structured organizations. The formal definition of status levels creates barriers to the upward flow of certain kinds of information and to the downward flow of other kinds of information. The establishment of lines of authority tends to channel communication vertically and to block lateral communications among departments. As a result, subordinates tend to receive the full impact of changes in policies and plans before they have acquired the information needed to prepare for and cope with the changes. Supervisors fail to learn about unsatisfactory conditions at the operative levels until the problems begin to affect operations adversely. The lack of communications along lateral lines tends to disrupt the coordination of activities. Avoidance of these three classes of difficulties requires continuous attention to the communication process. Stogdill and Haase (1957) have shown that the structure of interactions and working relationships between members of organization often departs markedly from the structure of communications specified by the formal organization chart.

Interexpectation. Research surveyed by Asch (1952), Bass (1960), Berg and Bass (1961), Bonner (1959), Cartwright and Zander (1953), Hare, Borgatta, and Bales (1955), Sherif and Sherif (1953), Stogdill (1959), Thibaut and Kelley (1959), and others indicates that members of newly created groups without acknowledged structure quickly perceive differences among members, form differential choices among members for leadership and companionship, and accord members different status rankings in the group. As members of such groups work and interact in carrying out the group task, they develop differential expectations regarding their own roles and other roles. As one member increasingly succeeds in playing a determining role in the group activities and interactions, he tends to reinforce the expectations of his ability to continue in the role. Productive work tends to diminish as long as the structure of positions and roles remains unresolved or a subject of conflict. Once the role structure receives acknowledgement, however, the group members are free to turn their efforts to productive output.

While the structure of positions and roles is being determined through the processes of interaction and reinforcement of intermember expectations, norms are also being developed relative to the conduct that is required, acceptable, and effective for the different roles. The member who achieves a position of leadership is usually accorded a higher degree of freedom for initiating action and structuring other roles than is accorded the occupants of other positions. When individual norms are changed, they tend to change in the direction that is in conformity with the norms of the group. The group norms constitute a mutually confirmed set of expectations regarding acceptable behavior. The group members tend to pressure deviant members to bring their behavior into conformity with the norms of the group.

It is obvious that intermember expectation is a powerful concept for explaining the development and maintenance of group structure. The differentiation and acknowledgement of role structure is based on the mutual reinforcement of member expectations in the process of interaction.

Interpersonal affect. Research reported by Moreno (1953), Jennings (1950), Bass (1960), Berg and Bass (1961), and Cartwright and Zander (1953) indicates that a position of leadership is most likely to be accorded the group member who exhibits spontaneity, initiates spontaneity in others, communicates easily with other members, tolerates freedom of action in other members, and expresses positive rather than negative feeling about the group task and group members. Findings such as these suggest that group members interact not only on the basis of overt action and communication but also on the basis of perceived feelings and personality characteristics (Bion, 1961; Thelen, 1954; Tagiuri and Petrullo, 1958).

Interpersonal affect is not usually regarded as a basic variable in group theory. Barnard (1948) has observed that the status system of the formally structured organization is designed in part to reduce the opportunity for interaction on the basis of feeling and personal considerations. The formal definition of structure, however, does not eliminate the operation or effects of interpersonal likes and dislikes. Research reported by Horwitz (1963) indicates that in interpersonal and inter-group situations where consensus is important, exchange of information about the feelings underlying one's actions that are generated by the other's actions tend to increase mutual identification and agreement.

As suggested by Barnard (1948), the formal definition of status levels tends to inhibit the communication of interpersonal affect. The status system tends to inhibit in particular the upward flow of unpleasant communications.

Intersocial comparisons.   Newcomb (1943), Sherif (1936), Merton and Kitt (1950), and others have developed the hypothesis that individuals tend not only to compare themselves with others but also to identify themselves with groups holding values and norms similar to their own. They tend to be dissatisfied in groups with policies and norms that differ from their own value systems, and they tend to be regarded as deviates in such groups. Research reported by Precker (1952), Fiedler (1954), Fensterheim and Tresselt (1953), and others indicates that individuals prefer as fellow group members those persons whose values are similar to their own. Groups tend to accept members whose value systems are in conformity with the value norms of the groups. Although individual value systems and reference group identifications are highly subjective in nature, it appears that they are easily perceived by individuals seeking membership and by groups considering individuals for membership.

Intersocial comparisons are important factors in the formation and composition of organizations. They can provide the basis for a har-monious or for a disruptive organization. The right of an organization to determine the composition of its membership may be a critical factor in its capacity for survival.

The *interpersonnel* panel of variables consists of interaction, inter-communication, interexpectation, interpersonal affect, and intersocial comparisons. It is basic to the formation and development of social groups. These variables in combination account for the mutual accept-ance and congregation of members to form groups and for the differen-tiation of structure (positions and roles) in newly formed groups. The operation of these variables accounts for the transformation of undif-ferentiated social interaction systems (groups) into structured systems (organizations) with positions and roles.

STRUCTURE

It seems clear that the variables in the *interbehavioral* panel account for the differentiation and maintenance of structure in newly formed groups. The structure that develops as a result of the operation of the interbehavioral variables differs from the processes that account for structure.

Social scientists have identified several aspects of structure that are disregarded in the classical theory, including interaction and communication nets, role structures, work-groups' substructures and norms, and various other subgroup structures and norms. Organization purpose is usually not treated as an aspect of structure, but it appears that it should be so treated.

Purpose and policies.   As stated in connection with the classical theory, the operation of purpose and policies is inferred from the characteristic activities carried out by a group in order to bring about a given class of outcomes. It was further suggested that some degree of community of purpose is maintained in the mutually reinforced expectations of the members. It is not necessary to assume that all members of an organization have identical expectations relative to its objectives. Identity of expectation is hardly possible in an organization of any size; nevertheless, a clearly defined structure of positions and the onrushing flow of operations may provide considerable unity of action. It is not safe to assume that these factors will provide unity of action in the absence of clearly communicated and agreed upon objectives, but it often does in long-established organizations where members can infer the operation of purpose and policy. Bass (1960) has reviewed studies that indicate that members are better satisfied with an organization when they have a clear understanding of its purpose and objectives.

Cyert and March (1963) suggest that organizational goals develop out of the bargaining process in the formation of coalitions. Thibaut and Kelley (1959) present a similar point of view. Managers and employees bargain not only about matters of payments and costs but also about matters of policy commitments. The formation of coalitions is not the assymetrical process usually assumed in the theory of the firm. While the manager receives a larger inducement than the operative employee, he also makes a larger contribution in the way of responsibility and accountability. Thus, inducements-contributions ratios tend to balance out, and the benefits for all can only be realized by mutual commitment to policy. Research reviewed by Bass (1960) and Berg and Bass (1961) indicates that group goals that are relevant to the members tend to modify their subsequent behavior. Participation in the formulation of goals and policies is a factor in subsequent conformity to them.

Task structures.   Ordinarily a variety of tasks must be carried out in order to accomplish the purpose of organization. These tasks are often referred to as functions of organization. Primary or direct functions define the operations necessary for accomplishing the primary purpose of organization. Indirect functions, such as finance, supply, sales, and personnel are necessary in large organizations for support of the direct functions.

There are usually fewer tasks or functions than there are positions in an organization (Shartle, 1959). That is, many members may occupy positions identified as accountant, salesman, lathe operator, and the like. The complexity of the task structure is likely to be related to the size of the organization and to the nature of the technologies involved in its operations.

Tasks themselves may be regarded as more or less highly structured. Job analysis and job description (Shartle, 1959) are methods for determining the structure and requirements of tasks. Triandis (1964) has suggested that member skill and complexity of task structure interact to affect the power structure of an organization.

Responsibility and authority are often treated as synonymous with function and status. Stogdill (1959) has suggested that responsibility and authority gain in utility as theoretical concepts when they are regarded as aspects of role performance rather than as attributes of position. It can be observed in organizations that as one executive succeeds another in the same position, they tend to exhibit different degrees of responsibility and authority although the status and functions of the position remain unchanged. Position can be clearly differentiated from role. The fact that successive occupants of the same position, although exhibiting different patterns of responsibility and performance, tend to perform in accordance with position specifications suggests that roles should be regarded as aspects of organization structure. Organizations consist of structures of positions and structures of roles. But since each member's role is defined in terms of what he does rather than what he is expected to do, role performance can also be regarded as an aspect of organization operations. It is the concept of role performance that connects structure with operations.

Positions and roles. Because of its deeply empirical orientation the classical theory provides an effective rationale for the prior structuring of an organization about to be brought into being. Because a chart can be drawn to specify the formal structure of an organization before personnel are recruited to man the organization, it has often been assumed that structure precedes operations. This assumption is not valid in a basic theory of organization. In newly created, undifferentiated groups structure develops as a result of individual and cooperative performance (operations) and as an effect of interaction and reinforced expectations (interpersonnel). The resultant structure of positions and roles defines organization. That is, an organization is a social interaction system (group) that is structured in terms of positions and roles. Although the view that function and structure develop simultaneously is of value in understanding the basic process of organization, it does not detract from the utility of the classical theory for the structuring of organizations.

The structure of positions can be clearly distinguished from the structure of roles. Positions are differentiated relative to function and status. Positions therefore define what the members are *expected to do* in the way of task performance and interaction with other members. Roles, on the other hand, describe what the members *actually are observed to do* in the way of task performance and interaction with other members.

Certain social scientists have tended to regard status, authority, and power as unnecessary evils in organization. This is an obvious and often admitted bias that leads to the rejection or misformulation of legitimate problems of organization. Although certain social scientists regard all status differences as undemocratic and detrimental to the dignity of the individual, Thibaut and Kelley (1959) suggest that the assent given by the members of an organization to its status system is of particular value to the less powerful members. Consensus in defining the status structure acts to constrain high status members from using their greater power to the disadvantage of those members in positions of lower status. Refusal to reach a consensus relative to the status system gives the most powerful members almost unlimited freedom to intrude upon the rights and privileges of less powerful members if they choose to do so. Refusal to acknowledge structure can be used as an effective means of gaining and maintaining power. It is apparent, then, that power structures and status structures are not identical dimensions of organization.

Neither are authority and power synonymous. Authority defines the area of freedom for initiative exhibited by the occupant of a position. Dubin (1957) maintains that power is concerned with the exclusive right to control essential functions of organization. Power struggles tend to center around such essential functions as controlling policy formation and the distribution of resources as well as the reinforcement of member expectations. In the long run, the member who gains exclusive right to reinforce member expectations can control all the other functions of organization.

Communication nets. Communication nets are specialized kinds of interaction structures. Research designed by Bavelas (1950) and modified by Leavitt (1951) indicates that small experimental groups in which all communications must be filtered through a position of centrality more quickly develop stable organization structures and make fewer errors than groups in which all members have equal access to information. But member satisfaction is higher in the latter groups. Guetzkow and

Simon (1955), using similar research designs but separating the operational problem from the organizational problem, found that different communication nets can operate efficiently if an effective organization is developed to carry out the operations. Communication nets with positions of centrality were better able to develop such structures than were nets that provided all members with equal access to information.

The vertical stratification of organizations tends to isolate operative members from information concerning changes in short-run operating policies and goals. But this is not a necessary consequence of stratification. Managements differ in their beliefs about the desirability of keeping employees informed. Plant bulletins and newspapers can be used in large organizations to let employees know what is happening. Even though the printed word carries somewhat less satisfaction value than face to face conversation, it is preferable to being in the dark.

In any organization where complex operations must be coordinated, a centralized information center is needed. The more carefully operations must be controlled, the greater the need for prompt and accurate information in the coordinating center.

Work-group structures and norms.   Just as organizations develop structures of positions and roles, each of the various work groups develops its own substructures of positions and roles. Members performing the same functions tend in time to acquire different status rank within the work group. Whether or not they perform the same functions, they tend to develop different roles. While differentiating its own status and role structures, each group also tends to develop its own set of norms.

Roethlisberger and Dickson (1939), Whyte (1955), Horsfall and Arensberg (1949), and others have found that work groups develop norms that set standards of conduct and regulate the work performance of group members. Among the functions served by such norms is the reduction of distressing inequalities of performance between members and the establishment of rates of performance that are tolerable day after day. Taylor (1911) referred to this process as "goldbricking." Needless to say, management has shown a reluctance to accept the norm concept as a legitimate dimension of organization theory because norms tend to regulate operations and are extremely difficult to change or control.

Other subgroup structures and norms.   It has been observed that the members of organizations associate with each other not only in the workgroup but also in a great variety of other subgroupings. Such groupings are usually referred to as "informal groups" or "informal organization" to differentiate them from the formal organization structure. Sayles

(1958) objects to the term *informal group*. He finds that friendship cliques, influence groupings, and other subgroups, when examined closely, exhibit leadership hierarchy, normative standards, and other characteristics of organization. Subgroups such as company teams, choral groups, and social clubs tend to become rather highly formalized. The labor union, a powerful system of subgroups in the industrial plant, cannot be regarded as an informal organization. It exists as an independent organization; yet it is an integral part of the industrial organization. All the kinds of subgroups discussed above should be assigned to the structural panel of organization theory. Every member of a large organization is a member of various subgroups and systems of subgroups, each with its own structure, norms, and activities that intermesh with those of the larger system.

Several writers have suggested that management should attempt to control the "informal organization" in order to bring the norms of the various subgroups into conformity with the primary purposes and policies of the parent organization. The author regards this as an extremely hazardous proposal. The best of organizations generates pressures and stresses from which the members need relief. The coffee break provides such relief. So do the norms of the various subgroups. So long as the norms of a subgroup do not constitute a direct challenge to the legitimacy of the purpose and structure of the organization, management will be better off leaving it alone. This does not mean that an organization should disregard the actions of overt enemies among its members. To deny it this right is to deny it the right to survive. If the management of an organization wants the loyalty and support of its "informal" subgroups, it should create the conditions that make such loyalty and support possible. Leavitt (1958) has outlined some of the measures that can be taken to create such favorable conditions.

OPERATIONS

Operations as a panel of variables was discussed in connection with the classical theory. Some additional comment is required in relation to the interbehavioral system. Performance, both individual and cooperative, is one of the foundation variables needed to develop a theory of organization. Without action (performance) by individuals there is no interaction among individuals. Without action and mutual interaction, a group cannot be said to exist. Continued action and interaction are necessary in undifferentiated groups for the development of group structure (organization).

In a group that does not deal with material objects of any sort, the operations of the group are described entirely by the performances (individual and cooperative) of the group members. For this reason, the operational panel of variables must be regarded as an integral part of the interbehavioral system.

THE INPUT-OUTPUT PANELS

Work in the fields of operations research and mathematical models has alerted social scientists to the fact that their complex theories can be represented in terms of a set of input variables, a set of mediating variables, and a set of output variables. The operational and inter-personnel panels have been treated tentatively as input panels of variables. These variables in combination generate group structure and operations. However, we shall find it convenient to redefine some of these variables for use as inputs in a theory of organization.

Following historical trends in the development of organization theory, discussion of the input and output panels will be postponed in this discussion until the Personal-Organizational Segment is considered. It is closely related to, or is a redefinition of, some of the panels in the Interbehavioral Segment.

❋   ❋   ❋

Organization has been defined as an interaction system that has become structured in terms of differentiated positions and roles. A convincing body of evidence indicates that experimentally created groups and other undifferentiated social aggregations develop structure as a result of the performances of the members interacting with each other at various levels of perception, communication, expectation, affect, and social comparison. In other words, *structure* is generated by two panels of variables identified as *operations* and *interpersonnel*. The three panels —interpersonnel, structure, and operations—comprise the interbehavioral orientation toward organization theory.

THE PERSONAL-ORGANIZATIONAL SEGMENT

In theory organization can be conceived as an abstract system. But organization depends upon the presence of living beings. The reality that organization theory tries to explain is the system of interrelated behaviors and expectations of the individuals who comprise the membership of the system. An individual's membership and position in an organization tends to identify him with a specific subgroup of persons. His membership in other organizations tends further to define his identity in the organization and in the community at large. These identities, as defined by his membership in various organizations, often determine whether he will be accepted for membership in a given organization.

The relationship between the individual and an organization must be regarded as an important segment of organization theory. This relationship can be more or less adequately described in terms of three panels of variables. These have been given the titles *Personal Characteristics,* *Identification with Organization,* and *Exchange with Organization.* The variables in these panels are listed in Figure 3.

PERSONAL CHARACTERISTICS

Physique and appearance. Various physical characteristics of individuals are of significance for membership in organizations. Individuals, for example, must meet certain minimum standards of height, weight, and physical condition in order to be accepted for membership in military organizations. The standards differ for commissioned and noncommissioned personnel. The standards for both categories of personnel differ

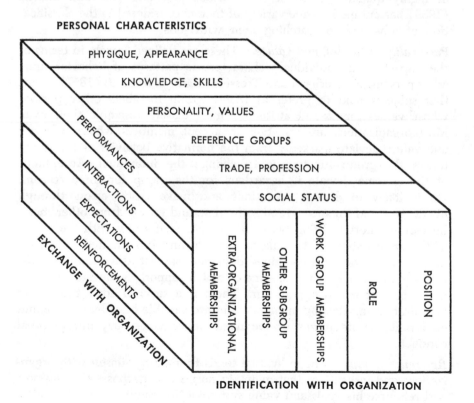

FIGURE 3
The Personal–Organizational Segment

under conditions of peace and war. Strength and physique are important in various industrial jobs (Harrell, 1958; Gagné and Fleishman, 1959). For many kinds of organizations physique and appearance are not important determinants of qualification for membership, but they tend to assume some importance in selection for high-level positions. An organization appears to prefer to be favorably represented in the person of its top leader.

Ability, knowledge, and skill.   These qualities are major factors in determining qualification for membership in industrial and governmental organizations. Sofer (1963) has observed that "just as different procedures are appropriate to the different phases of an organization's affairs, so are different sorts of people." A large organization needs members who differ in skill and level of ability in various technologies. Many organizations administer batteries of tests as aids in the selection of highly qualified personnel for various jobs and positions. Shartle (1959) has outlined a wide variety of factors considered in the classification of jobs and in matching men with jobs.

Personality, attitudes, and values.   These are defined largely in terms of the impact of an individual's characteristic patterns of behavior upon other persons. Fensterheim and Tresselt (1953) and Smith (1957) report that subjects tend to prefer as fellow group members other persons whose values (measured attitudes) most closely resemble their own. Most organizations are reluctant to accept members whose behavior and values deviate markedly from the normative behavior of the group unless the group function is to change the individual. Acceptance of the extreme deviate is hazardous for the group for three reasons. He is likely to disrupt operations and make costly errors through his deviant performance. He absorbs time and energy from other members in an effort to bring his behavior into conformity with the norms of the organization. If he fails to conform and is permitted to remain in the organization, his continued deviancy may act as a stimulus to the formation of divisive cliques, some of which support the deviant member and others of which oppose him. There is a survival advantage to an organization in selecting members who are capable of at least minimum conformity to its norms of technical performance and interpersonal conduct.

Reference groups.   The individual tends to identify himself with organizations and institutions that maintain norms and purposes that support and reinforce his goals and value systems (Newcomb, 1950). Organizations tend to attract and to accept as members individuals who identify themselves with other organizations that have similar and supportive, rather than hostile, purposes and norms (Sherif and Sherif, 1956). Since an individual's performance and conduct within an organization may be influenced by his membership in or identification with other organizations, the factor of external identifications may have an effect upon the cohesiveness and survival capacity of the organization (Etzioni, 1961).

Trade or profession.   Selection for membership in many kinds of organizations, and particularly for specified positions in organizations, is directly dependent upon an individual's training and experience in a trade or profession. This factor operates as a barrier to selection for positions that accept only persons who have been certified by an appropriate trade association or training institution.

Social status.   An individual's social status in the community may also be a factor that facilitates or hinders his acceptance for membership in various kinds of organizations. Kahl (1957), Davis (1949), Centers (1949), and others have shown that there is a parallel between the class structure of the community and the status structure of the organizations within the community. If an individual's value systems, patterns of social behavior, and reference-group preferences tend to identify him with a specific social class in the community, he will be more readily accepted by a stratum of organization with similar norms, behavior patterns, and reference group alignments. Membership in various racial and nationality subgroups within the community may operate as a barrier to membership in certain organizations.

The panel of variables entitled *Personal Characteristics* constitutes an integral part of organization theory. These variables in various combinations determine the acceptability of individuals for membership in organizations and for positions within organizations. The character and personality of two organizations that are similar in size and purpose may differ markedly depending upon the policies and procedures they adopt for the acceptance of members.

IDENTIFICATION WITH ORGANIZATION

An individual, when identifying his membership in an organization, is likely to say, "I work for the XYZ Company." But other persons like to identify an individual's membership in terms of the position he occupies in the given organization. That is, they like to know not only the organization to which an individual belongs but also his status and function in the organization.

Position.   A member's position defines the general nature of the contribution he is expected to make to an organization and his status level in the organization. Generally, but not invariably, members in higher-level positions tend to be better satisfied and more closely identified with an organization than do members in the lower echelons. Lenski (1956),

Merton and Kitt (1950), Renck (1955), and Yoder, Heneman, and Cheit (1951) have presented confirming evidence on this point. Leavitt (1958) found that members are better satisfied when they occupy positions in the communication structure that permit them to know what is being done in the organization. Such knowledge permits more effective performance and more adequate control over one's job.

Role. Herzberg, Mausner, Peterson, and Capwell (1957) have surveyed various studies that indicate that an individual's satisfaction with an organization tends to be associated with the role he is permitted to play. Once a member accepts the functions of his position, he likes to have enough freedom of action to carry them out in a satisfactory manner. If he is prevented from doing so, he finds it difficult to identify himself firmly with the organization. In other words, a member tends to feel that he is not a valued member of the organization when he is denied the right to play his expected role.

Subgroup memberships. If there are several work groups in an organization holding the same status and performing the same function, a member's satisfaction may vary according to the work group to which he is assigned. He may find some work groups more congenial than others. His satisfaction with the organization may also be determined in part by the values and norms of various friendship and influence subgroups that accept or reject him as a member.

Extraorganizational memberships. The closeness of a member's identification with an organization and the extent to which he accepts its goals and norms as his own may be determined by the goals and norms of the external organization with which he identifies himself. Merton and Kitt (1950) and Stouffer and associates (1949) found that members tend to be better satisfied with an organization when they identify themselves with it rather than with other groups that deny the legitimacy of the purpose and status structure of the organization. Kahn (1964) reports that role conflict is directly associated with the number and importance of the member's business contacts outside the organization.

The variables in the panel *Identification with Organization* are of importance in a theory of organization because members are identified with the organization in terms of these variables and because they determine in part the member's satisfaction with the organization.

EXCHANGE WITH ORGANIZATION

In a basic theory of organization the performances, interactions, and expectations of the members can be regarded as input variables, which combine to .generate group structure and operations. These same variables can be regarded as dimensions or avenues of exchange between individual members and the organization. The members, through their performances and interactions, carry out the activities (operations) of the organization and acknowledge a structure of positions and roles. The resulting operations and structure bring differing degrees of satisfaction and dissatisfaction to the members. The expectations of some members may be satisfied, while the expectations of others may be deflated. Some members pay higher expectational costs than do other members to maintain their membership in the group. In other words, some members receive less return (in the way of reinforcement of their expectations) for their contribution to the group than do other members. The tolerance of differential contributions and differential rewards appears to be a necessary condition for the development and survival of organizations.

Performances. A member's performance of his task represents a contribution to organization, which he exchanges for pay or some other form of satisfaction. Even when a member's contribution consists of little more than paying his annual dues, he usually expects some sort of return.

Interaction. There are writers who would have us believe that social interaction is always an unalloyed delight. The fact is that many members of organizations find interactions stressful and emotionally demanding. Certain members may refuse promotion to supervisory positions in order to avoid interactional stress. Moreno (1953) has shown that individuals differ in the number of interactional relationships they can maintain with ease and comfort. Interaction, like performance, can be regarded as a contribution by the members to the organization in which various satisfactions and dissatisfactions are immediately forthcoming.

Expectations and reinforcements. A member invests various expectations, fears, hopes, and ambitions in certain of the organizations to which he belongs. Whether or not they are valued or recognized as such, they are member contributions to organization. These variables largely determine a member's motivation to work. In general, individuals tend to work harder when in doing so their expectations are thereby reinforced. They tend not to exert themselves if: (1) exertion fails to result in reinforcement or (2) reinforcement occurs without exertion. Expectation as a dimension of exchange between a member and the organization is a determiner of organizational cohesiveness and morale.

An individual tends to evaluate the rewards from membership against the costs of being a member on the basis of his expectations. March and Simon (1958) have formulated a set of hypotheses that summarize the complex relationships between the inducements offered by an organization, the contributions made by a member, and the willingness of the member to remain in the organization. Both intraorganizational and extraorganizational factors are considered in estimating the inducement utilities and the contribution utilities.

*   *   *

Some of the variables in the personal-organizational segment are either variants of, or are closely related to, those in the Interbehavioral System. The panel *Identification with Organization* is composed of the same variables assigned to the structural panel of the Interbehavioral System; the former identifies a member's place in the organization (in terms of his position, role, etc.), while the latter describes the structure of the organization (in terms of positions, roles, subgroups, etc.). In real life the importance of an individual's identification with the organization is evidenced by the fact that a properly qualified member who is placed in a key position, particularly in the top leadership position, can transform a failing organization into a growing and prosperous one. Another person placed in the same position can bring about the collapse of the organization.

The *Exchange with Organization* panel is composed of some of the same variables that appear in the Interpersonnel panel of the basic system. The variables in the Exchange panel account for the contribution—reward relationships between a member and the organization. The same variables in the Basic System account for the operations of the organization.

The above discussion indicates that the same variables in a theory of organization can be regarded as an attribute of individual members or as an attribute of organization. It is a weakness of most formulations of organization theory that if they are built upon considerations of the organization as a system, attributes of the individual are rejected as unimportant or irrelevant to the system and *vice versa.*

The panel *Personal Characteristics* is composed of variables that are usually treated in textbooks on personnel or industrial psychology. Their importance to a theory of organization is evidenced by the fact that most large organizations establish personnel departments to deal with the problems arising in connection with these variables. The characteristics of individuals are important factors in personnel functions involving the recruitment, selection, assignment, and remuneration of members.

It is suggested that the characteristics of individual members, the identification of members with the organization, and the exchange relationships between members and organization should be considered in a theory of organization.

THE INPUT SEGMENT

On the basis of purely logical considerations, the input variables of a system should be considered first. They are the variables that generate the total system when they are operated upon in various combinations. But the present paper is not primarily concerned with the logical structure of organization theory. It is concerned rather with an examination of the scope and dimensions of the theory. For this reason it has seemed desirable to proceed along the lines of historical development rather than of logical sequence. This approach should enable us to determine what organization theory consisted of in the past, what it consists of at the present time, and what it is likely to become.

It was suggested in discussing the Interbehavioral Segment that performances, interactions, and expectations can be treated as input variables that generate group structure, operations, and interpersonnel. Parsons (1951) and Homans (1950) explain social structure and function on the basis of actions, interactions, and sentiments. Stogdill (1959) has suggested that three such inputs are appropriate and adequate for explanning the developmental processes in initially unstructured groups. It is not quite so apparent that these are appropriate inputs for organizations in which structure and operations have been fully determined before opening their doors to accept members and begin operations. In such cases structure and operations do not emerge directly from the performances and interactions of all the members. Even in previously structured organizations, however, the variables in the Interpersonnel panel tend to emerge as a result of member performances, interactions, and expectations. It is therefore not incorrect to regard these variables as inputs in any kind or organization. But for purposes of practical measurement, it is convenient to redefine the inputs for organizations in which structure and operations have already been designed.

The panels of variables (Measured Inputs, Interbehavorial System, and Personnel-Organizational Relations) in the *Input Segment* are shown in Figure 4.

MEASURED INPUTS

Organizations in which an employer-employee relationship exists between the organization and its members tend to measure member performance in terms of hours of work or piece-work rates. The performance of salaried members is measured in terms of level of technical, professional, or managerial skill. Job analysis and job evaluation are often used to establish levels of skill and differential wage and salary ranges. Thus it is apparent that the measurement and evaluation of performance and interaction can involve quite complicated procedures.

The variables in the Measured Inputs panel include both Human and Material factors. Not all organizations operate upon material variables as inputs. But most organizations for which a theory of organization is important are concerned with material and monetary inputs. Various kinds of organizations measure inputs and outputs almost entirely in terms of financial values. Material inputs may constitute the supplies operated upon, or they may provide the power equipment, facilities, and housing required for the performance of operations.

Human inputs. For purposes of measurement, evaluation, and remuneration, human inputs have been redefined here. As mentioned above,

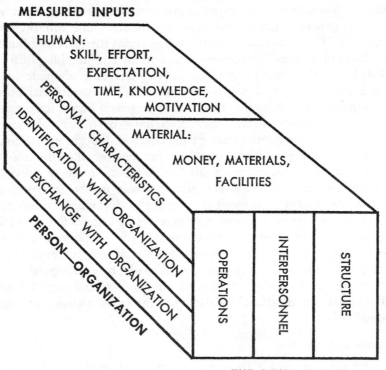

FIGURE 4

The Input Segment

remuneration for performance and interaction is usually based on hours of work, amount of work produced, or level of skill. Motivation and skill in personal interaction tend to be more carefully evaluated and more highly remunerated in the middle and top levels of organization than in lower levels. Some crude measure of member expectation and satisfaction can be obtained in a well constructed job-satisfaction survey. But such surveys seldom take advantage of the opportunity to obtain expressions of member expectation, ambition, and desire to make a contribution. It must be recognized, of course, that it is unwise to raise expectations that the organization is not prepared to satisfy. To do so merely increases discontent. For an organization that is expanding rapidly enough to utilize the ambitions and creative capabilities of its members, there might be some advantage in obtaining expressions of expectation. Member expectations are inputs and potential assets that are usually ignored in both theory and practice.

Material inputs. Theorists often ignore material inputs, which tend to be central concerns of managers. Accounting systems and economic models of organizations are based on dollar values of input and output. The survival of the firm depends on a sound financial structure. The models developed in operations research use raw materials as inputs and manufactured products as outputs. Raw materials, technologies, plant design and facilities, and operational procedures are evaluated and remunerated on the basis of hours of work, level of skill, effort, and the like. Remuneration is not measured in terms of performances, interaction, and expectations, as such.

It is apparent that the set of input variables that is used in a theoretical system depends on the kind of system that is to be developed. One set of variables is appropriate and necessary in accounting for group structure and operations. Another set of inputs is required to account for the evaluation, measurement, and remuneration of member contributions. All have an impact on the members of organizations.

THE BASIC (INTERBEHAVIORAL) SYSTEM

In the Interbehavioral System individual performances and cooperative performances are regarded as input variables that account for organizational operations. Interaction and interpersonal expectation, along with performance, are regarded as a set of input variables that accounts for Structure and Interpersonnel. In the Input Segment such variables as time and skill are regarded as inputs, but it is apparent that hours of work and levels of member skills are not in themselves variables that can generate group structure or interpersonnel. They are regarded as inputs in various theoretical models because they are easy to measure.

Variables such as knowledge, skill, and expectation are identified as Personal Characteristics in the Personal-Organizational Segment of organization theory. These same variables, along with time and effort, are treated as Measured Inputs in the Input Segment. As personal characteristics, they are regarded as variables that account for the willingness of members to join an organization and for the acceptability of individuals as members in an organization. When regarded as measured inputs, they account for, or provide a basis for, the evaluation and remuneration of member performance, interaction, and motivational expectation.

*   *   *

Performances, interactions and expectations have been regarded by several writers as complex input variables that, in combination, are capable of generating a theory of organization. However, for purposes of practical measurement, evaluation, and remuneration these human inputs are usually defined in terms of hours of work, volume of work produced, or level of skill. The fact that when a complex concept is used as an input it can be analyzed into different component subconcepts for different practical purposes makes the task of the organization theorists a difficult one.

THE OUTPUT SEGMENT

The input variables in a theory of organization not only account for structure, interpersonnel, and operations; they also generate a set of outputs. Structure, interpersonnel, and operations may be regarded as mediators between inputs and outputs, as illustrated below. These five sets of variables constitute the very core of organization theory.

$$\text{Inputs} \longrightarrow \left| \begin{array}{c} \text{Operations} \\ \text{Interpersonnel} \\ \text{Structure} \end{array} \right| \longrightarrow \text{Outputs}$$

When they are operated upon by the members of an organization, inputs are transformed into outputs. But some of the inputs are utilized in the development and maintenance of structure and interpersonnel. In addition, structure may impose restraining or facilitating conditions at various stages and loci of operations. Equally, if not more, important is the fact that various aspects of interpersonnel may affect operations. The productivity norms of work groups tend to regulate and pace operations, thus determining the rate of productive output. Considerations such as those discussed above suggest that the Input and Output panels of variables should be regarded as integral aspects of the basic system.

The outputs of an organization are usually measured in terms of its productivity. That is, productivity is often regarded as the only output that results from the group operations. Stogdill (1959) reports that a theory of organization achievement based on this point of view is neither logically consistent nor in conformity with the experimental evidence. He found that if *productivity*, organizational *integration*, and organizational *morale* are all regarded as outputs, the resultant theory appears to be logically consistent and accounts for the research findings. The three output concepts must be carefully defined in order to satisfy a basic theory of organization.

The panels of variables in the output segment are shown in Figure 5.

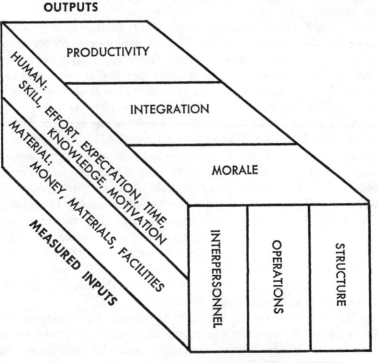

THE BASIC SYSTEM

FIGURE 5
The Output Segment

PRODUCTIVITY

Productivity is defined as the change in organizational expectancy values that results from the operations of the organization. If the operations of the organization do not involve money or materials, operations are described entirely in terms of the performances (individual and cooperative) of the members. The productive outcome is some resultant decision or action that satisfies in some positive or negative degree the goal expectations of the organization.

Military operations are usually regarded as successful if they win battles or take objectives without unreasonable losses of manpower and materials. An organization that conducts a drive or campaign usually evaluates its productivity in terms of the attainment of a specific objective. A social welfare agency evaluates its productivity in terms of the services it is able to provide its clients with the available staff and finances. Business organizations usually measure productivity in terms of dollar values.

Davis (1955) defines industrial productivity as "the change in product obtained for the resources expended." This definition is elaborated: "The measure of productivity which results from applying productivity accounting is the change in output value per dollar of input between given and base periods after price changes have been eliminated."

Gold (1955) has developed productivity indexes based on measures of physical output, man-hours, fixed investment, and productive capacity. Kendrick and Creamer (1961) discuss the methods employed and problems encountered in the measurement of company productivity. The use of dollars in the measurement of productivity would appear to provide a quite stable and objective scale of values. But this stability is illusory. A dollar is not valued alike by all persons. The purchasing power of the dollar varies from time to time. The monetary scale of values is subject to evaluation in terms of other scales of value that are more subjective and more difficult to define than the monetary scale. There is no ultimate or absolute scale of values for the measurement of input and outputs. The monetary scale is the most useful because it is the easiest to measure and define.

The U.S. Department of Labor (1954) measures productivity in terms of the change in man-hours required to produce a given volume of product in one period of time compared with the man-hours required to produce the same volume of product in a base period of time. This index is a measure of the utilization of productive capacity rather than of actual productivity.

The national economy is regarded as an input-output system in which national income is regarded as an input and the gross national product as the output.

Not all inputs are transformed directly into outputs. As has been shown above, some are utilized for the maintenance of the organization. Others are converted into organizational cohesiveness and morale as outputs.

INTEGRATION

Integration is defined as the maintenance of structure and function under stress. Stress may arise within the organization or be applied externally. The importance of the integration is particularly apparent in military organizations. The military commander attempts to penetrate or sweep the enemy lines while maintaining the integrity of his own forces. A similar strategy is employed in the game of football. In order to operate effectively and avoid defeat, it is necessary to maintain structure.

Although integration is difficult to measure quantitatively, the failure to maintain cohesiveness is readily observed. Sports writers report that "the team fell apart." Military dispatches announce that "enemy opposition crumbled under our attack." Political writers report that "the cabinet fell because Mr. X was unable to gain a vote of confidence for his policies."

The importance of integration in an industrial organization is not always readily apparent. But it is there nevertheless. The members of a highly cohesive organization will not willingly permit it to be invaded by the agents of other organizations intent upon capturing some of the leadership functions of the organization. If the members do permit their organization to be successfully invaded, it is usually because their leaders have failed to maintain a cohesive organization.

Any organization, regardless of size and purpose, must maintain structure and operational effectiveness in order to attain its objectives and cope with emergencies. The survival of the organization under stress and emergency may depend upon the strong support of its members. Members tend to support the organization more strongly when they derive positive satisfactions from it. Brayfield and Crockett (1955) and Herzberg and associates (1957) have analyzed the literature on the relationship of job satisfaction to productivity and other variables. Brayfield and Crockett found that individual job satisfaction was not related significantly to work group productivity in thirteen of fifteen studies analyzed. Herzberg and associates found small positive correlations between job satisfaction and productivity in fourteen of twenty-six studies analyzed. The remaining twelve studies showed zero to negative correlations. However, they found in twenty-one of twenty-four studies analyzed that positive job satisfaction is related to reduced personnel turnover. In twelve of thirteen studies, positive job satisfaction was related to reduced absenteeism. Stogdill's (1959) analysis of the literature suggests that whereas job satisfaction is not significantly related to productivity, it is rather highly related to variables that might be regarded as measures of integration. High rates of absenteeism and personnel turnover, for example, suggest a low degree of organizational cohesiveness. When many members are separating or absenting themselves from an organization, they are not giving it very strong support.

Differential rates of absenteeism and personnel turnover in the various departments and work groups of an organization may be regarded as useful measures of integration. Satisfaction with various aspects of membership and work assignment may be treated as an indirect but useful index of organization cohesiveness. Member satisfaction contributes to organizational integration, not to productivity.

As with most generalizations in the social sciences, those stated in the preceding paragraph must be qualified. Shils (1950) and Merton and Kitt (1950) report that a member's satisfaction with an organization may be conditioned to a high degree by expectations that he develops outside the organization and by feelings of relative deprivation that develop when he compares himself to persons with whom he identifies himself in other organizations. Zaleznik, Christensen, and Roethlisberger (1958) found that reward (acceptance) by the work group and reward by management exert differential effects on member satisfaction and productivity. Individuals who were rewarded by the group tended to produce in conformity with the group norms and were relatively well satisfied. Those who were not rewarded by the group tended to produce high or low and were relatively dissatisfied. Those members who were not rewarded by the group tended to produce low under conditions of reward by management, and to produce high under conditions of non reward by management. These results suggest that consistent nonreward may be less frustrating than conflicting rewards by two different reference groups that are important to the individual. Triandis (1959) has advanced the hypothesis that the relationship between job satisfaction and productivity will be at a minimum under extremely low and extremely high degrees of pressure for productive output.

Despite the fact that it is difficult to develop direct measures of organizational integration, it is not difficult to observe the presence or absence of cohesiveness. Research by French (1941) and Lanzetta (1955) indicates that experimental groups tend to strengthen their cohesiveness under conditions of threat. French (1944) also found organized groups to be more cohesive than unstructured groups. Festinger and associates (1952), Gerard (1953), and others have reported that the members of cohesive groups exert strong pressure on deviant members to conform to the group norms, and they obtain a higher degree of compliance than do members of less well integrated groups. Hare (1952) found small groups to be more cohesive than large groups. Mills (1953) reported more stable power structure in cohesive groups. Sherif and Sherif (1953) and Thibaut (1950) have shown that cohesive groups are better able than poorly integrated groups to repel external aggression. In most of these small group studies, observers were used to assess and evaluate the cohesiveness of groups.

Integration should be regarded as a result of organization structure and operations rather than as a variable that conditions structure and operations. In other words, it is an output of organization. Of course, cohesiveness, along with other outputs, may affect structure, operations, and interpersonnel through feedback effects.

MORALE

Morale as an output of organization is defined as drive or freedom from restraint in action toward a goal. Morale defines the motivational power actually being exhibited by the organization, but not necessarily the motivational capacity of the organization. Organizations usually possess greater motivational potential than they are able to utilize except in times of emergency and stress. Organizations that attempt to maintain themselves continuously in a high state of morale under routine operating conditions (when no emergency is threatening) tend to suffer a marked reduction in cohesiveness. In addition, subgroup norms begin to operate to regulate the performances of the members and to counteract the pressures exerted upon them. Many athletic teams, especially in baseball, basketball, and football, appear to represent exceptions to the generalization stated above. But in the field of sports, every game constitutes an emergency. If athletic contests required eight hours, rather than one or two hours, of daily play, group norms would almost certainly develop to slow down and routinize the game. Baseball fans sometimes complain that the game has become boringly deliberate.

Morale represents a loosening and goal-oriented result of organizational structure and operations. Cohesiveness, on the other hand, represents a tightening and conserving outcome of structure and operations. If this distinction between morale and cohesiveness is valid, then one might expect them to be correlated negatively. Research results suggest that there is no simple linear relationship between the two variables. Studies of the groups studied by French (1941), Lippitt and White

(1943), and others indicate that member freedom of action is greatest under medium, rather than under minimum or maximum, degrees of structure. Lanzetta (1955) found that groups under stress tend to increase their cohesiveness, but they exhibit less vigor and initiative in attacking their tasks. Factor-analytic studies of group performance reported by Cattell and Stice (1953) and Haythorn (1953) indicate that morale and cohesiveness are either loaded on different factors or are inversely loaded on the same factor.

Darley, Gross, and Martin (1952), Katz, Maccoby, and Morse (1950), and Likert and Katz (1948) report that task enthusiasm is positively related to measures of productivity and that productivity is facilitated by a type of supervision that allows group members an adequate degree of freedom for initiative in task performance. Lippitt and White (1943) found that group productivity tends to be highest under moderate rather than under extreme degrees of structure. Stogdill's (1959) analysis suggests that morale may be either positively or negatively related to productivity depending upon what the group members are attempting to do. Situations can be observed in which the members of a group sabotage productivity with as much enthusiasm as they exhibit in productive work on other occasions.

It will be noted that morale is not, and cannot properly be, defined as job satisfaction. Member satisfaction is positively related to organizational cohesiveness. Research reported by Bass (1954) suggests that the relationship between satisfaction and morale (drive) is complex. The relationship was found to be positive in pleasant groups but not in unpleasant groups. In general, highly satisfied individuals do not tend to exhibit high degrees of initiative and effort. This observation should not be regarded as constituting a justification for deliberately frustrating the members of organizations as a means of motivating them. This form of motivation tends to backfire, because it serves as a stimulus to resentment, to the lowering of workgroup-productivity norms, and to reduced cohesiveness of the organization. Sound organizational morale grows out of the conditions of organization that make morale possible. Among these conditions are (1) the clear definition of roles, which permits each member to know what he is expected to do, and (2) the provision of enough freedom for initiative so that each member can attack his task with confidence and a feeling of accomplishment.

OUTPUT BALANCE

It has been suggested that operations, interpersonnel, and structure act upon the human and material inputs as processors and mediators. The result of these processing and mediating actions is the creation of three sets of outputs. The outputs are identified as productivity, integration, and morale. Material inputs are not characteristic of all organization, but the three panels of mediating variables (Figure 2) and the three panels of output variables (Figure 5) are characteristics of all organized groups.

It has been shown that the relationships between the concepts in the operations, interpersonnel, and structure panels are complex and variable. Certain pairs of variables exhibit characteristically linear relationships, while other pairs usually exhibit nonlinear relationships. But what is usually true of these relationships is not invariably true. Since the outputs of organization are resultants of the three panels of mediating variables acting on the input variables, the relationships among the variables in these panels will affect the relationships among the three output variables. That is, relationships among the output variables will change as the relationships between the input and mediating variables change. In addition, departmentation and the variables in three panels (personal characteristics, exchange with organization, and identification with organization) of the personal-organizational segment will affect the outputs.

In view of the number of variables and the complexity of the interrelationships among the variables that affect the output, it is difficult to formulate any all-inclusive statement of relationship among the output variables. If inputs are held constant and operations become stabilized over a given period of time, it would appear that an increase in one output must necessarily be accomplished at the expense of one or both of the other outputs. This assumption is in accord with research results that indicate that an increase in productivity is often associated with a reduction in cohesiveness and *vice versa*.

In order to obtain an increase in all three outputs simultaneously, it would appear necessary to increase the inputs—human, material, or both. To test this hypothesis Stogdill (1963) conducted a study of six football games. A football game appears to represent a situation in which each team invests high but varying degrees of effort, skill, and expectation as inputs in play after play. Eight high school football coaches acting as observers rated the morale (amount of pressure exerted upon opposing team) and cohesiveness (maintenance of structure under stress) on each play. The number of yards lost or gained on each play was used as a measure of team productivity. The measures of productivity, cohesiveness, and morale were found to be highly and positively correlated for the team on offense. The coaches' ratings appeared with high loadings on a general factor. But yards gained, applied pressure, and maintenance of structure also appeared as specific factors in most games. These results indicate that the measures of productivity, cohesiveness, and morale were not identical variables. They also suggest that a high and variable rate of input constitutes one of those conditions under which productivity, cohesiveness, and morale may all be made high (or low) simultaneously.

*   *   *

It is not always easy for the theorist to break loose from several decades of habituated thinking in his science. The literature since World War I has usually defined morale as job satisfaction and has insistently presented the view that morale is a determinant of productivity. In other words, morale has been regarded as a mediating or processing variable in raising or lowering productivity. More recently in the social science literature cohesiveness has also been regarded as a mediating variable that affects productivity.

In this analysis an attempt has been made to sort out the different panels of variables and to differentiate the different segments—inputs, mediators, and outputs—from one another. The mediating variables were all assigned to the Interbehavioral System. Three panels of variables—Structure, Operations, and Interpersonnel—were considered to act upon the inputs as mediators and processors. Just as productivity is an output, cohesiveness and morale must also be regarded as outputs. They are not mediators: they are resultants of the mediators acting on the input variables. Of course, the outputs may feed back to affect both input and processing variables. Continued success or failure may affect the members' willingness to invest in the organization as well as their relationships with one another.

THE ENVIRONMENTAL-ORGANIZATIONAL SEGMENT

An organization is in part a product of its physical and cultural environment. The physical environment and the nature of the resources available may place constraints upon the kinds of activities in which the organization can engage. The societal environment may prescribe the aims and structure of organization, as well as the right to organize.

An organization engages in an exchange with its environment. The physical media of exchange will be determined in part by the resources and materials provided by the environment and in part by the social value placed on the available materials by the members of the larger society. All the panels of variables that have been discussed thus far constitute avenues of exchange between an organization and its environment.

The viability of an organization is firmly rooted in the relationships that it maintains with its environment. The survival of utilitarian organizations depends upon their ability to extract from the physical environment those materials necessary to sustain their operations. Unless an organization gains unusual power, its aims and activities must be such as are tolerated by the larger social system of which it is a part. In order to survive crises an organization must maintain the internal mechanisms necessary for coping with change.

The three panels of variables (External Constraints, Exchange with Environment, and Survival Capacity) shown in Figure 6 do not account in an exhaustive fashion for the possible relationships between an organization and its environment. But they appear to account for the most critical problems involved in those relationships.

EXTERNAL CONSTRAINTS

The environment imposes numerous restraints upon human organization. Despite man's inventiveness in exploiting his environment, climate and material resources have controlled the development of human societies to a marked degree. In Arctic lands only small, loosely organized bands have been able to find the food, clothing, and materials necessary for survival. Temperate lands provide enough food and materials to support large, complex, and densely populated societies. It is observed, of course, that societies differ in their utilization and exploitation of the same available resources. The kinds of organizations that develop in a society are determined to a very large degree by the technologies utilized for exploiting the environment. Udy (1959) in a study of 150 nonindustrial organizations found that tillage, construction, animal husbandry, and manufacturing tend to be carried out by permanent organizations; and hunting, fishing, and collection by temporary organizations. Tillage and construction tend to be more complex in task structure than hunting, fishing, and collection. Organizations carrying on complex processes tend to be more highly structured in regard to status levels than organizations carrying on simpler processes.

The social environment must be regarded as a far more potent force than the physical environment in determining the purpose and form of organization. Religious belief has played a major part in the development of large, complex, stable societies. The concepts of deity and moral principle have provided relatively stable standards for the legitimation of societal authority structures. The institutions and organizations of a society derive their rights and obligations from the still higher authority defined by the folk norms and religious doctrines of the dominant members of the society. Religious institutions have tended to support and stabilize governmental and economic organizations, as well as family

EXCHANGE WITH ENVIRONMENT

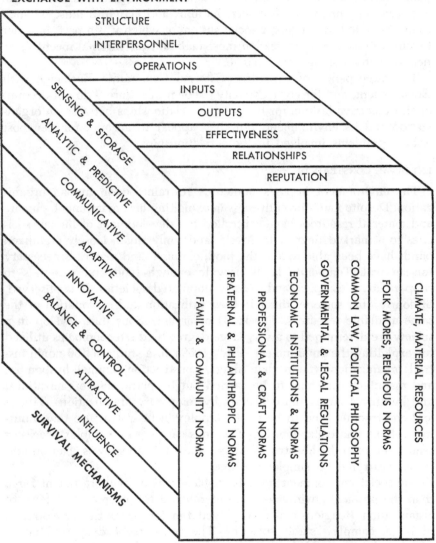

STRUCTURE
INTERPERSONNEL
OPERATIONS
INPUTS
OUTPUTS
EFFECTIVENESS
RELATIONSHIPS
REPUTATION

SENSING & STORAGE
ANALYTIC & PREDICTIVE
COMMUNICATIVE
ADAPTIVE
INNOVATIVE
BALANCE & CONTROL
ATTRACTIVE
INFLUENCE
SURVIVAL MECHANISMS

FAMILY & COMMUNITY NORMS
FRATERNAL & PHILANTHROPIC NORMS
PROFESSIONAL & CRAFT NORMS
ECONOMIC INSTITUTIONS & NORMS
GOVERNMENTAL & LEGAL REGULATIONS
COMMON LAW, POLITICAL PHILOSOPHY
FOLK MORES, RELIGIOUS NORMS
CLIMATE, MATERIAL RESOURCES

EXTERNAL CONSTRAINTS

FIGURE 6
The Environmental—Organizational Segment

structure. The reinforcement of religious belief at the family level has tended in turn to establish a wide base of legitimation among the individual citizens of the society (Parsons, 1951).

Even when rulers have succeeded in imposing a new religion upon conquered countries, they have seldom been able to displace the folk norms of the people. Governments fall, and one religion replaces another, but the folk norms and common law tend to endure. Their stability and power is such that as a social system becomes stabilized they can often be appealed to above the codified law of the land. They too provide a base for legitimation and support of the institutions and organizations of a social system and at the same time restrict their rights and privileges.

In recent centuries, particularly in Western cultures, religious doctrine has yielded considerably as the ultimate source of organizational and governmental authority. Common law and political philosophy have been utilized increasingly as bases or criteria for the legitimation of organization. The appeal of political doctrine appears to derive from the fact that it broadened the base of ultimate authority and formulated the rights of individual man as founded in folk norms and common law. The right of individuals to organize for the accomplishment of a common purpose that is sanctioned by the societal norms has provided an instrumentality for the economic, educational, artistic and cultural enrichment and advance of societies that maintain the right.

Governmental and legal regulations impose restraints on organizations in all societies with centralized governments. Udy (1959) has shown that "societies with centralized governments are more likely to possess complex hierarchies of general social stratification than are societies without centralized government." The stratification of a social system and of its component organizations provides an effective mechanism for the imposition of restrictions defined by laws and governmental regulations. Thus, the right of an organization to pursue its purposes is subject to some restraint in most societies. The same normative system that legitimizes the right to organize also legitimizes the imposition of restraints designed to preserve the social system as a whole.

The economic philosophy, norms and institutions of a society determine in part the purpose, form, and structure of the organizations it will develop. Udy (1959) has shown that the ownership, structure, recruitment practices, and reward systems of organizations are closely related to the major kinds of economic activity that support a society.

Most societies develop professional specialists who have influence and often authority by virtue of their specialized knowledge and skills. If the specialists are numerous enough to form a professional society, the society is likely to formulate norms and standards that regulate the conduct of its members and define the permissible relationships between specialist and client. Thus, the professional society and the trade association serve to protect their members in the maintenance of high standards of technical performance. Barnes (1960) reports that engineers in an industrial firm who identify themselves with the norms of their profession tend to be more productive and to present greater problems to management than do those who identify with the norms of the firm. Blau and Scott (1962) report similar findings.

The norms of the fraternal and philanthropic organizations of a society may permeate and influence the conduct of all organizations in the society. Family norms and local norms may also influence the practices and activities of the organizations in a community.

An organization is subject to great variety of constraints. Environmental factors, both physical and social, operate to delimit the aims and activities of organizations. But most of the constraining factors can also be converted by a resourceful organization into rights and opportunities for growth and achievement.

EXCHANGE WITH ENVIRONMENT

An organization may be regarded as an agent of exchange with its environment. The exchange may be of minimal character. However, governmental, economic, educational, and religious organizations tend to make major impacts upon the social system of which they are a part (Form and Miller, 1960).

All the panels of variables in the Basic (Interbehavioral) System constitute avenues of exchange between an organization and the larger social order. Contacts and negotiations between organizations tend to be carried out by members with similar functions and equivalent status rankings. The conduct of business is made possible by the fact that for almost innumerable kinds of transactions, single representatives are empowered to commit their respective organizations to binding agreements. Thus, organization structure may be regarded as providing an avenue of exchange.

The variables in the Interpersonnel panel provide several channels for exchange between the individual and the organization, as well as between the community and the organization. Mutual expectations between individuals and the organization are communicated and reinforced through interaction, intercommunication, and interpersonal affect. A member's identification with norms and reference groups in the community may affect his relationships with the organization, thereby facilitating or hindering effective exchange.

The operations of an organization provide the most easily observed channel of exchange between an organization and its environment. Many of the inputs of an organization are provided by the members of the larger society. The resulting outputs have some positive or negative social significance, even if minor in nature. If an organization operates on material objects, they must be extracted from the environment and may change it to a marked degree. The manufactured product, in turn, makes a major impact upon the society that utilizes it. Thus the variables on the Input and Output panels also constitute dimensions of exchange.

The relationships that an organization maintains with the community and with other organizations and institutions involve exchange of social values. Its reputation or image also may be regarded as involving an exchange of values. Riley and associates (1963) suggest that an organization has many publics and that its effectiveness in serving them may be determined by the differing images that it presents to its publics.

The exchange relationships between organizations and environments may change not only the social system of which they are a part, but even the surface of the earth that they inhabit.

SURVIVAL MECHANISMS

Often an organization is developed to attain a single specific objective. Once the mission is accomplished, the organization is disbanded. But many kinds of organizations have continuing objectives that extend into the indefinite future. Their failure might create hardships for large numbers of persons and in some cases for the society as a whole. Thus, many organizations regard survival as a fundamental objective, although it is not stated explicitly as such.

The survival of an organization is rooted in the relationships that it maintains with its physical-social environment. It must be capable of coping with environmental change. In other words, an organization should provide itself with the functions, arrangements, and mechanisms necessary to assess its internal condition, as well as those needed to assess the presence and trend of environmental change (Rice, 1963; Thompson and Bates, 1959).

There is a rather large body of literature on the problem of organization change. The principles of change are discussed by Ginzberg and Reilley (1957). Case studies are presented by Ronken and Lawrence (1952) and Jaques (1952). The readings edited by Lawrence and associates (1961) and Bennis, Benne, and Chin (1961) cover case histories, theory, and research. Baum (1961), Blau (1956), and Gouldner (1954) discuss bureaucratic structures that are resistant to change.

Organizations often appear more sensitive to the impact of external change than to the necessity for internal change. But this is not always true. The nature of organizational mechanisms for sensing internal and external change is not well understood. Organization analysts usually recommend the maintenance and encouragement of upward communication as a means of sensing the need for internal change. There can be no doubt of the value of this recommendation. But members in the lower and middle echelons of a large organization are not always aware of the exact nature and magnitude of internal problems. Top management seems to need to be better sensitized to the importance and operation of basic dimensions of organization. Problems arising in connection with variables that are not regarded as an integral and legitimate aspect of organization are likely to be ignored or rejected. This observation applies in particular to variables in the Interpersonnel panel.

The memory of an organization resides not only in the memories of its individual workers, but also in its repository of written records, when such are available. Ready access to information in storage often provides an important survival advantage. But memory may constitute a handicap as well as an advantage. Organizations appear particularly unable to forget unfortunate incidents and unfavorable outcomes. Such memories of unpleasant events often lead to the rejection of proposals for change and innovation without adequate consideration of their possible advantages.

Analysis, diagnosis, and evaluation are facilitated by a sound body of professional knowledge. Better methods are available for determining the need for change in structure and operations than for change in interpersonnel. Changes in structure are often recommended as cures for problems in interpersonnel. Systematic and comprehensive research is needed to isolate the conditions that determine and limit various problems in interpersonnel, as well as the relation of such problems to structure and operations. Remedial action should be based on diagnosis that considers the possible effects of, and the new problems likely to be created by, the action.

Certain kinds of organizations maintain such delicately balanced relationships with their environment that their survival depends upon the ability to predict change. Military organizations maintain departments of intelligence that are responsible for collecting and evaluating information that will be useful for predicting enemy action. The sales departments of large industrial and retailing organizations maintain departments whose function it is to anticipate consumer demand and ability to buy. It is costly and hazardous to manufacture or store more than can be sold. The maintenance of an effective arrangement for predicting change and trend is coming to be recognized as a prime necessity in various kinds of organizations.

The importance of communications has been discussed in connection with the problem of internal sensing. Communication provides a primary channel for sensing external conditions and for effecting an impact upon the social environment. All members of an organization constitute potential or active channels of communication between the organization and the community. Members of the lower echelons do not always communicate what members in the higher echelons would like to have communicated. Unofficial communications are often more potent than official ones in determining the public image of an organization.

Although numerous organizations maintain specialized functions or departments that are responsible for sensing, evaluating, and predicting change, few maintain specialized functions for adapting to change. The intelligence function may collect and evaluate information regarding the nature of change. The planning function may anticipate change and develop plans for coping with it. But these functions are seldom responsible for the initiation of action designed to cope with change. Such action is usually initiated in higher echelons, which are responsible for policy formation and coordination of activities. The physical separation of the executive function from sensing, predictive, and evaluative functions renders an organization vulnerable to breakdowns in communications. This vulnerability resides not only in the failure to communicate, but also in the frequent reluctance of higher echelons to accept as authentic the communications received from lower echelons. Lower echelons also exhibit reluctance to accept communications that involve changes in role performance. Once the structure and operations of an organization have become stabilized, all status levels tend to resist change. Research results suggest that the acceptance of change is facilitated when all members who will be affected are involved in the task of planning for change.

With rapid advances in technology, the survival of an increasingly large percentage of organizations depends upon the capacity for innovation. Product innovation often involves innovation in organization structure and operations. Organizations tend to be conservative. Changes in structure and operations always involve a cost to the members in that they must redefine their roles and change their ways of doing things. Members become accustomed to the fact that the coordinative requirements of the organization set bounds to the initiative and performance of each role. Innovation and creativity require that certain roles be defined with wider areas of freedom than is customary for routine operations.

One of the triumphs of the Classical Theory has been the development of principles and procedures for coordinating and controlling the operations of organization. Poor coordination in industrial organizations can result in bankruptcy. It would be foolishly costly, for example, to permit most departments to manufacture materials for a thousand assemblies if the department responsible for one critical part could make only enough to complete a hundred assemblies. As the operations of an organization become more complex and as its relationships with its environment become more sensitive, the demands for coordination tend to increase.

Organization control is a function designed to determine the extent to which performance corresponds with stated objectives. Accounting reports, productivity charts, progress reports, and related oral and written communications enable members in coordinative positions to assess the extent to which an organization is performing as it is expected to perform. The necessity for control increases as the margin between success and failure narrows. The higher the level at which first line operations are coordinated, the greater the need for prompt and accurate control procedures. Immediately and constantly available control information is needed for the effective operation of the automated plant.

Academic training and experience in operative positions of organization do not necessarily provide an adequate basis for understanding the extent to which coordination and control influence the definition of roles. Unsatisfactory role definition is usually attributed to the whim of supervisors or managers. This is often, but not always, the case. The greater the demands for organizational coordination and control, the more closely must role performance be defined, regardless of the personality or inclinations of supervisors. This fact has induced a number of large corporations to disperse their manufacturing operations. Each of several subunits can usually maintain a higher degree of freedom for initiative in role enactment for the attainment of a single subordinate objective than is possible in a larger organization that must coordinate operations for several subordinate objectives. Formalized control procedures are associated with complexity of operations. They are also associated with the depersonalization of performance.

Organizations differ in the mechanisms they devise for attracting members and customers. The purpose of an organization may be sufficient in itself to attract a closely defined category of members. Usually an organization must render a minimally satisfying service in order to attract members or customers. Many organizations depend primarily upon their reward (salary) systems to attract and hold members. But an adequate pay schedule does not necessarily guarantee the loyal support of members. Many other factors, such as recognition of performance, opportunity for contribution and advancement, security of position, and satisfaction of expectations, tend to strengthen member support of the organization. Advertising and a reputation for providing a satisfying product or service tend to attract customers.

As a society tends increasingly to grant legally defined privileges to organizations and to regulate their activities on a differential basis, they tend to develop mechanisms for influencing legislation and public opinion. Public relations departments and lobbyists have the specific function of influencing the environment to the advantage of the organization.

❉   ❉   ❉

The physical-social environment imposes a great variety of constraints upon an organization. The right to organize as well as the purpose and structure of organization may be determined to a high degree by the structure of the society of which the organization is a part. Organizations of all sorts engage in exchange relationships with their environments. Members take into an organization values acquired from the larger society. The organization in turn creates at least some minumum change of value that is carried back into the larger societal system.

Organizations maintain a great variety of arrangements, mechanisms, or functions for coping with internal and external change. The various mechanisms may not always be used simultaneously, but the survival of an organization may depend upon their being readily available when needed. It is a function of management to keep the effects of their use in balance.

SUMMARY

After a half century of development the classical theory has achieved a marked degree of sophistication in the analysis of organization. The development of structures for the effective management and control of complex operations is based on a highly rationalized system of thought.

Recent experimental and theoretical advances in the social sciences have also contributed to the understanding of organization. They have shown that intermember relations must be regarded as constituting an integral aspect of organization. The interaction concept is basic to the definition of social group; and the concept of intermember expectation is basic to the definition of organization. Our analysis suggests that the concept *interpersonnel* serves to bind structure, operations, and member interrelations into an *interbehavioral system* that processes inputs and generates outputs. The advantage of this formulation is that it incorporates a dimension of theory that has heretofore been regarded as alien and illegitimate, and hence to be ignored. Both experience and research have demonstrated, however, that it can be ignored only at a heavy cost to organizational cohesiveness, productivity, and morale. If it is a reality of organization, it should constitute one of the dimensions of organization theory.

Our analysis suggests that the relationships that an organization maintains with its members and with its physical-social environment involve problems that cannot be ignored in practice; nor can the impact of various norm systems that are applied in the evaluation of organization be ignored. If the organization must cope with problems of relationship and evaluation, then these problems should be recognized in the body of theory about organizations.

All the variables and problems discussed in this analysis are regarded as legitimate in one or more segments of theory in the fields of anthropology, business organization, economics, political science, psychology, and sociology. They must be dealt with in practice, if only blindly and resentfully when their legitimacy is denied. They can be dealt with more adequately in the long run if they are regarded as integral aspects of organization. The operations and interrelations of a set of variables are best understood when incorporated in a single theoretical system that can be subjected to logical analysis and experimental validation.

An attempt has been made to examine the scope of organization theory and to show that several panels of variables belong in the same multidimensional system. This is a study in breadth rather than depth. It has been concerned only incidentally with the logical structure of the system. However, research results have been cited that indicate that considerable progress has been made in determining the logical structure of certain segments or subsets of the theory.

Both the classical theory and social science research have produced various principles of organization that exhibit considerable general validity. However, accumulating research results suggest that exceptions are encountered in relation to each of these principles. Systematic research is needed to determine the limiting conditions attending the principles and the alternative actions required under various exceptional conditions.

Under the impact of systematic research and theoretical refinements, large amorphous systems tend to reveal structure that permits improved understanding, prediction, and practice. The hope for such benefits serves as a continuing stimulus to the development of an integrated theory of organization. But this is a task in which quite moderate aspirations can be easily frustrated. Moore and Snyder (1952) have cautioned that "no definition of organization will accommodate the jarring impact of the real world, but the utility of a definition does not depend upon that. An integrated theory of organization if and when it is attained, will not say everything everyone knows about every empirical organization."

A theory of organization is not necessarily a theory of management. Management theory can, and in fact must, be derived from organization theory. But management theory tends to involve philosophical assumptions and value orientations regarding the nature of human behavior that are not basic to a theory of organization.

A theory of management is a theory of practice. It is of course interested in facts and sound principles. But theories of practice regarding human nature and human relations almost always involve schools of thought that differ in their philosophical orientations. The disputes between social scientists and the classical theorists are concerned with differences in recommended practice. These differences are based on variations in philosophical and professional committment. While these differences are significant for the practice of management, they do not affect any of the realities regarding the dimensions of organization. It is argued that organization theory is an instrument not for conducting ideological dispute but for acquiring verifiable knowledge.

REFERENCES

ABBREVIATIONS

ASQ   *Administrative Science Quarterly*
ASR   *American Sociological Review*
JAP   *Journal of Applied Psychology*
JASP *Journal of Abnormal and Social Psychology*
HR   *Human Relations*

Allee, W. C. *Cooperation Among Animals, With Human Implications.* New York: Schuman, 1951.
Asch, S. E. *Social Psychology.* Englewood Cliffs: Prentice-Hall, 1952.
Baker, A. W. and Davis, R. C. *Ratios of Staff to Line Employees and Stages of Differentiation of Staff Functions.* Columbus: Ohio State U., Bureau of Business Research, Monograph No. 72, 1954.
Bales, R. F. *Interaction Process Analysis: A Method for the Study of Small Groups.* Cambridge, Mass.: Addison-Wesley, 1950.
Bales, R. F. and Strodtbeck, F. L. "Phases in Group Problem Solving." *JASP*, 1951, 46, 485–495.
Barnard, C. I. *Functions of the Executive.* Cambridge: Harvard U. Press, 1938.
Barnard, C. I. *Organization and Management.* Cambridge: Harvard U. Press, 1948.
Barnes, L. B. *Organizational Systems and Engineering Groups.* Boston: Harvard Business School, Division of Research, 1960.

Bass, B. M. "Behavior in Groups II. Increased Attraction to the Group as a Function of Individual and Group Goal Attainment." Baton Rouge: Louisiana State U., Dept. of Psychology, 1955. (Unpublished report.)

Bass, B. M. "Feelings of Pleasantness and Work Group Efficiency." *Personnel Psych.*, 1954, 7, 81–91.

Bass, B. M. *Leaadership, Psychology, and Organizational Behavior.* New York: Harper, 1960.

Baum, B. H. *Decentralization of Authority in a Bureaucracy.* Englewood Cliffs: Prentice-Hall, 1961.

Bavelas, A. "Communication Patterns in Task Oriented Groups." *J. Accoustical Society of America,* 1950, 22, 725–730.

Bennis, W. G., Benne, K. D. and Chin, R. *The Planning of Change.* New York: Holt, Rinehart Winston, 1961.

Berg, I. A. and Bass, B. M. *Conformity and Deviation,* New York: Harper, 1961.

Berger, J., Cohen, B. F., Snell, J. B. and Zelditch, M. *Types of Formalization in Small Group Research.* Boston: Houghton Mifflin, 1962.

Bion, W. R. *Experiences in Groups.* New York: Basic Books, 1961.

Blau, P. M. *Bureaucracy in Modern Society.* New York: Random House, 1956.

Blau, P. M. and Scott, W. R. *Formal Organizations,* San Francisco: Chandler, 1962.

Bonner, J. T. *Group Dynamics.* New York: Ronald, 1959.

Borgatta, E. F. and Bales, R. F., "Interaction of Individuals in Reconstituted Groups." *Sociometry,* 1953, *16,* 302–320.

Brayfield, A. H. and Crockett, W. H. "Employee Attitudes and Employee Performance." *Psychological Bull.,* 1955, 52, 396–424.

Brown, A. *Organization: A Formulation of Principle.* New York: Hibbert, 1945.

Cartwright, D. and Zander, A. *Group Dynamics: Research and Theory.* Evanston, Ill.: Row, Peterson, 1953 (2nd ed., 1960).

Cattell, R. B. and Stice, G. F. *The Psychodynamics of Small Groups.* Urbana: U. of Illinois, Laboratory for Personality Assessment and Group Behavior, 1953. (Mimeo.)

Centers, R. *The Psychology of Social Classes.* Princeton: Princeton U. Press, 1949.

Cooley, C. H. *Social Organization.* New York: Scribners, 1909.

Crisswell, J. H., Salomon, H., and Suppes, P. *Mathematical Methods in Small Group Process.* Stanford, Cal.: Stanford U. Press, 1962.

Cyert, R. M. and March, J. G. *A Behavioral Theory of the Firm.* Englewood Cliffs: Prentice-Hall, 1963.

Dale, E. *Planning and Developing the Company Organization Structure.* New York: American Management Assn., 1952.

Darley, J. G., Gross, N. and Martin, W. E. "Studies of Group Behavior: Factors Associated with the Productivity of Groups." *JAP,* 1952, *36,* 396–403.

Davis, H. S. *Productivity Accounting.* Philadelphia: U. of Pennsylvania Press, 1955.

Davis, K. *Human Society.* New York: Macmillan, 1949.

Davis, R. C. *Fundamentals of Top Management.* New York: Harper, 1951.

Dubin, R. "Power and Union—Management Relations." *ASQ,* 1957, *2,* 60–81.

Etzioni, A. *A Comparative Analysis of Complex Organizations.* Glencoe, Ill.: Free Press, 1961.

Fayol, H. *General and Industrial Administration*. London: Pitman, 1949.

Fensterheim, H. and Tresselt, M. E. "The Influence of Value Systems on the Perception of People." *JASP*, 1953, *48*, 93–98.

Festinger, L., Gerard, H. B., Hymovitch, B., Kelley, H. H., and Raven, B., "The Influence Process in the Presence of Extreme Deviates." *HR*, 1952, *5*, 327–346.

Fiedler, F. E. "Assumed Similarity Measures and Predictors of Team Effectiveness." *JASP*, 1954, *49*, 381–388.

Flament, C. *Applications of Graph Theory to Group Structure*. Englewood Cliffs, Prentice-Hall, 1963.

Follett, Mary P. *Freedom and Coordination*. London: Management Publications Trust, 1949.

Form, W. H. and Miller, D. C. *Industry, Labor and Community*. New York: Harper and Row, 1960.

French, J. R. P. "The Disruption and Cohesion of Groups." *JASP*, 1941, *36*, 361–377.

French, J. R. P. "Organized and Unorganized Groups under Fear and Frustration." *U. of Iowa Studies in Child Welfare*, 1944, *20*, 231–308.

Gagné, R. M. and Fleishman, E. A. *Psychology and Human Performance*. New York: Holt, 1959.

Gerard, H. B. "The Effect of Different Dimensions of Disagreement on the Communication Process in Small Groups." *HR*, 1953, *6*, 249–271.

Ginzberg, E. and Reilley, E. W. *Effecting Change in Large Organizations*. New York: Columbia U. Press, 1957.

Gold, B. *Foundations of Productivity Analysis*. Pittsburgh: U. of Pittsburgh Press, 1955.

Gouldner, A. W. *Patterns of Industrial Bureaucracy*. Glencoe, Ill.: Free Press, 1954.

Guetzkow, H. *Simulation in Social Science*. Englewood Cliffs: Prentice-Hall, 1962.

Guetzkow, H. and Simon, H. A. "The Impact of Certain Communication Nets upon Organization and Performance in Task-Oriented Groups." *Management Science*, 1955, *1*, 233–250.

Hare, A. P. A Study of Interaction and Consensus in Different Sized Groups. *ASR*, 1952, *17*, 261–267.

Hare, A. P., Borgatta, E. F. and Bales, R. F. *Small Groups: Studies in Social Interaction*. New York: Knopf, 1955.

Harrell, T. W. *Industrial Psychology*. New York: Rinehart, 1958.

Haythorn, W. "The Influence of Individual Members on the Characteristics of Small Groups." *JASP*, 1953, *48*, 276–248.

Hemphill, J. K. *Group Dimensions: A Manual for Their Measurement*. Columbus: Ohio State U., Bureau of Business Research, Monograph No. 87, 1956.

Herzberg, F., Mausner, B., Peterson, R. O. and Capwell, Dora F. *Job Attitudes; Review of Research and Opinion*. Pittsburgh: Psychological Service of Pittsburgh, 1957.

Homans, G. C. *The Human Group*. New York: Harcourt, Brace, 1950.

Horsfall, A. B. and Arensberg, C. M. "Teamwork and Productivity in a Shoe Factory." *Human Organization*, 1949, *8* (1), 13–25.

Horwitz, M. "Power Identification, Nationalism, and International Organizations." (Unpublished report, 1963.)

Jaques, E. *The Changing Culture of a Factory.* New York: Dryden, 1952.

Jennings, Helen H. *Leadership and Isolation.* New York: Longmans, Green, 1950.

Kahl, J. A. *The American Class Structure.* New York: Rinehart, 1957.

Kahn, R. L. *Conflict and Ambiguity: Studies in Organizational Roles and Personal Stress.* New York: Wiley, 1964.

Katz, D., Maccoby, N. and Morse, N. C. *Productivity, Supervision and Morale in an Office Situation.* Ann Arbor: U. of Michigan, Institute for Social Research, 1950.

Kendrick, J. W. and Creamer, D. *Measuring Company Productivity.* New York: National Industrial Conference Board, 1961.

Koontz, H. D. and O'Donnell, C. J. *Principles of Management.* New York: McGraw-Hill, 1955.

Lanzetta, J. T. "Group Behavior under Stress." *HR*, 1955, *8*, 29–52.

Lawrence, P. R. *Organizational Behavior and Administration.* Homewood, Ill.: Dorsey, 1961.

Leavitt, H. J. *Managerial Psychology.* Chicago: U. of Chicago Press, 1958.

Leavitt, H. J., ed. *The Social Science of Organizations.* Englewood Cliffs: Prentice-Hall, 1963.

Leavitt, H. J. "Some Effects of Certain Communication Patterns on Group Performance." *JASP*, 1951, *46*, 38–50.

Lenski, G. E. "Social Participation and Status Crystalization." *ASR*, 1956, *21*, 458–464.

Likert, R. and Katz, D. "Supervisory Practices and Organizational Structures as they Affect Employee Productivity and Morale." *American Management Assn., Personnel Series* No. 120, 1948.

Lippitt, R. and White, R. K. "The Social Climate of Children's Groups." In R. G. Barker, J. S. Kounin, and H. F. Wright, eds. *Child Behavior and Development.* New York: McGraw-Hill, 1943.

Luce, R. D., Bush, R. R. and Galanter, E. *Handbook of Mathematical Psychology.* New York: Wiley, 1963.

McGregor, D. *The Human Side of Enterprise.* New York: McGraw-Hill, 1960.

March, J. G. and Simon, H. A. *Organizations.* New York: Wiley, 1958.

Mayo, E. *The Human Problems of an Industrial Civilization.* New York: Macmillan, 1933.

Mead, G. H. *Mind, Self and Society.* Chicago, U. of Chicago Press, 1934.

Merton, R. K. and Kitt, A. S. "Contributions to the Theory of Reference Group Behavior." In R. K. Merton and P. F. Lazarsfeld, eds. *Studies in the Scope and Method of "The American Soldier."* Glencoe, Ill.: Free Press, 1950.

Mills, T. M. "Power Relations in Three-Person Groups." *ASR*, 1953, *18*, 351–357.

Moore, W. E. and Snyder, R. C. "The Conference on Theory of Organization." *Social Science Research Council Items*, 1952, *6*, (4), 41–45.

Moreno, J. L. *Who Shall Survive?* Beacon, New York: Beacon House, 1953.

Newcomb, T. M. *The Acquaintance Process.* New York: Holt, Rinehart & Winston, 1961.

Newcomb, T. M. *Personality and Social Change.* New York: Dryden, 1943.

Newcomb, T. M. *Social Psychology*. New York: Dryden, 1950.

Parsons, T. *The Social System*. Glencoe, Ill.: Free Press, 1951.

Parsons, T. and Shils, E. A. *Toward a General Theory of Action*. Cambridge: Harvard U. Press, 1952.

Petersen, E., Plowman, E. G. and Trickett, J. M., *Business Organization and Management*. 5th ed. Homewood, Ill.: Irwin, 1962.

Precker, J. A. "Similarity of Valuings as a Factor in Selection of Peers and Near–Authority Figures." *JASP*, 1952, *47*, 406–414.

Rapoport, A. "Forms of Output Distribution between Two Individuals Motivated by a Satisfaction Function." *Bull. Mathematical Biophysics*, 1947, *9*, 109–122.

Rapoport, A. "In Search of Quantifiable Parameters of Group Performance." In D. P. Eckman, *Systems: Research and Design*. New York: Wiley, 1961.

Rashevsky, N. *Mathematical Biology of Social Behavior*. Chicago: U. of Chicago Press, 1951.

Renck, R. "Morale in Four Key Groups in Industry." In *Conference on Employee Attitude Surveys*. Chicago: U. of Chicago, Industrial Relations Center, 1955.

Rice, A. K. *The Enterprise and Its Environment*. London: Tavistock Publications, 1963.

Riley, J. W. *The Corporation and Its Publics*. New York: Wiley, 1963.

Roethlisberger, F. J. and Dickson, W. J. *Management and the Worker*. Cambridge: Harvard U. Press, 1939.

Ronken, Harriet O. and Lawrence, P. R. *Administering Changes*. Boston: Harvard U., Graduate School of Business Administration, 1952.

Sayles, L. R. *Behavior of Industrial Work Groups: Prediction and Control*. New York: Wiley, 1958.

Shartle, C. L. *Occupational Information*. Englewood Cliffs: Prentice-Hall, 1959.

Sherif, M. *The Psychology of Social Norms*. New York: Harper, 1936.

Sherif, M. and Sherif, Carolyn W. *An Outline of Social Psychology*, New York: Harper, 1956.

Sherif, M. and Sherif, Carolyn W. *Groups in Harmony and Tension*. New York: Harper, 1953.

Shils, E. A. "Primary Groups in the American Army." In R. A. Merton and P. F. Lazarsfeld, eds. *Studies in the Scope and Method of "The American Soldier."* Glencoe, Ill.: Free Press, 1950.

Simmel, G. *The Sociology of Georg Simmel*. Trans. by K. H. Wolff. Glencoe, Ill.: Free Press, 1950.

Smith, A. J. "Similarity of Values and Its Relation to Acceptance and the Rejection of Similarity." *J. Psychology*, 1957, *43*, 251–260

Sofer, C. *The Organization from Within*. Chicago: Quadrangle Books, 1963.

Stogdill, R. M. *Individual Behavior and Group Achievement*. New York: Oxford U. Press, 1959.

Stogdill, R. M. *Team Achievement under High Motivation*. Columbus: Ohio State U., Bureau of Business Research, Monograph No. 113, 1963.

Stogdill, R. M. and Haase, Katheleen K. "Structures of Working Relationships." In R. M. Stogdill, ed. *Leadership and Structures of Personal*

Interaction. Columbus: Ohio State U., Bureau of Business Research, Monograph No. 84, 1957.

Stogdill, R. M. and Scott, E. L. "Responsibility and Authority Relationships." In R. M. Stogdill, *Leadership and Structures of Personal Interaction.* Columbus: Ohio State U., Bureau of Business Research, Monograph No. 84, 1957.

Stouffer, S. A., Suchman, E. A., DeVinney, L. C., Star, S. A. and Williams, R. M. *The American Soldier: Adjustment During Army Life.* Princeton: Princeton U. Press 1949.

Suppes, P. and Atkinson, R. C. *Markov Learning Models for Multiperson Interactions.* Stanford, Cal.: Stanford U. Press, 1960.

Tagiuri, R. and Petrullo, L. *Person Perception and Interpersonal Behavior.* Stanford, Cal.: Stanford U. Press, 1958.

Taylor, F. W. *The Principles of Scientific Management.* New York: Harper, 1911.

Thelen, H. A. et al. *Methods for Studying Work and Emotionality in Group Operation.* Chicago: U. of Chicago, Human Dynamics Laboratory, 1954. (Mimeo.)

Thibaut, J. W. "An Experimental Study of the Cohesiveness of Underprivileged Groups." *HR*, 1950, 3, 251–278.

Thibaut, J. W. and Kelley, H. H. *The Social Psychology of Groups.* New York: Wiley, 1959.

Thompson, J. D. et al. *Comparative Studies in Administration.* Pittsburgh: U. of Pittsburgh Press, 1959.

Thompson, J. D. and Bates, F. L. "Technology, Organization and Administration." In J. D. Thompson et al. *Comparative Studies in Administration.* Pittsburgh: U. of Pittsburgh Press, 1959.

Triandis, H. C. "A Critique and Experimental Design for the Study of the Relationship between Productivity and Satisfaction. *Psychological Bull.*, 1959, 56, 309–312.

Triandis, H. C. "Notes on the Design of Organizations." In James D. Thompson, ed. *Approaches to Organizational Design.* Pittsburgh: U. of Pittsburgh Press, 1965.

Udy, S. H. *Organization of Work.* New Haven, Conn.: HRAF Press, 1959.

U. S. Department of Labor. *Techniques of Preparing Major BLS Statistical Series.* Washington: Bureau of Labor Statistics, 1954.

Urwick, L. *The Golden Book of Management.* London: Newman Neame, 1956.

Whisler, T. L. and Harper, Shirley F., *Performance Appraisal: Research and Practice.* New York: Holt, Rinehart & Winston, 1962.

Whyte, W. F. *Money and Motivation.* New York: Harper, 1955.

Willner, Dorothy, ed. *Decisions, Values and Groups.* New York: Pergamon, 1962.

Yoder, D., Heneman, H. G., and Cheit, E. F. *Triple Audit of Industrial Relations.* Minneapolis: U. of Minnesota Press, 1951.

Zaleznik, A., Christensen, C. R. and Roethlisberger, F. J. *The Motivation, Productivity, and Satisfaction of Workers.* Boston: Harvard U., Graduate School Business Administration, 1958.

2

Notes on the Design of Organizations

HARRY C. TRIANDIS

Associate Professor of Psychology, University of Illinois.
This chapter should probably bear the names of all the participants in my group at the Seminar, for it contains many key ideas and approaches supplied by my colleagues. The broad framework of variables and the emphasis on organizational functions were supplied by Raymond Katzell, the contingency model of the prediction of leadership effectiveness by Fred Fiedler; the discussions were most ably led by Nathan Maccoby, who supplied innumerable insights that later developed into formal hypotheses; John Miner played the salutary role of reminding us to keep the individual in our developing scheme. Other members of the Seminar were also influential in molding this chapter. Ralph Stogdill's (1959) thinking blended well with our developing scheme; Herbert Simon's emphasis on organizational goals gave me an important new direction for thinking about organizations. A critical reading of an earlier version of this chapter by participants in my group at the seminar and by Robert Ewen, Martin Fishbein, and Charles Hulin is gratefully acknowledged.

This chapter focuses on the *design* of organizations. The emphasis on design suggests that consideration of the activities of design engineers, or other professionals concerned with design problems may prove helpful. For example, how does an engineer proceed when he designs a bridge? First, he obtains the information about the constraints of his problem—e.g., expected traffic patterns, geography and geology of the area, rates of erosion, weather characteristics that determine speed of winds, and expected weight of snow likely to accumulate on the bridge. Next, given the restraints of his problem, which specify the location, size, and load characteristics of the bridge, he determines the size and cost of the various structures that are likely to perform effectively under those conditions. Finally, he considers modifications in his original design that might reduce the cost.

If we consider this analogy and attempt to apply it to the problem of the design of organizations, it is obvious that we must answer a number of questions: (a) What are the dimensions that define the environments of organizations? (b) What are the dimensions that define the characteristics of organizations? (c) What are the criteria of organizational effectiveness? The first question calls on us to identify the constraints of our problem, the second to identify the different designs that are possible, and the third to evaluate the cost and utility of a solution.

This chapter will attempt to answer these questions, although because of the lack of systematic research the present answers can be no more than educated guesses. Nonetheless, even if they are partially or even totally wrong, they will perhaps constitute a beginning in the systematic research of organizations. This chapter is actually a series of interlocking research proposals, and it is hoped that the proposals are sufficiently specific to permit the immediate collection of data that will test the hypotheses and determine what modifications are necessary.

The organization of the chapter is as follows: First is presented a scheme for the classification of variables. This scheme groups variables into *inputs* (or constraints of the organizational problem) *structures, functions,* and *outputs* (or criteria of organizational effectiveness). Inputs are defined by characteristics of the environment and the resources available to the organization. Structures are defined by the relationships among key elements of the organization. Functions are processes that must occur in order to obtain a given output. Outputs are measures of organizational effectiveness. Second, the relationship among variables within each of the groupings is examined; for example, how the output variables relate to each other. Third, some illustrative hypotheses are offered, which connect some of the key variables to each other. Finally, a possible research strategy that will permit the sharper formulation of organizational theory is examined.

A THEORETICAL SCHEME

There have been many significant attempts to organize the data and thinking about organizations into theoretical schemes. Among the major attempts are those of March and Simon (1958) and the chapters of several theorists in Haire (1959). Most of these attempts have focused on some of the relationships among significant organizational variables. The present attempt is somewhat more inclusive, but also looser and possibly less valuable than the more limited attempts of other analyses. Nevertheless, it does represent the answers of our seminar group to questions such as: What are the major variables of organization theory? Can they be classified in any meaningful way? What are the major types of relationships that ought to be investigated?

The variables required to describe organizations are numerous, and only the most important will be considered in the present chapter. Table 1 lists some of those variables—a list not intended to be exhaustive. Consideration of the variables will, however, permit adequate though crude characterizations of any organizational design. Examination of the variables listed in Table 1 will not permit the reader in all cases to understand their intended meaning. For this reason, the discussion that follows describes some of the more obscure variables and give examples that will help the reader to conceptualize them.

INPUTS

The environment. The economic environment of the organization is defined by its position in the markets of its various products (e.g., competitive, oligopolistic, monopolistic), the demand for its products, the elasticity of this demand, etc. The political-legal environment defines limitations in organizational behavior (e.g., antitrust legislation) as well as factors that may provide enhanced motivation to the members to reach the goals of the organization (e.g., the presence of a common enemy, as in war, price war, or threat to the life of the organization).

The history. It is obvious that previous decisions relevant to organizational behavior have an influence on subsequent organizational behavior (e.g., previous decisions about wage levels are used as baselines for the determination of new wage levels). Thus, the organizational history is

TABLE 1
The Four Groups of Variables of the Theoretical Scheme

INPUTS	STRUCTURES	FUNCTIONS	OUTPUTS
ENVIRONMENT *Economic* *Political-legal* e.g., Presence of common enemy *Working conditions* ORGANIZATIONAL HISTORY *Previous decisions* *Existing structures* e.g., flat-tall *Climate of labor-management relations* OTHER CONSTRAINTS *Lack of* good new ideas know-how good people capital markets	INTERACTIONS AND COMMUNICATION *Type of* who to whom how frequently who initiates functional-emergent formal-informal SOCIOMETRIC *Position of leader in this structure* STATUS *Power structure* *Status congruence* ORGANIZATIONAL STRUCTURE *Tall-flat* *Span of control* *Division of labor* no. of roles/no. of men uniqueness of roles line-staff locus of decision locus of responsibility	LEADER *Promotive* (initiating structure) information receiving processing planning organizing integrating coordinating directing controlling measuring results training generating insights *Maintenance* (consideration) goal formulation role specification norm specification group identification rewarding reconciliation process facilitation *Monitoring* pressure for production norm enforcement	OBJECTIVE *Quantity of product* *Quality of production* *Profits* *Absenteeism* *Turnover rates* ATTITUDINAL *General satisfaction* *Intrinsic job satisfaction* *Self-actualization* satisfaction with extent of use of abilities satisfaction with responsibility and authority satisfaction with promotions satisfaction with self-development *Satisfaction with supervision* satisfaction with supervisory administrative abilities satisfaction with supervisory consideration satisfaction with workload and pressure

TABLE 1 (CONTINUED)

INPUTS	STRUCTURES	FUNCTIONS	OUTPUTS
RESOURCES	GROUP CHARACTERISTICS	EMPLOYEES	confidence in justice and interest of management
People	*Size*	*Participation*	satisfaction with communications
Demographic characteristics	*Cohesion*	in decisions	*Satisfaction with job security*
e.g., age, race, social class, rural-urban backgrounds, religion	*Permeability*	in norm formulation	*Satisfaction with working conditions*
Abilities	*Viscidity* (absence of strife)	*Use of skills*	satisfaction with work load and pressure of job itself
e.g., verbal, quantitative, perceptual	*Heterogeneity*	*Productive behavior*	satisfaction with work environment, including hours, shifts, health hazards, etc.
Personality	member abilities	exertion of effort	low fatigue or monotony
e.g., tolerance for uncertainty, persuasiveness, perceptive of least preferred co-worker	personality	exploration of environment	*Satisfaction with fellow employees*
Attitudes, interests, goals, values	attitudes	acquisition of information	*Financial satisfaction*
Reference groups of the employee and characteristics of these groups	goals	problem-solving	satisfaction with salary or wages
Habits	interests	*Obtaining rewards from using abilities*	satisfaction with vacation rules and fringe benefits
	FIT	*Obtaining rewards from social comparisons*	satisfaction with insurance plans
	Between job requirements and		satisfaction with profit sharing plans
	member abilities		
	personality		
	attitudes		
	behavior		
	Relation of individual and		
	group goals		
	leader goals		
	company goals		

TABLE 1 (CONTINUED)

INPUTS	STRUCTURES	FUNCTIONS	OUTPUTS
Normative resources e.g., ideas about appropriate power appropriate behavior of company toward employees appropriate behavior of supervisor toward subordinate company to public, customers, etc. *Financial Resources* *Technical know-how* TECHNOLOGY *Equipment* *Job characteristics* structure percent programmed by environment complexity visibility (can supervisor check performance?) requirements ability personality e.g., personal contacts with insiders—outsiders			*Pride in organization* *Morale:* Congruence of individual and group goals

one of the constraints of the design of a new organization. Other constraints, such as the lack of good new ideas, know-how, good people, capital, markets are also listed.

The resources.   The resources available to the organization are indicated under the headings "people," "technology," "financial," and "normative." Most of these variables are self-evident. In describing people, approximately sixty variables may prove useful (Cattell, 1957). Some of them deal with abilities, some with personality, and some with interests, attitudes, etc. In addition, it may be important to utilize special variables for the measurement of characteristics of persons having a particular role in the organization. For instance, Fiedler (1958) has found a variable employed with group leaders, which he calls "Esteem for the Least Preferred Co-worker" (LPC), that is very helpful for the specification of the conditions under which leaders have effective groups. To obtain this measure, Fiedler utilizes a series of bipolar seven point scales, such as intelligent-unintelligent, cooperative-uncooperative. The subject is asked to think of all his past coworkers and focus on the most undesirable coworker he has ever had. He is then asked to rate this particular coworker on the bipolar scales. The score is computed by measuring the extent to which the subject values this coworker. Subjects high in LPC rate the least preferred coworker as being relatively intelligent, cooperative, etc. In contrast, subjects low in LPC tend to make judgments in which they indicate that such a coworker was unintelligent, uncooperative, etc. Fiedler's (1958) early research showed that low LPC leaders who were sociometrically chosen by their important (key) team members had highly effective work groups. In contrast, low LPC leaders who were not sociometrically chosen and leaders who had high LPC scores tended to be ineffective. More recently Fiedler (1963) presented a model of leadership effectiveness, which specifies the conditions under which leaders of high or low LPC are likely to be effective. This model will be discussed in a later section.

Technology.   One important result of the technology employed by an organization is the specification of jobs having certain characteristics. The technology determines the extent to which the job may be programmed (i.e., employee behaviors may be precisely specified); this important variable is designated by Fiedler (1963) as the "task structure." It is possible to think of jobs in which the greater part of the employee's behavior cannot be specified in advance, such as research work or jobs in which much of the employee's behavior can be specified, such as repetitive jobs and unskilled work. The kind of leadership behavior required under low task structure, as in the former jobs, is not the same as the kind of behavior required under high task structure, as in the latter jobs.

From the point of view of our discussion of organizational design, it is necessary to impose the limitation that the inputs of Table 1 are fixed, and there is little that the manager can do to alter their values. This is a gross simplification, but it is necessary to permit us to complete the discussion in a reasonable length of time. Thus, the designer of the organization begins his study by obtaining information about those inputs that he regards as fixed and proceeds with his design accordingly.

STRUCTURES

Interactions. The importance of *interactions* has been adequately formulated in the literature (Homans, 1950; Whyte, 1959) so that inclusion of this variable needs no further justification. The distinction between functional and emergent interactions appears desirable. Functional interactions are those required by the technology or the nature of the job ("pass me the hammer"); emergent interactions are those that occur over and above such requirements. High frequencies of emergent interactions between two individuals are typically related to positive feelings between them. The distinction between formal and informal structures has been well illustrated in the Hawthorne experiments and needs no further defense.

Power. The concept of power is not sufficiently well understood, in spite of some helpful theoretical analyses (French, 1956; French and Raven, 1959). There is first, of course, power inherent in a job, which involves the ability to reward (reward power) or punish (coercive power). Legitimate power is based on an employee's belief that his supervisor has the right to prescribe his behavior or opinions. There is power inherent in the individual, such as power due to charm (attraction power) or due to expert knowledge (expert power). In analyzing power it is important to consider both what the position permits and what the person said to have power wants and what his subordinates permit. Power deals with both initiation and compliance. One possible index of an individual's power is the number of times others do what he suggests over the number of times he initiates suggestions. A finer index would consider both the number of suggestions and the initiator's perceived importance of his suggestions.

In addition to the *initiation power* just described there is also *negation power*. A measure of this power would be the percent of suggestions or requests that are denied or in which the supervisor refuses to concur. An analogous example of power in an academic profession is a person who writes many papers but whose work is not quoted. Such a person would have little initiation power. People who write critical articles that are highly effective have high negation power. Thus, the people who have most power are those who have both high initiation and high negation power, e.g., writers of original treatments of the subject matter of the profession whose books become widely used and whose acceptance or rejection of certain research findings set a pattern for the profession.

Status congruency.   Both experiments and theoretical discussions employing the concept of status congruency (Adams, 1953; Clark, 1960) amply illustrate the usefulness of this variable. *Individual status congruency* refers to the consistency of an individual's status characteristics (age, sex, race, religion, nationality, education, income, etc.) For example, a very young Negro from Africa living in the United States with three years of public school education earning a million dollars a year would be highly status incongruent, within American society. *Group status congruency* refers to the consistency of the status characteristics among the members of the group. A group consisting of members earning $5000 a year and $1 million a year, would be status incongruent on income. Research findings indicate that group members perceive individuals with high status incongruency as threats. Groups with status incongruency appear to have characteristics similar to noncohesive groups (i.e., groups whose members choose outsiders rather than insiders as friends).

Tall vs. flat organizations.   Tall organizations are those that have several levels of authority and responsibility; flat organizations have few such levels. The armed forces are good examples of tall organizations; universities often have relatively flat structures—professors to head of department to dean to president. Some companies have experimentally attempted to minimize the number of levels by reducing them to three. The vice-president of one such company [1] addressed the 1963 Pittsburgh conference and gave a glowing report of the results in this experiment.

Group characteristics.   Under group characteristics we cite those variables discovered by Hemphill and Westie (1950) as important dimensions of groups that do not already appear in other parts of our lists.

The heterogeneity of group composition appears to be an important variable. Member heterogeneity in attitudes is related to communication effectiveness and perceived liking (Triandis, 1959a) and to group creativity (Triandis et al., 1964); heterogeneity in abilities is also relevant to group creativity (Triandis et al., 1964).

1. Mr. Arthur Kuriloff, Vice-President, Non-Linear Systems, Inc., Del Mar, California.

FUNCTIONS

A function may be defined as an attribute or process that is hypothesized as intervening between some feature of organizational design (input, structure) and some organizational output. The term is similar to Bakke's (1959) "essential processes."

It is necessary to introduce such concepts in our theoretical scheme because the relationships between inputs and outputs are extremely complex and greatly dependent upon situational variables, such as the size of the plant or the degree of urbanization of the environment. (Katzell et al., 1961; Katzell, 1962). A taxonomy of situations, such as that proposed by Sells (1962), is not yet available. For this reason it would be almost impossible with present knowledge to develop a theory in which inputs are related to outputs using situational variables as the conditional variables. But if we obtain measurements of the function variables, it is possible to tap the effects of the situational variables since these variables have a distinct effect on functions. By measuring the functions we may avoid the measurement of each of the numerous situational variables that are influential in the determination of organizational behavior. Of course, a complete theory would have to describe how the situational variables are related to the functions, but for the purposes of our present limited attempt we may focus on the function variables and ignore the majority of the situational variables.

What is the nature of the function variables? Suggestions are obtained from the work of Bales (1950), Stogdill and Coons (1957), and others who dealt with the behavior of leaders. They found that leaders perform two classes of essential functions: (i) promotive functions that are relevant to the accomplishment of the job; and (ii) maintenance functions that are relevant to the perpetuation of the group. It is reasonable to assume that the employees are also engaged in similar functions. Productive behavior and the obtaining of rewards from participation in the group are two classes of employee functions that correspond to the leader promotive and maintenance functions. Employee participation in decisions and norm formulation appear to be related functions that are conceptually distinguishable from the productive behavior and obtaining-rewards functions. Additional functions, or modifications of the functions listed in Table 1, will undoubtedly be proposed as the theoretical scheme that is presented in the present chapter is put to an empirical test.

It may be desirable to give an example of the operation of functions. Consider the situation in which the personal goals of the members of the organization and the prescribed goals (external goals) are not the same. This is a situation in which the organization must seduce the individual into behaving in ways that are inconsistent with his goals. This may be accomplished with more formalization of procedures, more pay, an attractive environment, or compromises involving catering to some of the individual's goals. The leader obtains more formalization by planning, organizing, and integrating, and he employs the function called "rewarding" by recommending more pay or better environment. Thus, the intervention of certain leader functions may convert a disfunctional discrepancy between inputs and structure (group goals) to useful behavior that leads to favorable outputs.

OUTPUTS

Two major classifications of output have been considered: Objective, such as quantity and quality of production, absenteeism, turnover, and profits; and subjective or attitudinal, such as the satisfactions that the employees and managers derive from participation in the organization.

Job satisfaction is the sum of several satisfactions, including intrinsic job satisfaction, satisfaction with the supervisor, with the company programs, with one's achievements, with one's fellow workers, or with one's advancement (Dabas, 1958; Roach, 1957; Twery et al., 1958). The variables listed in Table 1 are extracted from several factor-analytic studies and are tentatively offered as the best list of job satisfaction components.

Morale. One of the most frequently used concepts in the literature of organization theory is the concept of *morale.* This concept has produced more confusion than perhaps any other concept in industrial social psychology. It seems to the present writer that a redefinition of the concept may lead to a clarification.

What is our definition of morale? Morale is a concept specifying the congruence of individual and group goals, the persistence of individuals in reaching the group goals, and the absorption of the individuals in the activities leading to reaching these goals. At the conference Katzell suggested that when a group of individuals exhibits a high ratio of group achievement to group resources, it is likely to have high morale. High morale will be present if the group's members have individual goals compatible with the group's goals, if they persist in reaching these goals in the face of difficulties, and if they are intensely absorbed and concerned in reaching these group goals. From this definition it follows that high morale does *not* necessarily imply high productivity. High productivity is a management goal and may or may not be a group goal. The definition implies that high morale exists when the individual works hard to reach the *group* goals, not the goals imposed by top management or some other group. In an industrial situation we might observe hard work, intensive activity, and persistence; all are characteristic of high morale. But further investigation may disclose that this intensive activity was not directed toward the production of goods but toward the creation of a "bank" of group products that could be used by the group to satisfy management demands during periods when the group is engaged in its favored activities, such as playing games. Thus, it is possible to have high morale and low *net* group productivity. It is also possible to have a group with low morale and no sense of *group* goals but consisting of individuals for whom productivity appears to be a path to success (Brayfield and Crockett, 1955; Georgopoulos et al., 1957). In such a case there may be high productivity without high morale. Similarly, there may be high morale without job satisfaction.

Of the output variables listed in Table 1 only the satisfaction with one's fellow workers is implied as a correlated aspect of group morale. There may be high morale groups in which the satisfaction with some aspect of the job, e.g., the supervisor or promotions, is clearly negative. In such cases "getting rid of the boss" might become a group goal, and the group might work enthusiastically, intensely, and effectively toward that end.

Thus, the concept of morale, as it will be used in this chapter, implies only high agreement of individual and group goals. However, some of its connotations may include the idea of being proud of one's group membership or feeling an élite.

ILLUSTRATIVE RELATIONSHIPS AMONG SETS OF VARIABLES

A complete statement of the theory implied by the classification of the variables of Table 1 would specify all the significant relationships among these variables. Such a statement would require several volumes. Furthermore, at present there is little empirical support for the majority of these relationships. Thus, the present section is presented purely as an illustration of what the theory might be like when, after many years of research, the empirical support for the propositions relating these variables becomes available.

It is convenient to discuss some of the propositions that relate the various groupings of variables under the following headings.
1. Relations of Inputs and Structures
2. Relations of Structures and Functions
3. Relations of Functions and Outputs
4. Reverse Relationships (e.g., Structures determining Inputs)
5. Relations of Inputs to Each Other and to Structures

6. Relations of Structures to each other and to Functions

7. Relations of Functions to Each Other and to Outputs

8. Relations of Outputs to Each Other as conditioned by Functions

In this section a series of hypotheses that correspond to these eight classes of propositions will be presented. Some empirical support exists for many of the propositions, but none are considered to be very firm at the present state of knowledge.

RELATIONS OF INPUTS AND STRUCTURES

This section presents some examples of relationships between inputs and structures. The relationships presented are not necessarily the most important or the best established. Since there are many potential relationships between variables of the input subgroup and the structure subgroup, only a small percentage of the total set of relationships could be presented. The purpose of this presentation is simply to illustrate a class of relationships that should be present in a complete theory of organizations.

The presence of a *common enemy,* as in war, or a threat to the life of the organization may create changes in the organization structure. There are case studies that show that when a company is in trouble and may become bankrupt, the interaction between labor and management becomes more intense. Adequate studies of the phenomenon do not exist, but there are enough experimental studies, such as the work of Sherif, to suggest that this is an important phenomenon. Thus, it seems likely that

Hypothesis 1: The presence of a common enemy will:
- a) increase the frequency of communication,
- b) increase the frequency of initiation of communication from the lower levels of the status structure,
- c) result in an increase in the congruence of the formal and informal communication structures,
- d) permit "tall" organizations to be more effective than similar organizations without a common enemy,
- e) lead to smaller group permeability,
- f) lead to greater group viscidity.

One of the most interesting input variables is the ability of the members. It is a variable that can be manipulated by the designer of organizations, provided that the labor supply for the level of ability he chooses is sufficient. The use of psychological tests in the ability area has long proven successful. Shifts in the cutting scores may permit changes in the average ability in the organization. Such shifts have to consider the validity of the tests used and the selection ratio (number selected over total number tested), but these considerations are beyond the scope of the present chapter. It is interesting to note that "training" can sometimes be substituted for "abilities" in the following hypotheses.

Hypothesis 2: An increase in member abilities will:
- a) result in a "flatter" status structure,
- b) result in job enlargement,
- c) lead to greater responsibility of the members,
- d) lead to more authority by the members,
- e) lead to a shift in the locus of decision toward the lower levels of the organization,
- f) lead to a larger span of control,
- g) result in fewer roles per number of people.

This hypothesis was suggested by Haire (1962).

Hypothesis 3: When the management philosophy is that workers are stupid, lazy, and unreliable:
- a) management will adopt a "tall" organizational structure,
- b) management will adopt an organizational structure with small spans of control,
- c) the locus of decisions will be higher in the status structure than when the management philosophy is that workers are intelligent, willing to work, and reliable.

Some of the propositions deal with the characteristics of the individuals that constitute the organization. Triandis et al. (1963) suggest that

Hypothesis 4: The higher the problem-solving ability of the members of a group the higher the problem-solving ability of the group.

However, when Triandis et al. (1964) were working with dyads, they found that in addition to individual ability it is necessary to consider the way the dyads are constituted. Thus, when the dyads are homogeneous in their abilities (both high or low or in the same combination of quality and quantity of individual outputs), and heterogeneous in their attitudes, dyadic creativity reaches a maximum; when they are heterogeneous in both abilities and attitudes the creativity reaches a minimum; when they are homogeneous in both or heterogeneous in abilities and homogeneous in their attitudes, their performance is average. The theoretical explanation of these findings led Triandis et al. to this next hypothesis.

Hypothesis 5: When the members are heterogeneous in their attitudes, there is:
    a) a greater variety of solutions initiated,
    b) less likelihood of agreement on the evaluation of such solutions

This view is in agreement with that proposed by Wilson (1964). Also,

Hypothesis 6: When the members are similar in their abilities, they work together more effectively than when they are dissimilar.

There are also some propositions that relate member personalities to organization structures. Thus,

Hypothesis 7: When there is a large number of group members who have a high need for power (Miner, 1963), the organization will tend to become taller than when there is a small number of persons with such needs.

Hypothesis 8: The behavior of the leaders will be influenced by the personality of the followers, and vice versa. (This hypothesis is suggested by Haythorn's [1956] study.)

The above hypotheses are illustrations of the kinds of propositions that relate inputs and structures. The next section will focus on propositions relating structures and functions.

RELATIONS OF STRUCTURES AND FUNCTIONS

Stogdill et al. (1956) found that the high-status members of a military organization spend more time in planning, coordinating, and controlling the operations of their departments than their subordinates or lower-level personnel did.

Hypothesis 9: The higher a member's status in an organization and the clearer the task structure, the greater the frequency of his performance of promotive (initiation of structure) functions.

The task structure is probably an important variable, since if the high-status member is leading a group in a highly unstructured task (e.g., research), he may actually spend less time initiating structure and more time showing consideration and encouraging his subordinates.

It seems likely that in tall organizations managers would have more time to devote to close supervision.

Hypothesis 10: The taller the organizational structure:
    a) the closer the supervision,
    b) the greater the pressure for production.

There is much evidence that the size of the work unit is an important organizational variable. It is likely that

Hypothesis 11: The larger the size of the work group, the lower the opportunity for member participation in the setting of group goals, hence the less the participation.

It is reasonable to expect that as the size of the group increases the leader will have to engage in leadership functions to an increasing extent; otherwise the group may simply disintegrate. Thus,

Hypothesis 12: The larger the size of the group, the greater the frequency of the leader promotive function behaviors.

Hypothesis 13: The larger the size of the group, the greater the frequency of the leader maintenance function behaviors.

However, with an increase in the size of the group the leader may simply not have the time to engage in monitoring functions. Thus,

Hypothesis 14: The larger the size of the group, the lower the frequency of the leader's monitoring of the behavior of individual group members.

Other propositions of the theory relate different kinds of structures, such as power, sociometric, communications, and locomotion (channels of advancement) structures, to different functions.

Hypothesis 15: The greater the freedom of communication in an organization, the greater the participation of members in goal setting.

RELATIONS OF FUNCTIONS AND OUTPUTS

Triandis (1959a) has argued that

Hypothesis 16: Other things being equal, the greater the pressure for production:
    a) the greater the quantity of production,
    b) the lower the job satisfaction.

However, within one range of pressure (slight to moderate), lower job satisfaction would lead to lower production. Hence, within this range, increased pressure would lead to lower productivity. A more general statement is

Hypothesis 17: Other things being equal, the greater the frequency of a supervisor's initiation of structure:

a) the greater the quantity of production,
b) the lower the satisfaction.

Hypothesis 18: The greater the frequency of a supervisor's use of consideration or maintenance acts, the greater the satisfaction.

Hypothesis 19: The greater the frequency of a supervisor's monitoring acts:
a) the greater the quality of production,
b) the lower the satisfaction.

Hypothesis 20: The greater the frequency of an employee's participation in goal setting, the higher his sense of self-actualization. (This hypothesis was suggested by Argyris [1957, 1959].)

Hypotheses 17–19 appear reasonable but lack empirical support. However, there are some empirical studies bearing on this topic. Anderson and Fiedler (1962) found that *supervisory* leaders had groups that were high in the quality of creative output; leaders who participated with their subordinates in the performance of the task had groups with a high quantity of creative solutions. But, as Anderson and Fiedler pointed out, there was one additional member in these groups, so that an additional supply of ideas was present. Kidd and Christy (1961) simulated an air-traffic-control center with three-man groups. They found that in that situation *laissez-faire* leaders had groups with high quantity; leaders engaged in close supervision had groups with high quality; and participant leaders (as in Anderson and Fiedler) had groups intermediate in quantity and very low in quality. Thus, the two empirical studies appear to agree that close supervision leads to high quality. If by close supervision is meant monitoring, then this finding is consistent with Hypothesis 19.

From experiments such as those of Schachter et al. (1951), Berkowitz (1954), and others it is clear that both cohesiveness and the pressure for production from other group members influence the extent to which a group member's productivity will be consistent with the group norm. In the case of such joint functions of two variables, it is necessary to discover whether the relative weights of the two variables remain constant across situations. It is probable that they do not, in which case it is necessary to discover the parameters that determine them.

Seashore (1954) found that high cohesiveness was related to less job-related anxiety, less variance in individual productivity (that is, greater control of output by the group), and less felt pressure for production.

Cohesion is a function of perceived job prestige, length of service, and small group size. In Seashore's study the productivity of the cohesive groups was determined by the confidence of the work group members in the management.

A number of interesting propositions are suggested by the work of Zaleznik et al. (1958). They found that groups with high status congruency and/or high cohesion consisted of individuals whose effort was specified by group norms. Thus they were "on the line" producers. However, such groups also gave high rewards to their members for social participation and hence showed much satisfaction with coworkers. Those workers who were not members of the group, the nonregulars, produced little or very much, depending on whether they identified or rejected the work group. The above studies suggest these hypotheses.

Hypothesis 21: The higher the group cohesiveness:
   a) the more will the productivity of the members be regulated by group standards,
   b) the higher the general satisfaction of the members,
   c) and, if there is high confidence in management, the higher the productivity (Van Zelst, 1952; Seashore, 1954).

Hypothesis 22: The higher the status congruency in the group:
   a) the more will the productivity of the members be regulated by group standards,
   b) the higher the job satisfaction of the members,
   c) and, if there is high confidence in management, the higher the productivity.

The effect of member participation in the setting of goals has been one of the central topics in industrial social psychology since the pioneering studies of Coch and French (1948). It recently became clear that their theory holds only when the employee perceives that such participation is legitimate (French et al., 1960). Likert (1961) makes participation the key concept of his organizational theory. His theory suggests these hypotheses.

Hypothesis 23: The greater the participation of the employees in group goal setting:
   a) the greater the productivity,
   b) the greater the similarity of individual and group goals,
   c) the greater the job satisfaction,
   d) the lower the probability of absenteeism (Hewitt and Parfit, 1953).

Strauss (1963) provides an extremely interesting analysis of participation, and distinguishes between decisions made by the superior (individual direction), decisions made jointly by the superior and subordinate (consultation), and decisions made by the subordinate (delegation). The analogs in the relationship between the supervisor and the group are (a) decisions made by the supervisor (group direction), (b) decisions made jointly (group meetings), and (c) decisions made by the group alone (group decision).

REVERSE RELATIONSHIPS

Here it is appropriate to clarify the following point: the presentation of the twenty-three hypotheses in the direction from left to right in Table 1 does not imply that all propositions of the theory will be of this form. It is clear that there are perfectly reasonable propositions that are directed from right to left in Table 1. For instance,

Hypothesis 24: Those members who are high in a status structure:
- a) are more likely to have normative resources suggesting "social service" than those who are at a lower level (Morse and Weise, 1962),
- b) are more likely to value opportunities for independence and self-actualization (Centers, 1948).

Several studies suggest that although there is a fundamental structure of similarity in the perception of jobs among managers and workers (Triandis, 1960), there are also some differences in the details of these perceptions and some significant distortions (Triandis, 1959c, d). Such studies imply that structural variables (e.g., position in a status structure) may influence input variables (e.g., perceptions). Other studies suggest that functions may influence structures that in turn influence other functions and hence certain outputs. The studies by Coch and French (1949) and French et al. (1960), for example, suggest that participation (a function) may, when the employees perceive it as legitimate, lead to congruence of goals between employees and the company (a structure variable). Such congruence is likely to lead to greater frequency of productive behaviors and hence to greater productivity and greater job satisfaction.

RELATIONS OF INPUTS TO EACH OTHER AND TO STRUCTURES

Under certain conditions satisfaction may be an input as well as an output. This happens for those elements of satisfaction that are not dependent on the employee's participation in the organization. For instance, when there is a favorable relationship between the normative resource "what is appropriate pay" and the financial condition "this is the pay that I will receive," there will be an input satisfaction. Other determinants of input satisfaction are reasonable job demands, pleasant working conditions, and a management that is "doing a good job." It may be noted that such satisfactions do not require the employee to participate in the organization but may be acquired by reading the newspaper or talking to other employees about the organization. Hence, they are inputs. Nevertheless, such input satisfactions may have consequences. For instance, they are likely to result in greater group cohesion(Seashore, 1954).

The reference groups of the individual employee determine to some extent his ideas about what is appropriate pay, how his supervisors should behave, etc. If job satisfaction is conceived of as a function of how much the employee expects from the job as well as how much he does in fact obtain from the job (Morse, 1953), then the employee's reference groups are crucial variables. Form and Geschwender (1962) have shown that sons who have reached an occupational level equal to or better than that of their fathers are more satisfied than sons who have reached an occupational level lower than that of their fathers. The same was true for occupational level relative to that of the brothers of the subjects. The higher the vertical mobility of the employees, the higher was their job satisfaction. Other input characteristics were also related to job satisfaction. Married employees were more satisfied than single employees; employees over forty years of age were more satisfied than those under forty; those earning more or having skilled as opposed to semi- or unskilled jobs were also more satisfied.

RELATIONS OF STRUCTURES TO EACH OTHER AND TO FUNCTIONS

The interactions between various kinds of structures may produce results that are inconsistent with some of the hypotheses relating structures to functions on an "other things being equal" basis. Thus, Hypothesis 10 suggested that managers in tall organizations would exert more pressure for production, and Hypothesis 19 suggested that high pressure for production would lead to low job satisfaction. It follows, therefore, that tall organizations would have employees who are less satisfied. Furthermore, Hypothesis 11 suggested that the larger the size of the work group the lower the participation, and hence, from Hypothesis 23c, the lower the job satisfaction. We would expect that when organizations are *both* tall *and* large, they would have employees who are particularly dissatisfied. However, the empirical evidence is exactly opposite. Porter and Lawler (1963), working with management employees, limited the generality of Worthy's finding that flat organizations are more effective. They found that in organizations with more than 5000 employees, tall structures were associated with high job satisfaction and flat structures with low job satisfaction; in organizations with less than 5000 employees flat structures were associated with high satisfaction and tall structures with low job satisfaction. The empirical findings could be translated into this hypothesis.

Hypothesis 25: The higher the congruence in the organization structures, the more likely it is that functions that will result in high job satisfaction will be observed.

In this proposition it is assumed that large organizations that are tall or small organizations that are flat have congruent structures.

Many additional propositions relating structures are reasonable.

Hypothesis 26: The smaller the group, the more cohesive it is likely to be.

Hypothesis 27: The more status congruency in a group, the greater the cohesion.

This hypothesis is supported by a laboratory study by Exline and Ziller (1959) in which status congruent groups were found to have more congenial social-emotional atmospheres, to show more agreement, and to have less interpersonal conflict.

Hypothesis 28: The greater the congruence of the power, sociometric, communication, and locomotion structures, the greater the frequency of productive behaviors.

It is probable that Likert's (1961) proposal for an organization consisting of interlocking committees would have exactly this effect, i.e., would increase the congruence in the various structures.

There is evidence that high status employees are more satisfied. It is likely that this is due to greater congruence in company and individual goals among high-level employees. Such congruence leads to greater productive effort, which, in turn, leads to higher productivity and also to higher satisfaction. Since it is technically impossible to compare the productivities of employees in different levels of the organization (since they are not doing comparable jobs), it may not be possible to test all aspects of this proposition.

RELATIONS OF FUNCTIONS TO EACH OTHER AND TO OUTPUTS

Hypothesis 29: a) The higher the frequency of rewards received by employees from their supervisor,
the higher the frequency of the employee productive behaviors;

    b) the higher the frequency of employee productive behaviors the higher the productivity.

These hypotheses are examples of propositions in which functions are related to each other and to outputs.

From Hypothesis 23b we have the proposition that the higher the employee's participation in goal setting, the greater will be the similarity of the employee's and the group's goals. To the extent that these group goals are formulated by discussions among the employees under the direction of the group's supervisor, it is reasonable to expect that the group goals will be similar to the goals of the supervisor. Thus, when there is high employee participation, there will be less need for the supervisor to monitor the employee's behavior since employee and supervisor goals would be similar. From these considerations we have:

Hypothesis 30: The higher the employee participation in goal setting, the lower the frequency of monitoring of employee behavior by the supervisor.

RELATIONS OF OUTPUTS TO EACH OTHER AS CONDITIONED BY FUNCTIONS

There is much evidence that relationships among the outputs are small or insignificant (Seashore et al., 1960). Brayfield and Crockett (1955) dispelled the assumptions concerning a necessary positive relationship between job satisfaction and productivity. Kahn (1960) traced the history of thinking at the University of Michigan Survey Research Center concerning this relationship. Back in 1947 Kahn and his colleagues began their research program with the implicit assumption that the two variables are, in general, positively and linearly related. After years of research it became clear that satisfaction is an output, not an intervening variable, and hence might be entirely independent of productivity. By 1960 Kahn was convinced that there is no relationship between the two variables.

The present writer agrees with the conclusion that there is no necessary relationship but is interested in the possibility of specification of this relationship by the conditional operation of functional variables. Consider the following arguments, which suggest that a relationship does exist between job satisfaction and productivity.

Triandis (1959a) suggested that a relationship exists between the two variables but that it is a complex one. He argued that the pressure for production exerted by the supervisor is a conditional variable determining the kind of relationship that exists between job satisfaction and productivity. Since the original article had not clarified how this pressure is to be measured, it may be desirable to do so here.

Consider the perceived pressure for production received by an employee from his supervisor (P) and the employee's expectation (E) of how much pressure for production "good" supervisors are likely to exert on their employees.[2] Now, consider the following "pressure for production index": $I = \frac{P\text{-}E}{E}$. When this index is negative, i.e., when the employee perceives that he receives less pressure than good supervisors are likely to exert, we designate this situation as State A. When the index is positive but low, we designate the situation as State B; when the index is positive but high, as State C; and when it is *extremely* high, we have State D.

Triandis' argument is based on the assumption that, other things being equal, the higher the pressure for production the higher the production but the lower the job satisfaction. Moreover, the correlations between pressure for production and job satisfaction will have different sizes for the three states. Thus, in State A the correlation would be very low, while in States B and C it would be much more substantial. This is because in State A the pressure is less than the amount that is considered "proper," so that even though any pressure for production may be considered undesirable, it is not nearly so undesirable as when it is greater than the perceived "proper" pressure. In State A, then, the greater the pressure, the slightly less the job satisfaction and the greater the productivity. Hence, in this state there will be a *low negative* correlation between job satisfaction and productivity. In State B the relationship between job satisfaction and productivity would be *positive,* as is suggested by commonsense assumptions. However, in State C, the relationship will be again *negative.* State C is a situation in which the supervisor tells the employee to produce or he will receive some important punishment. Here we might expect the employee to produce more in order to avoid the punishment but to be less satisfied than in State B. Furthermore, in this state, the greater the pressure the lower the job satisfaction but the higher the productivity; hence the negative relation between job satisfaction and productivity. In State D the employee finds the pressure intolerable and quits his job. Of course, at the points between State A and B, and between States B and C, the relationship between job satisfaction and productivity would be equal to *zero,* permitting a transition from negative to positive relationships and vice versa.

Triandis' arguments led to a complex curve (Triandis, 1959a, Fig. 1). They were based on a purely logical analysis of the influence of the pressure for production on productivity and job satisfaction. It so hap-

2. Measures may be obtained by means of ratings on a 9-point scale, or by development of appropriate scales.

pens, however, that the experimental data obtained by Katz et al. (1950, 1951) and by Morse and Reimer (1956) support this purely logical analysis.

It will be recalled that Morse and Reimer (1956) gave two experimental treatments to four divisions employing routine female clerical workers. Treatment I, which was given to two divisions, consisted of organizational changes designed to lead to greater employee participation. Treatment II, which was given to the other two divisions, was designed to increase the role of the supervisor. The first treatment was called "participatory" and the second "hierarchical." It is quite likely that the hierarchical treatment involved more pressure for production than occurred either before the experiment or in the participatory treatment. This is suggested by the fact that eight of the nine employees who quit their jobs because of dissatisfaction during the experiment were from the hierarchical divisions, and during the exit interviews they made comments about "the pressure for production and the work standards."

Morse and Reimer provide no information about the absolute value of the "pressure for production" variable before the application of the experimental treatments. However, Maccoby, who studied the same employees just before the experiment, reported at the Pittsburgh seminar that it is reasonable to assume that the pressure was in the middle of the possible range, i.e., somewhere between State B and State C. A reduction in pressure, as is likely with the participatory treatment, should place the work group in State B, while an increase in the pressure should place it in State C; therefore, the participatory treatment should result in high satisfaction and productivity (a positive relationship), while the hierarchical treatment should result in low satisfaction and high productivity (a negative relationship). This is exactly what Morse and Reimer obtained.

Another source of support is the laboratory study by Pepinsky et al., (1960) in which again the relationship between productivity and pressure was curvilinear.

More recently Ewen (1963) examined the responses of more than a thousand life insurance salesmen to a job satisfaction questionnaire. The instrument was administered anonymously to the salesmen and included questions about their productivity and the extent to which they felt pressure for production from their supervisors. It is a reasonable guess that with the distance existing between their supervisors and themselves, these salesmen operated in State A or State B as far as the pressure for production *from their supervisors* variable is concerned. In State A Triandis would predict no correlation between job satisfaction and productivity; in State B he would predict a positive correlation. Ewen's results showed that for those salesmen who report experiencing a low pressure for production the correlation was .17 (Not Significant) in the validation and .21 (N.S.) in the cross-validation group; for those experiencing medium pressure it was .15 (p<.05) and .33 (p<.01); and for those experiencing a high pressure for production the correlation was .26 (p<.01) and .23 (p<.01). These results and arguments are by no means conclusive, but they suggest that it is premature to abandon the quest for a relationship between job satisfaction and productivity.

It is probable that variables other than the pressure for production might also act as conditional variables. Harding and Bottenberg (1961) have found certain biographical variables to be important. Katzell et al. (1961) and Cureton and Katzell (1962) have shown that the size of the work force, the city size, the wage rate, and the degree of unionization might be conditional variables influencing the relationship between productivity and job satisfaction. Hulin (1963) has argued that relationships between affective responses, such as job satisfaction and responses connected with behavior *in* the work situation would be very strongly affected by situational variables, such as union-management relations, the pressure for production, etc. Situational factors that lead the workers to accept management goals should show positive relationships between satisfaction and productivity; situational factors that lead the workers to reject management's goals should show no such relationships. These situational variables should have little effect on the relationship between job satisfaction and behavior directed toward leaving the situation (lateness, absenteeism, and turnover), but the characteristics of the workers and the economic conditions of the area in which the plant is located should have a definite influence on this relationship.

Thus, we find that a function variable (Table 1), namely, pressure for production, plays a conditional role on the relationship between two output variables—job satisfaction and productivity—and that some input variables, namely, worker characteristics and economic conditions, influence the relationship between other output variables—namely, job satisfaction on the one hand and absenteeism, turnover, and lateness on the other. The above discussion should be illustrative of the complexity of the interrelationships among the variables of Table 1.

HYPOTHESES DEVELOPED AT THE SEMINAR

The previous section presented a series of hypotheses merely to illustrate the nature of the theory that was proposed by Katzell and elaborated in the group discussions at the seminar. The hypotheses were developed by the writer for this purpose and do not represent a carefully thought out system of theoretical propositions, such as the system that might be developed through painstaking empirical research. The seminar discussion group did develop some specific hypotheses in the course of the discussions. These hypotheses were discussed in considerable detail, and may therefore be stated with more confidence than the illustrative hypotheses of the previous section. They will be discussed in this section.

As is typical in conferences, different members of our group were interested in different variables. Maccoby, for example, was most interested in variables associated with *ésprit de corps* or the "pride in one's group." He asked: "What makes a group have a 'gung-ho' quality?" This variable is very similar to group morale as defined in the present chapter. Some of the hypotheses he proposed will be described in the present section. Fiedler was interested in the variables that relate leader behavior to group effectiveness. He presented a theoretical model, which summarizes many years of empirical research. Group effectiveness is related to leader characteristics, the power of the leader, the task structure, and the nature of leader-member sociometric relationships. This model will also be presented in this section. Miner stressed the importance of individual motivation variables. Since this interest is well presented in Miner's recent writings (Miner 1963, 1964) and has already been referred to in the previous section, it will not be discussed here.

RELATIONSHIPS BETWEEN PRIDE IN GROUP AND OTHER VARIABLES

Hypothesis 31: High pride in group is more probable when there are clear group boundaries and low group permeability.

Low group permeability is the condition that makes membership in the group difficult or possible only as a result of some achievement. Hemphill and Westie (1950) found that differences in permeability constitute an important characteristic of groups.

The hypothesis is probably correct, because group boundaries and low group permeability would permit the members of the group to acquire a clear "we" feeling and to experience some cognitive dissonance reduction (Festinger, 1957) when valuing their group. Specifically, the cognition that they have expended much effort in order to become group members would be inconsistent with the cognition that "this is not a particularly good group." Accordingly, it is likely that to increase consistency the latter cognition would be changed to become "this is a good group."

The group must have some training to tolerate partial failure, frustrations, and deprivations. The argument here is that without such training, the group will fall apart when it fails to reach some of its goals. If members have *"faith"* in their goals (i.e., have some reasonable hope of reaching them) but fail to reach them, they may continue as a group if they can obtain social reinforcement from each other, even in situations where the group's goals are absurd (Festinger, et al., 1956). Basically, the argument is that groups that always succeed or always fail either learn to devaluate their goals or despair of reaching their goals and therefore disintegrate. Thus,

Hypothesis 32: High pride in group is improbable when:
  a) the group is always successful,
  b) the group is never successful.

This hypothesis suggests that high pride in group requires a particular schedule of reinforcement. Further research must investigate what schedule is best for what kinds of groups. Stated differently, this hypothesis says that in order for a group to have high pride in itself it is necessary for most of the members to value the group goals highly and also to have some hope of reaching the goals.

Hypothesis 33: High pride in group is more probable when:
  a) the members perceive that they have similar goals,
  b) the members perceive that they *share* deprivations (a "common fate" phenomenon that would increase "we" feeling),
  c) the members perceive themselves as being status congruent.

In a sense, this hypothesis argues that the more the members perceive each other as being alike in terms of goals, past experiences, and characteristics, the more they will fuse their self-percepts with their perception of the group. Since most normal individuals value themselves, they will obtain cognitive consistency by also valuing their group.

RELATIONSHIPS BETWEEN LEADER BEHAVIOR AND GROUP EFFECTIVENESS

Fiedler (1963) has presented a theoretical analysis of the conditions under which different kinds of leader behavior lead to maximum group effectiveness. Fiedler's analysis is in terms of three major classes of variables, which specify these conditions. The first class of variables is related to the position power of the leader. Leaders high in position power, e.g., a general vis à vis a private, are contrasted with leaders having low position power, e.g., the elected president of a lady's volunteer organization vis à vis the members. The second class of variables is related to the acceptance of the leader by the members. Leaders that are accepted, e.g., chosen sociometrically, are contrasted with leaders that are rejected by their group members, e.g., underchosen sociometrically. The third class of variables is related to the structure of the job that the group has to do. Some jobs are highly structured; that is, most of their elements are programmed, as is the case with an assembly job; other jobs are very low in job structure; that is, there is no way of pre-determining the employee's activities, as is the case with research jobs.

Fiedler hypothesized that leader acceptance is by far the most important variable, followed by position power and task structure, in that order. His analysis applies only to interacting groups and not to coacting groups and is cast in terms of the LPC (Esteem for the Least Preferred Co-worker) scores of the leader.

Fiedler's research has shown that there are differences between leaders who score high or low on the LPC scales. Those who are high in LPC, i.e., indicate that they perceive their least preferred coworker more or less favorably, are warm, kind, tolerant individuals, deeply concerned with keeping good relations among the members of their group. By contrast, those who are low in LPC are managing and have a sort of "I will take no nonsense" attitude towards the members of their group. Julian and McGrath (1962) have shown that the low LPC members tend to interrupt group discussions and to put people back on the "right track" when the group discussion tends to be unproductive.

Fiedler argued that whether a leader will be more effective if he is warm, friendly, permissive, considerate, compliant, and concerned with interpersonal relations (high LPC or if he is managing, controlling, active, and more concerned with the task (low LPC) depends on the value of the position power, leader acceptance, and task structure variables. Thus, when every aspect of the group situation is in favor of the leader (high power, accepted, knows job needs) or when everything is unfavorable for the leader (low power, not accepted, job needs are unclear to everyone), the behavior of the leader that maximizes group effectiveness *relative to other groups operating under such conditions* are those that are typical of the behavior of low LPC leaders. When the conditions are intermediate, the high LPC leaders may be more effective. Fiedler (1963) analyzed a large number of research studies and found support for this view. Here is an intuitive explanation of why this is so: When the leader is powerful, accepted, and knows what has to be done, he is more effective if he tells his followers "go do it" than if he asks "what do you think is best for us to do?" Similarly, when the leader has no power, is not accepted, and the job is unstructured, the group will fall apart unless he behaves in a managing, directing manner. However, when these extreme conditions do not prevail, then some other types of behavior may be more appropriate. Fiedler found that when the leaders have no power but are accepted by the members and the job does not have much structure, the high LPC leaders are more effective. When the leaders do have power but are not accepted and the job has some structure, again the high LPC leaders are more effective.

This argument is also in agreement with Katzell's (1962) analysis, in which he concluded that complex tasks may require permissive supervision while simple tasks may require close supervision. Empirical support for this view was presented by Vroom and Mann (1960) and Bergum and Lehr (1963).

TASK STRUCTURE

In addition to the relationships described by Fiedler's model, which may all be stated as hypotheses for further research, Fiedler has presented a number of other findings that suggested to the seminar group members the following hypotheses.

Hypothesis 34: The higher the task structure, the lower the required member ability for a given level of output.

Hypothesis 35: The higher the task structure, the lower the required leader ability to obtain a given output.

These two hypotheses arise from the following considerations. When the job has much structure, it is possible to program most of the activities of both the members and the leader. Such programming may be done through instruction, through the introduction of mechanical or electronic aids, or by persons outside the group (who presumably have high abilities).

Hypothesis 36: The total power within a group is inversely proportional to the degree of structure of the task.

Theoretically, if the task is completely programmed, it is not necessary to have people doing it. Machines do not have power in the sense of producing or accepting new ideas. Thus, power over the goals of the organization is inversely proportional to the extent to which the jobs may be programmed.

Hypothesis 37: The greater the heterogeneity of the group member goals, the higher the correlation between task structure and group effectiveness.

This hypothesis reflects the idea that when group members are very heterogeneous in their attitudes, they may tend to move in contradictory directions, particularly if the task is not structured. The clearer it is what behavior is required for the task (i.e., the higher the task structure), the less important is this heterogeneity. Thus, when there is heterogeneity, group effectiveness requires high task structure, and low task structure is quite likely to result in low group effectiveness. Similar arguments support another hypothesis:

Hypothesis 38: The more the task structure, the less the intra-group conflict.

The reader should not make the mistake of equating task structure with task difficulty. It is possible to have highly structured jobs that are very simple, e.g., hammering a nail, or very difficult, e.g., firing a missile; it is possible to have low structure jobs that are relatively simple, e.g., answering letters received by a congressman, or low structure jobs that are relatively difficult, e.g., doing successful research. It is clear that different degrees of training are required for these jobs.

Hypothesis 39: The amount of training required on a job is proportional to the difficulty of the job and inversely proportional to the extent of task structure of the job.

Fiedler presented evidence that suggests that when a job has some structure and the leader has some power relative to the members, the I.Q. of the leader is positively correlated with group effectiveness (Fiedler and Meuwese, 1963). However, when the leader has little power or the job is unstructured, the member's I.Q. correlates with performance, while that of the leader does not.

CRISES IN ORGANIZATIONS

Disruptions in on-going processes in organizations will be considered as crises. When crisis conditions prevail or when the frequency of crises is high in the environment in which the organization is operating, the following hypotheses are reasonable.

Hypothesis 40: The greater the leader power, the greater the organizational effectiveness.

Hypothesis 41: The greater the tendency of the leader to consult his subordinates, the greater the organizational effectiveness.

Hypothesis 42: The greater the opportunity to change the jobs to a low task structure, the greater the organizational effectiveness.

Hypothesis 43: The optimal conditions would involve all three characteristics of the previous three hypotheses.

APPLICATIONS: HOW TO CHANGE AN ORGANIZATION

There are many ways in which an organization may be changed. Changes may be engineered through teaching or through therapy directed towards key people. Changes may be initiated by those members of the organization who have little success in reaching their goals, or by key people when they see that changes in external conditions (e.g.,

economic conditions) will preclude their goals. It is clear that the engineered changes will have relatively small influence on the members of
the organization, while the therapy changes will have relatively large
influence. The changes may be obtained by changing inputs (people,
money, technology), organizational structures (power, roles, communications, size of groups, group boundaries, tall-flat organizations, span of
control, clarity of group boundary), or by influencing key people in
certain positions within these structures (changing values, goals, attitudes, etc.)

In making these changes the designer of organizations is greatly
helped by the functional equivalence between certain characteristics of
organizations. For instance, increases in task structure are equivalent to
increases in the formalization of the procedures or to centralization of
the organization. In other words, the greater the degree of centralization
the lower the task structure *can be*, for the same effect. Increases in the
task structure may be obtained by either formalizing the work procedures
(writing time and motion standards), by planning the job so that most
of it is done mechanically (automation), or by close supervision (centralization). Another equivalent to task structure is member abilities. Other
things being equal, the higher the abilities of the members relative to
task demands, the less *can be* the task structure, the less supervision is
required, and hence the more decentralization is feasible. When there
is high task structure and high member ability, decentralization is very
effective (The Roman Catholic Church; the U.S. Forest Service as
described by Kaufman, 1960).

The above arguments suggest that certain organizational characteristics may compensate for the lack of other characteristics. This inter-
changeability is most helpful to the designer of organizations, since in
some designs he will have to consider the characteristics of the members
of the organization as given and can change only the task and the
structures, while in other conditions he might be able to change the
characteristics of the members through selection, placement, and transfer but have little opportunity to change the task structure because it
depends too much on the technology or because changes in the task
structure would be prohibited by financial considerations.

PROPOSAL FOR A RESEARCH STRATEGY

The previous sections of this chapter were directed to both the research
specialist in the area of organizational theory and the general reader
interested in the discussions that took place at the Pittsburgh seminar.
This section is explicitly designed for those interested in doing research

on organization theory. The research that will be discussed is likely to be of greater interest to social psychologists than to, say, economists or political scientists.

In the present section it will be argued that some relatively major changes in research procedure must take place in order to make progress in the area of organization theory. The key point of the previous sections is that the number of variables that are involved in the description of organizations is very large. It is a fairly sure guess that at least a hundred input variables are unrelated to each other and yet important, and that about fifty structure variables, thirty function variables, and close to twenty output variables are also involved. Furthermore, the specification of the relationships among these two hundred variables is by no means simple. Even consideration of the relationship between two variables— say productivity and job satisfaction—may take a researcher several years.

Thus, the research strategy must be a cooperative one. In the opinion of the present writer, the problem is that the variables of organization theory are not stated *sufficiently* clearly and their measurement is not *sufficiently* unambiguous for such a cooperative enterprise. In other words, we cannot have a science of organizations unless and until we improve both our concepts and our measurements.

COMMENTS ON THE MEASUREMENT OF VARIABLES

Consider the following case: Argyle, et al. (1957) did a study in which they were interested in replicating some of the American studies on the relationships between supervisory attitudes and productivity in England. They first combed the literature and discovered a number of replicated findings; then they settled on five dimensions of supervisory attitudes that they thought might be related to productivity. In the following list the pole that is related to high productivity is shown first.

1. *General* as opposed to close supervision.
2. *Little production pressure* on the employees rather than much.
3. *Employee-centered* as opposed to production-centered supervision.
4. *Democratic* as opposed to authoritarian supervision.
5. *The use of persuasion* as opposed to punitive disciplinary techniques.

Argyle and his associates hypothesized that these five attitudinal variables were positively related to the productivity of the groups headed by foremen having the desirable attitudes. However, they felt that the previous methods of measurement were inadequate. For this reason they decided to use *four* different methods for the measurement of *each* of these attitudinal variables.

First a pair of researchers had a half-hour structured interview with each foreman. The interview questions were designed to tap each of the ten poles of the five variables. The interinterviewer reliability was .74. Second, they administered an anonymous seventeen-item Likert-type questionnaire; again, each of the ten poles was represented by one or two questions. Third, they went to the various managers, who knew some of these foremen, and asked them to rank the foremen whom they knew on each of the five dimensions. The poles of the dimensions were described in great detail. Finally, they presented each foreman with five sets of two cards each. On each of the cards were typed the behaviors of a hypothetical foreman and the respondents were asked to choose the foreman they thought would do the best job in their shop. Each set of cards dealt with one of the five dimensions. The second phase of this procedure, which the researchers called the Foreman Description Preference Test, required each foreman to rank the five descriptions he had chosen, thus giving a measure of perceived relative importance of each dimension. The scoring reflected both the pole preference and the perceived importance of each dimension.

Thus, the researchers had four methods that *supposedly measured* the same thing. What were the obtained intercorrelations? They were:

		1	2	3
1.	Interview			
2.	Questionnaire	.09		
3.	Management ratings	.21	.05	
4.	Foreman Description Preference Test	.14	.04	.13

In other words, the intercorrelations were almost negligible. What went wrong?

The major fault, it seems to this writer, has to do with conceptual clarity. Some of the items in their interview and questionnaire were normative—of the type "a foreman *ought* to be/do such-and-such"—and some dealt with actual behavior—"*I* do such-and-such." Some may argue that the normative items are projective and may tell us more than the actual behavior items. This is possible, but it is clearly important to treat scores from normative and actual items separately. Many investigators have worked with differences between such scores (Porter, 1961; Ross and Zander, 1957) and have found most useful results. If the scores were highly correlated, difference scores would have provided no information not already present in the actual scores.

Furthermore, the interview and the questionnaire reported on the attitudes of the foremen as *they* see themselves, the management ratings reported on how *managers* perceive the foremen, and the Foreman

Description Preference Test reported on how a foreman perceives other foremen who might be operating in his department. These perceptions are by no means equivalent.

The questionnaire correlated least with the other measures—the correlations were less than .10. But note that this was the *only* method that was administered anonymously. It is fairly well established that in many situations anonymous procedures give different results than procedures involving identification of the subject. It is probably desirable to include an anonymous or at least an indirect procedure for the measurement of attitudes in each research project as a means of checking on the "true" attitudes.

The recent work of Sherif and Hovland (1961) may have opened the way for indirect measures that give the same results under anonymous as under identification conditions. They have shown that there are systematic distortions in the judgments of attitude items that can be related to extreme attitudinal positions. This would suggest a procedure in which the subject is instructed to do the relatively nonthreatening job of judging whether certain attitude statements belong to category A or to category B. From the frequency of placement of the statements in A or B, we would be able to infer the subject's attitude. This is an indirect approach that deserves further research.

The point of this lengthy discussion is simply this: If three competent investigators bent on measuring a particular variable by four different methods slip into so much conceptual unclarity, it is not surprising that different investigators, employing their preferred measuring instruments, obtain contradictory results. Contradictory results are often blamed on sampling or on the interaction of uncontrolled variables with the measured variables, but it may well be that they are due to the conceptual confusion that prevails in the measurement of variables. A few studies (e.g., Smith et al., 1961) have used several procedures with high concurrent validity and correlated their results with criteria measured by procedures also having high concurrent validity. But more such studies are urgently needed. There are some studies in which a serious effort was made to obtain conceptual clarity. On the matter of the relationship between foremen and workers, for instance, Foa (1955, 1957a, 1957b, 1958) has made such an attempt. In general, the use of Guttman's (1959) facet analysis is likely to be most helpful in the process of conceptual clarification in the area of attitude measurement. Again more such efforts are needed.

Another problem is the reliance of so many investigators on face validity. Rarely is the measurement of a variable such as job satisfaction studied from the point of view of construct validity. Factor analysis that shows that the items that sound as though they are tapping a particular variable load on the same factor is a necessary but not a sufficient step in the validation of an attitude instrument. It is necessary to use some external criterion, such as absenteeism or turnover rates, to establish the validity of the instrument. It is even better if we employ experimental procedures, e.g., when people are promoted there *ought* to be an increase in their job satisfaction. An instrument that supposedly measures job satisfaction but does not discriminate among such people and employees who have not been promoted ought to be considered suspect.

Much of the research in organization theory depends on attitude instruments. Yet the problem of the presence of so much stylistic variance in attitude tests seems to have concerned only a few (e.g., Wiggins, 1962) investigators. Much of the research on personality tests, which shows the presence of a variety of response sets, appears to be ignored by attitude-scale constructors. Examination of the currently used inventories suggests that some of their variance is determined, in part, by acquiescence, social desirability, the tendency to endorse items that are worded in the first person (Albright, et al., 1962), the tendency to "lie." etc. Edwards, et al. (1962) have shown that social desirability, acquiescence, and the tendency to lie are factorially independent. Messick (1960) has shown that social desirability itself is multidimensional. Elliott (1961) has shown that item construction and respondent aptitude are related to response acquiescence. The varieties of response sets have been discussed by Broen and Wirt (1958) and McGee (1962). Procedures for the separate measurement and control have been suggested by Helmstadter (1957) and have been widely used in research (Clayton and Jackson, 1961). In view of these developments, there is no excuse for continued use of those old attitude measurement instruments that do not permit the controls suggested above.

In many studies the investigators employ attitude measures without consideration of the correlation between employee attitudes and demographic variables such as age, type of job, level in the organization, etc. England, et al., (1961) and England and Stein (1961) have shown that such correlations exist. Furthermore, it is likely, though not yet shown empirically, that there are variations in the weights used by people at various levels in the organization when they weigh the various factors that are instrumental in creating their attitudes. For instance, the component "self-actualization" or intrinsic job satisfaction appears to be the major component in studies of the job satisfaction of management and professional personnel (Harrison, 1960; Herzberg et al., 1959) but is relatively unimportant in studies of workers (Wherry, 1958). In the next section we will present a procedure that permits the computation of these weights.

HOW TO PLAN THIS RESEARCH

The burden of the above discussion suggests to the present writer that it is necessary to reconsider the methods employed in doing research. The need for systematic, programmatic research in the small groups area has been pointed out by McGrath (1962). Such a need exists even more strongly in the area of the study of organizations. One possible solution is the following. The various professional societies interested in the study of organizations would appoint representatives to interdisciplinary committees whose function would be to study and report how each of the key variables of the proposed theoretical scheme is to be measured. Standardized procedures would be established. For those variables for which measurement requires special training, one of the representatives on the committee would be charged with the function of providing such training to researchers interested in the use of the variable. Such training institutes would, of course, be open to all qualified applicants.

This kind of standardization procedure is very common in the physical sciences. The units of measurement in those sciences are established through international conventions. There is a very large number of possible variables that might be measured in electricity, yet by international convention, the key measures—such as Volt, Ampere, Coulomb—and their interrelations to other variables are agreed upon. It might be said that "our field is too new" to freeze the variables at this point. The answer is that if we do not, there will be a continuation of this wasteful work, where each researcher measures most of his variables in the way he finds most convenient and where considerable confusion exists in the communication of obtained measures and results. Furthermore, something useful should result from the interdisciplinary committees suggested above, since they would at least obtain clarification of the meaning of the various variables.

If agreement on the methods of measurement of the variables is obtained, then different investigators might undertake to study different aspects of the interrelationships among the two hundred variables, utilizing the standard methods of measurement. As an example of the kinds of studies that might be undertaken at this stage, we present a research proposal for the study of individual differences in goals.

AN ILLUSTRATAVE RESEARCH PROPOSAL:
THE STUDY OF INDIVIDUAL DIFFERENCES IN GOALS AND JOB SATISFACTION

In his lecture to the seminar, Herbert Simon pointed out that it is imperative that we study the goals of organizations. He examined how organizational goals might be related to individual motives and how personal goals and role-determined goals might be related to each other. He reminded the conference that at any point in time an individual attends only to a limited number of characteristics of the situation in which he is operating. It is a characteristic of humans that they attend to different aspects of their environment, depending on their previous experience (Dearborn and Simon, 1958). Thus, sales managers see sales problems behind most major company crises, bankers stress the importance of cutting costs, production people the importance of more efficient production, and marketing people the importance of developing a new, more marketable product. Though all these sets of people have a vague, common goal—namely, to increase profits—they tend to substitute for this major goal subgoals that are entirely different in character. When a person joins an organization, there are a number of already determined behaviors that must become parts of his role. The role-determined behavior may or may not be consistent with the overall organizational goal; but the individual is likely to see direct connections. He faces a set of constraints, some of which are *generators*—they generate alternatives—but the solutions must be checked against various other constraints, which are *tests*. Further elaboration of Simon's thinking on the concept of organizational goals is provided in a recent publication (Simon, 1964).

When a person focuses on constraint B and ignores constraints A, C, and D, he employs B as a generator and A, C, and D as tests of his solutions. Now to the extent that the generators and tests used by person Alpha and person Beta are the same, to that extent we can talk about common goals. If many members of an organization have similar generators and tests, we can ignore their personal goals and talk about organizational goals (the overlapping generators and tests). If Alpha and Beta are doing related jobs, the variables employed by one will overlap to a certain extent with the variables used by the other. It is the job of higher management to so structure the situation that the goals of Alphas and Betas interdigitate without creating undue stress.

This conception of goals points to the fact that different people in an organization will employ different criteria of organizational effectiveness. For instance, the shareholders may simply consider return on investment and give it 100 percent of the weight. The customers may give weight to both the quality and price of the products produced by the organization and consider an organization effective depending on its success to provide good quality products at a low price. The workers may consider a host of factors including wages, security, "self-actualization," etc. Furthermore, different personalities, group memberships, family obligations could produce different patterns of loading of these factors. Management may consider profits or longevity of the organization as the major factors; and, again, the weights placed on the various factors may be influenced by such variables as the management level, the functions of the manager in the organization (sales, production, finance) and a variety of demographic factors that tend to create a common past experience.

The research that we are about to propose aims at discovering the relative weights placed by different individuals, differing in levels, functions, and having different demographic characteristics, on key aspects of their work environment.

Let us begin with an attempt to measure the relative weights of characteristics leading to job satisfaction. We may construct a questionnaire in which a series of hypothetical jobs are described in terms of their key characteristics. The questionnaire would begin with a definition of terms, such as what is meant by "good" working conditions, or "good" supervision. The hypothetical jobs would then be presented and the subject would be asked to judge their relative desirability (from his point of view). For instance, one hypothetical job may be described as follows: "A job that requires working under poor conditions, having high financial rewards, poor supervisory practices, and good conditions of personal development." The characteristics are presented with high and low values, in all possible combinations. This is a factorial design, and it permits analyses of variance. Such analyses may be undertaken for each subject, and may provide the following information: (a) whether the subject paid attention to a particular characteristic when making his judgments of desirability; e.g., some may not pay attention to working conditions, while others undoubtedly would pay attention to this characteristic of the job; (b) whether there are significant interactions between characteristics; e.g., it might be that the subject views a job having high pay and an opportunity for self-actualization as quite desirable in spite of the poor working conditions associated with the job, but when both poor working conditions *and* poor supervision are associated with the job he sees it as undesirable; and (c) how much variance is controlled by each of the characteristics; i.e., how much weight the subject places on that characteristic. It is our hypothesis that the weights obtained under (c) above will vary as we consider subjects differing in level and function of job in the organization, and in demographic characteristics. The hypothesis is plausible in view of the differences in individual motivation found among managers differing in level, function, and demographic variables (Porter, 1961; 1962; 1963a, b; Rosen, 1961; Rosen and Weaver, 1960).

The design suggested above has been found useful in a number of studies of social perception (Triandis and Triandis, 1960, 1962; Triandis, 1961, 1963, 1964; Rickard, et al., 1963). It is now being employed in investigations of job satisfaction by Robert Ewen.

In studies of goals, it might be fruitful to consider a variety of organizational goals, such as return on investment, quality of the product, low prices, control of a large portion of the potential market, perpetuation of the organization, large size of the organization, control over other companies, providing high wages, providing security for the employees, industrial peace, self-actualization of the manager, providing opportunities for self-actualization of the employees. For each of these conceivable goals we might consider some high and some low value. It should be possible to construct questionnaires employing complex stimuli varying in several of these characteristics simultaneously—e.g., how desirable is it to take a decision that will result in having an organization that has a high return on investment, low quality of products produced, a large size, and uncertain industrial peace? Analyses of the responses obtained from managers with different functions and at different levels should show differences in the relative weights they assign to the various outcomes, i.e., differences in their goal structures.

Another kind of project may employ psychophysical methods for the determination of the indifference curves (Thurstone, 1959) for various outcomes. Is, for instance, a change in the probability of a strike that will cost X amount from a probability of .30 to one of .50 subjectively equivalent to an increase in return on investment from 4 to 6 percent?

It is clear that a large number of research projects may be generated from the above suggestions. One may study the relationship between demographic variables and goals, or between structure variables and goals. One may look at how different goal structures are related to different manager behaviors—functions—and how these functions are related to different outputs. If several such studies are carried out, we might obtain a network of relationships that would permit the tracing of how inputs are related to outputs, and hence how organizations may be designed to maximize the desired outputs.

The above argument can be summarized as follows. First, a serious effort must be made to standardize our measurement of the key variables. Second, some of the major relationships among the two hundred variables should be investigated. Third, experience with the effect of changes of key inputs on structures, functions, and outputs and of key structures on functions and outputs must be accumulated. At that stage the organization specialists should be in a position to design organizations with the same kind of certainty that the engineers who design bridges exhibit at the present time.

SUMMARY

This chapter summarized some of the thinking of Fiedler, Katzell, Maccoby, and Miner, as well as the present writer, on the question of how to study organizations. We established that approximately two hundred variables are likely to be important in the description and study of the behavior of organizations. Some of these variables are presented in Table 1. Illustrations of the kinds of hypotheses that might involve these variables were presented. It became clear that the number of variables, the innumerable ways in which they could be measured, and the conceptual lack of clarity involved in the present procedures of measurement, require a drastic reorganization of the current research procedures. Comments on some of the methodological problems involved in the study of organizations were presented. It was argued that there is a need for standardization of the present measurement procedures in order to make the study of organizations a truly cooperative scientific enterprise. Some illustrations of useful approaches in the study of the interrelations of the variables were presented. In addition, some suggestions were made on possible applications of this knowledge, in terms of organizational design and organizational change.

REFERENCES

ABBREVIATIONS

ASR   *American Sociological Review*
ASQ   *Administrative Science Quarterly*
EPM   *Educational and Psychological Measurement*
HR   *Human Relations*
JAP   *Journal of Applied Psychology*

Adams, S. "Status Congruency as a Variable in Small Group Performance." *Social Forces*, 1953, 32, 16–22.
Albright, L. E., Porter, T. B., and Glennon, J. R. "Favorability in Employee Attitude Surveys as a Function of Item Personalization." *American Psychologist*, 1962, 17, 370.
Anderson, L. R., and Fiedler, F. E. "The Effect of Participatory and Supervisory Leadership on Group Creativity." Technical Report No. 7. Urbana: U. of Illinois, Group Effectiveness Research Laboratory, 1962.
Argyle, M. *The Scientific Study of Social Behavior.* New York: Philosophical Library, 1957.
Argyle, M., Gardner, G., and Cioffi, F. "The Measurement of Supervisory Methods." *HR*, 1957, *10*, 295–313.
Argyris, C. *Personality and Organization.* New York: Harper, 1957.
————. "Understanding Human Behavior in Organizations: One Viewpoint."

In M. Haire, ed. *Modern Organization Theory.* New York: Wiley, 1959.

Bakke, E. W. "Concept of the Social Organization." In M. Haire, ed. *Modern Organization Theory.* New York: Wiley, 1959.

Bales, R. F. *Interaction Process Analysis: A Method for the Study of Small Groups.* Cambridge, Mass.: Addison-Wesley, 1950.

Bass, B. M. *Leadership, Psychology and Organizational Behavior.* New York: Harper, 1960.

Bergum, B. O., and Lehr, D. J. "Effects of Authoritarianism on Vigilance Performance." *JAP,* 1963, *47,* 75–77.

Berkowitz, L. "Group Standards, Cohesiveness and Productivity." *HR,* 1954, *7,* 509–519.

Brayfield, A. H., and Crockett, W. H. "Employee Attitudes and Employee Performance." *Psychological Bull.,* 1955, *52,* 396–424.

Broen, W. E., and Wirt, R. D. "Varieties of Response Set." *J. Consulting Psychology,* 1958, *22,* 237–240.

Cattell, R. B. *Personality and Motivation Structure and Measurement.* Yonkers-on-Hudson, N.Y.: World Book, 1957.

Centers, R. "Motivational Aspects of Occupational Stratification." *J. Social Psychology,* 1948, *28,* 187–217.

Clark, J. V. "Motivation in Work Groups: a Tentative View." *Human Organization,* 1960, *19,* 199–208.

Clayton, M. B., and Jackson, D. N. "Equivalence Range, Acquiescence and Over-generalization." *EPM,* 1961, *21,* 371–382.

Coch, L., and French, J. R. P., Jr. "Overcoming Resistance to Change." *HR,* 1948, *1,* 512–532.

Cureton, E. E., and Katzell, R. A. "A Further Analysis of the Relations among Job Performance and Situational Variables." *JAP,* 1962, *46,* 230.

Dabas, Z. S. "The Dimensions of Morale: An Item Factorization of the SRA Employee Inventory." *Personnel Psych.,* 1958, *11,* 217–234.

Dearborn, D. C., and Simon, H. A. "Selective Perception: The Departmental Identification of Executives." *Sociometry,* 1958, *21,* 140–144.

Derber, M., Chalmers, W. E., and Stagner, R. *The Local Union-Management Relationship.* Urbana.: U. of Illinois, Institute of Labor and Industrial Relations, 1960.

Edwards, A. L., Diers, C. J., and Walker, J. N. "Response Sets and Factor Loadings on Sixty-one Personality Scales." *JAP,* 1962, *46,* 220–225.

Elliott, L. L. "Effects of Item Construction and Respondent Aptitude on Response Acquiescence." *EPM,* 1961, *21,* 405–415.

England, G. W., Korman, A. K., and Stein, C. I. "Overcoming Contradictions in Attitude Survey Results: The Need for Relevant Attitude Norms." *Personnel Administration,* 1961, *24,* 36–40.

England, G. W., and Stein, C. I. "The Occupational Reference Group: A Neglected Concept in Employee Attitude Studies." *Personnel Psych.,* 1961, *14,* 299–305.

Exline, R. V., and Ziller, R. C. "Status Congruency and Interpersonal Conflict in Decision-Making Groups." *HR,* 1959, *12,* 147–162.

Ewen, R. B. Some Determinants and Correlates of Job Satisfaction. Unpublished Master's thesis, U. of Illinois, 1963.

Festinger, L. *A Theory of Cognitive Dissonance.* Stanford, Cal.: Stanford U. Press, 1957.

Festinger, L., Riecken, H. W., Jr., and Schachter, S. *When Prophesy Fails.* Minneapolis: U. of Minnesota Press, 1956.

Fiedler, F. E. *Leader Attitudes and Group Effectiveness.* Urbana.: U. of Illinois Press, 1958.

————. A Contingency Model of Leadership Effectiveness. Technical Report No. 10. Urbana: U. of Illinois, Group Effectiveness Research Laboratory, 1963.

Fiedler, F. E., and Meuwese, W. A. T. "Leader's Contribution to Task Performance in Cohesive and Uncohesive Groups." *JASP*, 1963, *67*, 83–87.

Foa, U. G. "Behavior, Norms, and Social Rewards in a Dyad." *Behavioral Science*, 1958, *3*, 323–334.

————. "Foreman–Worker Interaction: A Research Design." *Sociometry*, 1955, *18*, 226–244.

————. "Relationship of Worker's Expectation to Satisfaction with Supervisor." *Personnel Psych.*, 1957a, *10*, 161–168.

————. "A Test of Foreman–Worker Relationship." *Personnel Psych.*, 1957b, *9*, 469–486.

Form, W. H., and Geschwender, J. A. "Social Reference Basis of Job Satisfaction: The Case of Manual Workers." *ASR*, 1962, *27*, 228–237.

French, J. R. P., Jr. "A Formal Theory of Social Power." *Psychological Rev.*, 1956, *63*, 181–194.

French, J. R. P., Jr., Israel, J., and Aos, D. "An Experiment on Participation in a Norwegian Factory." *HR*, 1960, *13*, 3–19.

French, J. R. P., Jr., and Raven, B. "The Bases of Social Power." In D. Cartwright ed. *Studies in Social Power.* Ann Arbor: U. of Michigan, Institute for Social Research, 1959.

Georgopoulos, B. S., Mahoney, G. M., and Jones, N. W. "A Path-Goal Approach to Productivity." *JAP*, 1957, *41*, 345–353.

Guttman, L. "A Structural Theory of Intergroup Beliefs and Action." *ASR*, 1959, *24*, 318–328.

Haire, M. "The Concept of Power and the Concept of Men." In G. B. Strother, ed. *Social Science Approaches to Business Behavior.* Homewood, Ill.: Dorsey, 1962.

Harding, F. D., and Bottenberg, R. A. "Effect of Personal Characteristics on Relationships between Attitudes and Job Performance." *JAP*, 1961, *45*, 428–430.

Harrison, R. "Sources of Variation in Manager Job Attitudes." *Personnel Psych.*, 1960, *13*, 425–434.

Haythorn, W. "The Effects of Varying Compositions of Authoritarian and Equalitarian Leaders and Followers." *JASP*, 1956, *52*, 210–219.

Helmstadter, G. C. "Procedures for Obtaining Separate Set and Content Components of a Test Score." *Psychometrika*, 1957, *22*, 381–394.

Hemphill, J. K., and Westie, C. M. "The Measurement of Group Dimensions." *J. Psychology*, 1950, *29*, 325–342.

Herzberg, F., Mausner, B., and Snyderman, B. B. *The Motivation to Work.* New York: Wiley, 1959.

Hewitt, D., and Parfit, J. "A Note on Working Morale and Size of Group." *Occupational Psych.*, 1953, *27*, 38–42.

Homans, G. *The Human Group*. New York: Harcourt, Brace, 1950.

Hulin, C. L. "Research Implications of Attitude Surveys in Large Organizations." Paper presented to Illinois Psychological Association, 1963.

Julian, J. W., and McGrath, J. E. "The Influence of Leader and Member Behavior on the Adjustment and Task Effectiveness of Negotiation Groups." Urbana: U. of Illinois, Group Effectiveness Research Laboratory, 1962.

Kahn, R. L. "Productivity and Job Satisfaction." *Personnel Psych.*, 1960, *13*, 275–287.

Katz, D., Maccoby, N., Gurin, G., and Floor, L. G. *Productivity, Supervision, and Morale Among Railway Workers*. Ann Arbor: U. of Michigan, 1951.

Katz, D., Maccoby, N., and Morse, N. *Productivity, Supervision, and Morale in an Office Situation*. Ann Arbor: U. of Michigan, 1950.

Katzell, R. A. "Contrasting Systems of Work Organization." *American Psychologist*, 1962, *17*, 102–108.

Katzell, R. A., Barrett, R. S., and Parker, T. C. "Job Satisfaction, Job Performance, and Situational Characteristics." *JAP*, 1961, *45*, 65–72.

Kaufman, H. *The Forest Ranger: A Study in Administrative Behavior*. Baltimore: Johns Hopkins Press, 1960.

Kerr, W. A. "Summary of Validity Studies of the Tear Ballot." *Personnel Psych.*, 1952, *5*, 105–113.

Kerr, W. A., Koppelmeier, G. J., and Sullivan, J. J. "Absenteeism, Turnover, and Morale in a Metals Fabrication Factory." *Occupational Psych.*, 1951, *25*, 50–55.

Kidd, J. S., and Christy, R. T. "Supervisory Procedures and Work: Team Productivity." *JAP*, 1961, *45*, 388–392.

Likert, R. *New Patterns of Management*. New York: McGraw-Hill, 1961.

McGee, R. K. "Response Style as a Personality Variable: by What Criterion?" *Psychological Bull.*, 1962, *58*, 284–296.

McGrath, J. E. *A Summary of Small Group Research Studies*. Arlington, Va.: Human Sciences Research, Inc., 1962.

McGregor, D. *The Human Side of Enterprise*. New York: McGraw-Hill, 1960.

Messick, S. "Dimensions of Social Desirability." *J. Consulting Psychology*, 1960, *24*, 279–287.

Miner, J. B. "Occupational Differences in the Desire to Exercise Power." *Psychological Reports*, 1963, *13*, 18.

Miner, J. B. *Studies in Management Education*. New York: Springer, 1964.

Morse, N. C. *Satisfaction in the White Collar Job*. Ann Arbor: U. of Michigan, 1953.

Morse, N. C., and Reimer, E. "The Experimental Change of a Major Organizational Variable." *JASP*, 1956, *52*, 120–129.

Morse, N. C., and Weiss, R. S. "The Function and Meaning of Work and the Job." In S. Nosow and W. H. Form, eds. *Man, Work and Society*. New York: Basic Books, 1962.

Pepinsky, P. N., Pepinsky, H. B., and Paulik, W. B. "The Effects of Task Complexity and Time Pressure Upon Team Productivity." *JAP*, 1960, *44*, 34–38.

Porter, L. W. "Job Attitudes in Management: I. Perceived Deficiencies in Need Fulfillment as a Function of Job Level." *JAP*, 1962, *46*, 375–384.

————. "Job Attitudes in Management: II. Perceived Importance of Needs as a Function of Job Level." *JAP,* 1963, *47,* 141–148.

————. "Job Attitudes in Management: III. Perceived Deficiences in Need Fulfillment as a Function of Line versus Staff Type of Jobs." *JAP,* 1963b, *47,* 267–275.

————. "A Study of Perceived Need Satisfactions in Bottom and Middle Management Jobs." *JAP,* 1961, *45,* 1–10.

Porter, L. W., and Lawler, E. E. "The Effects of 'Tall' versus 'Flat' Organization Structures on Managerial Job Satisfaction." *American Psychologist,* 1963, *18,* 431.

Rickard, T. E., Triandis, H. C., and Patterson, C. H. "Indices of Employer Prejudice toward Disabled Applicants." *JAP,* 1963, *47,* 52–55.

Roach, D. E. "Dimensions of Employee Morale." *American Psychologist,* 1957, *12,* 443.

Rosen, H. "Managerial Role Interaction: a Study of Three Managerial Levels." *JAP,* 1961, *45,* 30–34.

Rosen, H., and Weaver, C. G. "Motivation in Management: A Study of Four Managerial Levels." *JAP,* 1960, *44,* 386–392.

Ross, I. C., and Zander, A. "Need Satisfaction and Employee Turnover." *Personnel Psych.,* 1957, *9,* 327–338.

Schachter, S., Ellerton, N., McBride, D., and Gregory, D. "An Experimental Study of Cohesiveness and Productivity." *HR,* 1951, *4,* 229–238.

Seashore, S. E. *Group Cohesiveness in Industrial Work Groups.* Ann Arbor: U. of Michigan, Survey Research Center, 1954.

Seashore, S. E., Indik, B. P., and Georgopoulos, B. S. "Relationships among Criteria of Job Performance." *JAP,* 1960, *44,* 195–202.

Sells, S. B. "Toward a Taxonomy of Organizations." Technical Report No. 2, ONR Contract Nonr-3436(00). Fort Worth: Texas Christian U., 1962.

Sherif, M., and Hovland, C. I. *Social Judgment.* New Haven, Conn.: Yale U. Press, 1961.

Simon, H. A., "On the Concept of Organizational Goal." *ASQ,* 1964, *9,* 1–22.

Smith, P. C., Hulin, C. L., Macaulay, D. A., Kendall, L. M., and Locke, E. A. "Cornell Studies of Retirement Policies: Measurement of Satisfaction." Paper read at APA meetings, 1961.

Stogdill, R. M. *Individual Behavior and Group Achievement.* New York: Oxford U. Press, 1959.

Stogdill, R. M., and Coons, A. E. *Leader Behavior: Its Description and Measurement.* Columbus: Ohio State U., Bureau of Business Research, 1957.

Stogdill, R. M., Scott, E. L., and Jaynes, W. E. "Leadership and Role Expectations." Bureau of Business Research, Monograph No. 86, Columbus: Ohio State U., 1956.

Strauss, G. "Some Notes on Power Equalization." In H. J. Leavitt, ed. *The Social Science of Organizations.* Englewood Cliffs: Prentice-Hall, 1963.

Thurstone, L. L. *The Measurement of Values.* Chicago: U. of Chicago Press, 1959, Chap. 12.

Triandis, H. C. "A Critique and Experimental Design for the Study of the Relationship between Productivity and Job Satisfaction." *Psychological Bull.,* 1959a, *56,* 309–312.

————. "Categories of Thought of Managers, Clerks, and Workers about Jobs and People in an Industry." *JAP*, 1959b, *43*, 338–344.

————. "Differential Perception of Certain Jobs and People by Managers, Clerks, and Workers in Industry." *JAP*, 1959c, *43*, 221–225.

————. "Cognitive Similarity and Interpersonal Communication in Industry." *JAP*, 1959d, *43*, 321–326.

————. "A Comparative Factorial Analysis of Job Semantic Structures of Managers and Workers." *JAP*, 1960, *44*, 297–302.

————. "A Note on Rokeach's Theory of Prejudice." *JASP*, 1961, *62*, 184–186.

————. "Factors Affecting Employee Selection in Two Cultures." *JAP*, 1963, *47*, 89–96.

————. "Exploratory Factor Analyses of the Behavioral Components of Social Attitudes." *JASP*, 1964, *68*, 420–430.

————. "A Cross-Cultural Study of Social Distance." *Psychological Monographs*, 1962, *76* No. 21 (whole No. 540).

Triandis, H. C., Bass, A. R., Ewen, R. B., and Mikesell, E. H. "Team Creativity as a Function of the Creativity of the Members." *JAP*, 1963, *47* (2), 104–110.

Triandis, H. C., Hall, E. R., and Ewen, R. B. "Member Heterogeneity and Dyadic Creativity." *HR*, 1965, *18*, 33–55.

Triandis, H. C., and Triandis, L. M. "Race, Social Class, Religion, and Nationality as Determinants of Social Distance." *JASP*, 1960, *61*, 110–118.

Twery, R., Schmid, J., and Wrigley, C. "Some Factors in Job Satisfaction: A Comparison of Three Methods of Analysis." *EPM*, 1958, *28*, 189–201.

Van Zelst, R. H. "An Interpersonal Relations Technique for Industry." *Personnel*, 1952, *29*, 68–76.

Vroom, V. H., and Mann, F. C. "Leader Authoritarianism and Employee Attitudes." *Personnel Psych.*, 1960, *13*, 125–140.

Wherry, R. J. Factor Analysis of Morale Data: Reliability and Validity." *Personnel Psych.*, 1958, *11*, 78–89.

Whyte, W. F. "An Interaction Approach to the Theory of Organization." In M. Haire, ed. *Modern Organization Theory*. New York: Wiley, 1959.

Wiggins, J. S. "Strategic, Method, and Stylistic Variance in the MMPI." *Psychological Bull.*, 1962, *59*, 224–242.

Wilson, J. Q. "Innovation in Organizations." In James D. Thompson, ed., *Approaches to Organizational Design*. Pittsburgh: U. of Pittsburgh Press, 1965.

Worthy, J. C. "Organizational Structure and Employee Morale." *ASR*, 1950, *15*, 169–179.

Zaleznik, A., Christensen, C. R., and Roethlisberger, F. J. *The Motivation, Productivity, and Satisfaction of Workers*. Cambridge: Harvard U., Graduate School of Business Administration, 1958.

3

A Model for Viewing an Organization as a System of Constraints

VERNON E. BUCK

Assistant Professor of Industrial Administration, Yale University. In addition to expressing my gratitude to the Pittsburgh seminar members, I want to thank Professors R. B. Fetter, W. S. Gere and Messrs. G. G. Raymond, Jr., and R. A. Thurber for their stimulation, critical insight, and helpfulness. I especially want to thank Professor Chris Argyris for his generous support, which made possible the following approach. However, the author alone is responsible for any errors and inadequacies that remain.

The literature dealing with organizations and approaches to their study may be broadly grouped into three points of view (March and Simon, 1958, pp. 6–7). First there is the machine model, which views members of organizations as passive instruments that perform assigned tasks, receiving but not initiating action. This approach has tended to utilize structural variables as a way of understanding organizational behavior, studying variables such as task specialization, chain of command, unity of direction, and span of control. A second classification is the incongruency between the goals of the organization and the goals of the individual, at least for all but the chief resource-controlling individuals. A third classification, used principally by March and Simon, deals with the problem-solving activities in organizations.

The approach to model building taken in this chapter uses elements from each of the above points of view. The incongruency between the goals of the individual and the goals of the organization (Argyris, 1957) is accepted by the author. His belief is that much of the resulting conflict is avoidable; the desire to minimize the costs of this conflict led to research that tended to confirm this position. From this research came the idea of explaining organizational conflict in the Lewinian terms of induced and own forces, goals, barriers, and valences (Hall and Lindzey, 1957). After some experimentation with the research data and the Lewinian concepts and for reasons noted below, it seemed helpful to analyze all organizational behavior in terms of goals, costs, and resource capacity restrictions.

Because of its widely demonstrated capacity for dealing with goals, costs, and resource capacities in a meaningful way, a decision-making model known as linear programming was appropriated from the area of economic analysis for use in understanding organizational behavior. The application of a model developed in another setting tends to minimize the risk of intellectual myopia that might stem from the construction of an elegant ad hoc model to fit one's own data. The linear programming approach is a decision-making model of resource allocation that is neutral with respect to the nature of the inputs, i.e., it is unaffected by the content and indices of the data. If one's data or manner of viewing organizations can be grafted onto such a decision model without doing violence to either the model or the data, then one should be justified in viewing the outcome as a model of organizational behavior. This juxtaposition will be the approach taken below.

Since organizational structure and process are intended to define appropriate behavior under certain circumstances and are a chief ingredient in conflict situations, they will receive close scrutiny. Recent studies of organizational behavior have tended to emphasize the individual and the small group; for purposes of exposition, little attention will be paid to this research here. This chapter will reassert the necessity of considering an integrated structural-process approach to the study of organizations; it will take as valuable givens the importance of people-centered, adaptive activities, such as increasing the quality of an individual's social sensitivity.

The purpose of this chapter is to develop a model that will be a useful way of viewing organizational behavior and structure. The reader who rejects the incongruency dilemma may still find much to recommend the model as a way of enhancing knowledge and understanding in the area of organizational behavior. In particular, the model's potential for coping with the complex nature of organizational behavior and for illustrating clearly the total ramifications emanating from behavior in organizations is in itself a strong recommendation for its consideration. The chapter will consist of two major sections: (1) descriptive materials, which develop the origins and meanings of certain helpful (and necessary, for the model) concepts and illustrate the fit between this model of organizations and the data that led to this point of view; and (2) a more quantitative discussion of how linear programming can give one much greater explicative powers in the study of organizations, how this approach arrays the same descriptive data in a dynamic and interrelated but readily comprehensible fashion. An experiment using artificial data is conducted to point up this discussion.

The model builder should be able to generate and test the efficacy of his models on many types of organizations. Most of the materials below are from industrial organizations since that is where the author's research is centered. Furthermore, it was while doing the industrial research discussed below that it first appeared that the proposed model could be useful in studying organizational behavior. Using industrial organizations as a bench mark has some advantages because money is a relatively general standard of utility with which to measure and compare alternative actions.[1] It is felt, however, that the model is neither unique to industrial organizations nor unique to the author's particular

---

1. The relative ease of using money as an index for decision making can lead to difficulty if one neglects the importance of those factors for which it is difficult to assign monetary values. See Likert (1961), Chap. 5.

industrial experiences and that the model will be helpful in studying any organization with some valid method of assigning measures of utility to various possible decisions. Empirical proof of this contention as well as an empirical validation of the model on industrial organizations must rest on subsequent research.

In brief, the following discussion maintains that an organization is the interaction of people and other resources in a strategy intended to attain certain specifiable goals; that organizations, like people, seldom have available all the desirable or even necessary resources that would assure the certainty or ease of goal attainment; that some organizational strategy must therefore be determined for the allocation of resources among the various demands for them; that despite their widespread currency most decision rules for the allocation of resources are little more than rules of thumb; that many organizations, which largely ignore the costs, limitations of resource capacities, and goals in decision making, generate an excessive amount of conflict and inefficient solutions to the problems confronting them; that approaches to better and more responsive strategies of resource allocation can now be simulated and tested with the digital computer; that this increased facility for dealing with the complexity of organizational behavior and structure should now challenge organization theorists to abandon their earlier reliance on relatively static, descriptive, global, and normative models of organizations.

ORGANIZATIONAL BEHAVIOR AS A FUNCTION OF CONSTRAINTS: DESCRIPTION

ORGANIZATIONAL GOALS

Individuals themselves rarely have sufficient resources to attain all possible goals. In many circumstances, if goals are to be reached satisfactorily or at all, several individuals may have to pool their resources. At least initially, the entrepreneur, the civil servant, or the corner boy creates an organization to increase the speed, magnitude, and likelihood of his goal attainment. Each of these individuals plus those who pool their resources with them may see the business, bureaucracy, or gang as supplying them with the desired funds, ideas, extra hands, or free time they need to achieve corporate affluence, tax loss, elective office, high sense of self-esteem, or some other desired end state. These end states, which are valued by the resource controllers and for the attainment of which the organization was created and/or maintained, will be called the goals of the organization. This view of organizational goals resembles the view of classical economics, in which the goals of the organization were defined by, if not identical to, those of the entrepreneur. He who pays the piper calls the tune—presumably a preferred one. He who provides the organizational resources or controls them, decides what the goals are to be. By manipulating resources, those tasks that are necessary for attaining the goals of the organization but which the controllers of resources are unable or unwilling to perform are delegated to others in the organization.

Certainly the goals that were instrumental in the formation of the organization need not retain their importance over time; hence, the above expression "the organization was created and/or maintained." An entrepreneur who formed an organization to gain extra hands for profit making may continue to operate his factory at a loss for some time, hoping to avert the human costs of unemployed workers. Corner boys may flirt with politics; an organization founded to foster research on one contagious disease may be maintained to foster other medical research long after the original contagion was eradicated.

One can note from the above comments that there is no disembodied deification of organizational goals. The contents of organizational goals are the desired end states on which the resource controllers reach agreement. Just as organizational goals do not magically arise, neither does their content or form mystically drift from one time to another. If the resource controllers of a foundation decide that the end point has been reached in the research and cure of a contagious disease, then a series of decisions must be made for a change in goals to occur. These decisions may be as humanitarian as inquiring into the most pressing medical problem; as reprehensible as determining for what the public will contribute most; as trivial as deciding whether or not to meet next month's payroll and keep the organizational personnel together while searching for a goal. To an outsider, a major university may drift into coeducation. But unless by "drift" one means a series of major policy decisions and the allocation of substantial amounts of resources by the trustees, this view of organizations is not a helpful one.[2]

As major decision-makers in organizations, the controllers of resources find that they face as an organizational entity the same problems that they face as individuals: they have many possible paths down which to channel their resources, but they seldom have enough resources to take all those paths. An organization may desire to reach new customers through a $100,000 advertising campaign, but it also must have a $100,000 product redesign if the campaign is to be effective. If the organization

2. Having listed the caveats of imputing decision-making powers to the structure of the organization, there will be several occasions in which it will simplify the exposition to use the expression "organizations [verbs]" instead of repeatedly stating "those who control the resources of the organization [verbs]."

has only $100,000 to spend, some kind of preferred schedule of resource allocation must be developed. If the resource controllers decide that their future rests in mass production, then relatively more or all of the available resources might be spent in advertising for new customers to absorb the volume. If the resource controllers of the organization decide that the future of the company resides in its continued reputation for design excellence, then relatively more resources must be spent in product redesign. It is the decision to commit resources for certain activities and to withhold them from certain others that operationally defines the organizational goals. Verbal pronouncements are insufficient for defining goals: the speaker must put his resources where his mouth is if something is to be considered a goal. By using this resource allocation approach, one can usually determine what the organizational goals are, in spite of change and their seemingly trivial or complex nature.

The desirability of efficiency follows from the above discussion: if one has many needs and limited resources, relatively more needs can be satisfied only if resources are allocated so as to increase each fraction of output/input. This notion of efficiency is necessary for the model: one must have limited resources for which to develop satisfactory strategies of allocation. If one has a bottomless bag of resources, there is no cost for anything, and any strategy will do. It is precisely because of limited resources and the constrained uses that one can make of them that there is a problem.

GOALS, COSTS, AND CAPACITY RESTRICTIONS AS CONSTRAINTS

The concepts of cost (negative cost is profit) and resource capacity restrictions have accompanied the foregoing discussion of goals. Because goals, costs, and capacity restrictions are the inputs for the model of this chapter, it is desirable to elaborate upon the meaning of costs and capacity restrictions.

For the organization that desired both to advertise its products widely and redesign them, costs were easily defined. It is also possible to estimate one's expected profit from the strategy chosen. As we will note later, not all circumstances of interest to us will lend themselves to precise measures of costs-profits. However, we will assume in this chapter that some reasonably good measure of utility is possible in all situations of interest.

The organization that had $100,000 available for allocation but needed $200,000 to make the preferred strategy possible was facing a capacity restriction. In this chapter any limitation on resource capacity that could affect decision making and decision implementation will be called a capacity restriction. It will be useful to distinguish between absolute and relative capacity restrictions. If one has only $100,000 available and cannot raise funds elsewhere, this inability to raise extra funds becomes an absolute restriction on money capacity and will circumscribe the range of possible decisions. If one has only $100,000 but might be able to borrow additional funds, albeit at great cost, there is only a relative capacity restriction. Capacity could be increased, but only with great changes in the cost structure.

Capacity restrictions quite clearly constrain behavior. If one's absolute money capacity is $100,000, one cannot maximize both the redesign and the advertising plans. Even if the resource controllers could borrow the funds, the requirements stipulated by the lender become restrictions themselves. In a similar fashion, costs also constrain behavior when resources are limited. If aspects other than cost are equal for cheap A and dear B, efficiency will preclude the selection of B. The high cost of B relative to A has effectively partitioned B out of contention. Finally, goals themselves affect and are affected by the definition of the situation. The individual who has inherited a flour mill faces nearly insurmountable barriers against converting it into an electronics industry; becoming an electronics magnate is not really a goal that is open to him. Rarely is one able to set and attain goals that fulfill one's heart's innermost desires. To avoid constant failure, goals are adapted to the available alternatives. By the same token, choosing certain goals delimits the kinds of decisions and activities open to one. This is particularly so in organizations in which the goal selection activities and the goal attainment activities are frequently divorced and specialized. Since goals, costs, and capacity restrictions all have their constraining features, we will speak of them collectively as constraints that determine organizational behavior.[3] When we speak of constrained behavior, we will be discussing behavior that results from the current level of capacity restrictions, goals, and costs extant in the situation.

DECIDING BETWEEN PATHS TO GOALS

During some recent research into manufacturing operations the author encountered what were for him some interesting and revealing applications of decision-making techniques. One of these widely used techniques might be called a multiple-comparisons technique for decision making. By comparing all possible combinations of alternatives available, an individual could determine the least costly combination of paths to his goal or goals. While the most vivid application of this decision-making

---

3. Some economic-decision models reserve the term "constraint" to define what we are calling "capacity restrictions." However, since there is no clearly established convention, we will use constraints in the more inclusive sense.

technique was in an area devoted to the design of new products, the multiple comparisons approach seemed to be a particularly useful frame of reference for understanding how and why a large portion of organizational behavior and structure appeared as it did. As an example of this multiple comparisons approach to decision making, consider the issues involved in establishing a new product line. During the design phase of a product, some kind of balance would have to be reached between the various possible features that the final product might embody. Perhaps within the mind of a single project director decisions would have to be reached about appearance, versatility, capacity, durability, and safety so that the goal of a profitable product could be attained. Rarely can the project director maximize all possible features or functions of a proposed product and still keep within a competitive price range. Compromises must be made if the product is to come into existence at all.

Figure 1 is a schematic example of how a decision might be reached by comparing the possible combinations of features that a finished product might have. It should be noted that the greater the number of features (appearance, durability, safety) and the greater the number of options within each category of features (buffing, painting, plating), the greater the number of possible combinations of paths to the goal or goals. Even when one is dealing with discrete alternatives like buffing, painting, plating, the number of path-goal combinations becomes large. If features and options were not discrete but were different distances along a continuum, then of course the number of possible combinations would be conceptually infinite and a conceptual "listing" of all alternatives would be impossible.

While the multiple comparisons approach to decision making is complete, i.e., it lists all path-goal arrays from ADG to CFI, and while it may be efficient if one is dealing with a few simple, discrete sets of path-goal choices, there will be circumstances in which approximations to it must be made. In times of stress, ambiguity, or cognitive limits to rationality, it may only be possible to use what we will call a serial comparisons strategy. Instead of comparing 27 (3x3x3) complete strategies with a multiple comparisons approach, one compares single paths in a step-wise fashion. Instead of comparing strategy ADG with ADH with . . . CFI, one simply compares A by B by C; having done his best in that selection (say he chose B), he compares D by E by F; having done his best in that selection (say he chose E), he compares G, H, and I similarly. When he has chosen one of these (say I), he has defined a path-goal strategy BEI, and he has had to make many fewer and simpler discriminations than he would have had to make with the multiple comparisons strategy. Because of the simplicity of this serial method and the fact that it will sometimes yield the same result as the multiple comparison approach, particularly when one is dealing with noninteractive discrete variables, the serial method appears to be more efficient. We shall note later that this appearance may be illusory and that there is less justification for relying on this approach than there might have been two decades ago.

A general statement of the serial comparisons method might be the following: take the most rewarding single index or option open and optimize it; having done that, take the second most rewarding index or step facing one and optimize it; etc. The chief distinction between this rule and the multiple comparisons rule is in terms of cognitive inability to decipher stimuli, making it impossible to array all possible strategies for comparisons. Stimuli may all be present, but one cannot process them into a strategy; some of the subsequent paths needed may be undefined during the interval in which a commitment to action must be made; there may be too many stimuli to process with present facilities. Perhaps

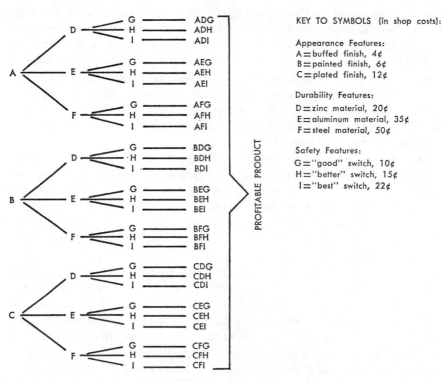

KEY TO SYMBOLS (in shop costs):

Appearance Features:
A = buffed finish, 4¢
B = painted finish, 6¢
C = plated finish, 12¢

Durability Features:
D = zinc material, 20¢
E = aluminum material, 35¢
F = steel material, 50¢

Safety Features:
G = "good" switch, 10¢
H = "better" switch, 15¢
I = "best" switch, 22¢

FIGURE 1
Examples of Possible Paths to Goals

one is confronted with a crisis; great costs are incurred by inactivity, but there is no time or facilities for developing a master strategy for action via multiple comparisons; the best option is taken and one attempts to maximize it for the time being. A diemaker may have to begin construction on a die if he is to meet delivery schedules; the customer may have decided on neither the composition of the alloy to be used in the die, nor the kind of machine in which the die will be mounted. Instead of being able to develop an overall plan for an optimum die, the diemaker must make important decisions in a step-wise fashion as the die construction progresses, relying on incomplete information; because there is an interaction of the features in die making, a better die is probable only when all the paths to the goals are known at the outset.

Quite common is the situation in which the stimuli are clear, the situation not critical, yet there is just too much information to process into a strategy. Rather than attempt the tremendous task of developing all the possible strategies of a 10x10x10x10 situation, one may attack the problem in a serial fashion. There are two aspects to this problem: a solution may exist but one is unable to find it or unwilling to spend the resources to find it; or because of present constraints or conflicting goals, no solution exists. It has been the author's observation that in situations characterized by changing demands, if no simple solution exists from the individual's point of view, he approximates one by the serial-comparisons method. While the multiple-comparisons method would guarantee the best approximation to a near-solution, in the face of change it may be too costly a process. Many employees seem to prefer at least doing their best on one option in order to defend themselves (among other motives—competence). They report feelings like the following: "I won't turn out junk. My work is 100% [quality]. I work just as hard for hitting the standards as I do for quality, but the rates are too tight. You can't do both!" In practice there may be little difference between a very complex situation in which a solution exists but is not solved for and the situation in which no solution exists. From the point of view of the individual, both situations are devoid of successful strategies.

With the multiple comparisons approach to decision making one has at least the conceptual opportunity to evaluate all possible total strategies. This is particularly important if there is any subtle interaction among subsequent paths. For example, one may choose a particular path-goal strategy that gives the most efficient overall results. This strategy has a very costly first step, which, when combined with a very costly fourth step, leads to a much more efficient result than any other path-goal strategy. But this best strategy would have never resulted from the serial comparisons approach because the initial costly step would have precluded it.

Whether one uses a multiple-comparison method or a serial-comparisons method in making decisions, there are factors that limit somewhat the difficulty of making decisions, although the difficulty may still exceed normal cognitive powers. Speaking of optimal strategies implies complete information, which is ordinarily unavailable. Not only is it unlikely that all possible alternatives are known, but time demands in organizations frequently also sharply limit the amount of searching for alternatives in which one can engage. Because of this lack of complete knowledge and the costs associated with trying to overcome this deficiency, one speaks of satisfactory solutions instead of optimal ones (March and Simon, 1958, pp. 140–141). Even granting this restriction, the potential number of combinations of known features and known options may be so great that it is impractical if not impossible to list and weigh all possible combinations. In practice one considers only a restricted subset of all the known alternatives, because decision rules can be developed about particular technologies that automatically exclude certain inefficient procedures without dwelling upon them. If a painted or chrome-plated product is customary in the market for this product, there is no point in spending resources even to evaluate paths originating at A. None of the paths utilizing buffing would yield a route to the goal of profitability. The company may base its reputation on high quality products; perhaps zinc (D) is an inadmissible path. This leaves us, in this simplified example, with open paths consisting of combinations of B, D; E, F; G, H, and I. But if the "good" switch, G, may fail and cause injury to the user, it may be summarily excluded from further consideration. The exclusion of poor choices at the outset sharply reduces the number of comparisons that must be made, whether by serial or multiple means. In this example these decision rules have eliminated all possible paths except those combinations of B, C, E, F, H, and I.

Regardless of the decision-making technique employed, the design and preferred schedule of decisions for the project director may not be fixed at this point. He may find that there are many others in the organization whose task is to limit even further the possible paths to the profitability goal. Marketing representatives may feel that a stainless steel product is necessary to prevent the problems of aluminum oxidation. Manufacturing engineers may wish to have the product fashioned from zinc since previously purchased zinc-working machinery is already available. The legal department may find that the company cannot manufacture a "best" switch because someone else holds the patent rights. The repair service representatives may press for using the "best" switch even if the company must pay a royalty for the design because the expected value of repair costs over the life of the product is lower for the "best" switch. Quality control representatives may want both stainless steel products and the "best" switch as a guarantee of the company's continued reputation for high quality products.

By the time the project director has achieved a finished design that is simultaneously a satisfactory engineering solution and a satisfactory solution from the points of view of all other members of the organization, he finds that the number of possible paths to the goal is greatly reduced. In fact, since some demands are mutually exclusive, there may be no solution that pleases everyone. One cannot have a zinc product and a stainless steel one at the same time. Compromises must take place, and the features that seem to be least important to the overall success picture of the product may be sacrificed if at least *a* path to the goal is to exist. It is at this point that many projects are shelved because no minimally acceptable complete path network to the goal does exist. If one's product must have the "best" switch and one can neither buy it, get a license to make it, design an equally effective substitute, nor risk the expense and notoriety of patent litigation, then one must shelve the project.

PATHS BECOMES GOALS

In spite of the large number of limitations on the freedom of the project director, he may be one of the most free individuals in an organization. Although many paths may be closed to him at a given time, it may not be true for all time on this product or for the next project on which he may work. Many others in the organization never have the same degree of opportunity or responsibility for deciding among alternative combinations of paths for goals, because the path (or paths) toward a goal (or goals) decided upon at one level changes from a path at that level into a goal at a lower level. This is true whether or not the lower level members of the organization have helped establish the goal.

Continuing the example of designing a new product, an organization's patent lawyer might take the position that it is impossible for his company to subvert the patent rights on the "best" switch and that to attempt this would be to suffer great damages. At this point he is a limiting factor on the choice of paths to the goal. But once a company officer has said that this path (use "best" switch) must and will be taken, then the goal of the lawyer must be to guarantee the taking of this path with least total cost to the company. The goal is a "given." He is no longer a consultant about the pitfalls of certain paths. His goal becomes the minimization of the costs of taking this path.

Figure 2 is a graphic example of how a path or paths at one level of decision-making becomes a goal or goals for subsequent levels of organizational structure. It does no violence to one's understanding of the real world to state that among other things stockholders are interested in profitable returns on their investment, goal g_1. At some point in the past various business ventures requiring capital were compared with one another on indices like profitability, public need, available resources, technology, trained people, and prior experience. For some reason or combination of reasons a decision was made to produce widgets. For the stockholders, making and selling widgets became a path (p_1) toward the goal of profitability (g_1). At this point making and selling widgets at a profit becomes the goal (g_2) of the president and the chairman of the board. They and their appointed assistants must define a suitable path

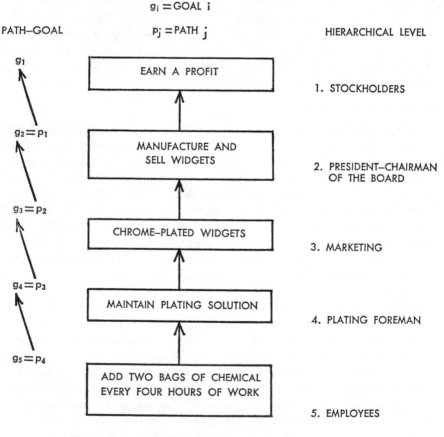

FIGURE 2
Examples of Paths Becoming Goals

to this goal. Perhaps the marketing representatives decide that the best current path (p_2) to the goal (g_2) is to introduce a chrome-plated widget. Following suitable paths for manufacturing and selling a chrome-plated widget now becomes the goal for many others in the organization. Maintaining the proper plating solution is an essential path (p_3) for achieving the goal (g_3) of a plated widget. Maintaining this solution is the goal (g_4) of the plating foreman. His path (p_4) to this goal is to have his employees periodically add chemical to the plating solution. Adding bags of chemical becomes the goal of the plating employees.

Because paths become goals for the subsequent levels of the organizational hierarchy, the degree of freedom in decision making becomes increasingly limited in lower-level positions. A decision made to take path 3 means that people at level 4 already have their goal (g_4) defined for them. They may have some discretion about defining how they shall achieve their prescribed goal; they may use some comparison strategy to evaluate alternative paths to the goal; but the fact that their goal has been defined severely limits the universe of alternatives open to them. This need not imply that the lower level workers labor under any more severe limitations in sum than do the upper level managers. Upper managers may feel fewer vectors of pressure from imposed paths, but the potency and saliency of these vectors stemming from the risk, ambiguity, and unprogrammed nature of their tasks may lead to an extremely limited set of conditions. For lower-level workers, however, the limited courses of action open to them result in highly programmed tasks with routinized activities, although there may well be less potency attached to any one of them. Their state of severely limited possible behaviors stems from the multiplicity of goals that are imposed upon them.

Figure 3 (an extension of Figure 2) indicates the impoverished pattern of goals available to employees at level 5. It is true, of course, that if the meanest employee does not do his job, the full realization of the goal will not be possible, but the paths-goals leading to the profitability goal are not very meaningful for the employee. The tie between dumping chemicals and the profit accruing to the company may be slight for the worker. Little individual ability is required to define the path to the goal "no smoking," but this kind of compliance may be one of the most important behaviors for the employee to emit.[4]

This is not to say that members of organizations have no influence over either minor events or major company policy. While the resource

4. There is great need for additional research on the implications of this paths-becoming-goals cycle for the mental health of organizational members. However, as stated at the outset of this chapter, this kind of inquiry will not be pursued here.

controllers bear the ultimate responsibility for determining an official resource allocation strategy, individuals at lower levels in the organization may develop their own strategies for changing those path-goal relationships that affect them. By attaching an additional cost of 25¢ per hour to spray painting, painters' unions have attempted to eliminate spray painting as a possible path to the goal. Trying to influence a change in paths selected by the higher-level decision-makers, a highly valued research director may threaten to leave the organization unless a higher priority is given to research and development work within the organization. Although in both of these cases higher-level managers can ignore these demands only at great cost, nonetheless the higher-level resource-controllers do determine the paths to be taken—the decision rests with them. Those lower can only attempt to influence the decision; they cannot make the decision. Once made, the decision selecting a path (spray painting at 25¢ per hour premium rate) becomes a goal to the lower-level painter, distasteful as it may be. The literature dealing with informal

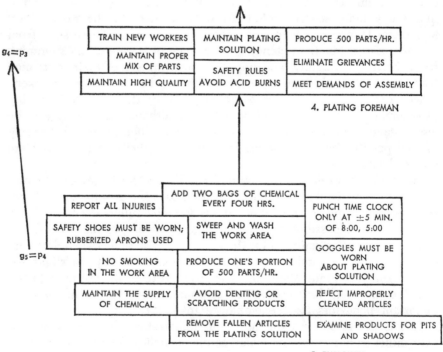

FIGURE 3

Possible Patterning of Paths—Goals

group behavior within organizations is replete with examples of how individuals attempt to redefine paths chosen by their superiors by increasing the cost of disliked alternatives (Whyte, 1955, chaps. 3 and 4). Whyte gives many examples of how quota restriction is adopted as a method of inducing change in paths, even if the desired change is as simple as retaining the present job structure but increasing the rate 10¢ per hundred pieces.

Paths and goals may eventually change in response to these demands. Other changes may be a function of something as impersonal as a changing level of the economy, e.g., dictating the cancellation of the deluxe-model product and the introduction of the economy-model product; or perhaps the highest level of decision makers decides to acquire additional product lines in order to satisfy certain power and dominance needs. Regardless of what data prompted the decision for altered goals and paths, these decisions become "givens" for subsequent levels of decision-makers. Premium costs, threats of resignation, quota restriction, state of the economy, and power needs of decision-makers may all be important data in the decision-making process, but the path-determining decision at that level defines the goals for the subsequent groups in the organization. This cascading effect of paths-becoming-goals permeates the whole organization. This is true in spite of the limiting influences at various levels that attempt to control goals by influencing the costs of certain path strategies.

CONFLICT IN COMPLEX GOAL STRUCTURES

In Figure 3 the mix of imposed goals for level 4 and 5 employees are examples of the limiting conditions faced by all members of organizations. For example, perhaps the shop superintendent has set stringent rules defining acceptable quantity levels of production; quality control insists at the same time that the products be free of defects; safety engineers refuse to let their rules be compromised in order to satisfy the other two demands; time and motion engineers may literally define each twist of the wrist. Furthermore, one frequently encounters special austerity campaigns, cost reduction campaigns, safety campaigns, quality campaigns, machine maintenance campaigns, further limiting the range of acceptable variations of behavior. One month may see a stringent enforcement of safety rules: goggles must be worn, all wounds must be reported to the nurse, spilled fluids must be immediately mopped up to prevent falls. Perhaps during the same period the quality control department decides to emphasize high quality standards of production; operators are urged to exert extra energy toward reducing the number of rejects during this campaign. Perhaps the budget for indirect labor has been cut and the amount of repair time available is sharply reduced; perhaps the production record is below its bogey and output must be increased if the performance record is not to look bad. All these vectors of pressure define paths toward goals with no room for official discretion on the part of the individual. Certainly at this level in the organization, as was the case for the project director, many of the induced paths-goals are mutually exclusive. In many instances one cannot reduce indirect labor expenses and produce at a level of quality that will satisfy the quality control people; one cannot produce at a high enough level of production to satisfy the shop superintendent unless one violates certain safety rules; a blatant violation of safety rules usually means discharge to the operator or cessation of production on that particular machine until the unsafe condition is corrected. None of these alternatives is satisfactory; no solution exists for all the demands simultaneously. Yet developing such a patterning of conflicting demands is a frequent strategy for "motivating" individuals.

Because of the difficulties in determining "best" strategies in many instances, many goal inducers develop a very simple control mechanism that they hope will "best" lead to their goals. This control mechanism for the goal-inducer is really a serial-comparisons strategy from the point of view of the goal-receiver. The superior simply instructs the subordinate to maximize every dimension of his job, whether such an approach is possible or not. Because of the aforementioned difficulties in making decisions this is usually not possible, and the subordinate finds himself in the no-solution situation. While in some no-solution situations a nearest approximation solution may be devised via multiple comparisons, in practice this maximize-all-parameters stratagem usually results in the subordinate applying the serial-comparisons method, with all the limitations inherent in this method. Since the manager himself cannot or does not determine a proper mix of activities and resorts to the maximize-all-parameters stratagem, his control tends to be displayed as a periodic exaggeration of first one parameter then another, followed by still another. The periodicity of this approach is not lost on the subordinate, and he develops a complementary strategy, really a sensitive varying of serial comparisons: take the parameter the supervisor is most interested in this period and maximize it; take the next most important parameter—probably last month's most important parameter—and maximize it, etc. The losses possible from this kind of periodic strategy and the upsetting effect on relationships within the organization are myriad. Yet there is widespread application of this approach to control of organizational behavior.

Most of these applications of "motivating" individuals are deliberate even if there is not a full awareness of the resultant impact. A widely used method of posing problems and demanding solutions that may not exist is to assign goals without the traditional or anticipated bundle of resources necessary for arriving at a solution. If a true solution exists and can be found to this dilemma, gains can be made. More often, however, the individual finds himself in the vise of incompatible demands, forced to "boilerhouse" or "gundeck" records, trumpet genuinely insignificant changes, or suffer poor marks from the resource controllers for his problem-solving ability. To the extent that an individual is a high achiever and is placed in tightly constraining networks of demands, it should surprise no one to find gentlemen's agreements, price-fixing arrangements, and other unholy alliances—unholy from the organization's point of view, perhaps, but with many saving features from the individual's point of view.

The JIC ("'Just In Case' the boss asks me") files reported by Argyris are a classic example of how organizational resources can be allocated to activities whose only function is the protection of the individual from impossible problem solving situations (Argyris, 1962, p. 48). This kind of misdirected activity and misallocation of organizational resources can occur because demands (induced goals) are made on the individual, but little is done to change the costs or constraints faced by him. Even managers who would reject any strategy smacking of unfairness or impossibility may be guilty of relying on such a strategy because they lack the cognitive powers, as do we all, to assess all the conflicting impact that all their demands may have, particularly if no honorable solution exists to the problems posed.

INTENDED RATIONALITY OF BEHAVIOR

We have noted that we can speak of organizational goals and paths to the goals; that paths at one level of the organization become goal–like for the subordinate levels of organizations; that in determining the path-goal strategy for any particular level one must account for the goals, the relative and absolute capacity restrictions on activities, and costs as perceived by the individual or individuals at that level. While one cannot underestimate the amount of confusion and the difficulty in making decisions in the face of all these frequently conflicting factors, one assumes that behavior is rational.[5] For our purposes we will define rationality as choosing that path-goal strategy from among all the known

5. See Simon, (1957b), p. 196. Professor Simon states: "A theory of administration or of organization cannot exist without a theory of rational choice. Human behavior in organizations is best described as 'intendedly rational'; and it merits that description more than does any other sector of human behavior."

alternatives that gives one the greatest total payoff.[6] Resource controllers
may choose to create an organization for earning profits instead of one
for religious teaching. This chapter is not concerned with why industry-
seminary choices are made, although they are assumed to be rational:
these kinds of organizational *raisons d'être* are given. The paramount
interest of this chapter is how one can rationally determine the most
efficient system with which to carry out the goals as they are determined
at the successive levels in the organization. We assume rational choices
at all these levels of decision making.

Some of the more interesting materials in industrial sociology have
described at length organizational acts that appeared irrational to others,
particularly others who were superior to the actors and who were accountable for their behavior (Whyte, 1955). Upon closer investigation,
however, these acts were frequently highly rational or "adaptive" from
the point of view of the actor: they were geared to give him the greatest
total payoff. The confusion that sometimes arises about whether a
particular act is rational surrounds the frame of reference of the interested parties and what motives they impute to others. If the sole motive
for a worker is financial reward, restricting production is indeed irrational when he is being paid incentive wages. The same act may be
less irrational if he is being paid day wages; and quota restriction may
be highly rational in times of unemployment and uncertain demand for
products. Painters who assign a 25¢ penalty for spray painting because
it is distasteful to them may be acting quite rationally from their point of
view; an economist viewing with alarm the falling demand for skilled
tradesmen may feel that the painters' strategy is highly irrational. It is
as Lewin and others have contended: if behavior is to be understood, it
must be from the point of view of the actor in question. Behavior that at
first glance seems quite erratic and goal-less could be seen to have quite
rational antecedents if the observer were omniscient.

The logical conclusion to this point of view of intended rationality is
that all organizational decisions are rational ones from the decision-
maker's point of view, given his state of awareness of the inputs to the
decision-making process. It is quite possible, of course, that the individual, while searching for a rational conclusion out of the morass of stimuli
confronting him, may make a decision that others in the organization
feel is detrimental to their own welfare or to the well-being of the
organization. While the likelihood of this happening is great in complex
organizations, it is still true that if better means of arraying the alternate

6. It will be noted that rationality and efficiency are related: the output/input ratio
   for a particular strategy determines the payoff, and the rational being chooses the
   strategy with the highest ratio.

strategies could be found the decision-maker would take the one giving him the greatest expected payoff. Organizational restrictions are fairly well defined in most circumstances: union rules, company policies, and governmental regulation leave little ambiguity. Goals are often less clearly spelled out as to specific action: increase sales 5 percent every year, increase dealer loyalty, etc. Finally, relative costs of alternatives may be only vaguely known once one attempts to go beyond purchased materials; total cost per finished product is frequently only approximately known, or it may be difficult to determine the costs of settling a grievance versus the probability of a three-week strike. Rationality may always be circumscribed by poor data. This is why we speak of "satisficing" solutions. But this should only spur the search for more and better data. Valid data on goals, costs, and constraints are essential for studying an organization as a system of constraints. However, with increasing appreciation of the importance of this kind of data, it will become more available; applications of models like the one under discussion should become more widespread.

THE DYNAMIC EFFECTS OF CHANGE ON STRATEGIES

Let us assume for a particular moment in time that all path-goal strategies have been determined and are in a state of functioning equilibrium. Perhaps workers at level 5 insist on having a 10¢ an hour wage increase because of intolerable heat. This one demand can theoretically change a whole series of path-goal strategies for many others, from labor relations to marketing to engineering. A demand of 30¢, plus eliminating shift work would probably cause more repercussions. Nearly any change in stimuli for the organization can change costs and constraints for some, perhaps affecting the goal strategies of others. Because of this potentially dynamic interdependency of all organizational stimuli, it is necessary to evaluate a change of a particular item in terms of possible effects on the whole organization. Many of the changes may be nonsignificant in their effects on other facets of the organization. However, dislocations of resources and impossible situations can be created by adding new variables to an otherwise stable situation.

This dynamic interrelationship is dealt with in the following way: when a decision-maker at a particular decision-making node in the organization receives a demand, he may translate it into constraints to see if the change in conditions is compatible with his existing strategy. If it is not, he must undertake some kind of search activity for a better solution. If he must change anything about his situation, this may mean changes for others above, below, and beside him in the organizational structure. This kind of adaptive change may resonate throughout the whole organization and perhaps even feed back to the original change and cause it to be altered. This process will continue until all participants have achieved their best possible solution, a circumstance that will define a new equilibrium. The next section deals with how to implement this descriptive model on the digital computer so that one can cope with the great complexity of interrelationships.

*   *   *

We have noted that an organization is the interaction of people and other resources in a strategy intended to attain certain specifiable goals and that the structure and process of an organization were created by its resource controllers because each believed that he could achieve more personal goal fulfillment acting collectively than acting singly. Organizational goals were defined as those end states that are valued by the resource controllers and for the attainment of which the organization was created and/or maintained; resources must be allocated for the attainment of an end state if it is to be judged a goal. There are no disembodied goals of an organization; organizational goals are a function of the amount of agreement between resource controllers about what constitutes a desired end state. Since this is subject to individual change, organizational goals can change over time.

Even having pooled resources for gain, most resource controllers of organizations find that they seldom have enough resources to achieve all their desired end states in optimal form. Being efficient—maximizing the output/input fraction—in the allocation of resources is therefore very important. For the resource controller the degree of efficiency is an important determinant of the amount of energy directed toward survival. Furthermore, behavior is seen as intendedly rational; if one had total knowledge about all the forces at work in the life of the individual, one could understand his behavior as rational; instead of developing a residual category of "irrational acts," one could make relatively more gains in the understanding of behavior by attempting to enlarge his understanding of these myriad forces at work.

Since resources are limited, the strategy for goal attainment must be one that allocates resources among the most favorable alternatives. In order to insure the best available strategy, information about alternatives must be processed and evaluated in terms of costs, resource availability, and goal orientation; decisions must be made between possible alternatives; resources must be allocated to enact the decisions. The advantages of using multiple comparisons as a decision-making technique were explored; while a serial-comparisons approach is a frequently used approximation to multiple comparisons, it could be a costly one. In the path-goal paradigm used in this chapter decisions are made about possible goals, and paths to these goals are determined; these paths become goals for all subsequent levels of decision making. As one descends the levels of decision making within an organization, accumulated barriers may so limit the alternatives available for consideration that there is little freedom for making decisions and little control over the orientation of one's activities. While subordinates can influence the costs of certain strategies —indeed, may drive up the cost of certain disliked strategies—once this strategy has been finalized for goal attainment by a superior, it becomes a goal for subordinates. In the final analysis, any strategy must be minimally acceptable to the resource controllers at the highest levels of the organization, because they can control costs and capacities and induce goals that will manipulate the desired changes in strategies.

Complex goal structures exist for large numbers of organizational members. Many of the demands are mutually exclusive; no solution, or no solution known to the incumbents, would allow all the demands to be met simultaneously. Large degrees of conflict are seen as resulting from these constrained circumstances. Conflict was seen to be frequently caused by a conscious over-inducement of goals and an under-allocation of resources. If innovation results, this motivational strategy can yield true problem solving in terms of increased efficiency. But what probably happens more often is that the situation has no known solution and merely has additional limitations, forcing crude serial-comparison strategies to be used. This kind of wastage of resources can occur even when the superior does not intend to create conflict; he is often unable to cope with the complexity facing him and so must resort to this approach.

At every decision-making node in the organization, each decision-maker is faced with a set of induced goals, a set of restrictions on his choices, and some measure of utility for each possible path-goal strategy. These three inputs of information lead to the decisions defining the resource allocation strategies and their execution. Assuming rationality, one can account for behavior in organizations using this resource allocation approach and having complete data on these three concepts. This does not imply that the resource controllers and other affected people will always, or ever, be pleased with all the allocation decisions and behavior, but they will nonetheless be able to account for them. At each node of decision making some minimal number of additions to or deletions in the set of constraints is possible by the individual, but the capacity for doing this customarily declines as one descends the vertical levels of decision making. No set of constraints remains stable for long; the goals, paths, and restrictions at each level define a system highly sensitive to change. But the strategies reached at each node of decision making in the organization affect and are affected by the decisions made at all other nodes in the organization. Any change in strategy at one particular node may lead to changes throughout the whole organization; each decision point in the organization is in a constant state of receiving input data, analyzing it, checking it for congruency with all other decisions, altering the present strategy where necessary, causing others to be modified where necessary. Because each of these decision points has its own set of constraints, because each of these sets of constraints can potentially affect every strategy in the organization, and because the sum of each of these constraint sets is a dynamically interrelated and interdependent system isomorphic with the complete organization, we speak of an organization as a system of constraints.

ORGANIZATIONAL BEHAVIOR AS A FUNCTION OF CONSTRAINTS: QUANTIFICATION

The previous descriptive material has shown how one can view much behavior in organizations in terms of resource allocation, given that the constraints—goals, resource capacity restrictions, and costs—are known. One who is familiar with linear programming will have recognized this as the implicit decision-making approach developed thus far. Even the terms themselves are consonant with the inputs of a linear programming model. The inputs necessary for the model are costs, capacity restrictions, and goals of various activities, defined in the fashion used in previous sections. We have spoken of being unable to maximize all features simultaneously; of having to "satisfice" or compromise on a balance of acceptable features; of having mutually exclusive events with no common solution existing; of facing limitations, boundaries, or constraints; of making decisions for determining path-goal strategies or resource-allocation strategies; of having complex goal combinations. These are precisely the situations in which linear programming is useful. We need only equate "complex goal combinations" with "objective function" in linear programming to make all the necessary terms consonant. Since the objective function is that expression of one or more terms defining what end state is sought by a particular activity, one can note that the fit of this term with goals is a good one.

THE LINEAR PROGRAMMING APPROACH

It is neither possible nor necessary to discuss the full rationale of the linear programming model in this chapter; it will suffice if the reader gains enough understanding of the model to appreciate its usefulness in coping with organizational complexity. Linear programming "is a method used to solve optimization under constraint problems. This is because . . . analysis using differential calculus breaks down when the constraint equations are systems of inequalities and, in any event, does not guarantee that the solution is non-negative" (Stern, 1963, p. 365).

The computational aids that will be available in the foreseeable future will not change this inability to use calculus to solve complex optimization problems. It is important, therefore, that one at least see if the linear programming method can give some power in dealing with organizational complexity. The interested reader will find several good introductory treatments of linear programming (Stern, 1963; Kemeny et al., 1957; Bowman and Fetter, 1961); let the casual reader accept the following conditions as necessary for the model to apply:

1. The function to be optimized (called the objective function) is linear in the independent variables.
2. The conditions of constraint are also linear in the unknowns.
3. All the coefficients and relationships in the problem are assumed to be known with certainty (Stern, 1963, p. 365).

Perhaps the best way to impart some understanding of linear programming is to consider the following exercise using the method:

An automobile plant manufactures automobiles and trucks. The plant is organized into four departments: (1) sheet metal stamping, (2) engine assembly, (3) automobile final assembly, and (4) truck final assembly—raw materials, labor, and other inputs being available at constant prices within the demand range of the plant.

Department capacities limited as follows:

Metal stamping   25,000 autos or 35,000 trucks per month
Engine assembly   33,333 autos or 16,667 trucks per month
Auto assembly   22,500 autos per month
Truck assembly   15,000 trucks per month

"The sales value of an automobile is $300 greater than the total cost of purchased materials, labor, and other direct cost attributable to its manufacture"; the truck yields $250 by the same measure. There are contributions to profit and overhead per unit [Bowman and Fetter, 1961, p. 103; from Dorfman, 1953].

In this exercise one has the manufacturing capacity restrictions and the cost data in terms of profit per auto and truck. If it is assumed that the goal is to achieve the greatest profit, the objective function becomes to maximize the sum [$300 (number of autos manufactured) + $250 (number of trucks manufactured)]. One must then determine the number of autos and trucks to be made to make this sum greatest.

Figure 4 illustrates how this problem could be treated graphically.

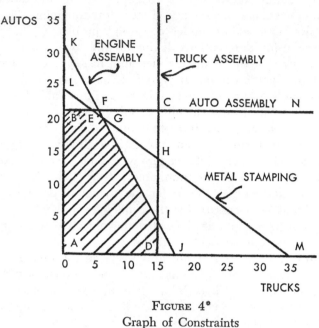

FIGURE 4*
Graph of Constraints
(Thousands)

*Based on Robert Dorfman, "Mathematical or 'Linear' Programming: A Nonmathematical Exposition," *American Economic Review*, December 1953, p. 799.

Any point on the metal stamping line LM could define the maximum number of combinations of auto or truck stampings possible; the area under that line and bounded by the coordinates (triangle ALM) defines the whole space of possible answers to the capacity restriction of metal stamping capacity for autos (25,000) and trucks (35,000). In the same manner the possible combinations of engine assembly are defined by the triangle AJK. Since absolute capacity restrictions on assembly limit the numbers of autos and trucks per month to 22,500 and 15,000 respectively, possible solutions must also lie under line BN for auto assembly and to the left of line PD for truck assembly. Note that there is substitutability of engine assembly and stamping capacity between autos and trucks: one unit of truck stamping capacity is equivalent to 5/7 unit of auto stamping capacity; one unit of engine assembly for trucks is equivalent to 2 units of auto engine assembly capacity. This kind of substitutability is possible all along lines KJ and LM, hence the term "linear" programming.[7] The intersection of all these spaces of possible

7. In practice, these relationships might not be linear at their extremities. Once again, however, the plea is for a useful model, not for the perfect, but improbable, mirror of the universe.

solutions is shaded in Figure 4. This intersection defines the region in which a solution that meets all the limitations could lie; nothing restricts any point within this region from defining a possible path-goal strategy. It will be stated without proof that each corner point, i.e., points A, B, E, G, I, and D, could be the "best" solution depending upon the cost associated with each strategy. In the problem as given point G defines the best solution. It can be shown by trial and error or by some other algorithm that given these profit figures, any other point would yield a lower value of the objective function, would yield less financial return, would thus be a less good strategy. It should be noted that there is some excess capacity with this solution at point G: while 6,480 trucks are built, 8,520 truck assembly units are not used; while 20,375 autos are built, 2,127 units of auto assembly capacity are not utilized. In spite of this slack capacity point G is still the most profitable one because of the current profit structures.

The difficulty with a graphical approach to solving these problems, apart from the difficulty in extrapolating values from graphs, is that if one is dealing with more than three possible goal states to which he is allocating resources (autos, trucks, buses, and bulldozers), the solution becomes impossible to visualize and difficult to deal with. Furthermore, this complexity increases as one must deal with other capacities, such as forging capacity, upholstery capacity, paint shop capacity, welding capacity. Fortunately, there are algorithms that simplify this task considerably after one has developed an algebraic system of capacity restrictions, costs, and objective function. Below is the algebraic form of the previous auto-truck exercise suitable for solution by algorithms:

where:

$$X_{as} + 5/7\ X_{ts} \leq 25,000$$

X_{as} = number of units of auto stampings
X_{ts} = number of units of truck stampings

$$X_{ae} + 2\ X_{te} \leq 33,333$$

X_{ae} = number of units of auto engines
X_{te} = number of units of truck engines

$$X_{aa} \leq 22,500$$

X_{aa} = number of units of auto assemblies

$$X_{ta} \leq 15,000$$

X_{ta} = number of units of truck assemblies

$$\text{Max } [\$300\ X_{aa} + \$250\ X_{ta}]$$

When one can formulate his problem in this general format of constraints, he can deal with a high order of complexity in problems of resource allocation, particularly if he has access to a digital computer.

PROGRAMMING AS AN AID TO RATIONALITY

Compared with many decision-makers, the manager in this exercise, who must determine how many autos vs. how many trucks to manufacture under the given circumstances, has a very simple life indeed. But even in such a simple problem as this the number of feasible solutions contained in the shaded area of Figure 4 is quite large. Correspondingly, a complete listing of multiple comparisons could become laborious if one considered all possible combinations in units from 22,500 autos and 3,500 trucks to 3,333 autos and 15,000 trucks. It is precisely because linear programming is equivalent to multiple comparisons, even in situations of great complexity, in selecting from all the possibilities the one (or few) best solutions that it is such a powerful technique. One need not make weaker approximations to multiple comparisons when confronted by diverse stimuli. By routinizing these stimuli into a linear programming model, one can cope with complexity. This is why it is such a highly attractive decision-making technique.

In spite of the ready availability of programming algorithms requiring only a slide rule or desk calculator, their usage remains limited. Even with the ease of computer techniques for solving such problems as the one above, rules of thumb are still the common way of solving them. Perhaps chief among these rules of thumb is what we have called the serial-comparisons method for decision making. Faced with the necessity of deciding how many autos-trucks to produce, a naive attack on the problem might be: since the profit on autos is greater by $50, produce all the automobiles one can; whatever capacity that remains can be channelled into truck manufacture. Following this kind of attack would lead to operation at point E (Figure 4) and to lose more than one and one-quarter million dollars a year in foregone profits. This is but one example illustrating the earlier statement that the gains made by using serial comparisons may be only illusory ones. This kind of loss is but one example of the costs incurred by being unable to consider or enumerate all possible combinations of paths to goals. Failure to cope with complex stimuli can be quite costly, and yet the failure and the cost can be unknown. Herein lies the great strength of the linear programming method: it is a powerful aid to rationality because it serves as a highly efficient generator of multiple comparisons, precisely gauging the worth of alternative strategies, in most cases precluding any reliance on serial comparisons. It can spell out in great detail the best path-goal strategy, the cost or profit of that strategy, and at what point it becomes worthwhile to alter one's strategy. The linear programming method is itself highly efficient because it does not have to compare every alternative, yet it gives the best solution(s) possible under the circumstances.

PROGRAMMING AND ORGANIZATIONAL BEHAVIOR

If linear programming is only infrequently used on such readily definable economic problems, it has never to the author's knowledge been applied to the understanding of organizational behavior problems. As we have noted thus far, from the incumbent's point of view many situations either do not contain, or because of complexity appear not to contain, any possible solution to the existing costs, constraints, and goals. This condition can result in a great deal of waste and misallocation of resources. While the multiple comparisons strategy is complete, one can rarely use it because of cognitive inability to "list" all the complex strategies that would result. Yet we noted that all substitutes for multiple comparisons had their own unique costs associated with their use. Since linear programming is highly efficient and yields results equivalent to multiple comparisons and since this is now a routine computing operation, it is important to see if this approach can be applied to the study of problems of organizational behavior. If one is to reduce the amount of avoidable organizational conflict, he must not rely on rules of thumb but must be able to make rational decisions and to solve problems confronting the organization using all relevant data. He must be able to derive the complex solution and assign the necessary resources to enact it. Barring that, he must be able to arrive at a clear realization of when truly impossible situations exist and, realizing it, be able either to reallocate resources sufficient to enable the application of that solution or to restructure the goals, constraints, and costs so that a true solution commensurate with available resources can be reached.

It is this necessity of generating and testing possible strategies or solutions that has led to the characterization of organizational behavior in terms of costs, goals, and capacity restrictions. If one can construct a composite model that (1) is a lamination of the richness of organizational behavior, not as simulated but as it is, and (2) has the power of the linear programming resource allocation model for determining the best possible path-goal branches available, he can truly speak of a constraint model of organizational behavior. By now, the congruency between the linear programming model and the view of organizational behavior as presented in the first section should be apparent. To strengthen the relationship, let us examine this congruency by treating with the linear-programming model some of the behavioral problems discussed earlier. Consider, in the linear-programming format, the issues confronting the project designer working on the desired characteristics of a new product.[8] In the simplified case described earlier the project director was dealing with three discrete parameters: appearance, durability, and safety. Recall that the buffed, zinc, "good" switch options were excluded at the outset as unsatisfactory selections. This allowed the possible

8. While we shall be examining simple graphical problems for purposes of exposition, recall that large, complex extensions of these problems are easily possible and solvable.

range of solutions to be limited to eight (2x2x2) out of twenty-seven (3x3x3). In this case the possible solutions are the corner points of the cube shown in Figure 5. It will be remembered, however, that this was just the beginning of the constraints confronting the project director. Members of quality control, repair service, marketing, manufacturing, legal department, etc., all wanted to impose constraints. Because many of them were mutually exclusive, it was noted that without some compromise on the restrictions, converting them from absolute to relative ones, no solutions would exist. Quality control may have to accept a less good product than they would like because of price considerations; marketing may have to accept a less attractive appearance in order to allow for safety and durability.

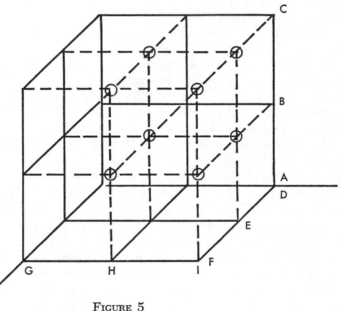

FIGURE 5
Design Constraints

As long as one can keep the problem relatively simple and in the discrete variable case, it is fairly easy to determine the points (see Figure 5) and to determine one's best solution; the same is true for continuous variables, although the number of possible solutions increases greatly. Figure 6 shows the dilemma faced by workers who must produce high quality products at a rapid rate, where quality and quantity are treated as continuous variables. The mix of quality and quantity produc-

tion open to them lies along line DK. However, quality control, manufacturing, repair service, and time and methods study groups have
added their own constraints. As a result of these constraints only the
shaded region in Figure 6 will contain acceptable solutions for all these
groups. Yet this does not intersect at all with the abilities of the worker
to perform. From the workers' points of view there is no solution to
the quality-quantity dilemma. Because of this workers develop a serial-
comparison strategy. They do the best they can with whatever index is
receiving the greatest amount of current attention, a strategy characterized by one respondent as "rolling with the punches." If the foreman
is demanding a high production rate, workers operate along line segment
GK. If he begins demanding higher quality, the workers shift their
efforts from near K to near G. Since the importance of quality products
has led to the institution of a quality control department, this department
adds its own constraints. If quality control people are on the work floor
demanding higher quality and rejecting a large amount of the current

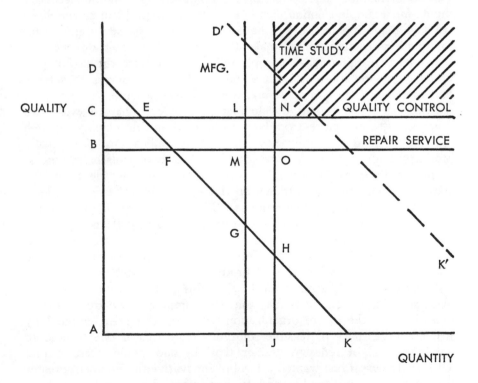

FIGURE 6
Constraints on Workers

production, then workers must change their strategy up to some point along ED. There is no way to keep all these groups happy simultaneously.

Such a picture of having no solutions and the resulting tugging and hauling for quality and quantity appears simple and trivial when viewed on such a diagram. For millions of workers, however, the situation depicted in Figure 6 is far from trivial. It is a chief contributor to the daily conflict that confronts them, conflict with which they must attempt to deal, always unsuccessfully in such situations. To be sure, if one could move line DK progressively toward the northeast corner, perhaps to line D'K', one could get a solution that was currently acceptable for all. As one might guess, this is what most resource controllers attempt to do. They take the position that (1) a solution always exists—find it; and (2) as in this case, if one could induce the workers to make more quality and quantity, all problems would be solved. This widespread point of view is itself only a rationalization for being unable to cope with complexity—one simply blames one's subordinates (since this is usually safer than blaming one's superiors) for not giving him the necessary inputs for a simple solution. Nor even now is the problem as simple as we have made it since workers have variables such as safety and norms for quota restriction, which make this whole issue multi-dimensional.

A final two dimensional example will help illustrate the use of programming to determine how one should allocate resources to get the best mix of activities. Suppose one were the vice president in charge of engineering research and development and were charged with two functions: keeping current products redesigned and developing research that would lead to totally new ideas and applications of company products. Suppose that the vice president had two pools of resources: draftsmen-designers and engineers-scientists. The president of the company added three constraints on the activity of the vice president: (1) no more than a certain amount ("Max" on Figure 7) of redesign should take place, because old customers get angry if they feel the model they recently purchased has just been changed and improved upon; (2) a minimum amount ("Min") of redesign must take place so that the company's whole line of products does not get the reputation of being stodgy; (3) a minimum level ("Min") of innovation must take place so that new products may join the company's line from time to time, keeping the dealer organization satisfied. The area bounded by ABCD is the space of feasible solutions. Note that if one wanted to obtain a level of redesign greater than B, one would need to hire more engineers; if one wanted a level of innovative development greater than point D, one would need to hire more draftsmen—or in both instances, somehow induce greater effort from them than heretofore possible.

COST DATA AND SCALES AS INPUTS

The graphic examples thus far have been functions of goals and capacities. The constraints have been fairly observable: the president of a company specifies the levels of redesign and innovation; various departments of an organization specify acceptable levels of performance. Any kind of barrier or imposed limitation may be considered as a restriction of capacity for action. Any desired end state to which the resource controllers would allocate resources for achievement may be considered a goal. The goals have been to maximize the utilization of resources and to get the best mix of redesign and innovation, quality and quantity possible. Goals and capacity restrictions have defined the space of feasible solutions and have defined the corner points in each case. While the corner points immediately define the best solutions, only the costs inherent in each solution can lead to a final determination of that point (or those few points) that define the best solution. Without this cost-profit data to minimize or maximize, one cannot define an objective

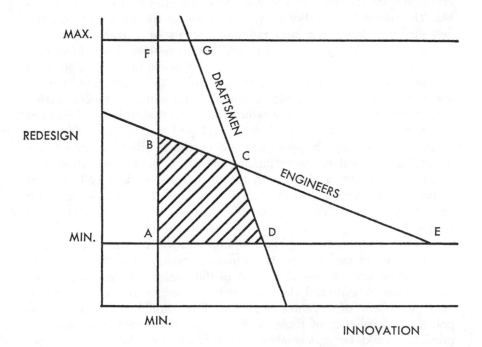

FIGURE 7
Constraints on Manager

function on which to operate with a linear programming model. Furthermore, just as goals and capacities may change, certainly costs may change. This means that no solution may ever be "best" for all time: whether one makes model Z or model X and how many of each may vary frequently in response to situational variables. In the autos-truck example, if the profit on autos dropped to $200 instead of $300 and the profit on trucks had risen to $600 instead of $250, then corner point I would have been taken as the best possible mix of products instead of point G. In the same fashion, it was also noted that workers frequently change their strategies in response to whether the foreman or the quality-control auditor is pushing the hardest during a particular period. The quality-control man makes it more costly for the worker to maximize a production strategy; the foreman reverses the cost picture.

These data on profits-costs associated with particular decisions have not been dealt with in the behavioral examples. Herein lies one difficulty in dealing with the linear programming model in organizational behavior problems: one needs cost-profit data in some form of utility that will encompass the diverse kinds of path-goal strategies that could be possible. The measure of utility must encompass at the same time quality and quantity, innovation and redesign, threats of strike, and technological change. Many industrial organization problems lend themselves to the dollar measure of utility; others must use subjective utility as a measure, even when comparing certain dollar inputs. This is not an apology: frequently the more meaningful questions that need asking force researchers to rely on measures of subjective utility. Techniques for measuring behavior are being developed and refined that give promise of allowing the quantification of the manifold variables one might find in his linear programming matrix. (Likert, 1961, chap. 13). Because this is not a chapter on the techniques of data collection or scaling of parameters, it will be assumed here that suitable data for measuring all constraints can be obtained for a linear programming model. Preliminary investigation by the author indicates that this is a reasonable assumption. While one must always remain respectful of the problems of cardinal utility—apples vs. oranges vs. grapefruit—this measurement issue is less significant in the context of this chapter because of the day in and day out kinds of conflict and pressures that many members of organizations face. For variables containing the potency and saliency of those conflicting ones we have discussed, this problem should be manageable. Members of organizations have considerable experience devising their own heuristic strategies, such as they are, and they are able to array variables along a dimension of subjective utility. Decisions of utility are the kinds of decisions that some individuals must make hourly. Is the single national advertising campaign equivalent to three and one-half regional marketing shows? Is one extra paid holiday equivalent to eighteen months of freedom from union organizing attempts?

This kind of measuring and comparison of subjective utility may never be so perfect as one would like, but this does not prevent a very helpful model from being built on such measures. Furthermore, it is not necessary for these measures to be perfect initially. One can view the linear programming technique as an iterative approach for dealing with organizational behavior problems, with subsequent iterations refining the parameters of the model. One can measure the relevant variables to the best of his ability and then develop a set of equations for applying linear programming. It may be that the linear programming solution is inconsistent or impossible, trivial, or fairly representative of the overall strategy desired. There is a significant amount of learning possible under each of these alternatives. If the solution and therefore the strategy defined by it is trivial or "out of line" with the desires of the resource controllers, then one at least learns the kind of dislocations, the kind of misallocation of resources that have been caused perhaps by the disproportionate emphasis that has been placed on certain factors. He may find that a very important variable to him does not even come into the solution; he may wish to add a constraint to assure that some minimal amount of the variable is present in the final solution. Perhaps he finds that the results indicate that he has overpriced the value of another variable, that this has lead to distortion in the overall strategy, and that this variable should not be emphasized as greatly in the future. In such a fashion, testing, comparing, reiterating, one approaches the "best" solution and strategy and learns a great deal about what are possible and impossible allocations of resources.

Perhaps the best way to bring together all the material thus far is to take a real example of an organizational behavior situation and deal with it completely in the linear programming fashion.

CASE DISCUSSION

The organization. In northern New York there is a small (400 employees) manufacturing company with which the author has been associated for three years in a research-consulting capacity. During that time he has gained intimate details about the operations of this organization. The data based on this experience are used in the case discussion below. The company is located in a rural environment and is largely family owned, with the family maintaining an integral position in the community. The company has no union; it hopes to do its best for the members of its organization by following the Golden Rule, devoid of "outside interferences." The company pays wages and benefits that compare favorably with the area and contributes additional funds to all employees from a profit-sharing plan. It markets its heavy capital goods equipment through a network of independent dealers. The family interests in the company are now largely controlled by the president of the company, who is also the son of the founder. When we speak of resource controllers in this example, we will be combining the first-level shareholders with the second-level administrative personnel (see Figure 2).

Organizational goals.   The goals of the organization have been determined by the family of resource controllers over time. These goals are now implemented by the president and are clearly spelled out in a widely distributed company publication. The official statement of the company's objectives maintains that the goals of the organization are:

> To render continually improving services to its customers with an intelligently managed, financially sound, progressive business organization *stimulated to practice high ethical standards* in all its relationships; thereby continually returning *well balanced* benefits to its employees, dealers, shareholders, suppliers, community and industry. (Italics in original publication.)
>
> We are certain this can be accomplished by coordinating the efforts of a group of people who sincerely believe that:
> 1. Customers determine our business success.
> 2. Security and opportunity are available, but have to be earned.
> 3. A reasonable profit is a cost of staying in business . . . a key to improved men, methods and machines.
> 4. Our owners are entitled to a fair return on their investment and the insured safety of their savings.
> 5. We should help others in their progress, including our suppliers.
> 6. We owe our physical and financial support to the community and government.
> 7. As a part of the . . . industry, we should continue to help increase the standard of living in the United States and in the rest of the world.
> 8. We should treat others as we would like them to treat us in all of our business relations.

In the terms of this chapter the goal of the organization is to earn a profit. This goal is achieved by (paths) satisfying the demands of customers, dealers, shareholders, suppliers, employees, and members of the industry and community.[9] If these diverse groups can be satisfied, the profits and success of the organization will take care of themselves. To

9. It will be recalled that for a desired end state to qualify as a goal of the organization resources have to be allocated for that end. Each of these above corporate objectives qualify as goals under that definition. While many industries give only a *pro forma* declaration of community support and interest, this company takes a very active role in this respect. The company recently made a substantial contribution toward improving the community's health facilities, exceeding the traditional tax support cited by most organizations.

maximize profits an optimal solution to the demands of these groups is organized; an organizational structure that can carry out the necessary organizational acts that lead to the satisfaction of those groups is created. In linear programming terms the objective function is to maximize the subjective utility to the company of the value stemming from satisfied customers, dealers, shareholders, suppliers, employees, members of the same industry, and the community. Since earning a profit is defined in these operational terms, hereafter we will speak of maximizing this objective function as the goal of the corporation. The necessary acts leading to satisfied customers, dealers, shareholders, suppliers, employees, members of the same industry, and members of the community become the paths. It was noted in earlier remarks that whether or not something is called a path or a goal depends largely on one's point of view. In this case it is most meaningful to consider the development of allocation strategies in this fashion.

Organizational paths. Elsewhere in the publication that defined the goals of the company there are extended discussions of how the organization endeavors to conduct its relationships with customers, dealers, shareholders, suppliers of materials, members of the same industry, employees, and the community in which it is located. Although the list is only representative, the following fourteen factors are repeatedly mentioned in connection with facilitating the organization's capacity to satisfy the demands of these groups: sense of fair play in dealings, stable level of operations, promptness in dealings, innovation, quality, service, price of product, courtesy in dealings, willingness to help solve problems of others, friendliness, warranties, high performance equipment, training available, and profits-wages. These are the paths to satisfied dealers, customers, shareholders, suppliers of materials, members of the same industry, employees, and the community. A totally satisfied customer is a function of path increments of fair play in dealings, promptness in dealings, a certain level of innovation of products, plus quality and servicing of the products, courtesy in dealings, willingness to help solve the customers' problems, friendliness in dealings, warranties available, high performance equipment, and training available. Similarly, the paths to all the satisfied others of each group may be defined in terms of these variables. This is a direct parallel of stating that an auto is a function of certain increments of stamping, engine assembly, and auto assembly.

Within the groups of customers, employees, dealers, shareholders, suppliers, members of the same industry, and members of the community, individual differences among the group members are certain to exist. For the purposes of this chapter, however, the coefficients that will be arrived at for each of the path variables will be average ones for each of these groups of individuals. In the same vein the subjective utility resulting from the satisfaction of any particular individual in any of these groups will also be an average value. If the individual differences are not large, using average values may be quite convenient for determining one's strategy of resource allocation. However, using average values is not a necessary simplification inherent in the linear-programming approach; in many instances it may not be desirable. If one has one hundred customers—two quite different industrial giants A and B and ninety-eight undifferentiable small customers—one may need to develop an organizational strategy that reflects the divergent needs and utilities of A and B and All Others. Instead of having as a goal the satisfying of one relatively homogeneous group of customers, one could have three customer goals: satisfying A, satisfying B, and satisfying All Others. All coefficients for the three groups might differ markedly, reflecting the divergent inputs and outputs in each instance. If the ninety-eight small customers were truly undifferentiable, one could use average values for the coefficients of the All Others group. To the extent that any customer, employee, dealer, shareholder, supplier, member of the same industry, or member of the community departs markedly from all other members of his group, it may be desirable to develop a special goal category for him. While enlarging the number of distinct goal variables in this fashion causes little computational difficulty, for purposes of exposition this chapter will deal only with average values for each fairly homogeneous group.

Programming organizational constraints.   At this point one has a set of organizational goals and a first level definition of what the paths to the goals are believed by resource controllers to be. One has the ingredients for a linear-programming solution for how resources should be allocated. The company does not have sufficient resources to make all customers, all dealers, all employees, the entire community, all suppliers, all shareholders, and all members of the same industry as happy as they might wish or as happy as the company might find desirable or necessary. Therefore the company is faced with a resource allocation problem: how to allocate its resources to get the maximum returns from keeping satisfactory relationships between the corporate entity and each of the other groups on which it depends.

As we noted earlier, empirical research that would allow the definition of costs and capacity restrictions in a meaningful fashion is needed. While the author is conducting research for this purpose, time has not permitted the analysis of the data. As a concession, the author acted as if he were the company president and deliberately contrived the path-goal values for the variables so that an example of the power of a programming model as an aid to rationality could be appreciated. Table 1 shows the matrix of goals, restrictions, and objective function. Because of the synthetic nature of some of the values, the results are not truly representative of this particular company; nonetheless, the strengths and opportunities for understanding available from using a linear programming model can be illustrated in the area of organizational behavior. For purposes of the following discussion, Table 1 defines the whole constraint structure from which the organization must devise a strategy to meet its goals; it defines any particular point in time that one may take as a base point from which to conduct comparisons. However, the reader is once again reminded that the values in Table 1 are artificial ones. It remains for subsequent research to validate procedures for assigning these values.

From Table 1 one learns that on the average a satisfied customer (X_1) requires 1.34 units of fair play (X_{14}), 3.38 units of promptness in dealings (X_{16}), 1.05 units of innovation (X_{17}), 7.43 units of quality (X_{18}), 9.01 units of service (X_{19}), 11.75 units of pricing policy activity (X_{20}), 0.92 units of courtesy (X_{21}), 1.62 units of problem solving assistance (X_{22}), 0.36 units of friendliness (X_{23}), 4.00 units of warranty policy activity (X_{24}), 8.80 units of high performance equipment (X_{25}), and 1.40 units of training (X_{26}). Each average satisfied customer (X_1) who receives this allocation of resources from the organization is worth an average of 44.0 units of utility to the organization. Each of the other groups' members may be satisfied in the same fashion. But the resources are not unlimited. There are only 16,000 units of sense of fair play (X_{14}) and only 1,600 units of innovation (X_{17}) available for all uses. The resulting deployment of resources for maximizing the objective function must be within the constraint limitations.

When one discusses the autos-trucks kind of economic problem, one customarily expresses constraints in terms of fixed capacity for welding, stamping, forming, and the like; but there may well be some instances in which a machine used primarily for one purpose has the capacity (perhaps at a marked reduction in efficiency) to perform another activity. Which facet of this versatility will be used will depend on the costs-profits and constraints present. While this variation increases the computations necessary to arrive at the best solution, this is a trivial increase with the use of computers. This convertible aspect of capacity is mentioned because many of the paths $(X_{14}$ through $X_{27})$ shown in Table 1 could have varying amounts of capacity assigned to them. Just as a machine might give 10,000 units of forming capacity *or* 6,000 units of stamping capacity, any particular worker may give two units of innovation or twenty units of courtesy. Which capacity one avails himself of will depend on the demands and the costs at that particular

TABLE 1
PROGRAMMING VALUES

X₁		Customers 1	Dealers 2	Shareholders 3	Suppliers 4	Employees 5	Mbr. of Indust. 6	Community 7			X₁
14	sense of fair play	1.34	1.15	00	2.30	2.46	.07	.42	≤	16,000	14
15	stable operations	00	00	3.50	00	8.56	00	8.45	≤	3,000	15
16	promptness in dealings	3.38	2.70	00	4.40	2.55	.22	.05	≤	3,500	16
17	innovation	1.05	9.10	00	00	00	00	00	≤	1,600	17
18	quality	7.43	2.51	00	00	00	00	00	≤	8,000	18
19	service	9.01	1.08	00	00	00	00	00	≤	10,000	19
20	pricing policies	11.75	5.70	00	00	00	00	00	≤	12,000	20
21	courtesy in dealings	.92	.42	00	.96	1.58	.77	.23	≤	5,000	21
22	problem solving aid	1.62	2.57	00	4.97	.68	1.57	.65	≤	2,200	22
23	friendliness	.36	.75	00	.36	1.91	1.09	.46	≤	6,000	23
24	warranties	4.00	1.29	00	00	00	00	00	≤	4,500	24
25	high performance equipment	8.80	5.35	00	00	00	00	00	≤	9,000	25
26	training available	1.40	00	00	00	7.44	00	00	≤	3,000	26
27	profits-wages	00	4.58	22.50	00	9.59	00	00	≤	12,000	27

MAXIMIZE $44X_1 + 17.6X_2 + 13.2X_3 + 2.2X_4 + 22X_5 + .88X_6 + .44X_7$

time for the worker as well as the machine. Rather than introduce this computational issue into the argument here, we will assume that the initial values are determined by their current availability, usage, and values—not necessarily the best allocation, but the current one. Defining a starting point thus would be the situation in a functioning company that attempted to investigate its own strategy of goal attainment via this programming technique. One would assess one's present capacities with respect to present demands; as incongruencies arose, substitutions of abilities could be performed within the limits of conversion.

From an investigation of the path variables (X_{14} through X_{27}) it appears that one is dealing with behavior an individual can and frequently does perform in combinations that are a function of his personality. An individual may be friendly, prompt, innovative, and concerned with quality simultaneously in whatever he undertakes. Under discussion here are the requirements and utilization of these behaviors, which are greater than one would customarily find solely as a function of personality—requirements and utilizations so great and necessary for the organization that it frequently institutionalizes them in order to guarantee a sufficient supply. Thus there are quality-control departments, research and development divisions, public- and employee-relations consultants, and marketing specialists. The salesman who smiles at everyone is not utilizing any organizational resources of friendliness when he smiles at a customer. But when he takes the customer night-clubbing as a gesture of organizational friendliness when he would much prefer to watch his daughter's piano recital, he is spending organizational resources for friendliness that may yield a sale. It is this extra-personality, organizationally determined act that is felt to be necessary for the satisfaction of the others that is being presented in Table 1. In this discussion one unit of friendliness uses up the same amount of resources whether it is spent on customers or on employees, dealers, etc. Distinctions are made in quantitative terms: 0.36 units of friendliness may be translated into two highballs and one steak dinner for a customer, or it might be equal to several inquiries about an employee's sick child by the foreman; and it takes an average of 1.91 units of this per time period to have an average satisfied employee.

The Meaning of Linear Programming Tables.   Table 2 shows the results of the first programming solution using the data of Table 1, the base point for our discussions, as the matrix of values.[10] In order to appreciate the substantial information available from linear programming, it will

10. The results are from IBM *1620 General Program Library 10.1.006* by C. P. Nichols, A. Nickel and L. Davis, "Linear Programming Code for the Card 1620 with Punched Card Option for Final Output."

TABLE 2
BASE POINT ITERATION

CASE BEHAV ITER No	FUNCTIONAL	VAR OUT	VAR IN	
001	5544936170	2000000000	0001044000	
002	5545351022	1600000000	0005022000	A
003	5552284930	2700000000	0003013200	
004	5552299242 h	1500000000	0007000440	
FUNCTIONAL	5552299242			

VAR/COST	ACTIVITY	LIM VAR	LOWER LIM	LIM VAR	UPPER LIM	
1400000000 a	9999.9000	2000	14.9374–	1500	.3199	
0007000440 b	120.3224	1500	.3211	0006	7.5808	
0005022000 c	16.4976	0006	16.0269	1500	28.0661	
1700000000	527.6596	0002	1.5351–	2000	21.3625	
1800000000	411.9149	0000	9999.9000–	2000	3.0189	
1900000000	798.2978	0000	9999.9000–	2000	2.4895	
0001044000 d	1021.2766	2000	21.5694	0000	9999.9000	B
2100000000	4006.6851	0006	.8081–	1500	.5976	
2200000000	456.1039	0006	.3362–	1500	.1868	
2300000000	5545.4816	0006	.5479–	1500	.2814	
2400000000	414.8936	0000	9999.9000–	2000	5.6076	
2500000000	12.7659	0002	12.1990–	2000	2.5489	
2600000000	1447.4704	1500	.8153–	0006	.8028	
0003013200 e	526.3016	2700 f	.0037	0006 g	27.2140	

VAR/COST	SHAD PRICE	LIM VAR	LOWER LIM	LIM VAR	UPPER LIM	
2000000000	1.9089	2500	17.0453–	0007	1254.2159	
0002017600	13.1879	1900	242.5840–	2500	11.8086	
2700000000	.5844	0007	6428.8843–	0003	9999.9000	C
0004002200 i	25.8784	0007	81.9970–	0005	9.4043	
1600000000 j	6.3814	0007	360.7871–	0005	41.3789	
0006000880	.5239	0007	1639.9418–	0005	188.0863	
1500000000	.0143	2200	5954.2390–	0007	1000.0486	

be necessary to devote a few paragraphs toward explaining the contents of Table 2. Looking first at paragraph B, the first column consists of the name of the variable (1400 is variable X_{14} or "sense of fair play") followed by a six-digit statement of the associated cost or profit, whichever is used (see a in Table 2). The decimal point is assumed to be in the middle of this six-digit field, i.e., XXX.XXX. Thus, 1400000000 indicates that the profit assigned to variable 14 is 000.000. The "activity" refers to either the amount of goal achievement possible (for goal variables X_1 through X_7) or the amount of slack capacity present (for path variables X_{14} through X_{27}). Thus variable X_{14} (sense of fair play) shows 9999 units of unused capacity [11]; variable X_7, which is part of the goal

11. In fact, there were 14,540 units of unused capacity of X_{14}. However, this particular computer program limits the magnitude of values in the output statements to ± 9999.900.

complex, has had 120 units achieved; 120 average members of the community were completely satisfied at an average profit to the organization of 0.44 units of subjective utility each (see b in Table 2). There were 16 totally satisfied average employees (variable X_5) each worth an average of 22.0 units of utility to the organization (see c in Table 2). There were 1,021 totally satisfied average customers (X_1), each worth an average return of 44.0 units of utility to the organization (see d in Table 2). There were 526 totally satisfied average shareholders (X_3) at an average of 13.2 units of profit each to the organization (see e in Table 2).

In paragraph B of Table 2, the lower and upper limit columns are the "limits of the cost coefficient over which the current solution is optimal" (Nichols et al., p. 13). The lower and upper limiting variables column lists the "variables which limit the range of the cost coefficient and will enter the basis if a limit is exceeded." (Nichols et al., p. 13). With respect to shareholders (X_3), therefore, we see that they are worth an average of 13.2 units of subjective utility to the organization; that one can satisfy 526 average shareholders under the current constraint conditions; that the programming solution is optimal in the face of profit changes unless the profit of 13.2 is reduced below .0037 (see f in Table 2), in which case variable X_{27} would enter the solution as unused capacity for profits-wages or unless the profit becomes greater than 27.2 (see g in Table 2), in which case X_6 would enter the solution as satisfied members of the industry.

In paragraph A the number of iterations necessary to determine the proper solution and the value of the objective function at each stage (called "functional") is shown, as well as the variables that are brought into the solution. The value of the functional, ΣX_1 (profit from each X_i in the solution), is equal to 52,299 units of subjective utility to the organization in this case (see h in Table 2). The leading two digits, i.e., 55, of the functional denotes where the decimal point should be located. In the "variable out" column the presence of path variables (X_{14} through X_{27}) exclusively in this column indicates that these variables were totally used; no slack capacity remains. Goal variables (X_1 through X_7) that remain in the "variable out" column indicate that there is no attainment of this particular part of the goal complex under current circumstances. Under "variable in" column, the presence of path variables indicates that they were not fully utilized and that subsequent iterations of the programming algorithm found it more profitable not to use the capacity so fully as had been anticipated in earlier iterations. Goal variables found in the "variable in" column indicate the amount of goal achievement possible under current constraints. The programming approach is equivalent to multiple comparisons instead of to serial comparisons because the algorithm is sensitive to all constraints and considers all paths that could lead to an optimal solution; it overlooks nothing included in the model.

In paragraph C the first column consists of the variable's identification and cost statement, just as in paragraph B. The "shadow price" is the penalty to the objective function of introducing a unit of that variable into the strategy. In this instance the upper and lower limits are stated in terms of activity (number of resource units instead of cost) over which the shadow price applies. If these limits are exceeded, the shadow price changes and the upper or lower limiting variable would be forced out of the solution, while the variable in question was forced into the solution. Thus there are no units of X_4 (satisfied suppliers) produced (see i in Table 2); it would reduce the value of the objective function by 26 units each time a unit of X_4 were forced into the solution. Variable X_{16} (promptness in dealings) is completely utilized; to introduce a unit of idle or slack capacity would be to reduce the objective function by 6.4 units of utility each time (see j in Table 2).

There are not enough resources to completely satisfy any of the dealers, suppliers, and members of the industry, variables X_2, X_4, and X_6 respectively. Given the present state of affairs, nothing can be done about this; because of scarce resources, one cannot be all things to all men simultaneously. If one wanted to please a dealer (X_2), one would have to divert resources from other areas to do so. All of variable X_{20} resources (pricing policies) are being taken to satisfy customers (X_1); to obtain the 5.7 units of X_{20} needed to please a dealer would require diverting them from customer usage, thus reducing the number of satisfied customers. Each time this was done, the overall subjective utility to the organization would be reduced by 13 units, a costly adjustment. Similarly, if one wanted to please a supplier (X_4), one would do so at the expense of one's employees (X_5); units of X_{16} (promptness in dealings) would have to be diverted from the employees into usage for the supplier. To do this would reduce the value of the objective function each time by 26 units of utility to the organization, a very costly process indeed. If one wanted to please a member of the industry (X_6), one would again have to divert units of X_{16} (promptness in dealings) from the employees to the industry members. This would reduce the objective function by .52 subjective utility units to the organization each time it was done. Note how any deviation from the strategy of 1,021 customers (X_1), 16 employees (X_5), 526 shareholders (X_3), and 120 members of the community (X_7) will be costly to the organization given the current constraints; if one cannot do everything, this is the best one can do with available resources.

Tables 1 and 2 give all the information necessary to preclude impossible demands. If one devotes all of resource X_{20} (pricing policies) toward maximizing the returns of utility to the organization, one can never totally please any dealers (X_2). If one tries to please dealers, one must be prepared to divert resources of X_{16} (promptness in dealings) from either customers (X_1), employees (X_5), or community members (X_7) and to divert X_{20} (pricing policies) from customers (X_1), employees (X_5), or some combination of these. The company president who tells marketing both to keep up the sales level (expected level of sales $= 1,021$) *and* to satisfy 100 dealers (X_2) must see that this cannot be done without reallocating resources for this purpose and that this reallocation would lead to a reduced number of satisfied employees (X_5), customers (X_1), or both. The president who tells the personnel manager to increase employee satisfaction must now be able to see that the personnel department would have to be allowed to divert resources of X_{15} (stable operations) and X_{16} (promptness in dealings) from other areas of the company if this is to be done. Purchasing department employees cannot please suppliers unless it is possible to divert resources of X_{16} from either customers (X_1), employees (X_5), or the community (X_7). The same thing is true about attempting to please members of the same industry (X_6). To pressure these people for results in the face of this impossibility is to invite misallocation of resources and costs to the whole organization.

Varying the resources available. Since some of the variables are being used at full capacity and are limiting the growth of the objective function, what would happen if one increased their capacities? One might be able to purchase additional resources, even if borrowing was necessary. It can be shown that if one increased the amount of X_{16} (promptness in dealings) available in Table 2 by 5,000 units, the total subjective utility to the organization would increase to 54,846.[12] One hundred and sixty employees (X_5) would now be satisfied, 278 members of the industry (X_6) would now be satisfied, the number of satisfied customers (X_1) would remain the same, and there would be 465 satisfied shareholders (X_3); but none of the satisfied members of the community (X_7) would remain.

On the other hand, if one reduced the amount of X_{16} (promptness in

---

12. This and the following discussions are based on the results of linear-programming tables generated by varying the indicated cell entries in Table 2. The generated tables, which are in the format of Table 2, have been omitted here because of space limitations.

dealings) available, some reduction in activity would have to take place. If one reduced the amount of X_{16} by 361 units, all hope of satisfying anyone except 929 customers and 533 shareholders would vanish because too little X_{16} would be available. The value of the objective function would fall to 47,905 units of utility. However, if one reduced the amount of X_{16} by 25 units, there would be a correspondingly smaller reduction in the objective function down to 52,140. This occurs because with a reduction of 25 units in X_{16} (promptness in dealings), a different strategy results, which leads to 531 satisfied shareholders (X_3) and 129 satisfied members of the community (X_7), but yields a 10 unit decrease in X_5 (satisfied employees), each unit of which is worth 22.0 units of utility. There remain 1,021 satisfied customers.

Similarly, one could reduce the amount of variable X_{14} (sense of fair play) by 10,000 units and have no effect on the overall strategy. But if one reduced X_{14} by 15,000 units, he would then reduce to 746 the number of satisfied customers (X_1) and eliminate all possibility of satisfying anyone else except 533 shareholders (X_3), because all other groups need increments of X_{14} but cannot compete with customers for them. The objective function would fall sharply to 39,876 units.

If one adds units of X_{25} (high performance equipment), there are no gains at all. There was a surplus of this variable to begin with. But if the amount of resources given to the payment of wages and profits (X_{27}) is reduced by 7,000 units, significant changes will be seen. The same number of customers remain happy (X_1), and the number of satisfied members of the community (X_7) increases to 251; but the number of satisfied employees (X_5) and the number of satisfied shareholders (X_3) drop to 14 and 216 respectively. The value of the objective function would decline to 48,208 units.

While one could purchase extra resources as a means of improving the overall position, the issues facing most organizations are complicated, because they must rely on their own present bundle of resources, particularly in the short run. Up to this point, we have assumed that the slack capacities of path variables X_{14} through X_{27} have no alternative uses. If slack resources could be converted to other uses in demand, however, additional gains could be made in utility to the organization. If one assumes that one unit of X_{14} (sense of fair play) could be converted into one unit of either X_{20} (pricing policies), X_{27} (profits-wages), X_{16} (promptness in dealings), or X_{15} (stable operations), then gains could be made. If one converted 10,000 units of resources X_{14} into 2,500 units each of X_{20}, X_{27}, X_{16}, X_{15}, the value of the objective function would climb to 57,198 units of utility. Further conversions could be made in an iterative fashion using programming until the value of the objective function reached a limit and all possible capacity was utilized.[13] While this is a trivial computation, research will be necessary on the substitutability of the organizational resources so that the conversion of resources from one form to another would be possible at more exact levels. While this undertaking will be difficult, it should be possible; the gains from programming and flexible reallocation of resources would certainly make research on this problem a worthwhile endeavor.

It is apparent that the more flexible and the more convertible one's resources are, the more likely it is that one can improve the value of his objective function. This convertibility will never be complete; some slack capacities will not have alternate uses. Units of variable X_{23} (friendliness) embodied in a marketing engineer may be convertible to units of innovation (X_{17}) for the research and development division; units of X_{23} embodied in the voluptuous marketing receptionist may have no transferability. The only usage to be made of the latter units of X_{23} might be to have the receptionist continue acts of friendliness toward customers (X_1) although it was known by the resource controllers that there were insufficient units of X_{20} (pricing policies) available to satisfy totally any additional customers (assuming other variables X_{14} through X_{27} had already been converted as completely as possible for usage toward achieving satisfied customers (X_1)). Rather than have this capacity of X_{23} (friendliness) remain totally idle, it may be best that the slack capacity be used for its most efficient end, even if a totally satisfied customer (X_1) never results, due to a shortage of necessary resources. This approach might give some residual good will even though under the present accounting procedure this good will would never increase the value of the objective function.[14] One would have many of the ingredients for a "shadow" strategy for pleasing others, like customers, requiring only some shift in organizational emphasis to free units of X_{20} (pricing policies) so that a real strategy of pleasing customers could be enacted.

Resource controllers might take the position that minimal increments of resources should be reserved for the satisfaction of some members of each group, regardless of the constraint picture. Thus one might take some organizational resources "off the top" to satisfy totally a few old customers; some faithful suppliers, conscientious dealers, loyal workers, stalwarts of the community, and fellow members of the industry who were a real credit to it. Once this was done, however, those resources

---

13. Using the data in Table 2, the author had made one-to-one conversions of resources that yielded an objective function of greater than 65,000 units of utility, and more conversions could have been possible.

14. However, a different approach for defining paths and goals might well account for this.

not siphoned off by this approach would become inputs into the programming model. One would continue to do one's best with the remaining resources, and the above remarks would remain pertinent.

Varying the profit. Programming one's organizational requirements gives one a great deal of flexibility in the face of change. We have noted that the goals of an organization can change: one might sell ones products directly to customers and eliminate the need for satisfying dealers; one might move one's factory into a large city and become totally unconcerned with satisfying members of the community. The flexibility of programming allows these kinds of factors to be added or deleted from consideration with very little difficulty. In the same fashion new paths to goals may develop and old ones may atrophy. New kinds of path activities may be called for; varying amounts of them may be called for as times change. One may find oneself constantly maneuvering such factors so that the objective function is as large as possible.

Up to this point it has been assumed that costs remained fixed and that one converted resources from one activity to another, purchased new ones, and sold or laid off unnecessary ones. Costs-profits may vary over time also. Just as the price of autos shifting from $300 to $200 and the price of trucks shifting from $250 to $600 made a difference in the solution of that problem, so will a change in the relative profit from the satisfaction of certain groups lead to a change in the returns of subjective utility. As circumstances vary, different profits may be assigned to certain activities. For example, most resource controllers today consider a satisfied work force more valuable than did their counterparts fifty years ago. At the very least, because of unions and legislation, a dissatisfied work force can cost substantial amounts of money. Having to deal with unions or hoping to preclude their presence has pushed up sharply the value of satisfied workers. Thus the value of X_5 (satisfied workers) is 22 units today; years ago it might have been only 5 units. In earlier years no value might have been placed on satisfied community members; today most organizations allocate resources to a specialized group for dealing with employees and community relations. Over the years shareholders may have lost status relative to other groups; in the days of the professional manager it is relatively less important to make shareholders totally satisfied. All of this points up the fact that a number of changes can occur in society that affect the cost picture to the organization and help dictate its final strategy.

Many organizations can cope with changes that evolve slowly, almost imperceptibly. It is dealing with more short-run changes that causes difficulty; how does one cope with changing circumstances when the time for search is short and the situation does not permit waiting for a sign from opinion leaders? It is in this instance that a programming technique can be very powerful. In fact, it is possible to develop in advance a whole series of possible strategies for coping with change in a rapid fashion. However, with the ease and speed of solving linear programming problems now possible by using computers, this would hardly be necessary. One could simply vary the cost data and iterate for a solution.[15] The more uncertain the matrix of possible inputs, the more likely one is to wait for developments and then compute. For example, suppose that competitors are raiding a company's dealer organization, trying to get its dealers to dump its line of products and take on that of the competitor. This has the effect of making satisfied dealers relatively more profitable. This causes a change from the equilibrium level of Table 2. If a resource controller feels that this threat is great enough to raise the profit from a satisfied dealer (X_2) from 17.6 up to 25.00, what strategy would result? It can be shown that if the threat to the dealer organization were considered no greater than this, no changes would be made by the organization. The present way of operating would still be best; this is so even if the threat pushed the return from a satisfied dealer to 30.0. But if the threat were great enough to move the value of dealers' satisfaction to 35.0 or 40.0, then major strategy changes would result. At a profit of 40.0 for a satisfied dealer (X_2), resources would be diverted away from customers (X_1), leaving 985 of them satisfied; no employees (X_5) would be satisfied because of the reduction in resources available; there would be a slight reduction in the number of satisfied shareholders (X_3) to 521 and a reduction to 61 in the number of satisfied community members (X_7). As a result of this diverting of resources, it would become possible to satisfy 62 dealers (X_2).

Suppose that one were operating in the base period of Table 2. Suddenly a rash of hostile grievances show up in the suggestion box, a union attempts to organize the factory, or an existing union threatens to strike. This raises the value of employee satisfaction (X_5). Suppose that the resource controller decides that the profit resulting from an average satisfied employee has risen from 17.6 to 30.0. The strategy resulting from this change in costs would have no effect on the number of customers satisfied; it would eliminate satisfied community members (X_7); only one disgruntled shareholder (X_3) might result; but one would

---

15. Note that the linear-programming solution is itself an iterative process. However, in the above context and in all instances not dealing directly with the mechanics of the programming algorithm, to iterate for a solution will mean to reiterate the whole solution process, which is itself iterative.

gain only 16 to 18 satisfied employees (X_5). If the value of a satisfied employee increases from 30.00 to 40.00, a change in overall strategy results. The number of satisfied customers (X_1) falls to 915, and the number of satisfied shareholders (X_3) is reduced to 465; however, it is now possible to have 160 satisfied employees (X_5) instead of the previous 16. Given the pattern of constraints in this case, it would not be possible to satisfy any members of the community (X_7), dealers (X_2), suppliers (X_4), or members of the same industry (X_6). If the value of a satisfied employee increases to 50.00, no change results. There is simply no way to manipulate existing resources to get more satisfied employees. Under these circumstances a resource controller who demands an increased number of satisfied employees (X_5) must be willing to allocate additional resources for that purpose.

Perhaps the shareholders (X_3) begin to get restive and the president thinks that the value of keeping them happy has risen from 13.2 to 30.0. If one re-evaluates the importance of satisfied shareholders in this fashion, one gains very little, an increase from 526 to 533 satisfied shareholders; the number of satisfied customers (X_1) remains the same, and its number of satisfied community members (X_7) rises from 120 to 134. One hundred eighty-eight members of the same industry (X_6) can now be satisfied with diverted resources. However, there are no longer any satisfied employees (X_5). If the returns from satisfied shareholders (X_3) are raised from 30.0 to 40.0, no additional gains result.

The preceding discussion has shown how one can use the pricing mechanism to alter organizational strategy. As a group like the dealers became more important, the amount of utility to the organization of achieving a satisfied dealer was increased. This one step alone caused strategies to vary where necessary to reflect this change in conditions. If circumstances changed so that dealers could be taken for granted, the procedure could be reversed. This would lead to a shift in resources elsewhere so that they would be more optimally used. It is important to note that this process can be looked at from another point of view. Suppose that the chief resource controller could not assign a value to a satisfied dealer (X_3), but that he knew he must have 62 satisfied dealers to stay in business, given the other conditions stated in Table 2. The only way the resource controller could achieve this would be to assign a value of 40.0 to a satisfied dealer (X_3). Thus he has been able to impute a value to a satisfied dealer.

Such examples of resource allocation could be multiplied many times in organizations, a large fraction of them highly fertile for conflict. The responsible organizational member confronted with changing demands for resources from his restive customers, employees, dealers can obtain increased resources only by diverting them from other uses. Confronted with his own demands, the demands of other members of the organization seeking to maintain or enhance their own bundle of available resources for their own ends, the responsible member of the organization finds very real limits to the strategies open to him, particularly in the short run. If the resource controllers insist on action for the restive groups without a corresponding reassessment of the current allocation of resources, the situation will demand innovation. Either the subordinate will generate new methods of getting increased quality from his employees, or he will have to resort to a serial-comparison strategy with its propensity for relatively low efficiency. This quality requirement may redefine the constraints. Workers who are often forced to yield this increased efficiency via speedups and rate reductions may make their own satisfaction a little more dear by inviting a union to organize their plant or by having a strike via the existing union. Thus the whole system of constraints is a very dynamic one with any one change having some probability of causing subsequent changes in constraints throughout the whole organization. For purposes of exposition, the changes thus far have been considered singly. However, one great strength in the programming approach is its facility for studying these dynamic interrelationships within organizations in order to be able to add and subtract goals, to change capacities and costs simultaneously. This flexibility for studying the dynamics of organizations by simultaneously varying the constraints can be shown.

Varying the profit and resources available. Suppose one faces threats from shareholders, employees, and dealers at the same time. How would the resource allocator use limited resources to confront this threat? What change in strategy from the base point would he use if indeed he could afford to change his strategy at all? It can be shown that a simultaneous occurrence of the events that have been discussed with respect to dealers, employees, and shareholders would lead to a strategy of 525 satisfied shareholders (X_3), 1021 satisfied customers (X_1), and 19 satisfied employees (X_5). There would be no totally satisfied members of the community (X_7), suppliers (X_4), members of the same industry (X_6), nor, in spite of the profit increase, any satisfied dealers (X_2). Customers (X_1) would still retain priority for all variable X_{20} (pricing policies) available.

If one increased from the base point the amount of available resources for variables X_{16} (promptness in dealings), X_{14} (sense of fair play), X_{25} (high performance equipment), X_{27} (profits-wages), and X_{20} (pricing policies) by adding 5,000.0, 10,000.0, 6,000.0, 7,000.0, and 1,000.0 units respectively, the following mix of activities would be most profitable for the organization: the number of satisfied customers (X_1) would rise to 1059; the number of satisfied employees (X_5) would drop to 12; the number of satisfied shareholders (X_3) would rise to 829; but it would no longer be possible to satisfy any members of the community (X_7); there would now be 54 satisfied dealers (X_2); there would now be 216 satisfied members of the same industry (X_6). No suppliers (X_4) would be satisfied.

What if one increased the capacities and the costs simultaneously? In terms of Table 2, variables X_{16} (promptness in dealings), X_{14} (sense of fair play), X_{25} (high performance equipment), X_{27} (profits-wages), and X_{20} (pricing policies) would be increased by 5,000.0, 10,000.0, 6,000.0, 7,000.0, and 1,000.0 units respectively; variables X_2 (satisfied dealers), X_5 (satisfied employees), and X_3 (satisfied shareholders) would be changed to 40.0, 50.0, and 40.0 respectively. By chance, these sample values selected for change would yield the same mix of activities for the organization as reported in the previous paragraph, where only the amounts of resources were varied. There, however, the increase in costs has affected the shadow prices and generally has increased the width of the limits on activities over which the current shadow prices apply.

Sensitivity of coefficients. The foregoing discussion has illustrated how different values in the objective function and varying amounts of resource capacities might lead to decisions differing from those shown in the base point iteration (Table 2). A further inquiry needs to be made into how sensitive decisions are to variations in values for the coefficients of the X_i's in Table 1. This is an important question because the greater the sensitivity of decisions to change in these coefficients of X_i's, the greater the burden for accuracy that must be borne by one's measuring instruments. While it is true that many strategies chosen could be re-evaluated and reiterated in terms of subsequent information, there will be circumstances in which this approach will not be satisfactory. It may be necessary to purchase expensive machinery or to make some other kind of irrevocable commitment for which there is no subsequent opportunity to change one's mind and adopt another approach. In such instances where a later iteration of strategy is merely academic, it is important to know how dependent decisions are on the present values and how one's chosen strategy would have changed had one known the "true" values.

One answer to this dilemma of measurement error is to iterate for all possible occurrences. One might take the measurements given in the base matrix as the best that can be done with this measurement process; one realizes that there may be some error in the process. If one has a large enough computer, it is possible to take these values and vary them systematically by increments. One could then see under what circum-

TABLE 3
RESULTS OF SENSITIVITY EXPERIMENTS

X_{16},X_1	% of X_{16},X_1	X_{20},X_1	% of X_{20},X_1	Trial	Results: X_1	X_2	X_3	X_4	X_5	X_6	X_7	Functional
4.06	120	14.10	120	A	851		527		15		121	44,788
4.06	120	11.75	100	B	862		533					44,971
4.06	120	9.40	80	C	862		533					44,971
3.38	100	14.10	120	D	851		465		160	454		47,511
3.38	100	11.75	100	E*	1021		526		16		120	52,299
3.38	100	9.40	80	F	1023		527		15		122	52,332
2.70	80	14.10	120	G	851		465		160	454		47,511
2.70	80	11.75	100	H	1021		465		160	278		54,846
2.70	80	9.40	80	¡	1023		465		160	277		54,909
5.07	150	17.63	150	J	681		520		89		50	38,791

* Original values from Table 2

TABLE 4
RESULTS OF SENSITIVITY EXPERIMENTS

Cells in Base Matrix	Original Base Values	I		II		III		IV		V		VI	
		Value	%Orig	Value	%Orig	Value	%Orig	Value	%Orig	Value	%Orig	Value	%Orig
X_{15},X_3	3.50	5.25	(150)					2.80	(80)			3.50	(100)
X_{15},X_5	8.56					12.84	(150)	8.56	(100)	4.28	(50)		
X_{15},X_r	8.45			4.23	(50)					6.76	(80)		
X_{16},X_1	3.38			5.07	(150)	4.06	(120)	4.06	(120)			4.06	(120)
X_{16},X_5	2.55	3.06	(120)	2.04	(80)	3.06	(120)						
X_{16},X_r	.05	.04	(80)	.04	(80)	.05	(100)	.08	(150)				
X_{20},X_1	11.75	9.40	(80)							11.75	(100)	5.88	(50)
X_{27},X_3	22.50	11.25	(50)			27.00	(120)	27.00	(120)	27.00	(120)	11.25	(50)
X_{27},X_5	9.59			9.59	(100)					7.67	(80)	4.80	(50)
Solution Values													
X_1	1021	1023		688		862		862		1021		862	
X_2													
X_3	526	571		533		444		444		440		857	
X_4													
X_5	16									14			
X_6													
X_r	120	196		268						206			
Functional:	52,999	52,716		37,440		43,798		43,798		51,164		49,245	

stances one would have arrived at decisions different from those in the base matrix, perhaps calculating the probability that one's own measurements are off by that amount. If one did not wish to use this complete listing approach, one might be able to use past experience as a means of reducing the computation of alternatives. Those values that experience indicated were unstable could be systematically manipulated; the stable ones could remain constant.

By inspection of Table 1 it is possible to determine which coefficients might be most critical in the making of a decision. For example, it can be shown that one could have considerable variation of coefficients for those path variables for which excess capacity existed without appreciably affecting the overall strategy. This is because unless the change were great enough to use up all the present capacity—and thus perhaps preclude the attainment of some previous goal variables—the same strategy would prevail, the same value of the objective function would result. Only a reduction in slack capacity (corresponding to the increased amount required for the strategy) would result.

On the other hand, certain critical points in Table 1—the cells defined by the intersection of goal variables decided upon (X_1, X_3, X_5, and X_7) and those variables which were used to capacity (X_{15}, X_{16}, X_{20}, X_{27})— could be much more sensitive to change since variations in these coefficients may determine whether or not certain goals remain in the overall strategy. For example, increasing the amount of X_{20} (pricing policies) necessary to please each customer (X_1) can only lead to fewer total customers being satisfied. If the amount of X_{16} (promptness in dealings) necessary to please a customer (X_1) is increased by twenty percent, the number of customers who could be pleased is reduced, but also possibility of pleasing any employees or members of the community is eliminated. This would be a major departure in strategy. It is sensitivity to this kind of shift in strategy that is sought.

Table 3 shows in tabular form what would happen to the overall decision strategy if the values of X_{16}, X_1 (amount of promptness in dealings required to satisfy a customer) and of X_{20}, X_1 (amount of pricing policies attention required for pleasing a customer) were varied. In three of nine trials, A, F, and J, the overall strategy would have remained the same; only in two trials, B and C, would the policies have differed markedly, with only two goals of the original four being possible.

Table 4 illustrates the results of varying the original base values by ±20% and 50% for those critical cells of the matrix. The 45 possibilities (50%, 80%, 100%, 120%, and 150% of each nine critical cells) were sampled randomly for five values, the only restriction being that the five values sampled not have any double counting for any one particular cell (e.g., one could not have X_{16}, X_1 be both 5.07 and 4.06 simultaneously.) Out of the six trials of this experiment, only in case V was the correspondence perfect, although strategies I and II are reasonably close. The resulting strategies in Cases III, IV, and VI indicate that if one's measuring instruments were no more sensitive to shifts than are these randomly chosen ones, one could get poor answers. It will be important, therefore, to have as refined measuring instruments as possible. However, if one did no more than explore as alternatives the worst possible outcomes that could happen, one would be making improvements on the common run of decision techniques in use today.

ORGANIZATIONS AS SYSTEMS OF CONSTRAINTS

The case discussion displayed the logic of using linear programming as an approach to the understanding of organizational behavior issues where one is confronted with the necessity of allocating scarce resources among available alternatives. When one defines organizational activities in terms of goals, costs, and capacity constraints—and it appears that large numbers of these activities can be—one can cope with substantial diversity and dynamism. The resulting solution is equivalent to a multiple-comparison strategy, but the iteration of a solution containing many path and goal variables requires only seconds on modern computing equipment. These are strong recommendations for experimenting with this model as an aid for coping with the size and complexity of organizational behavior problems.

In the case discussion, however, we have only begun to develop an overall organizational strategy. We have thus far dealt only with the top level of an organization. With paths becoming goals for subsequent levels of the organization, the whole process of goal and path definition must be done again at each level and at each decision-making node at that level of the organization. Each of the paths X_{14} through X_{27} becomes a goal for one or more others in the organization. Innovation may become part of the goal complex for the research and development division; courtesy may become a function of personnel, marketing, and public relations; warranties may become a function of manufacturing, service, and marketing; paths are now developed so that these higher level paths, which have become goals, can be reached in optimal fashion. Thus the manufacturing division may have received induced goals of providing a sense of fair play for workers and suppliers and a certain level of innovation in terms of production engineering. The paths it develops may be merit reviews, a policy of not taking advantage of suppliers' errors that benefit the organization, or promotion by seniority and ability. By fully exploring the range of relevant paths and goals, one is able to develop for every decision-making position a linear-programming table as shown in Table 1. The remarks applicable to the case study would apply throughout the organization.

As pointed out in the descriptive section, any particular change in strategy within the organization could potentially resonate throughout the whole organization. Thus a 10 percent reduction in variable X_{16} (promptness in dealings) led to changes at the top level of decision making. Since this decision would be taken as a given, the effects of having no resources with which to please the workers would soon be felt by the personnel manager. Hopefully, he would have the freedom to point this out to the top decision-makers so that a new strategy could be determined that might allow some resources to be allocated for

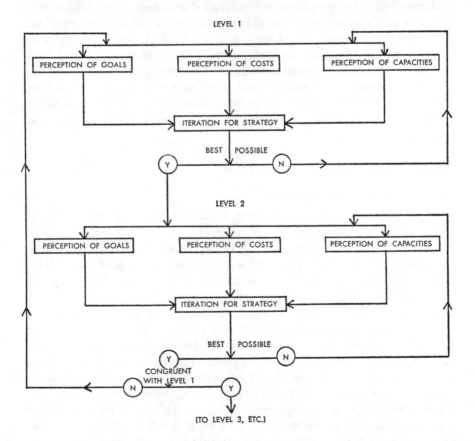

FIGURE 8
Organization as a System of Constraints

worker satisfaction. No solution at any level need remain an isolated one. Its ramifications may very well affect the price, capacities, and most certainly the goals of others. For this reason several iterations for solutions may be necessary at several decision-making nodes. This complex interrelationship is shown in Figure 8. One iterates at one level for the best solution that one can obtain; the solutions obtained at that point define the givens for subsequent levels. Having achieved a solution at one level, a subsequent level of iterations must be conducted until the best solution has been obtained; this solution may then be referred back to the organizational strategy determined by the resource controllers to see if the strategies are congruent. If so, levels 3, 4, . . ., are free to follow the same processes. Moreover, this is only the picture by levels; lateral comparisons within each level as well as vertical ones may be necessary and may begin to complicate interrelationships even more. Fortunately, this added consideration is trivial computationally. If one can transform data into the resource allocation format of Table 1, one can cope with complexity, the dynamic interrelationships between vertical and horizontal decision-making nodes. Because constraints are capable of defining the situations of interest and because the dynamic system (see Figure 8) resulting from the total integration of each set of constraints defines the organization, we speak of the organization as a system of constraints.

DISCUSSION AND CONCLUSIONS

RESOURCE ALLOCATION APPROACH

An organization, like an individual, cannot be all things to all people; yet it must be some things to some people if it is to remain viable. Confronted with this dilemma, the resources of an organization must be efficiently allocated. Today there are decision-making approaches that enable one to allocate resources optimally, given data on costs, goals, and capacity restrictions. The linear-programming model used in this chapter is one such approach. While its use is most common in the production, planning, and distribution phases of management science, it has been shown that to the extent that behavioral information could be quantified in terms of the linear-programming model, one could indeed speak of a constraint model of organizational behavior. Activity could be characterized as a function of costs, capacity restrictions, and goals defined in terms of appropriate inputs. Although the case discussion and examples came from the area of industrial organizations, any organization, whether on-going or in the design stage, could be characterized with this approach as long as the goals, costs, and capacity restrictions could be quantitatively defined. Furthermore, for important aspects in the life of the individual, it appears that it may be possible to measure the factors sufficiently well to use an iterative process that can yield increasing refinement. There is much less justification for total reliance on rules of thumb for problem solving even in the areas of organizational behavior; the programmed-constraints approach can yield the information necessary for viewing organizations as complex resource-allocation processes. The richness of factors exogenous and endogenous to the organization can now be manipulated.

MEASUREMENT PROBLEMS

Few scientific undertakings are free of measurement difficulties; this model of organizations is no exception. The common denominator of this chapter has been subjective utility and its perception; if the resource controller values something, we assign it a higher utility than we do something he likes less. To this extent the usefulness of the constraint model is a function of the measurement of subjective utility, and there should be no mistaking the problems in dealing with it. Much in this chapter depends upon the ability to measure utility meaningfully. Although researchers typically feel uncomfortable using a notion of subjective utility, members of organizations must frequently deal with it. The design engineer must use some implicit if not explicit scale of subjective utility and some kind of heuristic linear programming to aid in making decisions if he is to arrive at a finished product. If a kind of linear-programming process with subjective utility goes on with many people much of the time, it is important to invest some research resources in defining those items and regions over which it is meaningful to use such notions. If decision models are to be used, this difficulty must be confronted. For the issues about organizations under discussion in this chapter, it appears that better and better approximations to meaningful utility relationships can be obtained by psychometrics and programming iterations (Strother, 1963, p. 34). In the area of economics and production decision, there is some indication that managers' past decisions are consistent enough to be incorporated into a procedure that leads to improvements in their subsequent decisions, even though the coefficients are determined after the fact (Bowman, 1963). A similar approach could be taken by iterating the linear-programming approach. If a resource controller did not like the final result of a strategy iteration, he could simply change some of the inputs and iterate again. When he finally obtained an acceptable strategy, he would have automatically defined the value to him of certain paths and goals. In this fashion the manager could respond to stimuli internal and external to the organization; he could make subsequent decisions and changes around the initial determination of strategy, which was itself a function of earlier iterations with respect to his values.

A willingness to iterate for solutions can even allow the study of personality variables that are important in a particular situation. As a first approximation, one might determine initial values for programming (see Table 1) and by iteration (see Figure 8) develop a strategy that optimized the objective function. This very iterative process would help clarify the utility of various activities. As a result of a programming iteration it may appear that a manager tends to evaluate the worth of his group of satisfied employees more than he can really afford to in terms of contribution to the overall organization. He may find that when it comes right down to spending the resources, satisfied workers are not so important as some other end state. But he might not have realized this until he was forced to allocate resources in some systematic fashion and was then able to determine how much his strategy cost him in terms of the objective function. Furthermore, the manager may insist upon an activity because it increases his sense of dominance; he may insist on producing some of the old line of products for sentimental reasons. When confronted with a programming solution illustrating the costs associated with his demands, he may change. If he does not, he has implicitly assigned a higher utility value to dominance, sentiment, etc. The profit of the item may be a negative one hundred dollars, but it may be worth some x number of utility units to the president. Having this information out in the open and having to admit that something is costly —but demanding it nonetheless—is much different from insisting that something be done but not realizing what all the overt and covert costs are. With this programming approach it is possible to get a good measure of individuals' needs and an understanding about how these needs might otherwise confuse the decision-making process. The individual himself is able to be more aware of himself and his impact on others with this added insight; he may be able to modify his own behavior so that it is more appropriate to the situation. At a very minimum, he should blame others less for the costs of a poor strategy that he himself has dictated.

It will take some work before we are able to measure with facility the inputs that go into a linear-programming model of behavior. However, the gains are such that it is important to obtain this ability. If programming results look complicated, it may be best to consider such a model as necessary for coping with the richness of data generated by organizations and to consider how much information may be lost by relying on the traditional methods of researching organizations. The choice may not be to compute or not; it may really be to understand complexity or not.

It is important to break out of the mold of the classical "one independent, one dependent variable" research if we are ever to understand the complexity of organizations. This is really a reversal from the factor analytic approach; rather than appealing to a summary coefficient on some strangely named factor distillates, it is held here that it is better to reinsert all the original richness of values and determine what are the complex interrelationships of more simple variables.

Even after the matrix of inputs has been derived, there are still further assumptions to be met. At this point it seems likely that the relationships of variables will be linear enough to allow for improvements in our understanding of organizational behavior using the linear-programming approach. It is very likely, however, that the relationships will not be completely linear over their entire range; but this is true even in the purely economic uses of linear programming. The wish is for a model that will be helpful enough to justify diverting resources for improving it, not waiting before one commits oneself to the perfect—and therefore improbable—model. Having gained some experience with decision-making techniques, it may become possible to create or adapt better and better techniques for use. The question is not is the model best, but rather is it worthy of consideration, is it helpful, does it increase our understanding of some phase of the real world, does it increase our ability to predict events?

INCONGRUENCY OF ORGANIZATIONAL AND INDIVIDUAL GOALS

This chapter has assumed that there is an incongruency between the goals of the organization and those of the individual, although the use of this programming model of constraints is certainly not dependent on this assumption. While this disjoint, path-goal nature of individual and organizational goals results in a great deal of conflict and costly adaptive behavior, it is unlikely that the conflict will ever be entirely eliminated. Much of the unwitting incongruity caused by inconsistent demands requiring impossible solutions can be minimized by a more thorough understanding of organizational behavior as seen within the constraint framework. Most managers are men of good will who do not purposely generate excesses of conflict. Even an organizational Machiavelli might reduce much of the existing conflict if he could realize the extent of misallocation of resources that result. As Likert points out, such managers are simply liquidating some of their intangible—but, nonetheless, real—assets (Likert, 1961, p. 71). It appears, however, that even many managers of good will would remain unconvinced that a misallocation of resources was occurring unless some kind of organizational model could carefully delineate for them the possible ramifications emanating from the choice of a particular course of action. Programming organizational processes and being able to determine the impact on the whole structure of certain changes allow one to determine the relationship between certain acts and the resulting level of goal achievements.

To give but one example of conflict reduction possible from this approach, consider the impact on the industrial organization discussed above in the case material when a new vice president of manufacturing was appointed. This new executive had views of paths and goals for the manufacturing division different from his predecessor's. A stranger to the situation, he (and certainly the employees he inherited) was far from clear about the relative importance of available paths, to what extent the formerly accepted paths should be abandoned for new ones, what the costs and limitations of certain strategies were. This lack of specificity for organizational goals and paths led to a great deal of conflict and misallocation of resources for the first year of his tenure. Only by trial and error—a very painful process for all involved—was an approximate strategy developed and a general understanding of this strategy reached by his employees. Several of his employees remarked that the new executive had changed the "rules of the game" but had not changed them to anything yet clearly defined. With a programmed-constraints model in operation, strategies could have been determined much earlier by assigning values for the expected utility of various approaches. As all manufacturing personnel became more familiar with the operations, they could have proposed adjustments in the strategy if it appeared that the previously determined values could not be maintained advantageously. But the initial commitment could have served as a basis for comparisons and subsequent iteration. Even if the first approximation had been a poor one, at least the subordinates would have known the rules of the current game; there would have been less anxiety about their roles of strategy-evolvers vs. strategy-enactors. A much more efficient understanding of what was expected from all participants would have been gained. A computer could have been used to explore several tentative strategies during "dry runs." The misallocation of resources that occurred was largely unnecessary; each subordinate's JIC file (" 'Just In Case' the boss asks") was a waste of organizational resources. Unfortunately, being aware of these misallocations and comparing alternatives meaningfully, even when one is aware of them, is a difficult task —almost always an impossible one without some model for coping with the complexity.

Regardless of the method used for allocating resources, the individuals in many specialized functions will probably feel that they have not received all the resources to which their unique contribution to the company entitles them. Personnel and marketing groups may both feel that they should have received resources that were given to the other and that they cannot operate effectively without these additional resources; both may be correct. Using the constraints model, however, each group will at a very minimum be able to see how and why the resources were allocated and how their own particular contribution fits into the total strategy. Each group can more clearly visualize that beyond a certain point any gains they make can only come at the expense of some other organizational function. This kind of approach could greatly increase the awareness of the importance of one's own contribution to the total organization and increase interest in the overall welfare of the organization as opposed to isolated empire building. By the same token, the top resource controllers will have more realistic expectations about the performance of their subordinates because they will have weighed the extant constraints before coming to an allocation decision.

TRADITIONAL VIEW OF ORGANIZATIONS

This formulation has also considered certain aspects of the traditional approach to the study of organizations. Unity of direction and chain of command have been implicit throughout the whole argument. Given the motives that led to the formation of the organization, all strategies throughout the organization must be at least minimally acceptable to the resource controllers, with strategies dovetailing into a meaningful path-goal relationship. There are great possibilities for refinements of control techniques with the programming approach because of the speed and ease of computer techniques and the possibility for all iterative strategies to be tested for fit with others. There would be little effort required for resource controllers to monitor the strategies developed in the most remote recesses of the organization. To this extent, the span of control could be enlarged. This would not necessarily lead to more job autonomy for the individual worker, however, because of computerized aids for routinized decision making. With such control possible, the resource controller would have to determine whether he really felt there were intrinsic advantages in job autonomy and really wanted to continue in that fashion, or whether in fact he had only accepted this approach in the past because it had been difficult to monitor decisions and therefore much more costly than it currently would be. True motives would at least come to the fore. It is probable that the span of control would in fact become much larger and that the average organizational chart would lose much of its symmetry, which was a function of the traditional notions of span of control. With the increased usage of computerized decision-making techniques, true decision-making nodes would replace the routine levels of supervision; many decision-making nodes would no longer be necessary for the routine ingestion and simplification of information for transmission to the resource controllers. Much greater cognitive capacity could be available to fewer people at higher levels. In some ways this seems like a terribly mechanistic model of human behavior—and the computation of the model is so. This is one of its great strengths. There is frequently a strain toward studying what we want to find. Too often human relators forget that there is a job to be done; too often production men forget that people must do it. Programming allows both kinds of information to be fed into the matrix for the best possible solution the constraints allow.

There is a substantial capacity for change built into this model. Convertibility of resources in terms of layoffs and rehires will not endear change to anyone. While change in the higher echelons of the organization will frequently be changes only in the kinds of symbols being manipulated, changes in the lower levels of the organization may lead to loss of status-yielding skills. However, if stability of employment can be insured to some extent and if status and other rewards can be conferred on those who have learned many operations giving them convertibility, then it would appear that change as a function of convertible resources need not be a problem. It would appear that if the successes of job enlargement had taught us anything, it would be that change in tasks per se need not be disliked but could be desired.

Certain tasks may continue to be specialized and certain people will continue to be specialists. The research physicist might never be pulled off his research to hasten product deliveries; but a research technician for the physicist might be shifted about from time to time for such demands. The very notion of convertible resources reduces the importance of limiting one's activities to a single task. It is very important that these individuals learn many tasks so that this convertible feature can be used. It is no small bonus that the less skilled task is the very one on which job enlargement and job rotation have made gains. One would customarily make few gains in job satisfaction if one moved the physicist from his research and rotated him periodically to advertising or enlarged his tasks to include production methods. He is already using many of his abilities; but for the technician who is using fewer abilities and who may be faced with routine tasks, such gains in job enlargement might be considerable. The job horizons of the research physicist may need little enlargement and hence little would be gained. In the case of the technician, the organization gains flexibility by being able to utilize his abilities, and the individual may make many personal gains in self esteem via the same route of job enlargement and job rotation.

Using such a model, one should ultimately be able to determine the proper inputs of organizational variables for one's own organization. Strategies would no longer need be determined by guess work or by blindly copying some other organization's experience. No longer would decision-makers have to rely on open-ended statements that the concept of job enlargement is good, the unit-manager concept is good, short spans of control are good, participation is good, short lines of communication are good. The relative importance of each of these variables could be developed within each organization. Prior research might help minimize the search process for the correct values, but greater gains would be anticipated if the values assigned to one's strategy were the product of the individual organization's total definition of the situation. Flour mills can afford much different structures than can electronics firms. Consumer-orientated electronics firms will probably need different organizational structures and processes than would an electronics firm that based its operations on government contracts. It should be possible to design organizations that are much more efficient than those with which we are currently familiar. Constant attention to change and constant varying of strategies will preclude periodic upheavals such as a giant steelmaker slashing employment by 10 percent. Constant awareness of factors would never have allowed such a catastrophe.

It is possible for the traditional view of task specialization to interfere with the responsiveness of this model by limiting the individual's understanding of or concern for all the ramifications of his actions. While programming allows a multiple-comparison approach, task specialization frequently encourages a serial-comparison strategy simply because all relevant data are not known.

A particular person or department may be rewarded only for catching errors in quality; someone else may specialize in product design and output. The rewards under task specialization are for finding the errors of others, not for devising an integrated strategy that would maximize the objective function for the whole organization. With a constraints model it should be possible to assign to the same group meaningful weights for the relative importance of error-production and error-finding. This would obviate the need to use a serial-comparison approach specialized by group. Individuals in charge of production could know the relative weights of quality vs. quantity and adjust their strategies accordingly. Because weights can point out the relative importance of certain behaviors, there should be less misallocation of resources stemming from task specialization.

The constraints model places a premium on widespread dissemination of information. If the linear-programming model is to compare various strategies, all the necessary data must be available. Omitted items cannot be considered in the iterated strategy, and the strategy could not hope to be totally representative. In this vein, much openness between individuals at all levels of the organization would be desirable. Assembly workers should know about marketing conditions, since these conditions may have an impact on their induced goals; in the same fashion, higher levels in the organization need information from assembly in order to remain effective at the design, methods, and quality tasks to which they are assigned. Instead of periodic reviews on performance and expectations, each individual could know constantly what was expected of him, how his index of performance was computed, and what changes in variables affected him personally.

DECISION-MAKING VIEW OF ORGANIZATION

The decision-making approach to the study of organizations has been apparent. It is doubtful that any real gains can be made in the understanding of organizations as complex processes incorporating animate and inanimate resources unless one deals with the decisions determining the interaction and allocation of these resources. One cannot afford to have a structural chart, a machine model of organizations on the wall defining relationships and in one's head a human-relations model of what occurs. The process of organization must involve the decisions about both approaches simultaneously, and solutions to organizational difficulties must embody both; compromises must be made customarily for true solutions to exist. This point of view recognizes that changing the structure of the organization, e.g., reducing unity of direction via group participation or decentralization of facilities or going from functional approach to product lines, is not enough. Nor is changing the people via group dynamics, sensitivity training, small-group research enough. Being aware of the dynamic interaction of both views is vital and possible. It may be highly desirable to continue investing in the best selection techniques for people, machines, and materials, particularly since one wants the most convertible organizational resources possible. But polishing up the inputs without coping with the overall problems of the organization as a structure-process would do little to solve the problems of the organization. The position here is that any improvement in inputs to the organization is helpful, but that gains can be made from a more meaningful allocation of all these inputs and that one cannot accomplish one's desired ends if the conflict and issues surrounding allocations of resources are ignored. It does not matter that a plant manager has had sensitivity training if the constraints confronting him force him to attempt impossible solutions. This is the kind of day-to-day issue that one's organization must be capable of managing. It may even lead people to believe that in fact there are no answers to the dilemma of the individual vs. the organization. Admittedly, the issues of organization structure and process are difficult. In the past this has all too often forced researchers to doff their hats to the importance of organizations as structures and processes and has sent them scurrying to improve the individual as the solution. Nothing stated here would reduce the importance of schemes such as group participation. The data-generating, data-collection aspects of group-centered situations would still be quite desirable. The constraints model is only as effective as the inputs to it are; group participation approaches may be very efficient generators of necessary input data. While the model would do the iteration for the group, the group might still function as a judge for accepting or rejecting the efficacy of any particular iteration.

TOWARD RESPONSIVE ORGANIZATIONS

The constraints model views organizations as complex servo-mechanisms in a constant state of information processing and regulation. There is probably no ideal organization strategy, no "one best way" for organizational design. There are only better ones or poorer ones, given the existing constraint patterns. From the point of view developed in this chapter, perhaps the most important property of an organization is responsiveness, the ability to change in the face of shifting stimuli. The responsive, resiliant organization should be the more successful organization because it would have the capacity to reallocate its resources so as to maximize its objective function. To be sure, others have made similar pleas for flexibility. Argyris (1957, pp. 205–208) and Likert (chap. 14) have argued for varying patterns of leadership behavior so that one would have options available to draw upon for certain situations. But these strategies tended to be discrete strategies for behavior, saying relatively little about the form to be taken by the other organizational resources. Laudable as these approaches have been, it now appears possible to obtain a great deal more specificity about the nature of all resource allocation and the interrelationship of parts and not be forced to rely upon leadership variables. Having a strategy that was a function of the whole organization would free one of the periodicity of leadership styles and organizational structure styles. If this kind of responsiveness is not sought, one runs the risk of developing rules and strategies for yesterday's problems. Since many strategies are costly to derive, there is a reluctance to abandon them even after conditions have changed. Such strategies become patchworks of rules, demands, special exceptions, and temporary adjustments. It is likely that one could make savings simply by eliminating the enforcement of outmoded strategies.

Responsiveness is possible in the constraints model because subtle shifts can be sensed whether or not these shifts lead to changes in overall strategies. This sensitivity is desirable because even if a non-conflicting strategy is defined, subsequent changes in inputs may constrict and lead to impossible demands. However, if one is continually evaluating strategies, these subtle shifts from the possible to the impossible or costly could be detected. Not every single variation will lead to different strategies. This would lead to chaos; many changes will alter the predisposition for action (in the event that things should change a significant amount more) without dictating strategy changes in and of themselves.[16] Thus, when the importance of satisfied dealers rose from 17.6 to 25.0, no overall shift in resources occurred. However, the prices of possible strategies shifted, indicating a different predisposition to act if there should be any further changes. Thus, the new cost of forcing a satisfied dealer (X_2) into the solution was reduced from 13.1899 units to 5.7879 units. It can be shown that other changes in limiting variables also took place. The range over which the current solution is optimal for satisfying customers (X_1) has been reduced from 21.5694 to infinity to 32.0688 to infinity, indicating the changes in predispositions. Having an awareness of the potential impact on the organization of every change is important; having this precision without the necessity of reshuffling resources every time a single dealer gets unhappy indicates the administrative feasibility of this approach.

DEVELOPING AND WEIGHING ORGANIZATIONAL STRATEGIES

No claim is made that the view of organizations taken in this chapter is the only one, or even the best one. The position taken here is that some departure from the traditional approaches to the study of organizations is necessary. Certainly there is utility in studying many different kinds of organizations and determining the unique features of each. But the only conclusion that can usually be drawn is that each organization is like all others in some respects and like no other organization in other respects. But anyone could have guessed that before he began; this is an inefficient use of multiple comparisons. On the other hand, organizational relationships are too much a function of the particular situation to allow one to develop abstract, pure strategies for understanding all organizations. The point of view taken in this chapter is that one should make provisions for the inclusion of all possibly relevant

16. Where "a significant amount more" might be defined as exceeding the limit over which the current solution is optimal.

goals and paths in his study, being prepared to assign them zero values if need be. In this way one could allow for all possible variations without having to exhaust all possible variations existing in all companies. Several years ago Herbert A. Simon looked forward to assigning values for organizational variables; somewhat later he hardly hoped for an invariant set of weights (Simon, 1957a, p. xxxiv and 41–44). In a sense, we may be able to do better now. If one treated variables like span of control, unity of direction, task specialization and chain of command as path variables toward certain goal variables, one could determine whether or not to increase or decrease certain emphases on these factors. One might have a particular concept of unity of direction: if a union organizes the plant, the concept of unity of direction would undergo a substantial amount of change. With unity of direction being diluted by the union, different strategies might have to be proposed. With a different type of product being introduced, a different view of span of control might have to be introduced. It may now be possible to assign values to the particular variables in the particular organization that one has in mind. It may now be possible to design an organization and assign weights to various important parameters on the basis of the situation's own unique factors, not on the data gathered elsewhere, where the demand, technology, constitution of work forces, goals of the resource controllers may all have differed markedly. To some extent, organizational behavior has had only the serial-comparison strategies of varied researchers available to it; awareness of the difficulties in coping with all the necessary variables has led to the development of gross and varied typologies. Now it may be possible to use the multiple-comparison strategy with each organization, roughing out the outline of the organization with as many variables as necessary, filling in the matrix of values with coefficients determined by local research.

Blake and Mouton (p. 44) have written: ". . . realities being what they are in an industrial situation, the way a supervisor behaves is largely determined not by what could constitute ideal management, but rather by what the existing constraints and pressures compel as realistic problem solving for that situation." Being able to array more meaningfully the available strategies, being able to assess the interrelatedness of the constraints at work in each situation, should enable decision-makers to make more congruent their views of "ideal management" and "realistic problem-solving." Models like the one developed in this chapter should help mitigate the conflict and incongruency that now exist for all members of organizations and enhance our ability to understand organizations as structures and processes.

REFERENCES

Argyris, C. *Interpersonal Competence and Organizational Effectiveness.* Homewood, Ill.: Irwin-Dorsey, 1962.

————. *Personality and Organization.* New York: Harper, 1957.

Blake, R. R. and Mouton, J. S. "The Managerial Grid: Key Orientations for Obtaining Production Through People." (*Mimeo.*)

Bowman, E. H. "Consistency and Optimality in Managerial Decision-Making." *Management Science,* 1963, 9, 310–321.

Bowman, E. H. and Fetter, R. B. *Analysis for Production Management.* revised ed. Homewood, Ill.: Irwin, 1961.

Dorfman, R. "Mathematical or 'Linear' Programming: A Nonmathematical Exposition." *American Economic Review,* 1953, 43, 797–825.

Hall, C. and Lindzey, G. *Theories of Personality.* New York: Wiley, 1957.

Kemeny, J. G., Snell, J. L. and Thompson, G. L. *Introduction to Finite Mathematics.* Englewood Cliffs: Prentice-Hall, 1957.

Leavitt, H. J., ed. *The Social Science of Organizations.* Englewood Cliffs: Prentice-Hall, 1963.

Likert, R. *New Patterns of Management.* New York: McGraw-Hill, 1961.

March, J. G. and Simon, H. A. *Organizations.* New York: Wiley, 1958.

Nichols, C. P., Nickel, A. and Davis L. "Linear Programming for the Card 1620 with Punched Card Option for the Final Output." *1620 General Program Library 10.1.006.*

Simon, H. A. *Administrative Behavior.* 2nd. ed. New York: Macmillan, 1957a.

————. *Models of Man.* New York: Wiley, 1957b.

Stern, M. E. *Mathematics for Management.* Englewood Cliffs: Prentice-Hall, 1963.

Strother, G. B. "Problems in the Social Science of Organization." In H. J. Leavitt, ed. *The Social Science of Organizations.* Englewood Cliffs: Prentice-Hall, 1963.

Whyte, W. F. *Money and Motivation.* New York: Harper, 1955.

4

The Organization-Set: Toward a Theory of Interorganizational Relations

WILLIAM M. EVAN

Associate Professor of Sociology and Management, Sloan School of Management, Massachusetts Institute of Technology. This is a revised version of a paper prepared for the Seminar on the Social Science of Organizations, University of Pittsburgh, June 1963. It is printed with the permission of *Management Science*, where it first appeared. The author developed the concept of organization-set in a proposal entitled, "Law, Formal Organization, and Social Change," which was submitted to the Russell Sage Foundation in the Spring of 1959. He wishes to express his gratitude to the members of his conference group at the University of Pittsburgh for their many valuable comments. He is especially indebted to John MacDougall, Robert Melson, and Sheldon Stryker for their critical reading of the manuscript.

Social science research on organizations has been concerned principally with *intraorganizational* phenomena. Psychologists have studied the individual in an organization; social psychologists, the relations among the members of a group in an organization and the impact of a group on the attitudes and behavior of group members; and sociologists, informal groups, formal subunits, and structural attributes of an organization.[1] With relatively few exceptions, social scientists engaged in organizational research have not taken the organization in its environment as a unit of observation and analysis. Selznick's (1949) work on the TVA is a notable exception, as are Ridgeway's (1957) study of the manufacturer-dealer relationships, Dill's (1958) comparative study of two Norwegian firms, Levine and White's (1961) research on health and welfare agencies, Elling and Halebsky's (1961) study of hospitals, and Litwak and Hylton's (1962) study of community chests and social service exchanges.

The relative neglect of *interorganizational* relations is all the more surprising in view of the fact that all formal organizations are embedded in an environment of other organizations as well as in a complex of norms, values, and collectivities of the society at large. Inherent in the relationship between any formal organization and its environment is the fact that it is to some degree dependent upon its environment; in other words, it is a subsystem of the more inclusive social system of society. As distinct from a society, which in some respects is relatively self-sufficient in that it runs the gamut of all human institutions, a formal organization is a partial social system inasmuch as it defines only a specific set of goals and statuses as relevant to its functioning.

The phenomena and problems of interorganizational relations are part of the general class of boundary-relations problems confronting all types of social systems, including formal organizations. All such boundary relations tend to be enormously complex. Apart from sheer complexity, problems of interorganizational relations have been neglected by organizational analysts in part because of the concepts and propositions of various theories of organization. For example, the Weberian theory of bureaucracy is concerned largely with internal structural attributes and processes such as specialization of functions, allocation of authority, and

1. See, for example, Argyris (1957; 1964), Costello and Zalkind (1963), Haire (1964), Bennis et al. (1964), Kahn et al. (1964), Blau (1955), and Evan (1963).

formalization of rules. Taylorism and other kindred theories are also oriented toward internal relations among personnel. And the inducement-contribution theory of Barnard (1938) and Simon (1945) also has an intraorganizational focus. (cf. March and Simon, 1958, pp. 83–111.) A notable exception to the intraorganizational focus is the theoretical work of Parsons (1959, pp. 10–16; 1960, pp. 60–65) on formal organizations. As a social system theorist, Parsons is concerned with how organizations differing in their primacy of functions solve four system problems: adaptation, goal attainment, pattern maintenance, and integration. Any attempt to investigate how a particular organization solves these problems immediately involves considerations of interorganizational relations.

Nothwithstanding the general neglect of interorganizational phenomena by organization theorists, managers are greatly preoccupied with interorganizational relations. Some well-known examples of interorganizational practices are allocation of resources to public relations, cooptation of personnel of environing organizations into leadership positions in order to reduce the threat they might otherwise pose, acquisition of and merging with competitors, use of espionage against competitors, and recourse to litigation, arbitration, and mediation to resolve interorganizational disputes. These and many other interorganizational phenomena and processes await systematic inquiry by organization theorists. Millett's (1962, p. 3) general observation about organization theory is particularly relevant to this problem area: ". . . our practice has far outrun our theory. . . . The art of organization has much more to its credit . . . than has the science of organization." Impeding progress are problems of conceptualizing and measuring interactions among organizations. Prevailing organizational concepts and theories concerned with intraorganizational phenomena are probably not adequate for a study of interorganizational phenomena.

The purpose of this paper is to explore in a preliminary manner some conceptual and methodological problems of interorganizational relations. In the process we hope to extend the scope of organization theory and to draw attention to the potentialities of comparative research on interorganizational relations.

THE ROLE-SET

One point of departure in the study of interorganizational relations is to examine the utility of the concept of the "role-set," developed by Merton (1957, pp. 368–380), for analyzing role relationships (see also Gross et al., 1958, pp. 48–74). A role-set consists of the complex of roles and role relationships that the occupant of a given status has by virtue of occupying that status. A professor, for example, interacts not only with students but also with other professors, with the head of his department, with the dean of his school, and occasionally with the president or with the members of the board of trustees.

In all organizations the occupants of some statuses perform a liaison function with other organizations. Top executives in industrial organizations frequently confer with government officials, with executives of other firms within and without the industry, with members of trade associations, with officials in the local community. As guardians of the "public image" of the organization (cf. Riley and Levy, 1963), they are probably wary of delegating to subordinates contacts with representatives of other organizations that might have critical significance for the welfare of their own organizations.

The difference in orientation and behavior between liaison and non-liaison personnel is clearly brought out in a study by Macaulay (1963). In a study of the use of contract law among business firms, Macaulay found a high incidence of noncontractual relations. Among his other findings was a difference in orientation among the various departments in business firms toward the use of contracts, with the sales department being more negatively disposed to contracts and the comptroller departments being more positively disposed. When interdepartmental conflicts arise about the use of contracts, the house counsel, Macaulay observes, occasionally performs the function of an arbitrator.

A role-set analysis of the sales personnel as compared with the personnel of the comptroller departments suggests a possible explanation for the observed difference in attitudes toward the use of contracts (see Evan, 1963a). As the "foreign affairs" personnel of an organization, sales department employees come into recurrent contact with their "role partners" in other organizations, i.e., purchasing agents, with the result that nonorganizational norms develop, making for less recourse to contracts. In contrast, the role-sets of comptroller personnel involve a higher degree of interaction with others within the organization, thus reinforcing organizational norms—including the use of contracts. We may infer from Macaulay's study that systematic inquiry into the role-sets of boundary personnel will shed light on interorganizational relations as it bears on organizational decisions, whether pertaining to the use of contracts or other matters.

THE ORGANIZATION-SET

Analogous to the role-set concept is what I propose to call the "organization-set." Instead of taking a particular status as the unit of analysis, as Merton does in his role-set analysis, I shall take as the unit of analysis an organization, or a class of organizations, and trace its interactions with the network of organizations in its environment, i.e., with elements of its organization-set. In analyzing a particular organization-set I shall refer to the organization that is the point of reference as the "focal organization," (cf. Gross et al., 1958, pp. 50–56). In order to avoid the danger of reifying interorganizational relations, the relations between the focal organization and its organization-set are conceived as mediated by (a) the role-sets of its boundary personnel, (b) the flow of information, (c) the flow of products or services, and (d) the flow of personnel. As in the case of the role-set, conflicting demands by members of the organization-set may be handled by the focal organization with the help of mechanisms analogous to those described by Merton (1957), e.g., by preventing observation of behavior and by concerted action to counter the demands of other organizations.

An analysis of the organization-set of a focal organization (or of a class of focal organizations), could help explain: (a) the internal structure of the focal organization; (b) its degree of autonomy in decision-making; (c) its degree of effectiveness or "goal attainment"; (d) its identity, i.e., its public image and self-image; (e) the flow of information from the focal organization to the elements of its organization-set and vice versa; (f) the flow of personnel from the focal organization to the elements of its organization-set and vice versa; and (g) the forces impelling the focal organization to cooperate or compete with elements of its organization-set, to coordinate its activities, to merge with other organizations, or to dissolve. As an example of the possible explanatory utility of the organization-set concept we shall presently consider the effects of structural variations in the organization-set on the decision-making autonomy of the focal organization.

SOME DIMENSIONS OF ORGANIZATION-SETS

If we are to make any progress in analyzing interorganizational relations, we shall have to identify strategic attributes or dimensions of organization-sets. With the aid of such attributes we can formulate empirically testable propositions about interactions among organizations.

A provisional listing of dimensions of organization-sets follows; its principal value may lie in illustrating a possibly useful direction of conceptual analysis. Whether these dimensions are more heuristic than others that might be abstracted can be determined only by means of empirical research.

1. *Input vs. output organization-sets.* The focal organization's environment consists of an input and an output organization-set. As a partial social system, a focal organization depends on input organizations for

various types of resources: personnel, matériel, capital, legality, and legitimacy (Evan and Schwartz, 1964). The focal organization in turn produces a product or a service for a market, an audience, a client system, etc. For example, a private hospital may have in its input organization-set the community chest from which it obtains financial support, an association of hospitals from which it receives accreditation, and the department of public health of the local or state government from which it receives one or more licenses granting it the right to function. Its output organization-set may include other hospitals with which it cooperates or competes, medical research organizations, government agencies to which it sends data, etc.

2. *Comparative vs. normative reference organizations.* As in the case of an individual, the focal organization may evaluate its performance by using one or more organizations in its set—input or output, more likely the latter—as a standard for comparison, i.e., as a "comparative reference organization." On the other hand, if a focal organization incorporates the values and goals of one or more of the elements of its organization-sets, we would refer to it as a "normative reference organization" (Merton, 1957, pp. 283–284). For example, a firm manufacturing a particular kind of bomber might compare the quality of its product with other firms manufacturing bombers. Such outside firms would then be deemed "comparative reference organizations." Suppose, however, the Department of Defense indicates that the rapid production of a newly developed unmanned decoy bomber is urgently required by the United States. If the firm decided to convert its current bomber production into the production of an unmanned decoy bomber, it will have in effect incorporated as its goal the goal of the government and would be using a representative of the government, the Department of Defense, as a "normative reference organization."

3. *Size of the organization-set.* A focal organization may have a relatively large or a relatively small number of elements in its set. Whether it interacts with few or with many organizations presumably has significant consequences for its internal structure and decision-making. The size of the organization-set is to be distinguished, of course, from the size of the focal organization, although the two are presumably correlated.

4. *Concentration of input organizational resources.* The focal organization may depend on few or many elements in its input organization-set for its resources. Whether the concentration of input organizational resources is high or low would probably affect the structure and functioning of the focal organization.

5. *Overlap in membership.* Not infrequently there is an overlap in

membership of the focal organization with one of the organizations in its set. This is manifestly the case with (a) employees of an industrial organization who belong to a trade union with which the focal organization has a collective bargaining agreement, (b) scientists or engineers who are affiliated with a professional society from or through which an employing organization recruits its employees, and (c) members of the board of directors of the focal organization who are also directors of organizations in its set.

6. *Overlap in goals and values.* The goals and values of the focal organization may overlap with those of the elements in its set. To the extent that this occurs it probably affects the nature of the interorganizational relations that develop. For example, hostility might be engendered between an American military base overseas and a political party in the country in which the base was situated if the party did not share the assessment that the base was performing a "protective and deterrent" function rather than an "offensive and provocative" function.

7. *Boundary personnel.* Classifying the personnel of an organization into those concerned principally with domestic matters and those pre-occupied with "foreign affairs" is difficult, though not impossible (cf. Thompson, 1962). In a study of four manufacturing organizations, Haire (1959, pp. 272–306) analyzes the growth of external personnel in relation to internal personnel. Parsons (1959, pp. 10–16; 1960, pp. 59–96) distinguishes among three levels of personnel and functions in a formal organization: institutional, managerial, and technical. The first and third category probably involve a higher proportion of boundary personnel than the second category. In other words, top executives and some staff specialists such as sales, public relations, and house counsel are more likely to be engaged in boundary-maintenance functions than are junior and middle executives.

SOME HYPOTHESES ABOUT ORGANIZATION-SETS

Whether or not our preliminary consideration of some conceptual problems of interorganizational relations will prove useful only empirical research can establish. In the interest of stimulating inquiry in this relatively neglected area, several hypotheses on organization-sets, each assuming a *ceteris paribus* condition, will be formulated with the aid of the attributes enumerated in the foregoing section.

1. *The higher the concentration of input organizational resources, the lower the degree of autonomy in decision making of the focal organization.* A case in point is the difference in degree of independence between a public and private university. A public university probably

has fewer sources of revenue than a private university, and one member in its organization-set, the state legislature, probably accounts for the greatest part of its revenue. Consequently, public universities with a high concentration of input organizational resources probably exercise a lower degree of decision-making autonomy than private universities with a low concentration of input organizational resources.

2. *The greater the size of the organization-set, the lower the decision-making autonomy of the focal organization, provided that some elements in the set form an uncooperative coalition that controls resources essential to the functioning of the focal organization, or provided that an uncooperative single member of the set controls such resources.* Where there is a high degree of conflict among the elements of the organization. set, such conflict may tend to cancel out their effect on the focal organization, thus affording it more autonomy than would otherwise be the case. On the other hand, to the extent that there are coalition formations and to the extent that these coalition formations provide essential resources for or services to the focal organization, this does impose significant constraints on the degree of independence of the focal organization.

A striking example of a coalition formation against a focal organization is the boycott by druggists—organized by their trade association—of the Pepsodent Company when the latter withdrew its California fair-trade contracts (Palamountain, 1955, pp. 235–239). Also impressive is the action of the National Automobile Dealers Association, in the courts and in legislatures, to curb the power of the three large automobile manufacturers to dictate the terms of contracts and to cancel contracts (Palamountain, 1955, pp. 107–158; Evan, 1962, p. 179). By means of concerted action this trade association has become a countervailing power in the automobile industry. But size of organization-set, through an alternative sequence of variations, may produce an increase in the decision-making autonomy of the focal organization as well as the decrease hypothesized above. Quite likely there is a positive association between size of the organization-set and size of the focal organization. The larger the organization, the greater the specialization in liaison functions, the greater the number of boundary personnel, and so the greater the decision-making autonomy of the focal organization. However, some qualifications are necessary. To the extent that the proportion of boundary personnel is indicative of the *actual* rather than the *attempted* impact on the elements of its set, the greater the proportion of such personnel in the focal organization—relative to the proportion of such personnel in the set—the greater is its decision-making autonomy. Thus it may be seen that different mediators of the effects of size of organization-set yield opposite consequences for decision-making autonomy of the focal organization.

3. *The greater the degree of similarity of goals and functions between the organization-set and the focal organization, the greater the amount of competition between them, and hence the lower the degree of decision-making autonomy of the focal organization.* In their study of health and welfare agencies, Levine and White (1961, p. 598) observe that:

> . . . intense competition may occur occasionally between two agencies offering the same services, especially when other agencies have no specific criteria for referring patients to one rather than the other. If both services are operating near capacity, competition between the two tends to be less keen, the choice being governed by the availability of service. If the services are being operated at less than capacity, competition and conflict often occur. Personnel of referring agencies in this case frequently deplore the "duplication of services" in the community.

Another illustration of this hypothesis is the enactment of a law by Congress in 1959 requiring legislative authorization of major weapons programs of the armed forces. The enactment, Section 412 of the Military Construction Authorization Act of Fiscal 1960, substantially affects the process of policy-making in military affairs. Previously, major weapons procurement was authorized on a continual basis. Section 412, however, required that procurement of aircraft, missiles, and ships by all the services would require renewed authorization on an annual basis. Section 412 was authorized by the Senate Armed Services Committee, which was seeking to expand Congress' participation in defense policy-making. Here it may be seen that the common goal of the Defense Department and of the Armed Services Committee was the adequate defense of the nation, and that efforts to achieve that goal brought them into conflict, lowering the decision-making autonomy of the Department of Defense (Dawson, 1962, pp. 42–57).

4. *The greater the overlap in membership between the focal organization and the elements of its set, the lower its degree of decision-making autonomy.* A case in point is the overlapping membership of industrial organizations and trade unions. Overlapping membership, if accompanied by overlapping goals and values, may engender a conflict of loyalties that in turn probably diminishes the autonomy of the focal organization.

In Africa trade unions have become closely associated with nationalist parties, which have almost invariably provided governments of newly independent states with important personnel. Overlapping membership then occurs between a ministry of the central government and a trade union. These union leaders then face a dilemma in the concurrent needs to meet their members' demands for higher living standards and to cooperate with the government in promoting economic expansion. Their decision-making autonomy is thus reduced relative to the autonomy present when they were only union officials.

5. *Normative reference organizations have a greater constraining effect on the decisions of the focal organization than do comparative reference organizations.* The relations between trade unions of federal civil servants and the government illustrates this hypothesis. In the American public service it has been traditional not to strike; instead public servants have been satisfied to have working conditions determined by legislation or unilateral administrative action. This is probably due in large measure to the fact that the government department for which the civil servant works constitutes a very strong normative reference organization. Civil servants have apparently incorporated the goals of government, one of which is to maintain the continuity of the government in all circumstances. A trade union of office workers outside the government that threatens to strike will be seen only as a comparative reference organization whose members perform parallel duties with government workers. In the case of the civil servant, a normative reference organization clearly determines behavior to a greater extent than a comparative reference organization (Spero, 1962, pp. 1–4).

The foregoing hypotheses are but illustrations of the kinds of hypotheses that might be formulated with the help of the properties of organization-sets. These hypotheses revolve around the dependent variable of autonomy in decision making of the focal organization. Clearly, similar hypotheses are needed for various interorganizational processes, e.g., coordination, cooperation, competition, conflict, innovation, amalgamation (Thompson and McEwen, 1958). Several examples of such hypotheses will be briefly considered:

1. *The greater the size of the organization-set, the greater the degree of centralization of authority in order to prevent the "displacement of goals"* (Merton, 1957, pp 199–201) *generated by subunit loyalties and actions. In turn, an increase in centralization of authority results in an increase in the formalization of rules within the focal organization as a means of guarding against the displacement of goals.*

2. *The greater the similarity of functions between the focal organization and the members of its set, the greater the likelihood that it will compete with them. Overlapping membership, however, probably tends to mitigate competition. If overlapping membership is combined with overlapping goals and values, cooperative action that could lead to amalgamation might ensue.*

3. *The greater the complementarity of functions between the focal organization and the members of its set, the greater the likelihood of cooperative action.*

4. *The greater the capacity of the focal organization to invoke sanc-*

tions against the members of its set, the greater the likelihood of co-ordination and cooperation, provided that members of the set do not succeed in uniting in opposition to the focal organization.

5. *The greater the shortage of input resources on the part of the focal organization, the greater the likelihood that it will cooperate with the input organizations in its set and the more favorable its disposition toward amalgamation with one or more of them.* The academic "common market" being formed among midwest universities to pool their resources in graduate education is a case in point.

6. *The greater the competition between the focal organization and the members of the output organizations in its set, the more favorable is its disposition toward amalgamation, provided that the goals and values of the respective organizations are compatible.*

7. *If the members of the organization-set exhibit a high rate of technological change, the focal organization, in order to remain competitive, will be highly receptive to innovations.*

SOME METHODOLOGICAL PROBLEMS

Apart from the conceptual problems awaiting analysis in this area of research, there are measurement problems of considerable difficulty. Describing and measuring networks of interorganizational relations presents a substantial methodological challenge. Some gross behavioral indicators of interorganizational relations are number of contracts, number of clients or customers, volume of sales or services, volume of telephone calls made and received, volume of mail sent and received. Mapping interactions of organizations would require special attention to boundary personnel, as noted above, and to the patterns of interaction of organizational decision-makers. Such mapping operations of the behavior of boundary personnel and decision-makers could also yield sociometric data on which of the elements in an organization-set are perceived by different categories of members of the focal organization as "comparative reference organizations" or as "normative reference organizations." Two closely related methodological tools that may prove useful in the mapping of interorganizational relations are graph theory and input-output analysis.

GRAPH THEORY

One possible use of graph theory (Cartwright, 1959, pp. 254–271; Harary and Norman, 1953; Flament, 1963) is in the construction of an index measuring the amount of decision-making autonomy of a focal organization or of any of the elements in its set. Let us consider three highly simplified organization-set configurations approximating a "wheel," a "chain," and an "all-channel network" (cf. Bavelas, 1951; Leavitt, 1964, pp. 228–241). In the three digraphs shown in Figure 1, each point represents an organization, each line a type of interaction (a flow of information, of goods, of influence, or of personnel), and an arrow the direction of interaction.

If we take A as the focal organization in the three configurations, how do they differ in their degree of decision-making autonomy? Intuitively, we would expect that I_A ranks first in autonomy, II_A ranks second, and III_A ranks third. In the automobile industry the supplier-manufacturer-

I. WHEEL

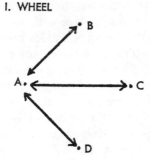

II. ALL–CHANNEL NETWORK

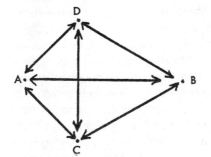

III. CHAIN

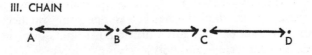

FIGURE 1
Three Organization-Set Configurations

dealer sequence of organizational relationships would suggest that the supplier is in a position comparable to III_A and that the manufacturers are in a position comparable to I_A (Ridgeway, 1957). Can we construct an index that would yield a "coefficient of interconnectedness" of elements in an organization-set—and hence decision-making autonomy—that would discriminate not only among the three simplified organization-sets shown in Figure 1 but also among other possible configurations?

INPUT-OUTPUT ANALYSIS

One input-output model that may prove useful in the study of interorganizational relations is that developed by Leontief (1953). In the study of the structure of the American economy, Leontief and his associates have, of course, concerned themselves with economic parameters such as prices, investments, and incomes. Is this mode of analysis applicable to noneconomic parameters of interorganizational relationships with which sociologists, social psychologists, and political scientists are concerned? Are the obstacles to an input-output analysis of interorganizational relations insuperable because the data most social scientists work with do not take the form of ratio scales, as is true of the data of economists? In most cases the data used by social scientists studying organizations—other than economists—frequently take the form of nominal or ordinal scales and, occasionally, interval scales, e.g., flows of information, flows of personnel, or flows of influence. Apart from the level of measurement, do noneconomic data permit the construction of "technical coefficients" of inputs to the outputs of the focal organizations?

One way of raising the question of the applicability of input-output analysis is to consider a highly simplified relationship between the members of an oligopolistic industry, such as automobile manufacturing. In Figure 2 we present a hypothetical input-output matrix consisting of the flow of influence on management decisions regarding the styling of new automobiles. It would appear from the hypothetical data in Figure 2 that G. M. is the "style leader." It receives the largest number of praiseworthy "mentions" in the minutes of management meetings of its competitors, and it in turn makes the fewest praiseworthy mentions in its meetings of its competitors' styles. Would an input-output analysis of matrices of the type shown in Figure 2—possibly in conjunction with additional data, e.g., share of the market—suggest any further operations for analyzing the data or yield any additional insights into the decision-making process concerning automobile styles?

An analogous matrix that might lend itself to an input-output analysis is shown in Figure 3. Once again it is clear from the hypothetical data that G. M. enjoys a commanding position: it has the smallest outflux of engineering personnel and the largest influx from the other automobile companies. Would an input-output analysis of this matrix, supplemented by data on other characteristics of the organizations, contribute to our understanding of the data?

The matrices shown in Figures 2 and 3 involve one point in time. Assuming that data are available for two or more time periods, can we

NUMBER OF PRAISEWORTHY MENTIONS RECEIVED BY

	A.M.	FORD	CHRYSLER	G.M.	TOTAL
A.M.		10	5	15	30
FORD	2		5	15	22
CHRYSLER	3	8		13	24
G.M.	0	4	6		10
TOTAL	5	22	16	43	

(left axis label: NUMBER OF PRAISEWORTHY MENTIONS MADE BY)

FIGURE 2
Hypothetical Matrix of Flow of
Influence on Styling Decisions in the Automobile Industry

(as Indexed by Frequency of Praiseworthy Mentions
in the Minutes of Management Meetings)

FLOW OF ENGINEERING PERSONNEL TO

	A.M.	FORD	CHRYSLER	G.M.	TOTAL
A.M.		15	5	40	60
FORD	5		5	25	35
CHRYSLER	7	8		35	50
G.M.	2	12	6		20
TOTAL	14	35	16	100	

(left axis label: FLOW OF ENGINEERING PERSONNEL FROM)

FIGURE 3
Hypothetical Flow of Engineering Personnel, 1955–1960

apply a Markov chain model to analyze the processes of change in interorganizational relations?

CONCLUSION

The foregoing methodological discussion together with the theoretical analysis may provide guidelines for new research on interorganizational relations. Of particular promise is comparative research on the organization-sets of different classes of organizations. How different are the organization-sets of economic, political, religious, educational, and cultural organizations? And what are the consequences of variations in organization-sets for the internal structure and for the decision-making process of different types of organizations? Do "coercive" organizations have a network of interactions with other organizations different from "utilitarian" and "normative" organizations (Etzioni, 1961)? How different are the organization-sets of habit, problem solving, indoctrination, and service types of organizations (Bennis, 1959, p. 299)?

Within the confines of any one class of organizations, how different are the organization-sets of, say, industrial organizations classified by industry? Similarly, what structural variations in organization-sets are observable among therapeutic versus custodial prisons (Cloward et al., 1960; Wheeler, 1961, pp. 229–259) or among hospitals differing in the importance they attach to the goals of treatment, teaching, and research?

Another possible use of organization-set analysis is in the study of intraorganizational dynamics. If each of the major functional areas in a business organization—production, sales, engineering, personnel, etc.—is taken as a unit of inquiry, an organization-set analysis would be applicable in studying interdepartmental relations. Such an approach would probably be especially useful in investigating the problem of innovation in industrial organizations (Evan, in press).

As is generally recognized, a formal organization is a particular type of social system. The study of interorganizational relations hence involves an analysis of intersocial system relations. Systematic inquiry into the interactions among various types of organizations may not only unearth new intraorganizational phenomena and processes, but may also provide the wherewithal for bridging the gap between the microscopic *organizational* and the macroscopic *institutional* levels of analysis. The solution of intersystem problems of the most aggregate level, viz., interrelations among societies, presupposes a knowledge of the nature of interorganizational interactions within and between the several institutions of a society.

REFERENCES

ABBREVIATIONS

APSR American Political Science Review
ASR American Sociological Review
ASQ Administrative Science Quarterly

Argyris, C. *Integrating the Individual and the Organization.* New York: Wiley, 1964.
———. *Personality and Organization.* New York: Harper, 1957.
Barnard, C. I. *The Functions of the Executive.* Cambridge: Harvard U. Press, 1938.
Bavalas, A. "Communication Patterns in Task-Oriented Groups." In H. Lasswell and D. Lerner, eds. *The Policy Sciences.* Stanford, Cal.: Stanford U. Press, 1951.
Bennis, W. G. "Leadership Theory and Administrative Behavior: The Problem of Authority." *ASQ,* 1959, *4,* 259–301.
Bennis, W. G., Schein, E. H.; Berlew, D. E., and Steele, F. I. *Interpersonal Dynamics: Essays and Readings on Human Interaction.* Homewood, Ill.: Dorsey, 1964.
Blau, P. M. *The Dynamics of Bureaucracy.* Chicago: U. of Chicago Press, 1955.
Cartwright, D. "The Potential Contribution of Graph Theory to Organization Theory." In M. Haire, ed. *Modern Organizational Theory.* New York: Wiley, 1959.
Cloward, R. A., Cressey, D. R., Grosser, G. N., McCleery, R., Ohlin, L. E., Sykes, G., and Messinger, S. L. *Theoretical Studies in Social Organization of the Prison.* New York: Social Science Research Council, 1960.
Costello, T. W. and Zalkind, S. S. *Psychology in Administration: A Research Orientation.* Englewood Cliffs: Prentice-Hall, 1963.
Dawson, R. H. "Congressional Innovation and Intervention in Defense Policy: Legislative Authorization of Weapons Systems." *APSR,* 1962, *56,* 42–57.
Dill, W. R., "Environment as an Influence on Managerial Autonomy," *ASQ,* 1958, *2,* 409–443.
Elling, R. H. and Halebsky, S. "Organizational Differentiation and Support: A Conceptual Framework." *ASQ,* 1961, *6,* 185–209.
Etzioni, A. *A Comparative Analysis of Complex Organizations.* New York: Free Press, 1961.
Evan, W. M., "Comment on Stewart Macaulay's 'Non-Contractual Relations in Business: A Preliminary Study.'" *ASR,* 1963a, *28,* 67–69.
———. "Indices of the Hierarchical Structure of Industrial Organizations." *Management Science,* 1963, *9,* 468–477.
———. "Organizational Lag." *Human Organization* (in press).
———. "Public and Private Legal Systems." In W. M. Evan, ed. *Law and Sociology.* New York: Free Press, 1962.

———— and Schwartz, M. A. "Law and the Emergence of Formal Organizations." *Sociology and Social Research,* 1964, *48,* 276–279.

Flament, C. *Application of Graph Theory to Group Structure.* Englewood Cliffs: Prentice Hall, 1963.

Gross, N., Mason, W. S., and McEachern, A. W. *Explorations in Role Analysis: Studies of the School Superintendency Role.* New York: Wiley, 1958.

Haire, M. "Biological Models and Empirical Histories of the Growth of Organizations." In M. Haire, ed., *Modern Organization Theory.* New York: Wiley, 1959.

Haire, M., ed. *Modern Organization Theory.* New York: Wiley, 1959.

————. *Psychology in Management.* 2nd ed. New York: McGraw-Hill, 1964.

Harary, F. and Norman, R. Z. *Graph Theory as a Mathematical Model in Social Science.* Ann Arbor: U. of Michigan Institute for Social Research, 1953.

Leavitt, H. J. *Managerial Psychology,* rev. ed. Chicago: U. of Chicago Press, 1964.

Leontief, Wassily W. et al., *Studies in the Structure of the American Economy.* New York: Oxford U. Press, 1953.

Levine, S. and White, P. E. "Exchange as a Conceptual Framework for the Study of Interorganizational Relationships." *ASQ,* 1961, *5,* 583–601.

Litwak, E. and Hylton, L. F. "Inter-organizational Analysis: A Hypothesis on Coordinating Agencies." *ASQ,* 1962. *6,* 395–426.

Macaulay, S. "Non-Contractual Relations in Business: A Preliminary Study." *ASR,* 1963. *28,* 55–67.

March, J. and Simon, H. A. *Organizations.* New York: Wiley, 1958.

Merton, R. K. *Social Theory and Social Structure* rev. ed. Glencoe, Ill.: Free Press, 1957.

Millett, J. D. *An Essay on Organization: The Academic Community.* New York: McGraw-Hill, 1962.

Palamountain, J. C., Jr. *The Politics of Distribution.* Cambridge: Harvard U. Press, 1955.

Parsons, T. "General Theory in Sociology." In R. K. Merton, Leonard Broom, and Leonard S. Cottrell, Jr., eds., *Sociology Today.* New York: Basic Books, 1959.

Parsons, Talcott. *Structure and Process in Modern Societies.* Glencoe, Ill.: Free Press, 1960.

Ridgeway, V. F. "Administration of Manufacturer-Dealer Systems." *ASQ,* 1957, *2,* 464–483.

Riley, J. W., Jr. and Levy, M. F., eds. *The Corporation and Its Publics: Essays on the Corporate Image.* New York: Wiley, 1963.

Selznick, P. *TVA and the Grass Roots: A Study in the Sociology of Formal Organization.* Berkeley and Los Angeles: U. of California Press, 1949.

Simon, H. A. *Administrative Behavior.* New York: Macmillan, 1945.

Spero, S. D. "Collective Bargaining in Public Employment: Form and Scope." *Public Administration Rev.,* 1962, *22,* 1–4.

Thompson, J. D. "Organizations and Output Transactions." *American J. Sociology,* 1962, *68,* 309–324.

Thompson, J. D. and McEwen, W. J. "Organizational Goals and Environment: Goal–setting as an Interaction Process." *ASR*, 1958, *23*, 23–31.

Wheeler, S. "Role Conflict in Correctional Communities." In D. Cressey, ed., *The Prison: Studies in Institutional Organization and Change*. New York: Holt, Rinehart & Winston, 1961.

5

Innovation in Organization: Notes Toward a Theory

JAMES Q. WILSON

Associate Professor of Government, Harvard University.

I am more than ordinarily indebted to colleagues. Several of the central hypotheses presented here were formulated in a discussion group that was part of the Ford Foundation Seminar on the Social Science of Organization, held under the auspices of the University of Pittsburgh in June, 1963. Members of that group, other than myself, were Thomas Wisler of the University of Chicago, Herbert Kaufman of Yale University, Irving Abramowitz of Ohio State University, and Dalton McFarland of Michigan State University. I, of course, must bear responsibility for the manner in which I have used their ideas.

An earlier version of this paper was given at the annual meeting of the American Political Science Association, held in New York City in September, 1963. Useful comments were received at that time from the discussants, James Robinson and James Davis, as well as from Allen Schick, Edward C. Banfield, Martha Derthick, and Peter B. Clark.

The process of organizational change is perhaps the least developed aspect of organizational theory. Innovation (somehow defined) occurs, as we all know, but it has rarely been studied systematically except at the small group level (Blau and Scott, 1962, p. 223). It has always seemed easier, and even more interesting, to analyze organizational "failures" to adapt, the displacement of goals, and the dysfunctional consequences of bureaucratization.

Although more has been written about innovation in the firm than in voluntary associations or government agencies, the state of the literature in economics is not much more satisfactory than in sociology or political science. For example, there appears to be little agreement as to whether monopolistic or competitive firms are more likely to innovate; for every case of a monopolistic firm that does innovate (e.g., du Pont introducing synthetic fibers) there is another monopoly that does not (e.g., General Electric failing to introduce the fluorescent lamp or Western Union failing to introduce the telephone). For every competitive industry with a high level of innovation (e.g., electronics firms) there seems to be another with a low propensity to innovate (e.g., textile firms) (Nelson, 1959; Fellner, 1951; Phillips, 1956; Brown, 1957; Maclauren, 1950).

Not only can little be said about the effect of market structure on innovation, but little can be said about the correlation between firm characteristics and innovation. Mansfield has shown that for certain industries firm size and the expected profitability of an innovation are positively correlated with the rate of innovation, but for these same industries there seems to be no statistically significant relationship between innovation and a firm's rate of growth, profit level, liquidity, profit trend, or age of management. Further, there is only a slight tendency for the same firms to be consistent innovators; the leaders in one innovation are very often the followers in another (Mansfield, 1961, 1963).

Although few comparably systematic studies have been made of organizations other than firms, historical and case study evidence has been assembled to show that some voluntary associations (such as the National Foundation for Infantile Paralysis, the YMCA, and the Red Cross) have adapted "successfully" to a changed environment, while others (such as the WCTU and the Townsend Movement) have not (Sills, 1957, pp. 253–270). Among government agencies, the New York

195

City Fire Department rarely innovates, while the Port of New York Authority continually innovates (Sayre and Kaufman, 1960). Innovation in a federal enforcement agency has been extensively analyzed (Blau, 1955).

It may be, of course, that what Wilbert Moore has said about theories of social change applies also to theories of organizational innovation: a "pure" theory of change, independent of some specification of *what* is changing, would be either impossible to formulate or, if formulated, empirically uninteresting (Moore, 1960). Nonetheless, there is some point in trying to think in the broadest terms about innovation generally, if only to prove that not much can be learned that way.

ORGANIZATIONS

We begin with a conception of any formal organization, the central analytical attribute of which we assume to be its economy of incentives (Clark and Wilson, 1961). An incentive is any gratification, tangible or intangible, in exchange for which persons become members of the organization ("the decision to participate") and, once in the organization, contribute time, effort, or other valued resources ("the decision to work") (March and Simon, 1958). Whatever the purpose, product, or technology of the organization, this inducements-contributions balance must first be maintained.

The executive of the organization is that person who (whatever else he does) has particular responsibility for maintaining the inducements-contributions balance. The executive may be more than one person, of course (e.g., a committee or a partnership).

Each person in the organization is performing a task (a task is all those activities that add up to the full time in the organization of one member). It is assumed that all members of the organization endeavor to act rationally, i.e., to minimize the costs and maximize the benefits to themselves of performing an organizational task, but that no two members may have precisely the same preference orderings. What is a cost to one member (e.g., the need to spend much time in conferences) may be a benefit to another (Homans, 1961).

An innovation (or, more precisely, a major innovation, since we are not concerned with trivial changes) is a "fundamental" change in a "significant" number of tasks. What is "fundamental" and "significant" cannot be given a precise, *a priori* definition, for in our scheme the meaning of these terms can only be determined by the organizations themselves. Each organization, we assume, can rank proposed (or actual) changes in terms of how "radical" they will be (or are). A change in tasks performed by ten typists may be less "important" (i.e., less radical) than the change in the task of one vice president. The executive measures proposed or actual changes in tasks in terms of the inducements-contributions balance. The greater the cost in scarce inducements, the more radical the innovation, regardless of the prospective benefits. Since these incentives include not only money payments but also prestige or status in the organization, the power of office, opportunities for rewarding social relationships, organizational purposes, and the like, the cost of an innovation is the extent to which any of these incentives must be redistributed or their supply increased. Loosely speaking, the executive of the organization assesses the cost of any innovation in terms of how much must be done to keep affected parties happy or (if the innovation calls for adding new members to the organization) what must be done (or "spent") to induce new members to contribute. Money costs are often very important, of course, but other costs may be of equal or greater importance: soothing ruffled fur, reducing uncertainty-induced anxiety, bolstering members' self-conceptions, appealing to their sense of duty, eliminating interpersonal tensions and hostilities, changing the norms of informal work groups, familiarizing workers with new technologies, finding ways to compensate demoted members for their loss of prestige and power, reformulating statements of organizational purpose. The more of these expenditures of money and effort that are required by the innovation, the more radical it is.

The prospective benefits of an innovation are assessed in the same way. The expected utility of an organizational innovation is the product of amount by which, if successful, it will enhance the supply of incentive resources and the probability that it will be successful. For some organizations wages and salaries may be the prime incentive to members, and thus net money income will be the prime incentive resource; for other organizations (including, perhaps, some business firms under certain circumstances), an intangible gratification such as organizational or personal prestige may be a crucial incentive for essential members, and thus opportunities for enhancing the organization's social standing, or the deference accorded members of it, will be the incentive resource in terms of which the benefits of a proposed innovation will be assessed.

The remainder of this paper will be an effort to indicate, in the perspective of the foregoing model of organizations, how proposals for innovations arise and how likely is their adoption. The "theory" of innovation here presented will be, of necessity, an indeterminate one. Since the members (and especially the executives) of large organizations differ in both their personal preferences for incentives and their tastes for risk, it will be impossible to say that under a specified set of circumstances any single organization or any class of organizations will respond in a particular way. All that can be said is that various circumstances increase or decrease the probability of innovation. Furthermore, we make no assumption that innovation is always good for organizations, and we do not intend our description of why some organizations are more likely to innovate to be taken as a prescription for other organizations that in some sense "ought" to innovate.

The unit of analysis is the organization, not the organization in its environment. For a variety of reasons we will not attempt to specify how environmental changes (for example, the action of a competitor or a change in the availability of resources) "cause" or "require" innovations in the organization. One reason is that we are not certain that they do in any obvious sense; the problem to be explained is why some organizations and not others respond adaptively to environmental changes. Further, we hope to show that for purposes of analysis it is useful to conceive of the organization as "sensing" its environment by means of a certain mechanism—the incentive system and the task structure—and as assessing environmental changes not directly but indirectly as they are presented to it through the demands of organization members.

We make two assumptions about the environment: that it is organizationally complex and that it is rich in potential resources (capital, skills, consumers, attentive elites). What is said here about organizational innovation may thus be wholly inappropriate for other societies (or even parts of our own society) that have relatively few organizations and a scarcity of potential resources.

THE CENTRAL HYPOTHESES

Innovation in an organization occurs in three stages: the conception of the change (strictly speaking, this is invention, not innovation), the proposing of the change, and the adoption and implementation of the change. We hypothesize that the probability of innovation activity at any of these three stages is principally a function of the diversity of the organization. Diversity in turn is a function of both the complexity of the *task structure* and the *incentive system*.

The *task structure* (i.e., the sum of all tasks, or one-man duties, in the organization) increases in complexity as the number of different tasks increases and as the proportion of nonroutine tasks increases. By nonroutine tasks we mean tasks that involve a minimum of prescribed, repetitive operations. If all operations in a given task are prescribed in advance and if those operations are essentially repeated from day to day, the task is entirely routine. In Herbert Simon's terminology, the task is highly "programmed." Routine or programmed tasks are more easily made subject to organizational control than are nonroutine tasks, either through supervision (checking on the performance of prescribed operations or on the attainment of certain rates of production, a certain quality of production, or both) or through mechanical and organizational "linkages," e.g., linking a number of routine tasks by arranging them on an assembly line moving at a predetermined pace.

The *incentive system* (i.e., the sum of all rewards given to members) increases in complexity as the number of sources of incentives increases, and these in turn increase in number with an increase in the number of groups (both membership and reference groups, both inside and outside the formal organization) with which each member is affiliated. Affiliation with any group is based (in accordance with the general conceptual framework underlying this theory) on receiving gratifications from that group; the more different groups with which the member is affiliated, the more potentially varied the kinds of satisfactions the member receives. Naturally, not all affiliations are relevant to organizational innovation; only those affiliations that require the member to conform to some extent to expectations relevant to the innovating organization's activities in return for whatever gratifications he receives will constitute an affiliation that acts as a constraint on his behavior in that organization.

Obviously one important source of an increase in the complexity of the incentive system is an increase in the complexity of the task structure, and thus the two aspects of organizational diversity are in part related. If the task structure becomes more complicated, it will in the typical case require the creation within the organization of subunits, the adding of more supervisory positions or levels, and perhaps the decentralization of operations. The creation of such subunits, particularly ones that are geographically dispersed or organizationally decentralized, normally results in the generation of subunit loyalties among members of the organization. If the subunit is sufficiently autonomous, more than simple loyalty may be at stake: the subunit may play as great or greater part than the organization as a whole in determining salary, promotions, and assignments. Thus, the larger the number of organizationally defined subunits, the greater the diversity of the organization—because both the task structure and the incentive system become more complex.

But the incentive system may be complex for reasons having nothing to do with the task structure. Organization members may be affiliated with (or identify with) informal work or social groups within the organization or with external associations and groups, such as trade unions, professional societies, colleague groups, political factions (Blau and Scott, 1962, pp. 60–74; Gouldner, 1958). The number and strength of such attachments complicate the incentive system by providing rewards that are not under direct organizational control. These extraorganizational (or nonorganizational) incentives are important to the extent the member values them and to the extent that the behavior they reward is clearly defined. Some such groups (e.g., an association of professional educators) may provide rather vague cues to action; others (e.g., an association of mathematicians) may provide very explicit ones. Further, some persons may value such rewards very highly (e.g., an economist who plans to return on the strength of his professional reputation to a university he left for service in a government agency), while others value them only slightly (e.g., an economist who has decided to forsake academia in favor of a position in private enterprise).

These two attributes of organizational diversity—task structure and incentive system,—are, of course, related. The tasks of the member are the costs he must bear; in exchange for so doing he receives rewards. The task structure is the manner in which the organization (more precisely, its executives) has allocated effort; the incentive system is the manner in which the organization and other groups and associations over which the organization is likely to have little control have allocated rewards. Organizational maintenance requires the executive constantly to find and distribute incentives. The role would be a simple one if there were a perfect "fit" between effort and reward such that a task once defined would be repeatedly performed by an individual once induced. This is rarely the case. The act of performing the task generates over time slightly different expectations, which are met with slightly altered incentives. The effort to find incentives for others (e.g., by making the organization increase in productivity) alters the existing distribution of effort and rewards, and further—indeed, endless—adjustments are necessary. Incremental changes are thus a constant feature of organizational life.

We argue here that the greater the diversity of the organization (in either its incentive system or its task structure or both), the *greater* the likelihood that some members will *conceive* major innovations, the *greater* the likelihood that some members will *propose* innovations, and the *less* likelihood that the organization will *adopt* the innovations. The reasoning behind these hypotheses follows.

Hypothesis 1: The greater the diversity of the organization, the greater the probability that members will conceive of major innovations.

A highly complex task structure inhibits close supervision, the precise specification of operations, and the linking of tasks in some mechanical fashion. Either ends or means will be only vaguely specified. (In the most complex task structure of all—organizationally uninhibited "basic" research—neither the ends nor the means of the member's task can be specified at all.) In a complex task structure each member's task will to some extent be tailored by him to suit his own methods and style. There will be few standards the organization can use to maintain conformity among members. Each member can plausibly claim some justification for conceiving his job differently than others conceive their outwardly similar jobs. This complexity means that activity anywhere in the organization will probably affect its members differentially. In the absence of clear performance criteria and in the presence of a variety of conceptions of nominally identical tasks, each member will try to define his own job for himself.

A highly complex incentive system maximizes the probability that each member will be confronted with slightly—even considerably— different expectations governing his membership and performance. The greater the variety and complexity of rewards, the greater the incentive to conceive of ways in which one's task can be altered to maximize the attainment of some particular mix of rewards that the member values.

The most diverse organization, such as a collection of loosely organized scientists conducting basic research in a variety of fields, will produce the highest number of innovative conceptions.

Hypothesis 2: The greater the diversity of the organization, the greater the probability that major innovations will be proposed.

A task structure and incentive system that encourages new ideas will tend to encourage proposals embodying these new ideas. Behavior in a large formal organization is likely to be different from behavior in a small group—in part because in a small group tasks are (at any given moment) likely to be simple and the incentives almost entirely intra-organizational. But in addition, the suggestion of new ideas in the small group is likely to be low if any member feels threatened by the possibility that his idea will be rejected or even scorned. He has no support other than his own daring and the possible good-will and approval of his associates. In a large, diverse organization with many subunits there are likely to be many innovative proposals that are likely to find support in some face-to-face group even though they run the risk of organizational rejection. In short, the more diverse the organization, the greater the likelihood of finding allies. Further, in a highly diverse organization the social distance between members and executives is likely to be great; proposals can be made and rejected impersonally, thus minimizing the cost of both proposing and rejecting.

Proposals are made both to adapt tasks so that costs (i.e., effort) are reduced and to increase rewards. The greater the diversity of the organization, the greater the likelihood that costs and benefits are in an unstable equilibrium. Since diversity means that any activity, including an innovation, is likely to affect members differentially, new activity will require a widespread readjustment of efforts and rewards. This is the chain-reaction effect. The chain reaction does not continue indefinitely, of course, because (as explained below) there are limits to the tolerance organizations will extend to even those innovations that are adaptive responses to changes it has already approved.

If members make proposals only after balancing the expected utility of the change against the costs of proposing it, then it may not be self-evident that even a highly diverse organization encourages innovative proposals. If, as we shall argue below, organizational diversity *reduces* the probability that a proposal will be adopted, and if a rejection would be counted as a cost by the person making the proposal, then it could be argued that diversity, by minimizing the chances of getting a proposal adopted, also minimizes the likelihood that anyone will make it.

There are several answers to this. First, many proposals must be rejected not because their prospective benefits to the organization are negligible but because the cost of obtaining consent to them is too high. In short, many are rejected, not "on their merits," but for essentially political reasons: it is too costly to concert the wills of organization members sufficient to implement the proposal. Thus, the proposer may be rewarded (by being thought a "bright fellow") even if his idea is turned down. Second, the greater the diversity of the organization, the greater the incentive members and subunits have in acquiring bargaining power, one against another. Whatever value a member attaches to the probability of being made better off by an innovation, he will invariably have an interest in avoiding being made worse off. To protect the status quo, the member will make counterproposals, offer suggestions to acquire bargaining power, or initiate limited changes in order to forestall greater (and less desirable) changes.

Hypothesis 3: The greater the diversity of the organization, the smaller the proportion of major innovative proposals that will be adopted.

To adopt a proposal the executive of a large organization must exercise influence over affected organization members. The more complex the task structure and incentive system, the greater the difficulty (i.e., the greater the cost) in wielding the influence. A complex task structure makes detailed control of the members' activities by the organization difficult: either means or ends or both will be difficult to specify. To the extent that such specification and supervision are not possible, it will be difficult to make the distribution of rewards dependent upon changing behavior. Further, the more complex the task structure, the less likely it is that the executive will be sufficiently knowledgable about members' work to run the risk of instituting an innovation without obtaining their consent (Clark, 1961). Only to the degree that he understands the organization's technology can he innovate entirely on his own authority; lacking this understanding, he must rely to some significant extent on the opinions of subordinates as to the feasibility, costs, and benefits of the proposed change. But a complex task structure also means that many members will be affected differentially by any major change; this in turn increases the probability that there will be disagreement among members about the merits of the change. Unless the executive has a high taste for risk, he must attempt to resolve this conflict, usually by redistributing incentives in such a way that aggrieved members are somehow compensated for the losses they will incur because of the innovation.

But if the organization also has a complex incentive system, such compensating moves by the executive will be difficult to carry out. The larger the number of incentives from extraorganizational sources (or other sources not directly subject to the executive's control), the greater the difficulty in using incentives to induce members to accept innovations (except, of course, in those cases where there happens to be a congruence between the activities required by the innovation and the activities rewarded by the extraorganizational incentives). The greater the value members attach to rewards they receive from informal work groups, professional societies, external colleague groups, trade unions, and the like, the less the relative value of those rewards the executive controls (e.g., pay, definition of purposes, prestige of office).

The process of adopting innovations can be looked upon as essentially a political one characterized by bargaining; the more diverse the organization, the more bargaining must occur before changes can be made. Inasmuch as incentives are by definition scarce, gratifying one member's demands for change (i.e., adopting his proposals) can usually be done only at a cost to other members—and the cost rises with increases in task complexity. Such proposals therefore elicit counterclaims (resistance, alternative proposals, threats). The executive seeks to reconcile the competing claims by mediation, by slowing the pace of events to insure that all affected parties are heard from, by finding new or alternative incentives to compensate members for losses (in game-theory language, by distributing side payments to convert zero-sum games into non-zero-sum games), and by searching for information that will indicate the limits of "tolerable" innovation.

The winning of consent for proposed innovations is costly to the executive *at the level at which the innovation is to take effect.* A highly diversified organization may also be a decentralized organization, that is, one in which authority over a predetermined range of choices is delegated to particular subunits. A certain proposal may more easily be adopted if it is dealt with by a subunit rather than by the organization as a whole because in the subunit there are fewer wills to concert. This fact might lead one to suppose that decentralization (and thus diversity) increases, rather than decreases, the probability of adoption of innovations. This supposition, however, is unwarranted, for it is based on a confusion of levels of analysis. The diversity of the organization must be determined for the unit or level to be affected by the innovation; the problem of adoption is a problem for the executive(s) of the unit affected. That a subunit of a decentralized organization can adopt a proposal does not mean that diversity has facilitated adoption, for the diversity of the whole organization is irrelevant to the politics of the subunit so long as the adoption of the proposal is irrelevant to the whole organization. In short, the application of all three central hypotheses requires first a careful specification of the organizational level to which they are to refer.

Finally, the limited resources available to the executive prevent the chain-reaction effect discussed earlier from continuing without end. In the short run, however, there will be a chain reaction; viewed retrospectively, innovations will seem to have occurred in clusters (Sofer, 1961). This is in part because the price of obtaining the consent of members to one innovation is often to adopt other innovations that will benefit them (or at least reduce the cost to them of the original change). A "package deal" will be negotiated. The chain-reaction effect may also be in part the result of a temporary lowering of the resistance to change: the organization is seized with an enthusiasm for change, perhaps because the successful adoption of one change encourages others to think that further changes are not so costly as they had believed. As with human passions, however, the enthusiasms of organizations are typically short-lived.

SOME RELATED HYPOTHESES

This general orientation (it is too much to call it a theory, since its main elements have not been stated in "operational" form) to the study of innovation suggests certain more specific hypotheses:

1. *If organizational diversity is directly proportional to the rate of proposals and inversely proportional to the rate of adoptions, little can be said about the total number (or the frequency) of adopted innova-*

tions in organizations. The net effect of these contrary tendencies would depend entirely on the steepness of the two curves; all that can be suggested from a theoretical point of view is their direction. This in itself may explain why the evidence on whether large or small organizations are more innovative is inconclusive. Nor can practitioners of organizational design find much use in the theory presented here; unless (as seems unlikely) numerical values could be attached to the rates of proposal and adoption for whole classes of organizations, there will be no way to determine an optimum point where, in effect, a marginal increase in the probability of additional proposals will just equal the marginal decline in the probability of their adoption.[1]

Such considerations as these may shed light on a problem familiar to the author: how can one compare the innovative capacities of two city governments, one of which is characterized by a high degree of centralization, the other by a low degree? Chicago's government is informally centralized by a political boss whose machine has almost complete control of the incentive system of key members of the administration and of almost all members of the city council (Banfield, 1961). New York has a city government that is decentralized; the formal, legal dispersion of power is not overcome by informal centralization under party auspices. Key administration members are attracted by a wide variety of rewards over which the nominal head of the administration, the mayor, has little or no control, e.g., the possibility of an independent political career, of advancement to higher posts within semiautonomous boards and commissions, of conforming to internally valued or externally rewarded professional expectations and standards, of entering into alliances with civic associations and newspapers for whatever benefits they can bestow, and so forth. In New York, new proposals are constantly being generated by many persons within the administration; each proposal, however, "must run a gauntlet that is often fatal" (Sayre and Kaufman, 1961, p. 716). There are literally scores of opportunities for others to intervene and register a decisive veto. In Chicago there is no such gauntlet; only the mayor's (i.e., the boss's) views count, and what he decides becomes policy. At the same time, relatively few proposals are generated within the administration; the real sources of innovations are private associations and groups that compete for the mayor's attention. (Such outside groups are also active in New York,

1. This is not merely a difficulty, but an impossibility. Material incentives are the cornerstone of economics precisely because they may have money prices—and hence numerical values—assigned to them. Once nonmaterial incentives are introduced (as they almost inevitably must be in a discussion of organizational innovation), such values cannot be calculated and determinate solutions cannot be obtained.

of course, but there they can usually count on having a governmental agency or bureaucrat as their overt ally.) Whether Chicago or New York is more innovative depends on the result of the operation of these contrary tendencies (Banfield and Wilson, 1963, chap. xxiii).

Although the inverse relationship between the rate of proposals and the probability of their adoption makes it difficult to predict in the ordinary case which of two organizations is more likely to be innovative, *extreme* differences in organizational diversity seem to be clearly related to differences in the level of innovation. A university research team is probably more innovative than a stenographic pool; apparently there is some (unknown) point beyond which further increases in diversity cause the rate of proposals to increase faster than the difficulty of securing their adoption—at least for some kinds of tasks. (The researchers' innovations may not be more significant, however, if the cost in inducements of their adoption is lower than is the cost of the adoption of the stenographers' innovations. The significance or radicality of the innovation from the organization's point of view should not be confused with its significance from society's point of view.) The pessimistic conclusion that organizational designers cannot use this theory of innovation to make any given organization "more innovative" must be modified to allow for the gross differences in levels of innovation between two quite dissimilar organizations. (In practice, of course, this concession probably will not offer much real solace, for the task of organizational designers is typically to introduce marginal changes in a single organization, not to convert it into a wholly different kind of organization. The theory does not permit one to predict whether diversifying a stenographic pool will make it more innovative; reality does not permit one to convert stenographers into physicists.)

There is considerable evidence that organizations with large proportions of "professional" personnel are more innovative than those with small proportions of professionals.

Stinchcombe (1960) has shown that "progressive" firms (impressionistically determined) have a higher proportion of professionals among their top workers than "stagnant" firms. Hill and Harbison (1959) have shown that industrial firms that innovated extensively between 1947 and 1955 also increased their employment of professionals during that period. Stinchcombe (1960) has reanalyzed their data to show that the innovating firms not only hire more professionals but also entered the period of innovation with more professionals.

Browning (1963) has compared two departments in a state government, one of which was (by a variety of measures) more innovative than the other. The innovative agency was far more "professionalized" than the other and had (in my terms) a much more complex incentive system (for example, the innovative department subscribed to 105 professional journals and sent its personnel on 281 trips to 91 out-of-state professional meetings; the other departments subscribed to only eleven journals and sent its personnel on only nine trips to five different meetings). Browning concludes that neither political nor technological changes accounted for the innovative department's behavior, but rather its own incentive system: "The main sources of new policies for the innovative, rapidly growing Welfare Department are neither local clientele demands nor shifting technology. They are the members of several professions, usually working in . . . universities, in private nonprofit welfare institutions, and in [other government agencies]" (p. 14).

That persons who are "cosmopolitans" are more likely to adopt innovations than "locals" has been well established for individuals outside the context of large formal organizations (Rogers, 1962, pp. 42, 44, 51, 228, 310). Carlson (1961) has shown that school superintendents recruited from outside the system are more likely to propose innovations than those recruited from inside. Few studies exist, however, relating the implementation of innovations within organizations to the professional or cosmopolitan character of the personnel. And as Benson (1961) has suggested, the great complexity of the instructional task and difficulty of supervising its execution have been two important reasons for the slowness of schools to innovate despite the professional orientation of the staffs.

2. *It is easier (less costly) to increase an organization's capacity to generate new proposals than it is to increase its capacity to ratify any given proposal.* The former requires adding new and somewhat differently motivated personnel, increasing the autonomy of subunits, or increasing the number of different tasks being performed, but the latter requires assembling power (enhancing the supply of valued incentives at the executive's disposal). Furthermore, increasing the proposal-generating capacity of the organization may not only make adoption more difficult by increasing the number of wills to be concerted but may also make it harder by increasing all member's valuation of the status quo. For example, in an effort to get new ideas introduced into the organization, "idea men" (e.g., a Vice President for Innovation) might be hired. The cost of such a move may well be an increased resistance to change by other members, who feel threatened by this move; it seems to increase the probability of unpredictable changes, so members respond by taking whatever steps they can to reduce that probability (e.g., by bestirring themselves to point out to others the risks of change).

This hypothesis may help account for the finding by Mansfield (1961) that the productivity of expenditures on research and development is lower in the largest firms than in the medium-sized ones (holding the absolute amount of such expenditures constant). While it is true that for any given firm size bigger R&D expenditures lead to more significant inventions for the firm, firms whose R&D expenditures are a larger proportion of the firm's total budget are more inventive than firms in which the proportion is smaller. Mansfield suggests that may be due to "looser controls and greater problems of supervision and co-ordination in a very large organization" (p. 15). In terms of the present theory, this apparent anomaly would be explained by the fact that the political influence within the firm of the R&D unit, and thus the ability of the unit to win acceptance for its proposed innovations (and for its research plans), increases the larger the share of the firm's resources it commands. Sheer size may produce more ideas, but insofar as innovation requires getting persons to accept the ideas, influence is necessary; the greater the *share* of the firm's resources spent by R&D, the less the diversity of the firm *as a whole*, and thus the less the influence required.

3. *Proponents of a particular innovation are not likely to perceive fully the difficulties that stand in the way 'of successful innovation* (Levitt, 1963). The proponent of a change is likely to see the benefits of the proposal in personal terms and the costs in organizational terms; everyone else is likely to see the benefits in organizational terms and the costs in personal terms. To the proponent the prospective benefits are (in most, though not all, cases) direct and easily conceived; the costs are remote, something "the organization" will deal with. To organization members who will be affected by the change the costs to them are likely to be directly and immediately felt; the benefits are something that will accrue remotely to "the organization." The executive is the person who must discover whether there are any terms on which objections can be overcome; he is likely to be the only person (or persons, if it is a collective executive) to whom *both* costs *and* benefits are directly perceived in personal terms—success or failure of the innovation is ultimately his responsibility, and the effort to adopt it is inevitably his task.

4. *Many organizations will adopt no major innovation unless there is a "crisis"*—an extreme change in conditions for which there is no adequate, programmed response. A crisis increases the probability that innovations will be ratified by increasing the cost to any member of opposing the ratification. If all members are persuaded that a crisis exists (if, for example, the firm cannot meet its payroll, or if the voluntary association is in danger of losing most of its members), then those who resist adopting the most favored innovation place themselves in the position of, in effect, favoring the death of the organization and therefore favoring the imposition of heavy costs on all other members.

Further, a crisis leads members to devote themselves to *organizational interests* rather than to task interests; the diversifying influence of the task structure is thereby temporarily set aside. Similarly, the crisis tends to eliminate the normal discrepancy between individual and organizational objectives, which it is the function of the incentive system to reconcile. The short-term value of organizationally controlled incentives increases because they are being threatened by the crisis; other incentives are presumably not in jeopardy, and, although their long-term value may remain unchanged, they are in effect discounted in the short term.

Empirical studies of the relationship between crisis and innovation have shown that an economic crisis led to faster rate of adoption of local industrial-development commissions in Iowa towns and that labor shortages led to a faster rate of adoption of a cotton-spinning innovation in English firms and to increased farm mechanization in Louisiana (studies summarized in Rogers, 1962, p. 125).

5. *Organizations that rely primarily on intangible incentives (as do voluntary associations, will display in exaggerated form the contrary tendencies that determine the innovative capacity of all organizations.* They will have a higher level of diversity and, as a consequence, the number of innovative proposals will be higher than in organizations that rely primarily on material inducements (such as business firms or government agencies). In the typical voluntary association, for example, the organization occupies a position of relatively low salience in the lives of most members; within the association, roles and tasks are less specialized, less clearly defined, and less demanding of a member's time than is typically the case in an organization that offers gainful employment to the member. As a result, demographic and personality variables (e.g., class, education, political affiliation, religion, marital status) become highly important as sources of diversity. The less structured the role, the less likely that individual behavior can be predicted on the basis of role occupancy; the personal characteristics of the member control behavior to a much greater extent, producing thereby a highly diverse organization. Furthermore, the organization has less opportunity to control behavior because it can only utilize incentives that are more general or indivisible than specific, money incentives (if a general incentive is given to one person, it must be given to all) and because such incentives are often not so highly valued as money incentives. Finally, the organization convenes in *meetings* rather than *around tasks*; in the nature of the case, the organization's business is everybody's business, and members are typically expected to make proposals.

All of these factors might be summarized by saying that a non-pecuniary organization must tolerate a great deal of foolishness if it is to survive. Whether it will adopt a greater or lesser proportion of these innovative proposals than will a pecuniary organization depends on the case. If the organization has a high salience for members (as, for example, the Socialist Party had for its members in the 1920's), a high value will be attached to the costs and benefits of new proposals and—lacking control over comparably highly-valued incentives with which to obtain compliance—the executive will find it exceptionally diffi- cult to ratify any new proposal that is not widely supported (and few proposals *will* be widely supported). If, on the other hand, the associa- tion has a low salience for its members, few may care enough what the organization does to block any plausible proposal (although they may well care how they are regarded personally by other members, and thus actively make proposals).

Looked at in organizational rather than in individual terms, a volun- tary association with broad, diffuse goals (typically associated with relatively low salience) will adapt more readily to environmental changes than will organizations with narrow, precisely stated goals (typically associated with high salience). Zald and Denton (1963) found that broad, diffuse goals contributed to the adaptability of the YMCA; Messinger (1955) suggested that the precise goals of the Townsend Movement inhibited its adaptability. In the former case the organization was able to offer a wide range of membership inducements without alienating any significant group of members; in the latter case, a change in inducements could only be accomplished at the cost of driving out one set of members in favor of another.

6. *Environmental changes that to the outside observer "objectively" seem to "require" innovation by the organization are likely to lead to such innovation only insofar as these changes alter the preferences of mem- bers for incentives (by changing present or prospective costs or benefits of participation in the organization).* The many organizations that ob- servers describe as having "failed" to "adapt" are often organizations that are being judged exclusively in terms of their goals (and then only in terms of their public, stated goals) and what is "objectively" necessary to attain those goals. Whether a failure to attain a goal will lead to innovation depends on whether members regard attainment of (or work toward) that goal as a reward of participation. Many organizations, of course, do have such goals (we call them "purposive" or "ideological" organizations); many more do not.

The distinction between goal and incentive may help account for the oft-noted tendency of many business firms to sacrifice short-run profit maximization for other objectives. As William Baumol suggests, many—

perhaps most—oligopolistic firms act as if they were trying to maximize sales revenue (or, perhaps more correctly, growth of sales revenue) subject to a minimum profit constraint (Baumol, 1959, 1962). Among the reasons for this is that the interests of management are often better served by a sales, rather than by a profit, objective; a favorable sales position produces more rewards for management than a favorable profit position, particularly if management has only a minor equity stake in the firm. Declining sales (whatever the profit level) may create a state of affairs in which certain members (such as distributors and salesmen working on commission) threaten to withdraw, in which firing rather than hiring becomes the order of the day, thus making personnel relations in the firm unpleasant, and in which management salaries may suffer (since salaries are empirically more closely correlated with the scale rather than with the profitability of operations [Roberts, 1959]).

The goal-incentive distinction also suggests some crucial differences in the behavior of voluntary associations that help explain why some associations "adapt" while others do not. Some associations are "enrollment" organizations, while others are "membership" organizations. The YMCA (Zald and Denton, 1963) and many adult education programs (Clark, 1956) are examples of the former; reform political clubs (Wilson, 1962) are examples of the latter. Organizations that sustain themselves by enrolling "users" are sensitive to user tastes for programs. They view the organization as a source of divisible benefits; they use services rather than attend meetings, they feel free to select their satisfactions from among those offered, and they withdraw if nothing suits them. Membership organizations, on the other hand, offer largely indivisible benefits; members benefit from, and identify with, the whole organization rather than consume its services. It is the total character of the organization—particularly its goals and general associational attractiveness—that constitute its inducements. Under such circumstances the organization's executive finds it harder both to know the tastes of the members (they can vote, but only in elections, not in a service "market") and to change goals and associational attributes to meet altered tastes. Thus, although the nominal goal of two organizations might be the same (e.g., serve the neighborhood), failure to attain the goal—or environmental changes that require new strategies to attain it—is more likely to lead to organizational innovation in the enrollment organization, in which the value of incentives are precisely measured against users' tastes, than in the membership organization, in which the value of incentives depends on members' *commitments* rather than tastes.

7. *Decentralization can be regarded as a method for increasing the probability of ratification of new proposals by confining (in advance)*

their effect to certain subunits. It is often regarded as a means of increasing efficiency (i.e., the ratio of valued output to valued input), and, of course, that is frequently the case; but it can just as easily be viewed as a way of reducing the obstacles to ratification without seriously increasing the risk. By decentralizing an organization, that is, by giving to subunits a high degree of autonomy in the control of their own incentive and task structures, the organization as a whole reduces the number of wills that must be concerted before a proposal generated within the subunit can be adopted. A subunit can ratify a proposal that would be smothered if it had to compete with all proposals from all subunits. There is a cost to such decentralization of course: the parent organization, by increasing the autonomy of subunits, may make it more difficult for it to manage these subunits with respect to those matters over which the parent organization retains control. In addition, only certain kinds of organizations—generally those that have tasks and objectives that can be unambiguously specified and measured—can risk extensive decentralization. If subunit performance cannot be precisely assessed, its behavior cannot be controlled and thus kept consistent with overall objectives.

The decentralization of the YMCA, according to Zald and Denton (1963), facilitated the adoption of innovations by various local units before other, apparently similar, units were even aware of the need for such changes. The National Foundation, on the other hand, was sufficiently centralized so that, according to Sills (1957), the *entire* organization was able to innovate quickly in response to a threat to its very existence even though no subunit had previously experimented with such changes.

8. *The extent to which "participative management" will stimulate the production of proposals or facilitate the adoption and implementation of innovations will depend upon, among other things, the extent to which the decision-making group itself becomes a highly valued source of incentives and the extent to which these group-based incentives are congruent with those offered by the larger organization.* The great theoretical importance attached by certain students of organization to group decision-making, participative management, and power equalization in organizations (especially business firms) stands in rather sharp contrast to the meager empirically verified results of the application of such theories. Strauss (1963) and Bennis (1963), summarizing the literature on this approach, conclude that it is by no means clear how likely or under what circumstances participation will improve worker satisfaction, increase productivity, or stimulate organizational innovation.

Substituting collegial for hierarchical methods of making decisions is widely advocated, yet there has been little effort to specify the organizational conditions under which collegiality will facilitate innovation; furthermore, few clear data have been produced to establish a relationship between the method by which a change is developed and improvements in the performance of the individual or the organization (Bennis, 1963, p. 159). Such devices as "T-group" training conducted under laboratory conditions often change the behavior of the subjects of the experiment, but we cannot be certain that this altered behavior persists after the subjects return to the organization or, if it persists, that it facilitates organizational change. Shepard's evaluation of his work with the Esso Company suggests that the laboratory experience was "slightly more helpful than useless" in changing the organization (Bennis, 1963). The experiment of Morse and Reimer (1956) was one of the few done in an organization rather than in the laboratory. While the group of clerical employees subjected to participatory supervision seemed to manifest more worker satisfaction, the group exposed to hierarchical supervision was the more productive. Likert (1961), on the other hand, indicates some evidence favoring the belief that organizational as well as personal benefits flow from participation.

On the basis of the theory of innovation presented here, one would expect a well-established participative management group would propose a larger number of innovations than isolated individuals working in a hierarchy in which innovative suggestions are rewarded by the group. In short, the organization has been made more complex by increasing the diversity of sources of incentives. One would also expect, however, that the probability of the adoption (including implementation) of any given proposal would depend on (a) whether the incentives offered by the decision-making group were valued sufficiently to induce members to alter customary behavior in order to obtain them and (b) whether the behavior induced by group incentives was compatible with that required by organizational incentives. As critics of the participative management movement point out, not everyone has the same taste for collegial decision-making and the opportunity it supposedly affords for cooperation, problem-solving, and "self-actualization." Some persons have a taste for routine, deference, power, and certainty or a desire to reserve for nonorganizational settings their self-expression.

That the effect of participative management on organizational change depends on member preferences for certain incentives is suggested by Strauss's explanation (1963, p. 67) of the difference between the results of the Harwood and Norway experiments. In the Harwood case (Coch and French, 1948) participation led to higher productivity because the opportunity to participate was highly valued by low-status rural female employees; participation did not lead to productivity increases in Norway (French, Israel, and Dagfinn, 1960) because such inducements had a much lower value for the more sophisticated urbanized male workers.

Participation in the simplest case may reduce resistance to planned change insofar as it provides an opportunity whereby certain *dis*incentives can be eliminated or reduced (by giving members a chance to talk out their grievances, discharge generalized resentment, and partially overcome feelings of inferior status). Whether participation can go much further cannot be predicted in advance for all cases, because too much depends on preferences for incentives. The fact that the theory of participative management, seen from the present theoretical viewpoint, cannot lead to unique predictions about outcomes might be grounds for qualifying some of the claims made on its behalf. It is worth remembering that informal work groups that *restrict* production and enforce quotas are also examples of a kind of participative management.

9. *Innovative proposals will be more frequent in organizations in which a high degree of uncertainty governs the members' expectation of rewards.* If incentives are not routinely received for the performance of specified acts, there will be a tendency for members either to quit the organization (having a low taste for risk and uncertainty) or to bid competitively with one another for a share of available incentives by advancing proposals. This pattern of management has been institutionalized, as Burns and Stalker (1961) point out, in certain British electronics firms. Committee management and group decision-making were instituted in the first place to deal with a special organizational environment—one characterized by a high rate of technological invention, a high level of competition, and the domination of a single, unpredictable buyer (the government). These electronics firms attempted to deal with their highly uncertain environment by organizing themselves in such a way as to maximize the flow of information, extend the search for alternatives, and develop a generalized commitment on the part of all members to the survival of the firm. The cost of this management system is a high degree of personal insecurity, because members have no clear conception of their duties, status, authority, or prospects. These costs must be met by the incentive system in some way. In this case one would expect the firm to stress that the unstructured situation eliminates seniority barriers to advancement, to distribute widely such intangible gratifications as titles and opportunities for access to the president, and to emphasize the importance of the work to the scientific community and to the nation as a whole. Once instituted, these arrangements (a highly complex task structure and incentive system) could be expected to increase markedly the number of innovative proposals but reduce

(whether by a corresponding amount is not clear) the ability of the organization to win consent for any single proposal.

Burns and Stalker draw the contrast of certain rayon textile firms (also in Great Britain) whose environment was much more stable (they dealt with a large number of small buyers with predictable tastes) and who could consequently organize themselves along more traditional, hierarchical lines with little reliance on nonmonetary incentives and a heavy emphasis on highly specific tasks.

10. *To the extent that members of a society attach a high value to extraorganizational, particularly nonmaterial, incentives, there will be an increased number of inventions (i.e., proposals) but a decreased probability of organizational innovation.* This may be an important policy implication of the foregoing analysis. In an affluent society in which a high standard of living is coupled with government measures that tend to equalize income (a steeply progressive income tax) and to prevent citizens from receiving private gain for performing public tasks (the elimination of political patronage, for example), organizations—especially those that act in the public sphere—may find themselves relying on incentives that stimulate invention but hamper the adoption of innovations. As money payments diminish in value (at the margin) and nonmoney payments increase in value, the organization will rely more and more on the latter. This will not only make life more difficult for the social scientist (behavior is harder to predict unambiguously when unmeasurable objectives, such as prestige, power, and ideology, are being sought), but it will also weaken the influence of organization executives, partly because nonmaterial rewards are less specific in their effect and partly because they are harder to bring under the control of the organization.

This may account for the apparently paradoxical fact that communities with high proportions of persons who individually favor such innovations as fluoridation and urban renewal are also communities with the lowest rates of adoption of such proposals (Hawley, 1963; Pinard, 1963). Banfield and Wilson (1963) have suggested that since the preference for such controversial innovations is higher among middle-class than among lower-class individuals and that since communities with a high proportion of middle-class citizens are more likely to be governed in accordance with the "good government" ideal, the inability to translate personal preferences into public policy may be the result of the weakness of the political structure. The political and governmental arrangements characteristic of middle-class communities tend to emphasize honesty, efficiency, and impartiality but are often incapable of assembling the amounts of influence necessary to adopt a controversial innovation. Perhaps this is because a preoccupation with procedural proprieties makes it impossible for the government to offer specific, material incentives to politicians and voters in order to permit the centralization of influence sufficient to ratify any but generally accepted proposals.

To the extent that innovation involves interorganizational relations (such as relations between political parties and interest groups), the changes described in the preceding paragraph may make such relations less stable as executives find it increasingly difficult to control the behavior of members and thus to deliver on commitments made to other organizations. Such considerations may in turn have the profoundest implications for social change generally, and not simply for innovation within organizations.

REFERENCES

ABBREVIATIONS

ASQ   *Administrative Science Quarterly*
HR   *Human Relations*
ASR   *American Sociological Review*
JASP *Journal of Abnormal and Social Psychology*

Banfield, E. C. *Political Influence.* New York: Free Press of Glencoe, 1961.
————— and Wilson, J. Q. *City Politics.* Cambridge: Harvard U. Press, 1963.
Baumol, W. J. *Business Behavior, Value and Growth.* New York: Macmillan, 1959.
—————. "On the Theory of Expansion of the Firm." *American Economic Review,* 1962, 52, 1078–1087.
Bennis, W. G. "A New Role for the Behavioral Sciences: Effecting Organizational Change." *ASQ,* September 1963, 8, 125–165.
Benson, C. S. *The Economics of Public Education.* Boston: Houghton Mifflin, 1961.
Blau, P. M. *The Dynamics of Bureaucracy.* Chicago: U. of Chicago Press, 1955.
————— and Scott, Richard M. *Formal Organizations.* San Francisco: Chandler, 1962.
Brown, W. H. "Innovation in the Machine Tool Industry." *Quarterly J. Economics,* 1957, 71, 406–425.
Browning, R. P. "Innovative and Non-Innovative Decision Processes in Government Budgeting." Paper read before the annual meeting of the American Political Science Association, New York City, September 1963.
Burns, T. and Stalker, G. M. *The Management of Innovation.* London: Tavistock, 1961.

Carlson, R. O. "Succession and Performance Among School Superintendents." *ASQ*, 1961, *6*, 210–227.

Clark, B. R. *Adult Education in Transition*. Berkeley and Los Angeles: U. of California Press, 1956.

Clark, P. B. "The Business Corporation as a Political Order." Paper read before the annual meeting of the American Political Science Association, September 1961.

———— and Wilson, J. Q. "Incentive Systems: A Theory of Organization." *ASQ*, 1961, *6*, 129–166.

Coch, L. and French, J. R. P., Jr. "Overcoming Resistance to Change." *HR*, 1948, *1*, 512–532.

Fellner, W. "The Influence of Market Structure on Technological Progress." *Quarterly J. Economics*, 1951, *65*, 556–577.

French, J. R. P., Jr., Israel, J. and Dagfinn, A. "An Experiment in Participation in a Swedish Factory." *HR*, 1960, *13*, 3–19.

Gouldner, A. W. "Cosmopolitans and Locals: Toward An Analysis of Latent Social Roles." *ASQ*, 1957–1958, *2*, 281–306 and 444–480.

Hawley, A. H. "Community Power and Urban Renewal Success." *American J. Sociology*, 1963, *68*, 422–431.

Hill, S. E. and Harbison, F. *Manpower and Innovation in American Industry*. Princeton: Princeton U. Press, 1959.

Homans, G. C. *Social Behavior: Its Elementary Forms*. New York: Harcourt, Brace & World, 1961.

Levitt, T. "Creativity is Not Enough." *Harvard Business Review*, May–June 1963, pp. 72–73.

Likert, R. *New Patterns of Management*. New York: McGraw-Hill, 1961.

Maclauren, W.R. "The Process of Technological Innovation." *American Economic Review*, 1950, *40*, 90–112.

Mansfield, E. "Technical Change and the Rate of Imitation." *Econometrica*, 1961, *29*, 741–766.

————. "The Speed of Response of Firms to New Techniques." *Quarterly J. Economics*, 1963, *77*, 290–311.

————. "The Expenditures of the Firm on Research and Development." Working paper prepared at the Graduate School of Industrial Administration, Carnegie Institute of Technology, Pittsburgh (n.d.).

March, J. G. and Simon, H. A. *Organizations*. New York: Wiley, 1958.

Messinger, S. L. "Organizational Transformation: A Case Study of a Declining Social Movement." *ASR*, 1955, *20*, 3–10.

Moore, W. E. "A Reconsideration of Theories of Social Change." *ASR*, 1960, *25*, 810–818.

Morse, N. C. and Reimer, E. "The Experimental Change of a Major Organizational Variable." *JASP*, 1956, *52*, 120–129.

Pinard, M. "Structural Attachments and Political Support in Urban Politics: The Case of the Fluoridation Referendums." *American J. Sociology*, 1963, *68*, 513–526.

Phillips, A. "Concentration, Scale, and Technological Change in Selected Manufacturing Industries, 1899–1936." *J. Industrial Economics*, 1956, *4*, 179–193.

Roberts, David R., *Executive Compensation*. Glencoe, Ill.: Free Press, 1959.

Rogers, E. M. *Diffusion of Innovations*. New York: Free Press of Glencoe, 1962.

Sayre, W. S. and Kaufman, H. *Governing New York City.* New York: Russell Sage Foundation, 1961.

Sills, David L. *The Volunteers.* Glencoe, Ill.: Free Press, 1957.

Sofer, C. *Organizations From Within.* London: Tavistock, 1961.

Stinchcombe, A. L., "The Sociology of Organization and the Theory of the Firm." *Pacific Sociological Review,* 1960, *3*(2), 75–82.

Strauss, G. "Some Notes on Power Equalization." In H. J. Leavitt, ed. *The Social Science of Organizations.* Englewood Cliffs: Prentice-Hall, 1963.

Wilson, J. Q. *The Amateur Democrat.* Chicago: U. of Chicago Press, 1962.

Zald, M. N. and Denton, P. "The YMCA: From Evangelism to General Service." *ASQ,* 1963, *8,* 214–234.

Afterword

The editor of a volume such as this has a certain advantage over its authors because he sees the collected results of their individual efforts. No one knows what they might have written had they been asked to collaborate, but my position in the publishing process gives me an opportunity to read between the lines or, more precisely, between the chapters and a chance to express some biases of my own in the guise of a summary. I believe there are some implications worthy of brief mention.

These chapters—especially the encompassing one by Stogdill—make painfully clear that organizations as considered here are variable-rich phenomena. Many variables—Triandis estimates two hundred—are known to "make a difference," and the study of anything that complex requires a strategy. I believe this volume raises three strategy questions that often are faced, but seldom faced up to, in interdisciplinary conferences.

1. *What scientific approach is appropriate for variable-rich phenomena?* The question is perhaps most clearly implied in the chapters by Triandis and Buck. Triandis argues that the task is so huge that we need standardization of measurement in order to divide the work among many researchers in a cooperative effort. Buck, who believes that with effort the measurement problems can be solved, puts his faith in new, more powerful tools for data manipulation to handle the richness of complex organizations.

Starting with the observation that the complex organization is too rich for its resource controllers to fully comprehend with traditional tools, Buck would introduce more powerful tools for obtaining and handling the richness of detail. A similar starting observation has led other re-searchers (March and Simon, 1959; Cyert and March, 1963) to analyze the devices resorted to by organization executives in simplifying and making manageable their demanding situations. These studies have produced search theory and the satisficing concept.

The initial observation that complex organizations are variable-rich phenomena thus brings two very different responses and marks alternative paths we might pursue. With scarce resources, should we follow one path or the other or hedge? No scientist would argue against more and better data, and better tools for the precise manipulation of data clearly are also an asset. But if we pour our energies into the substitution of hard data for rough estimates and replacement of heuristic problem-solving with analytic precision, do we run the risk of contributing to the fine-tuning of present models of organizations and have little or nothing to say about the design of those that should be developed for new aspirations and new conditions?

2. *Are traditional research designs adequate for the analysis of complex organizations?* Ashby (1958) observed that the traditional touchstone of what is properly scientific is the rule "analyze into parts, and study them one at a time." Given a system, he says, physics and chemistry promptly break it to pieces in order to study the parts. This approach, which may be epitomized by the controlled experiment, Ashby contrasts with the study of the system as a whole and asks what methods there are for the study of intact systems.

We now have useful tools for the investigation of some complex phenomena when the one-variable-at-a-time rule is not empirically feasible—including multiple regression techniques, principal component analysis, Latin square disigns, and computer simulation. Still, as Triandis points out, even consideration of the relationships between two variables, such as productivity and job satisfaction, may take a researcher several years, and there may be two hundred variables that make a difference.

Perhaps we have no alternative but to get on with the laborious and tedious task, even though it requires a huge commitment of resources. But before making that allocation, we might pause to consider possible alternatives. These are not easily identified, if they exist, because they are departures from well-worn traditions. Ashby suggests the alternative of general systems theory, and perhaps there are or can be others.

If we take the traditional path of reduction—of breaking systems down into their elements—where do we stop? The sociologist might be willing to stop dissecting the organization when he reaches the level of roles or norms. The social psychologist probably would want to continue to the level of attitudes. Who knows where the psychiatrist would stop?

But each would be willing to stop before the final possible reduction; each would be willing to work at some level of abstraction.

Are there rules for selecting appropriate levels of abstraction? One rule might have us reduce as far as available techniques permit. A more economic rule might have us reduce until the costs of further reduction exceed the benefits, but we would still need to know how to measure costs and benefits. One suspects the rule actually employed is more traditional than calculated. As Newcomb (1954, p. 228) has pointed out in examining relations between sociology and psychology:

> At each level (of inclusiveness) the specialist is less concerned about the "internal" structure and functioning of his elements than with their interrelations; for certain purposes, at least, he accepts them as undifferentiated entities. By the same token, he has only a limited interest in the relatedness of what is for him a total system to other like systems. At the same time, he tends to be critical of his neighbors in characteristic ways: of the more inclusive specialist, for casualness in taking the properties of his elements for granted, and failing to realize that properties vary with internal structure and process; of the less inclusive specialist, for ignoring influences "from above" according to which intra-system relationships are in part controlled by inter-system demands.

The fact that a system is variable-rich does not necessarily mean that all variables are equally significant, that all operate continuously, or that they are interrelated in invariant patterns. Perhaps before we invest in systematic exploration of all (above some specified level of reduction) variables and interactions, we should invest in consideration of our strategies for tackling complex systems. An adequate system model might suggest, for example, that some of our variables are governed by step-functions, becoming constants within a given range of conditions. The "zone of indifference" or of "acceptance" in the inducements-contributions theory of Barnard (1938) and Simon (1961) is an example of how the step-function notion might simplify the task of exploring variables and their permutations.

If organizations can be understood as something other than the combined effects of many discrete elements, the task of building that understanding may be considerably simplified.

3. *Are traditional measures adequate to our task?* The answer hinges on how that task is defined by answers to the preceding questions. If we must establish the magnitude and interactions of a great many variables already well recognized in the several disciplines, then the types of measures typically used in those disciplines may indeed be the appropriate base, and the effort called for by Triandis to standardize measures might indeed be the heroic effort.

But if the approach to organizations is that of the total system as such, perhaps new measures are needed to operationalize newly conceived dimensions. At the very least, the panelization of variables offered by Stogdill suggests the possibility of measures summarizing rather than merely adding the values of a panel. The chapters by Evan and Wilson illustrate this rather clearly. Evan conceives of an organization set and speculates about dimensions of that set that are not simply the sum of the values of elements of that set. Wilson works with the dimension of organizational complexity, which must be measured as a characteristic of the organization, not simply as the sum of characteristics of its elements.

The best-known example of the issue, in the social sciences, is probably the impetus given by Kurt Lewin to measures of properties of groups as distinct from the combined properties of their members. The issue has been analyzed more recently by Lazarsfeld and Menzel (1961), who distinguish three types of properties that describe collectivities: analytical properties based on data about each member, structural properties based on data about relations among members, and global properties not based on information about the properties of individual members. Barton (1961), working with organizational research from several disciplines, classified the measures used as additive, distributional, relational-pattern, and integral.

The distinction of types of measures is not merely an interesting academic exercise; it becomes crucial when we venture beyond the measurement of element states and attempt to compare organizations in process. The social sciences dealing with organizations are much better at inferring processes than at describing and analyzing them. The simplest approach to process is in terms of the results we think it produces; e.g., we infer something about the process of attitude change when we describe attitudes before and after the process has operated. We can report that an organization has successfully adapted to a changing environment, but if we want to design a characteristically adaptive organization, we must have more sophisticated ways of describing and measuring *processes*.

These are issues that, in my opinion, face all of us interested in the scientific study of complex organizations. How they will, or should, be resolved remains to be seen. But the fact that the Seminar on the Social Science of Organizations (1963) moved us closer to identifying some basic issues speaks for the Seminar's success.

REFERENCES

Ashby, W. R. "General Systems Theory as a New Discipline." *General Systems*. Vol. III. Ann Arbor, Michigan: Society for General Systems Research, 1958.

Barnard, C. I. *The Functions of the Executive*. Cambridge: Harvard U. Press, 1938.

Barton, A. H., *Organizational Measurement and Its Bearing on the Study of College Environments*. New York: College Entrance Examination Board, 1961.

Cyert, R. M. and March, J. G. *A Behavioral Theory of the Firm*. Englewood Cliffs: Prentice-Hall, 1963.

Lazarsfeld, P. F. and Menzel, H. "On the Relation between Individual and Collective Properties." In A. Etzioni, ed. *Complex Organizations*. New York: Holt, Rinehart & Winston, 1961.

March, J. G. and Simon, H. A. *Organizations*. New York: Wiley, 1958.

Newcomb, T. M. "Sociology and Psychology." In J. Gillin, ed. *For a Science of Social Man*. New York: MacMillan, 1954.

Simon, H. A. *Administrative Behavior*. 2nd ed. New York: MacMillan, 1961.

Methods of
Organizational Research

Methods of
Organizational Research

EDITED BY VICTOR H. VROOM

KARL E. WEICK

LOUIS B. BARNES

TOM BURNS

THORNTON B. ROBY

UNIVERSITY OF PITTSBURGH PRESS

Participants

1964 SEMINAR IN THE SOCIAL SCIENCE OF ORGANIZATION

THE UNIVERSITY OF PITTSBURGH

J. STACY ADAMS, Behavioral Research Service, General Electric Company
LOUIS B. BARNES, Graduate School of Business Administration, Harvard University
BERNARD M. BASS, Graduate School of Business, University of Pittsburgh
SELWYN W. BECKER, Graduate School of Business, University of Chicago
L. VAUGHAN BLANKENSHIP, School of Business Administration, University of California, Berkeley
PETER M. BLAU, Department of Sociology, University of Chicago
TOM BURNS, Department of Sociology, University of Edinburgh
GEOFFREY CLARKSON, Alfred P. Sloan School of Management, Massachusetts Institute of Technology
DEXTER C. DUNPHY, Department of Social Relations, Harvard University
ROBERT HAMBLIN, Department of Sociology, Washington University
L. RICHARD HOFFMAN, Department of Psychology, University of Michigan
ROBERT C. JOYNER, Department of Psychology, University of Toronto
KENNETH E. KNIGHT, Graduate School of Business, Stanford University
EDWARD E. LAWLER, Department of Industrial Administration, Yale University
PRESTON P. LEBRETON, College of Business Administration, University of Washington
FREDERICK MUNSON, Graduate School of Business Administration, University of Michigan
ANTHONY OBERSHALL, Department of Sociology, University of California, Los Angeles
LYMAN PORTER, Department of Psychology, University of California, Berkeley
THORNTON B. ROBY, Department of Psychology, Tufts University
W. RICHARD SCOTT, Department of Sociology, Stanford University
ERIC TRIST, Tavistock Institute of Human Relations, London, England
STANLEY H. UDY, Department of Sociology, Yale University
VICTOR H. VROOM, Graduate School of Industrial Administration, Carnegie Institute of Technology
RICHARD E. WALTON, Krannert School of Business, Purdue University
KARL E. WEICK, Department of Psychology, Purdue University
STANTON WHEELER, Department of Sociology, University of Washington

Contents

Figures

Foreword

The last ten years have witnessed a marked increase in the amount of interest shown by behavioral scientists in the systematic study of large-scale formal organizations. One has merely to examine the titles of recently published books to be convinced that first-class scholars and researchers are now directing their energies toward the explanation of organizational phenomena.

A closer examination of the contents of some of the recently edited volumes in this field—such as Haire's *Modern Organization Theory,* Cooper, Leavitt, and Shelly's *New Perspectives in Organization Research,* or March's *Handbook of Organizations*—permits a second inference about the present state of this area of knowledge. One cannot help being struck by the fact that there is substantial disagreement among contributors on such matters as the boundaries of the field of inquiry, the most pressing problems for study, and the relative usefulness of different research methods or theoretical systems. The widespread use of such terms as "organization theory" and "organizational behavior" conveys to the outsider a misleading image of a collection of social scientists jointly engaged in the construction of a stable edifice of knowledge with general agreement about its final shape and the building materials to be used. But, in fact, it can be argued that different contributors are working from vastly different sets of architectural plans and that many are ignorant of or unsympathetic towards the activities of large segments of other contributors.

If the latter representation is more accurate, it probably stems, at least in part, from the fact that the contributors to the study of organizational behavior are themselves representatives of several different academic disciplines, mainly psychology, sociology, political science, economics, and business administration. While some contributions may be described as truly interdisciplinary, most investigators of organizational behavior have tended to "borrow" their problems, theories, and research methods from their basic disciplines and publish their results where they will be read and recognized by others in the same discipline. In addition to this disciplinary insularity, there is some evidence, particularly in major centers of organizational research, of an institutional insularity. Investigators from the same institution tend to share common perspectives of and approaches to the field and, judging from their citations of the literature, are often unaware of relevant work done in other institutions.

The diversity in approaches to the study of organizations on the part of persons from different disciplines and/or institutions does not in itself constitute a serious problem for the development of the field. The systematic study of organizations has too short a history to warrant universal agreement concerning aims, methods, or theories. The diversity that currently characterizes the field may provide a needed protection against a tendency to "put all eggs in one basket" and may increase the probability that the resources expended will contribute viable knowledge. The unfortunate aspects of disciplinary or institutional insularity stem not from diversity per se but from the fact that investigators all too frequently conduct their research in ignorance of relevant research methods or theory in other disciplines or institutions. The consequence of the many channels of publication and the multitude of methodological and conceptual systems is redundancy in research output and inadequate coordination among the various approaches.

There is pressing need for the articulation of alternative points of view so that readers may see them in juxtaposition, weigh the arguments for themselves, and make their own judgments. In this volume, we seek to accomplish this goal with respect to the problem of methods of organizational research. It contains papers by four social scientists each of whom explores the potentialities of a particular research method for examining organizational processes.

The paper by Karl Weick deals with the increasing adaptation of the laboratory experiment for studying organizational behavior. The possibility of creating in the laboratory, at least in its simplest and most elementary forms, the basic properties of an organization and studying the activities under highly controlled conditions is an attractive one. The laboratory offers the indisputable advantages of precision of observation, and internal validity and replicability. Although the communication net studies of Bavelas and Leavitt date back almost two decades, the potentialities of this research method for illuminating a variety of organizational processes are just being realized.

As Barnes notes in his paper, experimentation is possible not only within the confines of the laboratory but also *in situ*. As behavioral scientists, with increasing frequency, have been called upon to apply their accumulated knowledge to changing organizations or to evaluate the change attempts of others, the opportunities for experiments in naturalistic or field settings have improved markedly. Although sometimes lacking in elegant controls, efforts to study organizations experimentally in ongoing settings provide desirable checks both against causal inferences from non-experimental research and against the applicability of generalizations from the laboratory to the real world.

In most investigations of organizational behavior the researcher has assumed the role, not of an experimenter in the strict sense of that term, but of a relatively passive observer of naturally occurring phenomena. These investigations vary in such respects as the number of systems being observed, the size of the systems being observed (individuals, groups, and organizations), whether the observations are made at single or multiple points in time, and whether the observations are quantitative and systematic or non-quantitative and unsystematic. A relatively recent development is the use of observational field methods to measure the attributes of total organizations. Analyses of the interrelations among organizational attributes provide the basis for inferences concerning the processes that give rise to different organizational forms. This approach, termed the comparative study of organizations, is discussed in detail by Tom Burns. The promise of this approach lies in the possibility of understanding phenomena, such as the impact of the external environment on the organization, which do not become the focus of attention in more microcosmic approaches.

While strictly speaking computer simulation is a method of stating theories rather than a system for collecting empirical observation, it is another potentially valuable addition to the armamentarium with which behavioral scientists approach the systematic study of organization. The invention of the electronic computer less than twenty years ago has major implications for the development of science and technology. One of the sources of the appeal of this innovation to the social sciences stems from the possibility of stating theories about complex behavioral events in the form of computer programs and testing theories by comparing computer output with behavioral observations. To date, the most extensive applications of this mode of theory construction have been on thinking and problem solving by individual human subjects. In his paper, which concludes this book, Thornton Roby concerns himself with the potentiality of computer simulation for formulating and testing theories concerning a wide range of organizational processes. Although this approach, as previously noted, is not a research method in the same sense as are laboratory experiments, field experiments, or comparative field studies, it does have considerable implications for research methodology. Formulation and verification of theories stated in computer languages will undoubtedly require much more extensive observation of the processes intervening between system inputs and outputs than is true of theories stated in verbal and mathematical terms.

One of the factors undoubtedly retarding progress in organization research is the limited power of existing empirical tools in relation to the richness and complexity of the phenomena that they are expected to examine. Few would dispute the fact that the organizational researcher has a difficult task trying to explicate organizational processes with the degree of precision characterizing the work of his colleagues in the physical and biological disciplines or even in some of the social sciences. Accordingly, it is important to recognize both the potential and the limitations of present methods and to be alert to further methodological developments when they occur.

What is the best way to learn about organizations?—by creating them in the laboratory and studying their activities under controlled conditions, by trying to change "ongoing" organizations and measuring the consequences of change attempts, by observing the properties of organizations and correlating these observations with one another, or by constructing computer models of organizational processes? The reader will find not one but four answers to these questions on the following pages. While each author states and develops his own bias, this set of papers sharpens rather than obscures the differences in assumptions underlying the approaches described. The choice among them in any given situation rests with the reader, but, hopefully, the following pages will make it a more informed choice.

Victor H. Vroom
Carnegie Institute of Technology

Preface

This book is an outgrowth of a seminar in methods of organizational research held on the campus of Chatham College from June 8 to June 18, 1964. The Seminar was supported by a grant from the Ford Foundation to the University of Pittsburgh. Twenty-six social scientists attended including ten psychologists, nine sociologists, and seven with their primary training in business administration and allied disciplines. Participants spent approximately two-thirds of their time in small working groups devoted to an intensive examination of one of the following research methods: laboratory experiments, field experiments, comparative field studies, and computer simulation. The remainder of the time was spent in lecture and seminar presentations involving the entire group.

Following the seminar, one member of each of the small groups was given the task of writing a paper on the subject considered by his group. His task was not to summarize the discussions, but rather to present his own perspective on the issues after having had the opportunity to discuss them extensively with others. The four papers contained in this book are the results of that work.

The seminar from which this book is derived is the final one in a series of three sponsored by the Ford Foundation and held during the summers of 1962–1964. Two books emerged from these earlier seminars. *The Social Science of Organizations*, edited by Harold J. Leavitt, was published by Prentice-Hall in 1963, and *Approaches to Organizational Design*, edited by James D. Thompson, was published by the University of Pittsburgh Press in 1966. In the judgement of the committee, the primary objective of these seminars—to stimulate interaction and collaborative efforts among persons from diverse disciplinary backgrounds who share an interest in organizational behavior—has, in large measure, been achieved.

The planning committee for the third seminar wishes to express its appreciation to the Ford Foundation for its financial support, to the Graduate School of Business of the University of Pittsburgh under whose auspices the Seminar was held, and to the participants themselves whose lively and informed interest contributed to its success.

HAROLD J. LEAVITT (Chairman)

BERNARD BASS

PETER BLAU

DANIEL KATZ

VICTOR H. VROOM

Methods of
Organizational Research

1

Organizations in the Laboratory

KARL E. WEICK

University of Minnesota

Eight people enter an experimental room and sit at separate desks. One of them silently reads through the following passage twice.

MODIFICATION OF SPECIES

One objection to the views of those who, like Mr. Gulick, believe isolation itself to be a cause of modification of species deserves attention, namely, the entire absence of change where, if this were a *vera causa*, we should expect to find it. In Ireland we have an excellent test case, for we know that it has been separated from Britain since the end of the glacial epoch, certainly many thousand years. Yet hardly one of its mammals, reptiles or land molluscs, has undergone the slightest change, even though there is certainly a distinct difference of environment, both inorganic and organic. That changes have not occurred through natural selection is perhaps due to the less severe struggle for existence owing to the smaller number of competing species; but if isolation itself were an efficient cause, acting continuously and cumulatively, it is incredible that a decided change should not have been produced in thousands of years. That no such change has occurred in this and many other cases of isolation seems to prove that it is not itself a cause of modification [Bartlett, 1932, p. 166].

The financial support of the National Science Foundation, Grant number GS–356, is gratefully acknowledged.

1

After reading the excerpt, the subject spends a few minutes performing an unrelated task and then writes the story from memory. Next, his version of the story is given to the second subject who reads it twice, works at another task, and then reproduces it. Each subject responds similarly.

The story written by the last subject reads as follows.

> Mr. Garlick says that isolation is the reason of modification. This has been proved by the fact that snakes and other reptiles were once in Ireland [ibid., p. 167].

Several things have happened to the story. The content has been simplified rather than embellished. Conventional phrases have replaced unusual details. Details have been personalized. Titles have been dropped making it more difficult for persons to place the event. In short, the subjects have tried to "justify whatever impression may have been left by the original" (ibid., p. 176).

The important question here is what relevance, if any, does this experimental exercise have to the study of organizations? Do the eight men constitute an organization? Can we learn about organizations by studying the fate of stories as they are passed from person to person? What can be learned? Questions such as these, phrased in terms of the simple task of serial reproduction, point to several issues involved in learning about organizations through laboratory experiments.

Some persons might contend that experiments on serial reproduction *are* relevant to organizational research. Stogdill (1950) and Vroom (1964) argue that differentiation of positions and a division of labor are defining attributes of an organization. If the eight subjects have different assignments (e.g., one attends to grammar, another attends to plausability) or if they differentiate themselves according to the responsibilities for accurate transmission of the story (e.g., the "first man" must be accurate, the "middle man" must add content because some will be lost), then it is conceivable that the situation of serial reproduction is like an organization. Guetzkow (1961) argues that mediated interaction distinguishes organization from small groups. Since interactions in serial reproduction are seldom face to face, the exercise qualifies as an organization by Guetzkow's standards. A related distinction is suggested by Bass (1964) who maintains that an organization consists of relations among positions, while small groups are relations among persons. It is unclear whether Ss perceive each other in positional or personal terms but, again, if positions are salient, serial reproduction has relevance to organizations.

Zelditch and Hopkins (1961) would probably describe the serial reproduction experiment as a "simply structured unit," meaning that it is neither complex nor does it have distinctive organizational properties. However, this type of unit still is relevant to organizations according to Zelditch and Hopkins because (1) it operates like a *subunit* in an organization, and (2) it has certain characteristics of a social system just as an organization does. It might also be argued that a serial reproduction exercise constitutes organizational research because it reproduces a common organizational phenomenon, "uncertainty absorption." March and Simon (1958, p. 165) comment that "uncertainty absorption takes place when inferences are drawn from a body of evidence and the inferences, instead of the evidence itself, are then communicated." This process is much like that observed in serial reproduction.

In each of the preceding instances, the task was potentially an organizational exercise because it resembled a natural organization in some respect or because it tested a proposition of relevance in organizational theory. However, there are other reasons why serial reproduction may not be an organization experiment.

Some of these reasons are definitional. Serial reproduction does not include properties that several investigators regard as crucial to the definition of organization. It does not contain technology (Leavitt, 1964), multiple groups (Simon, 1960), an external environment (Becker, 1964; Krupp, 1961), hierarchy of authority (Schein, 1965), or formality of policies (Zelditch and Hopkins, 1961).

Aside from definitional shortcomings, the task also has the disadvantages of many contrived situations. The interactions between subjects are transitory (Lorge, Fox, Davitz, and Brenner, 1958) and there is little time or reason for group traditions, rituals, and norms to develop. The laboratory group probably is not of the subject's own choosing (Sherif and Sherif, 1964) although neither are many groups in natural organizations. Tasks may appear trivial (Mechanic, 1963), their performance may have few consequences for the subjects (Cook and Selltiz, 1964), and the subjects, if they are students, are probably excessively compliant (Proshansky and Seidenberg, 1965, p. 13).

This brief examination of serial reproduction suggests a few of the issues that arise when attempts are made to study organizations in the laboratory. These issues are especially sharp in the case of serial reproduction because the task is not conceived with organizations in mind. Yet even this task has some relevance, given certain definitions of an organization, and the exercise can be modified to make it more relevant. If eight persons are not enough to constitute an organization, more could be added. Participants could be supplied with selected information about the other communicators (e.g., one is ambitious, a newcomer, skilled, suspicious, trustworthy) and structural or status distinctions could be made explicit. Instead of stories, persons might reproduce communications about controversial issues within the organization. The first person in the chain might observe an event and report his observations rather than read an intact story. Subjects might be given access to earlier messages or spend the time interval prior to reproduction on some activity *related* to the content of the communication.

This introduction suggests three very general conclusions about laboratory studies of organizations.

1. Experimental Organizations are Simplified

The preceding review suggests that any laboratory experiment involving interacting persons contains both features that are typical of natural organizations and features that are not. Thus the same experiment can be seen by some investigators as relevant to the study of organizations, by others, as irrelevant. It all depends on which characteristics of organizations are regarded as crucial.

It is unlikely, however, that any experiment will fully satisfy the investigator who values fidelity between laboratory and natural events. Fidelity typically must be compromised to gain clarity and control. If a person wishes to use experiments, he probably will have to choose among the several characteristics of organizations that he regards as important. To gain control, simple tasks in simple settings are often required. Selectivity need not be detrimental, it may compel the investigator to be more explicit.

2. Tests of Organizational Theory do not Require Organizations

Experiments are often used to test propositions derived from organizational theory. When an experiment is used for this purpose, its content is determined by the theory, not the referent event. This is one of the reasons that a surface resemblance between laboratory organizations and natural organizations often is absent and unnecessary. The relationship between contrived and natural events in hypothesis testing is aptly summarized by Zigler (1963, p. 353).

> What the experimenter is saying is that if such and such holds in the real world because of the principles expounded in the particular theory under investigation, then such and such should hold in the world which the experimenter has created. This translatability is what gives theoretical import to experiments which involve phenomena which, taken in isolation, not only appear picayune but seem to have little relationship with what one observes in nature.

It should not be assumed that Zigler's description affords a blanket justification for all experiments. Instead, it sharpens those things for which an experimenter should be held accountable and those for which he should not. It is clear that the experimenter must be explicit about the "world that he has created." Recent research concerning the social psychology of experiments (Rosenthal, 1963) suggests that it is more difficult to be explicit about the world that one creates than many have expected. Only if an experimenter is explicit can an observer judge if the intended conditions have been created and whether equivalent opportunities exist for "real world" principles to operate. The experimenter's claim is that his design permits these same principles to operate and that the only changes in conditions are minor ones.

While it is probably true that the experimenter can muster a stronger argument for the generality of his findings if the experiment resembles the real world, all this really does is reduce the size of the deductive leap he must make and defend. Assuming that the principles from the real world are explicit, that the experimenter is rigorous in his deductions, and that he has intimate knowledge of the world he has created, he may be less concerned with creating a close replica of the natural event.

3. Organizations can be Created Experimentally in Several Ways

Although this point has some overlap with the first summary statement, it is included to indicate that organizational experiments assume many forms. For example, organizations can be created by appropriate choices of subjects. Any experiment that uses as subjects members of ongoing organizations (e.g., Bass, 1963; French and Snyder, 1959; Maier and Hoffman, 1961) may qualify as an organizational experiment. The subjects do not have to be members of organizations, they could be aspirants as in the case of students of journalism (Lyle, 1961), business (Bass, 1963), or international relations (Guetzkow, 1959). Even further removed from actual membership, but still potentially relevant, are experiments in which subjects either explicitly role play persons in organizations (Rosenberg and Abelson, 1960), engage in activities similar to those of persons in organizations (e.g., Cohen, 1958; Strickland, 1958), identify with one organizational member in a tape recorded interaction (Ring, 1964), or read about the activities of persons in organizations and react to what is read (DiVesta, Meyer, and Mills, 1964).

Organizational experiments also may be constituted by the inclusion of trappings found in actual organizations. Such experiments may range from actual organizations that are created in the laboratory and exist for several days (Wager and Palola, 1964), through partial organizations (Evan and Zelditch, 1961), down to experiments that have a plausible but minimal set of props (Cyert, March and Starbuck, 1961). It could also be argued that any experiment testing a proposition derived from or relevant to organization theory is an organizational experiment (as is one that is multi-person), permits interaction between groups, involves coalitions (Thibaut, 1964, p. 88), or exists for an extended period of time. Clearly, these criteria include most social psychological experiments.

In one sense, arguments over whether an experiment is organizational or not are unnecessary. This judgment depends on the extent to which the specific research promotes understanding of organizational processes. Our reason for illustrating various definitions of these experiments is to suggest some ways in which organizations can be studied in the laboratory and, indirectly, to suggest the flexibility of the laboratory.

SUMMARY

At the outset, it is important to realize experimental organizations seldom resemble natural organizations. Experiments permit persons to look more closely at some problems, but not at others. However, it is the experimenter's theoretical preferences, his preconceptions about experiments and his ingenuity that define the range of problems that are susceptible to experimental inquiry. It is the purpose of this chapter to detail how laboratory studies are created, and what they can and cannot accomplish.

The chapter will contain the following sections. First, characteristics of experiments will be described in terms of the fictions and nonfictions that have emerged about laboratory experiments. Next, various means to construct organizational settings in the laboratory will be examined. The exercises to be discussed range from complex simulations that are property-rich to minimal tasks involving virtually no organizational trappings. Then a comparison between field and laboratory studies of a common problem will introduce an extended discussion of the strengths and problems associated with conducting experiments. Primary emphasis will be placed on problems.

THE NATURE OF ORGANIZATIONAL EXPERIMENTS

Formally, it is possible to define experimentation as "experience carefully planned in advance" (R. A. Fisher, quoted in Kaplan, 1964, p. 147) or as "a process of observation, to be carried out in a situation especially brought about for that purpose" (Kaplan, 1964, p. 154). While these definitions do imply that experiments are intentionally structured "so that the effects of the independent variables can be evaluated unambiguously" (Underwood, 1957, p. 86), they do not hint at some of the controversial issues associated with experimentation. These issues are best portrayed by selections from the folklore about experiments:

> The social science laboratory with its sense of innovation, its mission of experimental proof and its direct, personal confrontation between subject and experimenter, is the highly charged home of chance, accident, hope, fear and danger [Mills, 1962, p. 24].
>
> What can be observed reliably is socially meaningless and what is socially meaningful cannot be observed reliably [Lewin, 1951, p. 155].
>
> No one believes an hypothesis except its originator but everyone believes an experiment except the experimenter [Beveridge, 1950, p. 47].
>
> Some social scientists will do any mad thing rather than study men at firsthand in their natural settings [Homans, 1962, p. 259].
>
> Man is evidently more efficient in his everyday life than in experimental rooms. . . . It is needless to point out how difficult it is for us to make threshold judgments, to not be tricked by an optical illusion, to remember nonsense syllables, and for a rat deprived of cues for proper discrimination to behave properly in a maze. Man and rat are both incredibly stupid in an experimental room. On the other hand, psychology has paid little attention to the things they do in their normal habitats; man drives a car, plays complicated games, designs computers, and organizes society, and the rat is troublesomely cunning in the kitchen [Toda, 1962, p. 165].

While this folklore is rich, colorful, varied, at times polar, and often accurate, it also serves to perpetuate certain fictions about experiments. Generally these fictions suggest that experiments are more fallible, less conclusive, and apply to a more limited range of problems than need be true. Certain myths in the folklore about experiments are sufficiently compelling that, once persons are familiar with them, they shun experiments and thereby forego any opportunities to disconfirm these myths. Therefore, it seems relevant to look briefly at some beliefs about experiments that might otherwise deter the organizational theorist from working in the laboratory.

FICTIONS ABOUT EXPERIMENTS

The four points that follow are not entirely fictions. Occasionally, they are problems in conducting experiments and in generalizing to the real world. However, their potency and disruptiveness is often overrated, hence they are not the deterrents to experimentation that persons believe they are.

1. Experiments Demonstrate the Obvious

A common belief is that laboratory experiments serve mainly "to demonstrate what you are already pretty sure of" (Homans 1962, p. 264).

While there is some support for this belief, it also represents a limited view of what can be accomplished in an experiment.

The impression that experiments amplify obvious phenomena arises from several sources. Experimental tasks often are sufficiently simple that the results appear straightforward and expected. Sometimes experiments are designed to produce a single phenomenon, no additional phenomena can occur in the same setting, therefore, the outcome seems obvious. Furthermore, when only a single variable is manipulated, observers often argue that an outcome is obvious because all the other crucial variables were controlled. It is also probable that the amount of work that precedes an experiment fosters the impression of obviousness. So much information is required to identify the variables, refine the predictions, and create the experimental situation, that it often seems that there is little more to be learned by actually executing the experiment. The important thinking about the problem has already occurred. The claim that obviousness pervades experiments also appears in conjunction with the argument that experiments test theory, but seldom generate hypotheses. As will be shown later, this view is too narrow.

There are several features of experimentation which suggest that obviousness is not as pervasive as many have imagined. And where experiments are obvious, this is often a strength rather than a weakness. Experiments furnish more occasions for hypothesis generation than is often realized. Seldom do the outcomes of an experiment unequivocally confirm a hypothesis. There are usually some measures or deviant cases that are inconsistent and require explanation. Attempts to account for these discrepant data often generate new hypotheses. But experiments can often generate hypotheses in a much more direct manner.

Discovery of hypotheses can be planned and it is in this sense that controls, hypotheses, contrived situations, and simple tasks—all prominent features of the laboratory—can facilitate the discovery of new relationships. It is likely that many potentially important hypotheses go unnoticed in field studies because there are too many distractions. These distractions are reduced in the laboratory and, even though there may be fewer occasions for novel relationships to occur, those that do occur are more likely to be noticed. Thus controls may aid rather than hinder hypothesis generation, and the laboratory may be a more appropriate setting for this activity than the field.

Several examples of planned hypothesis generation can be cited. Each of these is a very general hypothesis that can be explored directly in the laboratory. March and Simon (1958, p. 169) propose that "the basic features of organization structure and function derive from the characteristics of human problem-solving processes and rational human choice."

But, whether structure actually is constrained by human cognitive abilities is an empirical question. One way to explore this question is to vary systematically the composition of a group along some cognitive dimension (e.g., abstract-concrete) and observe differences in the structure and process of problem solving that emerge (Tuckman, 1964). If the problem is one of discovering the processes that perpetuate and disrupt group traditions when membership changes, a more explicit answer is likely to be found in the laboratory than in the field (Jacobs and Campbell, 1961; Kuethe, 1962). Frequently, the laboratory permits one to ask questions in an uncommon fashion and create conditions to arrive at the answers. In order to study what produces change, one could ask, "What does it take to keep an organization from changing?" The experimenter could allow experimental groups to have planning sessions (Shure, Rogers, Larsen and Tassone, 1962), could assign organizational structures that are intolerable and compel change (Bass, 1963, p. 152) or instruct participants to change their work structure every twenty minutes, and then determine what was required to *terminate* the changes that were instigated by these three procedures. A mechanism that terminates changes is apt to be a mechanism that also affects the adoption of change. Or, to study the relationship between organizational structure and motivational phenomena, such as inequity (Adams, 1963), the experimenter could vary organizational structure by creating different communication networks and determine in which kinds of networks participants experience greater and lesser inequity when payment differs from expectancy.

An additional sense in which experimentation aids discovery is implicit in the phrase, *experiment as metaphor*. By metaphor is meant "an implied comparison between things essentially unlike one another. . . . One image is superimposed upon another in order to provide a perspective or better understanding of the subject at hand" (Bruyn, 1964, pp. 101–102). Experiments often provide a means to visualize a complex event. Instead of trying to imagine the effects of different antecedents in the natural event, the experimenter visualizes what would happen if some feature of the experiment were changed. While in a sense such usage of experiments may be nothing more than the manipulation of a verbal model, it does have one important difference. If the experimenter's thinking does generate a potentially valuable observation concerning the real world, it is possible to verify this impression in the very situation where it was generated, the experiment. Errors in translation from one level of abstraction to another are thereby avoided.

Aside from the fact that experiments generate hypotheses, there are other reasons why obviousness is a fictitious shortcoming of experiments.

Whether or not an outcome is obvious is a relative judgment. Findings that are obvious in terms of one set of beliefs are often unexpected in terms of another set. It is one of the truisms of experimentation that unequivocal support for one proposition seriously endangers other propositions. However, many of these disconfirmations are unseen because premises are not made explicit. Intuition is a notoriously misleading basis for prediction, and criticism of obviousness often masks a failure to make intuitions explicit.

In short, the claim that experiments demonstrate the obvious may represent a confusion of explicitness with significance. As experimental operations are made more explicit, experimental outcomes often seem less surprising. This is desirable because it probably means that the findings are less ambiguous to interpret. Unfortunately lack of ambiguity is sometimes mistaken for lack of importance or significance. This is one of the reasons that experiments may appear to add little information.

Aside from the issue of mistaken interpretations of explicitness, there is the fact that experiments are not merely a means to demonstrate phenomena; they also aid hypothesis generation. Hypotheses may be suggested either indirectly by analysis of unexpected findings or directly by exploratory experimentation. The use of experiments for exploration has often been neglected, but this usage seems especially important given the continuing development of organization theory.

Whether or not one can make discoveries seems to depend less on where he looks than on how he looks. It is possible that during a given period of time less may happen in the laboratory than in the field. To some this means that laboratory events are less significant, to others it means that there are fewer distractions from observing the event.

2. Experiments are Artificial

One of the most pervasive fictions about experiments is that they are artificial. This view often is held because novelty is confused with artificiality. Laboratory tasks and settings may be unfamiliar to the subject, but this has nothing to do with the significance of his responses. The laboratory situation is still real, the subject must make some adjustment to it, and there is no reason to believe that his responses will differ from those in other unfamiliar situations. As Kaplan (1964, p. 169) observes, "the experimental situation is not to be contrasted with 'real life' but at most only with everyday life."

It is also true that the novelty of experimental exercises is sometimes exaggerated. There are many organizational processes that have high "ecological validity" in the laboratory setting. Milgram (1964, p. 850), for example, stated that the laboratory "is one social context in which compliance occurs regularly" and, therefore, is an apt site in which to study obedience. Thus, whether the laboratory setting contains events that are novel or events that are expected, the settings coerce behavior and in this sense are not fictitious.

Artificiality, however, may become more of an issue when one considers the goals of people who participate in experiments. Subjects often are concerned with more than just the task assigned by the experimenter. It is this spread of concern to issues such as deciphering the purposes of the experiment and predicting what is a "healthy" or "safe" response, that many persons equate with artificiality.

Once again, however, artificiality is not the problem. The problem is one of control. The subject's motives are in no sense feigned, they simply encompass a larger portion of the experiment than the experimenter intended. The subject's plight is essentially that he knows he is being watched and evaluated while he does not know what is being observed. It is these doubts that lead to "evaluation apprehension" (Rosenberg, 1965) or the "deutero-problem" (Riecken, 1962). While the fact of being observed and evaluated in terms of unstated criteria is not uncommon in organizations, it does cause problems in the interpretation of experimental outcomes. It is sometimes difficult to disentangle the effects of trying to gain clarity from the effects of the experimenter's intended manipulations.

Apprehension, however, is not an unsolvable problem. One way to reduce its effects is to conceal the fact that data are being collected (e.g., Sherif and Sherif, 1964). Another way is to promise the subject *in advance* that information about the experiment, his responses, and those of others, will be provided at the conclusion of the exercise, and then to provide this information. Experiments are an unusually good chance for subjects to learn about themselves, about other people, and about research methods, and these learnings are typically regarded as a fair exchange for participation. Much of the difficulty in experiments occurs because the experimenter faults on his portion of the exchange.

A further characteristic of experiments that is often mistaken for artificiality is the population that is studied. It often appears as if college students are not people. A typical objection to the subject population found in experiments is voiced by Dill (1964, p. 52): "What college sophomores do, alas, may not be much more relevant than the behavior of monkeys for predicting how executives, nurses, or research scientists will perform."

Although college students differ from executives in many ways, they also have many similarities. Thus the question of appropriate subjects resolves to one of "are the ways in which he [the college student] differs from other people correlated with the effects investigated" (Zelditch and Evan, 1962, p. 59). In some studies college students do differ in relevant dimensions. Jensen and Terebinski (1963, p. 87), for example, report that in their simulation of a railroad system, "a PhD with system experience lost interest after four or five sessions in which he learned the . . . appropriate strategies. College sophomores used different heuristics and never seemed to understand the system in the same way as the others; they remained interested much longer." Thus, when system experience is a potential determinant of an effect, sophomores may be inappropriate *unless* the experimenter wishes to hold this variable at a value of zero. Also it is possible that the railroad simulation made demands unlike those of most "systems" which sophomores encounter. It is certainly true that sophomores have some "system experience." If they did not, they would be unlikely to survive in college.

It is unlikely that one could ever find a subject population that is equivalent to a typical organizational member. The reason is simply that there is no such thing as a typical member. Members vary just as subjects do. Observing executives to learn about foremen would be just as suspect as observing college students to learn the same information. Unless the experimenter is explicit about personal variables that moderate his phenomenon, and unless these variables assume quite different values in his subject population and his referent population, the use of a college student is not a serious limitation.

It is possible that most objections to the use of sophomores are really objection to recruitment procedures rather than to the abilities of this particular population. Conditions under which subjects participate in experiments often affect their behavior. Rosenthal (1963) and Hood (1964) detail the ways in which volunteer subjects respond differently than non-volunteers. Gustav (1962) describes the resentment that occurs among subjects when they are required to participate in experiments. The form in which this resentment may be shown is interesting. Subjects often regard the requirement to serve in experiments as "one more harassment imposed by the university." To the extent that they equate experiments with waiting in line for meals and with restrictions on hours and automobiles, they probably exhibit a common response—rebellion and indifference. Thus, students may be less appropriate as subjects for experiments, *not* because of their skills and experiences or lack of them, but rather because the conditions under which they participate influence their reactions to laboratory events.

It can be concluded that even though there are many reasons why laboratory findings may not generalize to other settings, artificiality is not among these reasons. Furthermore, artificiality is a dangerous label to attach to experiments because it focuses attention on pseudo issues and suggests self-defeating solutions. If a situation seems artificial, the only thing to do is make it more real or natural. And this usually means that more "props" are added so that the setting *looks* more natural. But, as more props are added, controls founder and it becomes more difficult to observe what happens. The behavior that is evoked is made no more real by these additions and, in fact, the experimenter has probably made his propositions less accessible.

3. Laboratory Contexts are Oversimplified

Since natural events have multiple determinants, it may not seem helpful to study laboratory events that fail to retain this complex context. If a social system is the unit of analysis, then events "isolated" for study in the laboratory lack crucial properties. Dalton (1964, p. 56), in describing his preference for field methods, comments that "where the problem was inextricably inter-twined with others, I felt that too much injustice would be done to the whole to wrench it out for the sake of sampling and scaling theory. In such cases one might objectively relate the mutilated part to a subjectively established criterion and in doing so inflate the part out of all proportion to the interlinked parts discarded because of quantitative inadequacy."

Although few people would deny that behavior has multiple determinants or that it is embedded in a system, many would disagree about how to act once this fact is acknowledged. That an event has multiple determinants still remains a hypothesis, and whether "wrenching it out" will drastically alter its properties is at least a question that can be tested. It is not necessarily true that factors in close proximity to a natural event affect its course. Human perception is sufficiently affected by considerations of economy (Heider, 1944) that causal attributions made under field conditions may differ from those made in the laboratory.

Aside from the issue of how many determinants there are of natural events, and whether these judgments are susceptible to perceptual bias, it should be noted that laboratory exercises "create a context of their own which is not incompatible with what is being modeled" (Meier, 1961, p. 241). Assuming that laboratory events have some resemblance to natural events, it is not uncommon to find that subjects enrich the laboratory event and invest it with some of the meaning associated with the natural event. While this creates problems for the experimenter, it also indicates that context is not insufficient or unrepresentative.

Laboratory events often look simple because the experimenter has used simplifying assumptions in testing a theory or because a simple replica is an obvious place to launch an investigation. Blalock (1963, p. 402) notes that, even though a formulation or experiment may initially be unrealistic, "by beginning with grossly oversimplified models a cumulative process can be set in motion in which one successively modifies the model or theory until it becomes more and more complex and provides a better fit to reality." There is no implication that the experimenter will retain his simplification indefinitely. He may tarry in complicating the model and demand clear evidence that more variables are needed, but he can add them. And he has the further advantage that it is easier for him to observe the effects of these additions.

Simply because natural events exist in a system and have multiple determinants, they are not thereby disqualified as objects for laboratory experimentation. Laboratory events often generate their own systemic properties and, even when they do not, the experimenter can add them to his model and experimental operations *when he is ready to observe their effects.*

4. Hypotheses Induce Myopia

One reason experiments are avoided is that they all involve hypotheses. It is sometimes assumed that hypotheses retard rather than hasten understanding for they force selective attention toward events. In the quest for hypothesis confirmation, important relationships may be overlooked. Dalton (1964, p. 54) presents an especially colorful picture of this possibility: "A prematurely publicized hypothesis may bind both one's conscience and vanity. . . . A hypothetical statement is also one's attempt to be original. Having once made such a statement, one more easily overlooks negative findings or, on having them pointed out, one's emotional freight often limits creativity to ingenious counterarguments."

Hypotheses serve several functions, one of them being to structure observation. It is inconceivable that an observer can give undivided attention to everything that occurs. Selectivity intrudes in one form or other. And a hypothesis derived from a theory is one means to order observation. The order imposed by a hypothesis extends further than many persons realize. In many experiments incidental phenomena take on added meaning because, if the hypothesis is true, these secondary events should assume a particular form. Hypotheses, in other words, frequently direct attention to new areas rather than force a neglect of them.

The question of how an investigator responds when a hypothesis is not supported is important, but this question must be separated from the issue of whether or not hypotheses are helpful. Even if a hypothesis is retained longer than some observers think it should be, this is no reason for hypotheses to be avoided. Furthermore, it is much more difficult to judge when a hypothesis has outlived its usefulness than Dalton implies. There are numerous occasions when hypotheses have been dropped prematurely more for reasons of taste than of error or disconfirmation (Abelson, 1964; Boring, 1964; Weick, 1965). And experimental results that do not support a hypothesis can occur for many reasons other than an error in the hypothesis. Incorrect independent variables may be chosen, manipulations may be unsuccessful, measurements may be insensitive, effects may be too weak to be observed, or the wrong outcomes may be observed. Even if a hypothesis receives continued negative evidence, it still may be useful to an investigator as a way to think about problems. However, one should not forget that seldom do good investigators propose just one hypothesis in a lifetime. Investments in any given idea tend to be less intense than Dalton suggests. And investigators also are mindful of "the cardinal principle of experimentation . . . that we must accept the outcome whether or not it is to our liking" (Kaplan, 1964, p. 145).

A conclusion about the value of hypotheses is advanced by Blau, a field worker who has used them: "It is all too easy to obtain impressionistic evidence for our broad theoretical speculations. Such evidence, therefore, helps us little in discriminating between diverse or even conflicting theoretical principles. My endeavor to stipulate hypotheses . . . and to collect at least some quantitative data served the purpose of furnishing a screening device for insight. Those ideas that survived this screening test, while still only hypotheses . . . were more apt to be correct than the original speculations" (Blau, 1964, p. 20). Hypotheses, in other words, may uncover problems as often as they obscure them.

Conclusion

Laboratory events are different from everyday events in many ways. But these differences do not always imply that the laboratory event is any less real or any less significant as a means to learn about people. Relationships among variables are suggested in the laboratory just as they are in the field. Laboratory controls do not restrict the richness of data; they frequently make it easier to detect the unexpected when it occurs. There are considerable problems in conducting laboratory studies. But the problems of incomplete knowledge of variables, artificiality, simplicity of events, and focused observation are not among the major drawbacks even though they are often represented as such.

NON-FICTIONS ABOUT EXPERIMENTS

Once the investigator separates crucial from non-crucial issues in experimentation, he can concentrate on ways to cope with these more enduring features of experiments. The following discussion samples the "styles" of thinking associated with the use of the laboratory, styles often taken for granted by experimenters. When these stylistic features are made explicit, they provide a more complete view of demands imposed by experimentation and assumptions made by those who use the laboratory.

1. External Influences on Laboratory Events

Experimenters sometimes overestimate the amount of control they have over the conditions of the experiment. Lewin, for example, propounded the view that the laboratory is an island. "Experimentation in the laboratory occurs, socially speaking, on an island quite isolated from the life of society. Although it cannot violate society's basic rules, it is largely free from those pressures which experimentation with 'life groups' has to face daily" (Lewin, 1951, p. 166). Experimenters currently are giving added attention to the fact that experiments are not as isolated as they would like. Experiments do exist in environments. The ways in which subjects act in experiments are frequently determined by the meaning of the experiment in the larger system. This can be an especially important issue in organizational experiments.

For example, an increasing number of organizational experiments are conducted at human relations training laboratories (e.g., Bass and Leavitt, 1963). Several rather explicit norms emerge in these laboratories and they undoubtedly affect the behavior of trainees when they participate in experiments. Egalitarian norms prevail, shared leadership is valued, status distinctions are discounted, previous experiences are irrelevant, and momentary feelings are expressed. In addition to being exposed to new and possibly unfamiliar norms, the trainees typically become more adept at working in groups.

Given these characteristics, it is not surprising that organization experiments conducted in training settings show that less highly structured organizations are superior to those with high structure. But the influence of the external system is not even this simple. Norms do not develop immediately; their clarification and acceptance take time. Thus it is probable that a person who has been in training for only a short time would feel more comfortable with a structured group since it closely resembles other groups with which he is familiar. As the training progresses, structured conditions probably create increased ambivalence, resentment, and frustration among participants because these conditions are contrary to those valued in the training sessions. Thus it is not surprising that experiments with the "link-pin organization" show superior results when they are conducted during the latter stages of training sessions. The important point is that this superiority may be the result, not of structural characteristics, but of uncertainty in the structured group concerning how they should act.

A further environmental influence in training laboratories is that most group exercises have a moral, and a task that "makes a point" is probably biased toward a particular outcome. If the results of the training exercise are then treated as experimental data, their significance should not be overestimated. It is probably safe to conclude that data collected during the early stages of a training laboratory are more representative of the population at large than are data collected later.

Experiments conducted at training laboratories are not the only ones susceptible to influence from the social system. Some effects of university settings have already been detailed. The point is that the experimenters must not ignore the setting in which experiments occur. The extent of this influence is suggested by Mills (1962, p. 22): "By examining the experiment's place within the institutional settings, its significance for the lives of the subjects, its operations as they represent interaction between observer and observed, by formulating the structure of role relationships and by interpreting the significance of events for this inclusive system, sociological analysis can . . . [help distinguish] that component in our raw data which should be charged to what experimenter and subject are doing to and for one another and that component which should be charged to the experimental group itself as an object of investigation."

2. Psychological Representation of Variables

The same feeling, belief, or perception can be created in several ways. For example, a person may experience uncertainty because he follows a bizarre and confusing route to arrive at the laboratory (Sherif and Harvey, 1952), is misinformed about physical symptoms that he experiences (Schachter and Singer, 1962), or meets persons who mistake his identity (Garfinkel, 1963). Experimenters typically exploit the fact that the same condition can be created in several ways and, as a result, they often expose subjects to contingencies that appear unusual and artificial. Experimenters assume that the critical problem in an experiment is to create the desired state in the subject. It is far less important what the manipulations that create this state look like.

Observers often believe that an event will be represented psychologically only if it unfolds in a manner familiar to the subject. In other words it is assumed that a physical resemblance between the laboratory and the real world is necessary if the input is to make a difference to the subject, i.e., to be represented psychologically. While it is a hypothetical

question whether psychological representation can be created by unfamiliar stimuli, most experimenters assume that it can. This simplifying
assumption is an important one.

Occasionally experimenters find that subjects become suspicious or at
least more attentive when uncommon events are used to create common
experiences. But the very uncommoness of these laboratory events prevents accurate labeling of their purpose, with the consequence that the
suspicion tends to be "free-floating." As long as suspicion takes this form
it is less likely to exert a *systematic* effect on the results.

The implication of these remarks is that any experimental manipulation is a theory. Manipulations represent an experimenter's hunch about
the conditions necessary to create psychologically the phenomenon of
interest. The manipulation also implies what the experimenter regards
as the most important properties of the phenomenon. In the example
involving uncertainty, each of the manipulations exploits a slightly different component of uncertainty. One exploits the desire for clear external
frames of reference; another, the desire for consistent impressions of
self; and the other, the desire for knowledge of the rules that guide the
behavior of others. But always the criterion for choosing a manipulation
is whether it makes a difference to the subject, not whether it is familiar
to him. Lewin's concept of life space is a valuable caution to the person
who believes that simulating the visible, physical components of a natural
event is sufficient to induce psychological representation. "I do not consider as part of the psychological field at a given time those sections of
the physical or social world which do not affect the life space of the
person at that time. The food that lies behind doors at the end of a maze
so that neither smell or sight can reach it is not a part of the life space
of the animal" (Lewin, 1951, pp. 57–58). Unless the object makes a
difference to the subject, it is not a part of the life space. And simply
creating a physical likeness is not sufficient to insure that an object is
included in the life space.

3. Parsimonious Explanations

Experimenters prefer simple explanations and they adopt more complex propositions only when the simple ones prove inadequate. This does
not mean that experimenters refuse to study complex propositions. Demands for parsimony have nothing to do with hypothesis testing. As
Marx (1963, p. 21) has stated, "the doctrine of parsimony is relevant
only to the acceptance of propositions—not to their testing or development. As a matter of fact, it should serve as a spur to scientific advance,
since it puts the burden of proof on those who prefer the more complex
alternatives; let them find some evidence which *requires* it." Most ex-

periments, therefore, attempt to study "fundamental processes which presumably underlie the behavior of humans in a broad range of organizational [and other] settings" (McGrath, 1964, p. 538).

A somewhat different (and less charitable) view of the experimenter's preference for simple explanations is expressed by Mills (1962, p. 23). He argues that experimenters are disenchanted because their experiments do not tell them more about groups and that, to defend against this disenchantment, they adopt simple models. The rationale for adoption is this: "the less there is to a group, the more we know about it. The more machine-like groups are, the more we can control them." Whether motivated by the strengths or the weaknesses of experiments, pressures toward parsimony are evident in the laboratory.

Among the basic organizational processes studied in the laboratory are delegation, decisions to participate, decisions to produce, and interdependence. Experimenters argue that if these processes are understood a great deal is known about organizations. Delegation is a good example. It is an important property of natural organizations (Selznick, 1948), it assumes several forms (Roby, 1962), and it can be studied in the laboratory (Solem, 1958).

Knowledge about the factors that led a person to join a firm is knowledge that helps predict what to expect from him. The decision to participate is a basic process in organizations, and the bases on which this decision is made can sometimes lead the person to exhibit high productivity (Weick, 1964) or low productivity (Adams and Rosenbaum, 1962). In a sense, any experiment can provide information about determinants of organizational productivity as long as the basis for participation is made explicit. Experiments involve the acceptance, performance and assessment of tasks just as do organizations. Conceivably a portion of the subject's performance is influenced by the conditions under which he accepted the task. At least this possibility can be examined if the bases of participation are known.

Interdependence (Miller and Hamblin, 1963) is also a basic fact of organizational life. Its effects are found everywhere. Events ramify widely, compensatory as well as retaliatory changes take place (Leavitt, 1964) and unanticipated consequences occur in unexpected places. Interdependence is a process that is especially well suited to exploration in the laboratory (e.g., Kelley, Condry, Dahlke, and Hill, 1965; Kelley, Thibaut, Radloff, and Mundy, 1962), and it can be created simply by putting each person's outcomes under at least the partial control of another person (e.g., Raven and Eachus, 1963; Weick and Penner, 1966).

One drawback in studies of basic processes is that they promote patchwork conceptions of organizations. The organization appears to be a set of independent processes or a set of dimensions. These properties are studied individually, and occasionally other dimensions serve as dependent variables. Although such an approach does not yield direct data on the interdependence of dimensions, this shortcoming is not serious at this stage of inquiry. The proposition that processes are complex is also subject to considerations of parsimony. It is probable that processes have multiple determinants; it is also probable that not all these determinants carry equal weight.

4. Experimenter as Artisan

The creation of conditions that establish, control, measure, and disentangle variables requires resourcefulness and imagination. It is difficult to prescribe ways to attack these problems. Precedent is less important in experimental design than in many scientific activities. Although the experimenter examines earlier experiments to learn about factors that may confound the results, he typically must devise new procedures to deal with these sources of error.

Examples of procedural twists that aid measurement and control are plentiful. To combat problems of scoring open-ended remarks, the experimenter can have subjects select their remarks from a prepared list of comments (Pilisuk, 1962; Thibaut and Riecken, 1955). To insure that vacillation in making judgments is recorded, the experimenter can have subjects write their answers with pencils that have no erasers (Krugman, 1960). To help subjects see all the alternatives open to them in a coalition task, an accomplice of the experimenter can suggest different alternatives by his actions (Hoffman, Festinger, and Lawrence, 1954). To control impressions of mutual liking among group members, the experimenter can have subjects rate each other, can scan and then discard these ratings in a wastebasket, and finally retrieve a "planted" set of ratings which are returned to the subjects (Dittes and Kelley, 1956). Perhaps the most important skill of the experimenter-artisan is his ability to embed crucial manipulations and measures in an expected or plausible sequence of events. If embedding is successful, fewer suspicions are aroused and the manipulations may be more potent (Schachter, 1951). Surprises or irrelevant instructions may induce caution or indifference. Festinger (1953, p. 155) states that, unless experimental instructions "are plausible in the sense of being integrally related to the experimental activity in which the subjects are to engage," their impact will be slight. Potential implausibility occurs when "the subjects could have done everything the experimenter required of them without these instructions ever having been given" (ibid., p. 159). It may make little difference to subjects whether they are matched on intelligence, testing a new product, starting a new organization, generating normative data, or competing with other groups, if they can perform the experimental task without knowing this.

A good example of the importance of embedding is found in the methods used to obtain measurements of attitudes before and after attempted persuasion. Attempts to embed the post-persuasion measurement have included interpreting the pre-measure as a "warmup" (Aronson, Turner, and Carlsmith, 1963), obtaining post-measures in a different experiment (Rosenberg, 1965), obtaining post-measure for an unrelated purpose (Festinger and Carlsmith, 1959), or presenting attitudinal items in different questionnaire formats (Hovland and Weiss, 1952). The crucial requirement is that the measurement not attract undue attention. Subjects must regard the event as a legitimate demand, i.e., they must see a rationale for its inclusion.

The consistency with which experimental events unfold affects subject behavior. Attention to subtle procedural details is necessary to maintain consistency. There are several examples in laboratory experiments where theoretically important contingencies were created, but aroused suspicion among subjects because of their implausibility. Ring (1964) varied status (high or low) and compliance (complies or fails to comply) and found that subjects were made uncomfortable by the high-status person who complied and the low-status person who did not comply. These contingencies were unexpected and, in *both* instances, the stimulus persons were regarded unfavorably. The compliant-high-status person was seen as timid and weak, the low-status-noncompliant person as brash and tactless. French and Snyder (1959) report that subjects in a work group found it difficult to comprehend why their supervisor in another room first sent them messages to slow down their work pace and, shortly thereafter, sent messages urging a speedup. Much of the suspicion may have occurred because the notes gave little explanation for the change in policy (e.g., "It's going fine. Forget about mistakes and try for speed"). The point is that tests of some propositions may impose considerable strains on plausibility. It should be noted that this argument does not contradict the earlier discussion of a confusion between novelty and artificiality. The earlier discussion dealt with unfamiliar events, whereas the present concern is more with incongruous events. It has been reasonably well demonstrated (e.g., Carlsmith and Aronson, 1963; Harvey, 1963) that mildly incongruous events are experienced as pleasurable but that marked incongruity evokes negative evaluations.

Demands for consistency and plausibility do not mean that the experimenter must forgo important controls or measurements; but these demands do require ingenuity and revision of earlier procedures. It should be noted that requirements of consistency, plausibility, and embedding can be met in contrived situations. There is no implication that these ends are accomplished only in highly realistic experiments. It does not take an elaborate simulation to achieve satisfactory embedding. What is required is that subjects be given a rationale for the experimenter's demands and that this rationale be acceptable to them. The necessity for being an artisan arises from trying to provide subjects with legitimacy for experimental operations while retaining maximum control over what occurs.

Conclusion

Experiments are responsive to external influences. Experimenters acknowledge this fact when they try to integrate experimental demands with demands of the larger social system and when they legitimate experimental operations for subjects. If external influences are ignored, important sources of error are not controlled. Experimentalists, however, are concerned with problems other than confounding external sources. They are concerned with choosing experimental conditions that make a difference to the subject. These choices are not influenced by considerations of realism and artificiality. Concepts and propositions are continually reexamined for excessive simplicity or complexity. Frequently the act of translating a concept into experimental operations aids this conceptual refinement. Even though the experimenter may seem to dwell on simple methods to study simple explanations, in reality he examines continually the adequacy of these explanations and his methods to insure that they do not generate misleading data. These then represent some of the non-fictitious features of experiments.

THE STRUCTURE OF LABORATORY ORGANIZATIONS

An organization may assume many forms when it is constructed in the laboratory. The purpose of this section is to describe some of the variations that are possible. Several tasks, arranged crudely along a dimension of the number and explicitness of organizational properties contained, will be described. The tasks range from those with virtually no explicit organizational content (minimum content) to those that involve the creation of an actual, ongoing organization (maximum content).

The use of the dimension of minimum-maximum content is to impose some order on the discussion. In actuality no one dimension is involved because, as one moves from task to task, *several* features vary.

Abstract experimental tasks tend to be concerned with a single, basic process. Explicit organization content is at a minimum. Neither the setting nor the task suggest organizational analogies to the subject. The process observed is presumably prominent in organizations, but is stripped of its usual accompaniments. The more concrete laboratory replica includes such salient organizational properties as structure, technology (e.g., telephones), and work activities (e.g., problem solving and conferences). The most concrete replicas involve simulated organizations with several participants, long time spans, tangible products, and hired subjects. A summary listing of tasks that represent these gradations is found in Figure 1.

The remainder of this discussion includes brief descriptions of each of

FIGURE 1

Organizational Replicas in Laboratory Exercises

Abstract Replicas

Group reaction time (Zajonc, 1965)

Common target game (Leavitt, 1960)

Anagrams (Ammons and Ammons, 1959a)

Detective story (Burns, 1964)

Group discussion (Hoffman, Harburg, and Maier, 1962)

Card sorting (French and Snyder, 1959)

Railroad game (Jensen, 1961)

Community exercise (Schein and King, 1964)

Aircraft maintenance (Enke, 1958)

Proofreading (Adams and Jacobsen, 1964)

Concrete Replicas

the benchmark tasks listed in Figure 1. Additional information about laboratory tasks to study organizations is found in Weick (1965).

GROUP REACTION TIME (ZAJONC, 1965)

Undoubtedly one of the most versatile group tasks yet devised is the group reaction timer designed by Zajonc. The subject's task is exceedingly simple. When a colored light goes on, the subject is to depress a key as quickly as possible. If his reaction takes longer than a preset interval, a failure light goes on. If the reaction is quick enough, the failure light remains off. A group task is formed by connecting several individual timers to a central timer. When this is done, numerous contingencies can be created. For example, in a seven man group, the clocks can be set so that each person must exceed an absolute time or all will fail; or each person must exceed his own average or all fail; or at least four of the seven persons must achieve a particular speed for all to succeed. Feedback of group results, division of labor, role structure, and cooperation-competition can all be manipulated with this apparatus.

Even though the reaction time task explicitly resembles few, if any, organizational activities, it has one decided advantage over most other tasks. It involves "individual behavior that is reasonably well understood, behavior extensively examined in individual psychology, behavior whose antecedents are reasonably well known" (Zajonc, 1965, p. 73).

Most tasks, especially those in complex simulations, can be performed adequately only with a rather complex mix of ability and effort. This makes it more difficult to interpret experimental outcomes. Fewer problems of this kind occur with abstract tasks. The principal benefits of the timer task are that it enables the experimenter to create a host of theoretically important contingencies and also incorporate a sensitive measure. It replicates the important organizational property of interdependence. Other tasks especially suitable because they increase the visibility of interdependence are minimal social situation (Kelley, Thibaut, Radloff, and Mundy, 1962), spirit leveling (Raven and Eachus, 1963), target identification (Miller and Hamblin, 1963), and word formation (Cottrell, 1963).

COMMON TARGET GAME (LEAVITT, 1960)

The properties of structure and differentiation, important variables in organizational theory, can be added to the property of interdependence in a strikingly simple exercise, the common target game. Three persons who cannot see each other, hold up fingers when the experimenter calls out a number between one and thirty. The object is for the fingers to sum to exactly the number that the experimenter has announced. If the subjects fail to hit the number, they try until they are successful. The necessity for differentiation occurs with numbers that are not divisible by three. If the experimenter calls the number 11, this number could be achieved by 3–3–5, 4–4–3, or 10–1–0. It is the group's task to arrive at a structure that will solve each problem on the first try.

Variations of this basic exercise have been used to study several organizational problems. Bass and Leavitt (1963) studied differences in productivity when plans were imposed or generated by the group. Zand and Costello (1963) used the situation to study group learning, Joyner (1965) to study concept formation, and Leavitt (1960) to study the effects of problem-solving history on the emergence of structure. The exercise seems appropriate to understand how subsystems in organizations function. Once a group is able to contribute numbers consistently so that a target is achieved on the first try, they may be regarded as having a stable, efficient, asymmetrical, shared decision plan. The relevance to organizations occurs both because of the product and because of the way in which the members achieve it. Joyner (1965, p. 4) characterizes the exercise this way: "Persons have worked together to acquire a structure for coordinating a set of diverse functions and have carried out these functions frequently enough that they constitute a stable set of problem-solving or decision-making procedures."

ANAGRAMS (AMMONS AND AMMONS, 1959a)

Somewhat more task content and complexity of assignment occurs when persons are presented with a set of letters and are instructed to form as many words as possible from these letters. The basic property of the task is that the sets of letters are problems, norms for the number of words derived can be established, and there is no single correct solution. Variations of the basic anagram exercise have been used in several organizational experiments (e.g., Bass and Vaughan, 1962; Kennedy, 1963), partly because the exercise lends itself well to delegation and a division of labor.

Ammons and Ammons (1959b, p. 719) have detailed the similarities that subjects see between the anagram task and real life problem solving. The following list summarizes some of these similarities:
1. Rearrangement of elements into new combinations is called for
2. Many solutions are possible, and differences among them are easily distinguishable
3. Problems vary in difficulty as perceived by Ss
4. Solutions are perceived by Ss as being more or less satisfactory
5. Informed ("literate") Ss can find some solutions, but never all; solutions are not seen as simple

6. Greater flexibility of attack on a problem leads to more solutions

7. Solutions vary in originality

Thus, it appears that some properties of problem solving are retained in this task, and appropriate structural features, such as are present in the next task, can be added easily. These additions would then provide conditions for studying organizational problem solving.

DETECTIVE STORIES (BURNS, 1964)

Seven persons are arranged in a three-level hierarchical structure. The only way they can communicate is by telephone. An intact detective story is divided into forty pieces, the pieces are scrambled and then distributed among the seven members. The task is to assemble the complete story as quickly as possible. Each person can talk to only one person at a time and lateral communications are prohibited. If equal power is desired, then conference calls can be permitted.

There are several reasons why this exercise has more organizational content than the anagram task. At a superficial level, it involves telephones which are a common item for transacting organizational business; but, more importantly, the telephone permits the person to clarify his remarks immediately if they are misunderstood. Unlike note-writing, which is the preferred means of communication in many organizational studies (e.g., Kelley, 1951), phones do not encourage cryptic communiqués. Furthermore, phone conversations enable one to detect, from verbal cues, how a message is received. The phone study also involves a larger group than is commonly found in networks (maximum of five persons). Since a participant can talk to only one person at a time, he must contend with the possibility that workers will devise other problem-solving procedures that involve less dependence on him. In the telephone task, persons in central positions have to do more work to get crucial items of information. In the network, they can set their own pace because they receive notes simultaneously from several persons and can respond when they are ready. In the telephone task, time may be taken from problem solving to try to contact a worker who is already talking to someone else.

Because of the several alternatives that it unfolds and the contingencies involved, this task has several properties found in natural organizations.

GROUP DISCUSSION (HOFFMAN, HARBURG, AND MAIER, 1962)

A considerable portion of organizational activity involves talking. Dubin (1962, pp. 13–14) reports the following two observations: "In the sheer volume of all activities demanded of him verbal interaction is the No. 1 form of contact, consuming upward of 80 percent of all the executive's time. . . . Only 12 times in 35 days of observation was this chief executive able to work undisturbed alone in his office during intervals of 23 minutes or longer." Although the telephone task captures some of this verbal interaction, a more direct means is to have several persons discuss face to face a problem of relevance to organizations as if they were members of the organization. Hoffman et al (1962, p. 206) studied the Change of Work Procedure problem which is a "role playing situation involving a conflict between a foreman and his subordinate workers about the relative merits of two work methods."

The use of group discussion is relevant to organizational theory, not because the group is regarded as a model of an organization, but because it replicates a common occurrence in organizations. Variables that affect the content and form of group discussions are apt to be variables of considerable importance in organizational theory. Assuming that persons implement group decisions, knowledge of the antecedents of these conditions assumes considerable importance. In addition, a group discussion task is equivalent to an all-to-all communication network, so it can be analyzed for its structural implications. Central structures can be allowed to emerge (Hutte, 1965) or they can be imposed by the experimenter (Delbecq, 1965). The meetings need not consist of role playing; they can be used for members to report on the progress of their work.

CARD SORTING (FRENCH AND SNYDER, 1959)

With the possible exception of the anagram task, none of the tasks sampled so far have content that explicitly models a production situation. The card sorting task involves a tangible product, supervisor-subordinate relations, a work-group, group outputs, and mediated interaction. Three workers are given the task of hand sorting a large pile of IBM cards into one of five trays depending on how many punches they contain. Each card has from 21 to 25 punches. This range was chosen purposely to prevent subjects from sorting each card simply on the basis of a quick glance; instead, the workers have to count the holes on each card. Yet the time to sort each card is short enough that partially completed units will have little effect on the productivity measure. Since all three workers sort cards into a common tray, individual contributions are obscured and it is not possible for members to compete with each other for favor with the supervisor who is in another room.

Because of the simplicity of the exercise, individual differences in learning and ability have little effect on the results. Measures of quality (number of cards sorted incorrectly) and quantity are readily available. Finally there is the extremely important property that there is room for an increase or decrease in productivity to occur. The authors state that they wanted the task to be "as routine and uninteresting as possible so that the restraining forces of satiation would prevent maximum performance even during the short time of the experiment" (French and Snyder, 1959, p. 131). It is important to build in satiation so that differences in productivity can occur. A common problem in many experiments is that all subjects work up to full capacity throughout the exercise with the result that dependent variables are insensitive to the manipulations.

Although the subjects still are clearly in an experiment, they experience several contingencies that are quite similar to those in natural organizations. This task represents a transition from the abstract laboratory task of remote relevance to organizations, to studies that are property-rich in organizational features.

RAILROAD GAME (JENSEN, 1961)

Two persons are given the task of running a simulated railroad system for six days (three actual hours). Their task is considerably more comprehensive than that of persons who were sorting cards in the French and Snyder task. The railroad system has ten stations connected by six railroad routes and trains run between all stations every day. The task itself is a scheduling problem and is described to subjects in this way. "You are on the night shift. During the shift you will receive orders to send a certain number of carloads of merchandise between various points. It is your job to determine how this merchandise is to be sent, i.e., in what kinds of cars and over what routes" (Jensen, 1961, p. 61). Subjects are paid a fee for each shipment depending on the car used and the route taken. The object of the exercise is to earn as much money as possible.

Unlike any of the exercises up to this point, subjects must contend with unpredictable events in the environment. Agents at stations follow erratic schedules in sending requests for cars, and changes in the weather affect both the roadbed of the railroad and the date when crops are ready for shipment. Since the decisions made by the subjects actually affect the state of the game, they must cope with their own ineptness and misscheduling later in the game. The exercise has the appearance of a natural organization, it is labeled an organization, and the instructions legitimate this impression.

However, as complexity and realism have increased, so have the problems of knowing what determines the subject's decision. The initial instructions to the subject do not specify the tasks, positions, or functions required to perform the task. Subjects, therefore, are forced to handle organizational problems as well as scheduling problems. While these multiple demands are life-like, it becomes more difficult for the experimenter to know whether the results are due to the ways in which subjects handle the problem of organizing themselves, the ways they handle the scheduling problem, or both.

An additional characteristic of simulations such as the railroad game is that they involve hypothesis generation rather than hypothesis testing. Usually the simulation is started and observers wait to "see what happens." Although hypotheses sometimes emerge from these studies, they are often imprecise, oversimplified, and provide few leads to be followed up under more controlled conditions. This evaluation is not so much an indictment of simulations as it is a caution to investigators who believe that the simulation of an organization is equivalent to understanding it. Simulations often invite tampering, but they seldom invite rigor.

COMMUNITY EXERCISE (SCHEIN AND KING, 1964)

Somewhat more elaborate, but still ideally suited to laboratory administration over a finite period of time, is the two-part community exercise. During the first part (2½ hours) subjects design and build houses from tape and 3×5 cards in competition with other firms. Frequent profit reports, bonuses for novel design, declining prices when the market is glutted, short production periods, pre-exercise planning, strict rules concerning acceptability of construction, group election of the manager, and the manager's appointment of his assistant lend both credibility and interest to the exercise. The second part of the exercise requires each group to plan and draw on a large piece of wrapping paper, a model residential community complete with parks, trees, and the houses built during the first part of the exercise. When the community has been designed, the manager must make a five-minute sales presentation "emphasizing the valuable features of the community design." The proposals of competing groups are judged on functionality, attractiveness, and the presentation.

Execution of the community task is complicated by a major change which is made between periods one and two. The managers and assistant managers of the winning and losing groups assume new positions. The manager of the winning group is transferred and now manages the losing group; the manager of the losing group is demoted to assistant manager of that group; the assistant manager in the losing group is transferred to the winning group as assistant manager "to gain experience" and the assistant manager in the winning group is promoted to manager. These changes pyramid the problems of the losing group. Not only do they have the stigma of losing and a greater desire to win, but they also "desire to defend their general manager who has been 'demoted,' [and] desire to show up their new general manager from the winning group" (King, 1964, p. 2)

One of the advantages this and similar exercises (e.g., Bass, 1963; Bass and Vaughn, 1963; Kennedy, 1963) have is that a tangible product is involved. Errors in production are more apparent, progress is evident, differences in tasks are clear, time is occupied, and management and production distinctions are more obvious. Despite the fact that the exercise covers a relatively short time, the problem is scaled down sufficiently that participants still deal with several organizational activities—finance, engineering design and layout, production, sales—without being overwhelmed by their magnitude. Basically, the exercise is simple, and it becomes complicated only as participants try a greater number and variety of strategies. The community exercise also involves considerable visible activity. The planning discussions, construction activities, evaluations of profit and other activities, permit the experimenter to observe what occurs. This is not always possible when a very small number of persons are involved or when the task requires considerable silent calculation. Because of the simplicity of the exercise, manipulations do not "get lost" in the proliferation of activities, controls can be made explicit, and measurements are less ambiguous. However, the cautions voiced earlier are still relevant. Simulations often induce method-centering rather than problem-centering. It is interesting to note that there is possibly less temptation to stand and gaze at a simple simulation than at a complex one. Manipulations are more plausible and should have more impact on a simple system than on a complex one. Or at least the effects of the manipulation will be easier to trace.

AIRCRAFT MAINTENANCE (ENKE, 1958)

In order to determine the feasibility of three new logistics policies at Air Force bases, Enke constructed two sets of air defense interceptor squadrons that were similar in every way except for the policies. The simulations were extensive. Not only were air bases, overhaul depots, parts repair departments, storage sites, and headquarters offices created, but also factory, transportation, and storage facilities where problems of delay and increased costs could occur. Each hour of laboratory time was the equivalent of one day of flight activities. The experiment lasted the equivalent of five years of the expected life of the aircraft. Each squadron "had the same aircraft, with the same parts, which malfunctioned on the same numbered flight" (Enke, 1958, p. 287). The major dependent variables were costs and number of aircraft in commission and combat-ready under each logistics system.

Such an elaborate simulation is a close approximation to a real organization, the major differences being the reductions in time and number of persons operating each facility. These losses are compensated for by the lengthy run of the system and the multiple contingencies that participants have to handle. It is especially important to have long runs when policy innovations are being tested. Enke (1958, p. 291) reports that it took some time for the managers to become familiar with the new policies and accept them. These problems of learning and acceptance, incidentally, are valuable clues to what may occur if the procedures become adopted throughout the Air Force. For example, one of the new policies required that each base transfer its inventory and record-keeping activities to a data processing center that was several hundred miles away. Reorders were made by the computer, not by the men at the base where the stock was housed. This policy represented a rather drastic change in job control and content for base personnel. When attempts are made to study the effects of new policies by using short-term laboratory studies (e.g., Bass, 1963), participants may be forced to use these new policies before they understand how they work. This means that the success of failure of the new policy may be difficult to interpret.

Enke's work is valuable because it illustrates the use of an elaborate simulation to test explicit hypotheses. He discovered that even though the new policies were responsible for considerable savings, they left the system vulnerable when a "war" occurred unexpectedly. Although fewer parts were destroyed under the new system because the inventory was dispersed, a policy of deferred purchasing led to an inadequate number of parts being stocked. The war occurred before the deferred purchase had been made.

Enke (1958) also hints at a subtle problem in managing a simulation of this magnitude that may affect the generality of the results. Because time and personnel were reduced, some additional procedures and forms were needed to permit the simulation to run. The missing people were replaced by forms. Enke reports that these forms and procedures "would not have been practical in actual Air Force organizations" (p. 292). Therefore, to the degree that the success of the newer policies was due to these procedural shortcuts rather than to the superiority of the policy itself, different outcomes might be anticipated. Fortunately, there is every possibility that the adequacy with which the other features were replicated simply "washed out" any major effect of these shortcuts. Just as it may be harder to generate a manipulation that has a strong impact on a complex simulation, so it may be harder for a single error or change to alter it.

PROOFREADING (ADAMS AND JACOBSEN, 1964)

One way for an organization to be created in the laboratory is for the experimenter to build it. Another way is for the *subject* to build it. This is essentially what occurs when a subject is hired "through normal channels" to work in what appears to be an actual, ongoing organization. If the hiring procedures are plausible and authentic, few additional organizational props are needed. The subject will "fill-in" the appropriate superstructure from the supervisor's "orientation" lecture and from his own experiences with other organizations. The replica is concrete *to the subject*, it only looks artificial and incomplete to the outsider. Psychological representation assumes considerable importance under these conditions.

Several persons have used hiring procedures to manipulate organizational content (e.g., Adams and Jacobsen, 1964; Evan and Zelditch, 1961; Wager and Palola, 1964). Adams and Jacobsen hired persons for part-time employment to proofread a manuscript on human relations. As part of the orientation procedure, the subject completed an application form and took a bogus test of proofreading ability. Undoubtedly the subjects saw the organization to be quite small since they were not exposed to any other members. This is in contrast to the situation created by Evan and Zelditch (1961) where "workers" actually saw other persons who presumably worked at other jobs within the organization. However, even these exposures were minimal because the subjects' contacts were mainly with one person, a supervisor, and these contacts were made by telephone. Extensive and extended contact with fellow workers and various levels of the organization is most apparent in the attempt by Wager and Palola (1964) to actually start and maintain an organization in the laboratory.

Although studies in which subjects were hired seldom explore the degree to which the subject felt he was in an organization, it appears that the channels through which the job was announced, as well as the orientation activities, should not have aroused suspicions. Undoubtedly a student who works part-time for a company during the summer or a university holiday is less concerned with job security, job content, and hours, than is a person for whom the job is a more significant portion of his life space. As yet, there are few data concerning how important this difference in setting is. However, given the experimenter's concern with activating organizational concerns in the laboratory, hiring manipulations seem to be especially potent.

CONCLUSION

To learn about organizations, an experimenter can create relevant processes with varying degrees of attention to the context in which they occur. The process can be established with virtually no explicit tie to organizational properties and in a form different from that in which it naturally occurs. Or both the form and context of the process can assume increasingly natural forms. Since many experiments are tests of theory, resemblance is less important than observability. However, when organizational properties can affect the hypothesized relationship, they may be added to the design if they do not render the measurements meaningless. The principal differences among the preceding tasks are summarized by McGrath (1964, p. 537). He notes that laboratory experiments (abstract tasks in the present discussion) contain discrete trials; the situations are unaffected by the responses of subjects, and generic structures and processes are not closely modeled after everyday life. Simulations (concrete tasks) have continuous stimulus situations that are modeled after real life in which the subject's responses determine the nature of subsequent stimuli.

GAINS AND LOSSES IN THE LABORATORY

While laboratory experimentation as a method of investigation solves some problems, it creates others. The purpose of this section is to detail several problems that may plague the organizational researcher when he turns to the laboratory. These problems are not unsolvable, but they must be identified before anything can be done about them. The advantages of laboratory methods have been well documented elsewhere (e.g., Campbell and Stanley, 1963; Festinger, 1953; Weick, 1965; Zigler, 1963). We will be content in this discussion to suggest some of these gains by means of an example comparing a laboratory and field experiment of the same organizational process. Although the example suggests some gains in the laboratory, it does so more by pointing to faults of the field than by pointing to strengths of the laboratory. After the two experiments have been compared, several problems will be described.

EMOTIONAL DISRUPTION IN THE FIELD AND LABORATORY

Many investigators have puzzled over the question, "Why do changes in organizational procedure often disrupt activities for extended periods of time?" To learn more about changeovers, Schachter, Willerman, Festinger, and Hyman (1961) studied the effects of emotional arousal on the performance of manual tasks before and after the task had been changed. It was hypothesized that harassments would have little effect on habituated or stereotyped activities such as assembly-line work because these activities are executed with little concentration. Even if the harassment disturbs thinking processes, there should be no visible effects. However, when a change in activity occurs, the new task would require close attention until it is learned. A history of prior harassment would be likely to hinder the learning and performance of the new task. The purpose of the field experiment was to test these predictions.

Actually a relatively simple situation is required. "It was the intent of the manipulations to make one set of groups disturbed and upset and the other set as happy as possible" (Schachter et al., 1961, p. 203). The basic experiment was replicated three times using matched assembly lines. The "disfavored" groups received almost daily annoyances for periods ranging from two-to-four weeks before the changeover. Because of considerations of appropriateness, the content of the harassments differed markedly although they apparently had in common continual criticisms of the quality of work performance. Criticisms seldom involved problems unrelated to work. Favored groups were fussed over and sheltered from irritations during this period.

In the execution of the studies, problems were legion. As the authors modestly note, "the problems of attempting to keep tight control of the experimental situation in the hubbub of a major industrial operation forced us to abandon many of these [methodological] niceties if we were to have any experiment at all" (ibid. p. 205). To minimize plant-wide disruptions during the changeovers, rigid schedules were made and could not be changed. When a snowstorm occurred on the day of the planned changeover in one study, only a very few of the experimental subjects could get to work. Replacement operators filled in for the workers who were absent and thereby destroyed the harassment manipulation. Additional groups were lost because workers had instituted an informal job rotation system and, therefore, were not "habituated" prior to the changeover. To conceal the fact that an experiment was being conducted, workers were not interviewed, meaning that valuable data were lost. Favored and disfavored groups occasionally worked different shifts. It was impossible to control discussions among workers off the job. Although no information is given about how the changeover was explained to the workers, it is possible that the results were due to a subtle difference introduced here, and not to the previous harassments. For example, in one of the replications, the change involved "dropping one of the seven assembly workers from the line. Her job was redistributed among the remaining assemblers" (ibid. p. 206). Since all experimental groups had supposedly been together at least six months, it is conceivable that the choice of the person who was removed could have affected the reaction to the changeover. By chance, an informal leader might have been removed in the "disfavored" group, but not in the "favored" group.

Despite such problems, data were collected and the hypotheses seemingly were confirmed although no statistical tests were performed. The complications in this study make it more difficult to know what mechanism mediates these results, or even if there is a stable result that needs to be explained. Although the three studies were described as replications, the situations, tasks, and measures were sufficiently different to raise questions of comparability.

An attempt was made by Latane and Arrowood (1963) to test the identical hypothesis under laboratory conditions. Subjects were presented with a display containing three switches and three lights. Their initial task was to anticipate which light would turn on next by pressing the appropriate switch. The lights followed a simple repetitive sequence that was easily learned and that was paced by the subject. After the task changeover, subjects were to press the switch of the same *color* as the light which was to come on. Previously, they had responded to position.

Harassment occurred after twelve minutes on the first task and arrived in the form of complaining, hostile female (subjects were male) who soundly criticized the subject for the way in which he had filled out a questionnaire at the start of the experiment. The non-harassment condition involved the same instigator, although now she mildly approved the subjects. After the unfriendly female left, the subjects continued the task for three minutes and then changed to the new task which they performed for eight minutes.

The results indicate that the female's harangue left the subjects significantly more tense, but not any more anxious, irritated, content, or happy than the control group. The differences in productivity following the changeover confirmed the predictions. The harassed group did significantly more poorly than the non-harassed group, although the effect was short-lived. Furthermore, the harassment did not affect performance before the changeover. Both groups performed equally well after the encounter but before the change to the new task.

These results are interesting, partly because they demonstrate similar findings in a field experiment and in a contrived laboratory situation. But even more striking is the fact that these similarities occur even though there are marked differences in time span. "While Schachter et al. prolonged their emotional manipulation over 2–4 weeks, we used 2 minutes, while their subjects had become stereotyped on the same job for untold months, ours had to learn a task in 12 minutes. It is not inconsistent, then, that the emotion-produced decrement on nonstereotyped production which they observed lasted from 1 to 3 weeks after changeover, while we obtained effects for only 3 minutes" (Latané and Arrowood, 1963, p. 326). The experiment was not without its shortcomings. The performance curves for the first task were still increasing when the changeover occurred, thereby rendering more questionable the argument that stereotypy had developed. The lesser impact of the emotional disruption may have been due to a weaker manipulation, but it may also reflect stoicism among the male subjects. It will be recalled that the study by Schachter et al. involved mainly females.

It is worthwhile to speculate on how the laboratory findings would be regarded if the related field experiment did not exist. The outcomes are similar and the procedures in the laboratory experiment provide fewer bases for alternative explanations. Schachter et al. have some indication that the effect holds across industrial situations, across tasks, and with subjects who are probably older and more experienced than those in the laboratory. Juxtaposition of the two studies increases the plausibility of the hypothesis. It also indicates the distinct differences in time and financial costs between the laboratory and the field. Perhaps the most apparent fact from this comparison is that controls such as randomization and replication (Blalock, 1963, p. 401) are important and that they can be attained with more certainty when the experimenter can create the situation to his liking than when he is concerned about disrupting factory production.

It is also valuable to compare the question of motivation in the two populations of subjects. McGrath (1964, p. 537) contends that "one important feature of data obtained from a 'real-life' situation is that the humans in that situation are operating under natural (not necessarily stronger) motivational forces, since the phenomena being studied are a part of their actual lives." Our earlier discussion of similarities between the laboratory and the field would suggest that both situations create "natural motivational forces" that are "part of actual lives." It is possible that the harassments were more meaningful in the field because they occurred in a familiar context and because they had implications for the amount of money the worker would earn. It is not clear, however, that there was any less suspicion in the field than in the laboratory. A sudden upswing in harassments is just as apt to be unnatural in the field as in the sudden arrival of a bellowing female in the laboratory. The harassment may be dealt with in different ways. For example, subjects in the laboratory had to solve the problem themselves whereas the workers in the field study could talk with their fellow workers. To argue, however, that the subject's concern in the field is any more real or relevant is to deny that subjects ever get involved in laboratory exercises. And evidence suggests that they do and that experimenters can heighten this involvement.

PROBLEMS OF INTERNAL VALIDITY

Having suggested some of the reasons why persons might wish to use the laboratory, we will describe some additional reasons why they might not. The problems to be discussed are some that are particularly bothersome in conducting organizational experiments. Using Campbell's (1957) classification, the errors will be divided crudely into those that affect internal validity and those that affect external validity. Internal validity is the basic minimum that any experiment must possess. The criterion by which it is evaluated is, "Did in fact the experimental stimulus make some significant difference in this specific intance?" (Campbell, 1957, p. 297). It is not infrequent for some variables other than the ones manipulated to influence systematically the results. If the experimenter fails to realize this, the findings he reports are incorrect in the sense that they are not a function of the manipulated antecedent. Internal validity is concerned with constructing experiments so that it is clear precisely what is controlling changes in the dependent variable. The problem of internal validity, in short, is to establish that the experimenter has actually found what he thinks he found.

Campbell (1957) discusses several quite general hindrances to internal validity. The present listing differs in that it is representative rather then comprehensive, specific rather than general, and, therefore, may apply only to certain kinds of experiments. The errors discussed below are intended to suggest the kinds of procedural subtleties in an organizational experiment that could render the results equivocal. It is anticipated that, with these few examples in mind, the reader will be alerted to a general kind of problem and will be able to locate many additional instances of such errors.

1. Esteem and Degradation

When a subject agrees to be looked at, he naturally wants to know what people see. If they withhold this information, require unpleasant activities, treat him as an object, or violate other social contracts, then it is likely that the subject will become concerned about his esteem as well as the experimenter's instructions. Subsequent behavior may be affected by either or both of these sources. An internally valid experiment exists only if instrumental behaviors are disentangled from those that are expressive.

Expressive behaviors are more likely, for example, when manipulations unintentionally threaten the status of subjects. Pepitone (1964) argues that experiments on aggression, consistency, and conformity often pose dilemmas for the subject in which he feels uncertain, incompetent, or belittled. The existence of these feelings constitutes an alternative explanation for the obtained results. For example, the requirements that subjects write strong arguments opposed to their private beliefs may generate something other than cognitive dissonance. "Inconsistent behavior increases the probability of social rejection. Since rational, intelligent behavior is highly valued by other people, the individual tries to reduce or at least conceal his irrationality for fear of losing status and power or even love and security" (Pepitone, 1964, p. 46). While this explanation seems more applicable to responses that are made in the presence of peers than those made in private, it does imply that persons worry about social censure and ridicule.

Concerns about esteem often undercut attempts to have subjects actually criticize each other or report to the experimenter that they dislike another person. Jones and DeCharms (1957) reported an unwillingness among subjects to dislike a person who obstructed progress. Jones (1964) found that subjects rate a disapproving interviewer quite favorably. Sampson and Insko (1964) used most of a two hour experimental session to get a subject angry. Mills (1962) suggested that the experimenter may have little difficulty creating dislike, but he may have considerable trouble directing it. He suggested that the well known experiment by Schachter (1951) on deviation can be interpreted as displacement onto a stooge of hostility actually felt toward the experimenter. The stooge became a scapegoat because the experimenter failed to fulfill his promises to the subjects concerning the agenda of their meetings.

While one implication of these remarks is that it is difficult to create dislike in the laboratory, the more important point is that the experimenter may get some indication that dislike is present but, overriding its effects, may be actions directed toward maintaining esteem.

Esteem also affects confederacy. Paid accomplices are often used to establish experimental conditions. If subjects are unwilling to be hostile or to deviate, the experimenter can hire someone to act this way in a group. Confederates, even when adequately trained (Efran, 1961), often find their antics costly and present a less explicit and compelling performance than the experimenter requires to test his predictions. Much of the discomfort felt by accomplices occurs because they forget that the attacks which their behavior elicits are directed at *the role*, not at them personally. Professional actors (Milgram, 1963) may be successful at making this distinction, but most amateurs are not. The stooge's discomfort may be increased even more if he has some doubts about his ability to play the role. Suppose he has been trained to be a belligerent manager in a simulation and, when he acts this way, his subordinates express strong resentment. If the stooge feels that he did not play the role well and yet provoked negative reactions in the other subjects, he may convince himself that he did a good job of role playing after all, *or* he may wind up believing that he really is an unattractive person. It is not the objective adequacy of the role playing so much as the stooge's

feeling of adequacy that controls this process. It is difficult to institution-
alize psychopathy. To insure reliability and intensity in stooge behavior,
it is necessary to realize the costs of confederacy and to provide appropriate supports in the form of adequate pre-training, props and scripts
during the presentation, and decompression aimed at maintaining a separation of the role from the person.

Threats to esteem are often threats to internal validity. As long as these
threats are randomized across treatments they are not a major problem.
However, these threats can easily operate *differentially* within the same
experiment because they are sensitive to slight differences in manipulations. When these differential effects occur, manipulated variables become clouded. Legitimation of instructions, the promise of an informative
decompression, and foreknowledge of the general aims and value of
experimentation may enable the subject to postpone concerns about
esteem.

2. Detachment in Dyads

Field researchers report that when they become friendly with their
informant, they are tempted to see the world solely from his point of
view. If this occurs, the field man finds less and less that requires
explanation. A related problem exists in the supposedly minimal and
"programmed" contact between an experimenter and a subject. That
this contact is not standardized has been suggested by several persons
(Back, Hood, and Brehm, 1964; Criswell, 1958; Friedman, 1964). The
problem of interest here is the way in which the number of subjects that
an experimenter confronts at one time produces subtle differences in his
behavior.

Schachter (1959) has discussed this problem. He noted that when subjects faced imminent electric shock, they were more anxious when this
threat was made to groups of five to eight than when it was made to a
single subject, even though the instructions were identical. The following
is proposed as an explanation.

> Despite the experimenter's deliberate attempt to behave identically in
> both experiments, inevitably a more personal relationship resulted in the
> two-person experiment. In this two-person study, the subjects felt free
> to ask questions and make comments and frequently did so, resulting in
> a relationship more informal than in the group setting, where almost no
> subject seemed to feel uninhibited enough to comment freely [p. 23].

Thus as the size or intimacy of the group changes, subjects may feel
more or less comfort in seeking clarification of instructions, expressing
dissatisfaction, or approving the experimenter. The experimenter also
may act differently in small groups. He may express more interest, be

more responsive, and provide more cues about the desired response. If he has any reservations about the reasonableness of demands made upon the subject, these doubts are apt to be sharpened in a dyad and the experimenter may feel greater pressure to weaken the demands.

Obviously several of these problems decrease if all comparisons involve groups of similar size. However, many organizational experiments, especially large-scale simulations, require the experimenter to give different instructions and feedback to small subgroups. When subgroups are instructed, this increases the chances that the experimental outcomes are due not so much to the manipulated variable, as to the fact that selected portions of the instructions were better understood, that distasteful requirements were made less painful, or that some of the hypotheses were more apparent. These influences may be partly countered in simulations simply because subjects have so much factual material to remember. Furthermore, in contrast to Schachter's study, the demands on the experimenter in a simulation are more complex and, therefore, individual requests are not as likely to receive undivided attention.

Aside from the simulations, organization theorists are interested in small groups. Frequently, groups of many differing sizes are lumped into this category, and comparisons are made among experiments in which size varies. The present argument is that size may be a subtle threat to internal validity because it mediates the ease with which the experimenter can remain detached from subjects. As intimacy increases, the number of alternative explanations for a finding also increases.

3. Task Substitution

Subjects frequently work on several problems in addition to the one they have been assigned; this problem has been discussed elsewhere as the problem of redefinition (Weick, 1965). The present discussion focuses on a different aspect of the problem. It is concerned with this phenomenon solely as a problem of internal validity and seeks to avoid the implication that the subject accepts the experimenter's definition before he alters it. Sometimes the subject's task is totally different from the one assigned by the experimenter. Hence, the label "task substitution" is used. While task substitution takes many forms, some are more relevant to organizational research than others. For example, there are several reasons why the internal validity of studies of novel structures might be suspect. Persons who perform novel tasks in unfamiliar structures often feel uncomfortable. Unfortunately, they often interpret this discomfort as a sign of inefficiency, and they proceed to alter the task and/or the structure "to make it more efficient." "Players will equate uncomfortable or strange relations with ineffective relations and fail to give innovative schemes a fair trial. Their behavior is quite rational. They want to win, and the game will last a short time. All the pressure is to convert the new scheme into the old, tried-and-true way of doing things." (Bass, 1964, p. 4). Alterations to increase efficiency do not have to be drastic. They may even go unnoticed. Nevertheless, if alterations are present, the intended structure is not and the experimental outcomes have different antecedents.

There are occasions when just the opposite problem occurs, when persons retain intact a task they are supposed to change. Persons may be given a task but not enough information to complete it (Evan and Zelditch, 1961), they may be placed in a structure that contains contradictory requirements, they may be placed with a partner who is ill suited for a job. The reason for these assignments is that the experimenter wants to force the subjects to make some changes. It is assumed that if persons are bothered by these circumstances, they will try to make them more acceptable. The experimenter wants to find out what is more acceptable and how it is adopted. Unfortunately, persons tend to invest their environment—whatever its content—with meaning, and typically they are reluctant to make changes. They may presume that the experimenter would not have assigned them a structure unless he thought it to be worthwhile. Guetzkow and Bowes (1957) suggest that subjects rarely revise imposed requirements because they are uncertain which revisions are within the rules of the game and which are not. This uncertainty is especially pronounced when lengthy instructions precede task performance.

In short, subjects often make sense out of experimental conditions when they are not supposed to. If subjects "rationalize nonrational requirements" internal validity is lessened. When a novel structure affects behavior, the effect may be due to the reasonableness of the structure instead of its novelty.

Task substitution may also originate in triviality. Many experimental tasks require little concentration and permit the subject to think about other things while he is working. These distractions often become more interesting than the task at hand and the outcomes of the experiment reflect a preoccupation with the substitute task. Rather than working on two tasks simultaneously, the subject may simply change the trivial task to make it more interesting. Schultz (1964, p. 397) argues that a considerable portion of a subject's behavior in experiments can be viewed as an attempt to vary the pattern of stimulation that reaches him. Thus a subject may alternate his responses in order to introduce a change in the number, nature, and temporal sequence of stimuli in his surroundings. Conditions that are especially prone to produce alternation behavior are

(1) no reinforcement and/or knowledge of correctness of response, (2) great similarity between stimuli, (3) prolonged exercise of one response alternative, and (4) a short intertrial interval.

Thus, a simple cooperative game may be made competitive to increase its interest. Friedell (1964, p. 7) suggests that this is a common occurrence. "In many experimental games cooperation is boring and competition is interesting. Cooperative behavior may be represented by monotonous sameness of choice, while competition may involve variety. A structural reason for this is that effective competition often requires that one's opponent cannot predict one's strategy. In symmetrical games competition presents the attraction of testing oneself against a peer rather than a simple situation. Thus, subjects may actually cooperate by tacitly agreeing to compete."

Substitution because of triviality implies that simulations have an advantage because the subject has no time to make substitutions; too many things are going on. Herein lies one of the dilemmas in an organizational experiment. Presumably a simple task is preferable to a complex one and a simple environment is preferable to one with multiple happenings, because the subject can understand the assignment more quickly, there are fewer sources of distraction and, therefore, the independent variables should be less ambiguous. But, when these conditions exist, the subject also may have time on his hands and dream up variations of the basic task. A complex simulation leaves little time for fabrication, but it generates a different kind of substitution. The more an experimental setting resembles a real-life organization, the more an individual is prone to act as if the organization were real and not contrived. This may aid involvement, but it also means that the subject will impose constraints and definitions where none exist, ignore experimental requirements and definitions not in the actual organization, and redefine his position so that it accords with his position in natural organizations. In short, simulations encourage assimilation, simple settings encourage contrast. In both cases, substitutions make the experiment even less like an organization than it really is.

A substitute task is, by definition, not the task assigned by the experimenter or the one he wanted to study. If the substitution is undetected, the experiment has less internal validity.

4. Counter-Reference Demands

Experimental demands often require subjects to perceive or act in ways that are contrary to those which are valued in their reference groups. These contradictory demands may unintentionally produce ambivalence, uncertainty, or vacillation. When these conditions exist, they provide alternative explanations of experimental outcomes.

It may be argued that reference groups are not salient when a subject participates in experiments. However, it is probable that there are more cues that reinstate reference groups than are realized. For one thing, subjects are typically recruited from a homogeneous population. If they had not been members of a particular group, they would not have been contacted for the experiment. Thus, recruitment makes reference groups salient. Furthermore, the experimental instructions often remind the subject of a reference group. He is told that his responses are of interest because he is a typical college student, an engineer, a sophomore, a male, an adult, a psychology student, or an average human being. Although these instructions are usually intended merely to distract or heighten plausibility, they may lead the subject to act as if he is a member of that group. Relevance of a task or a dilemma to specific groups should also heighten their prominence as determinants of subsequent behavior. Jones and DeCharms (1957) report a study involving naval cadets where norms that were created experimentally clashed strongly with existing cadet norms. Subjects were asked to decide what disciplinanry actions should be administered to a turncoat. In one condition, the subjects were told that the norms for judging whether or not a person was a turncoat were unclear. The cadets, however, simply could not accept this information. Undoubtedly the combination of recruitment of a specific group plus a relevant issue contributed to the weakening of this manipulation. Loyalties to the Navy may well have been pitted against felt obligations to the experimenter. Ambivalence was clearly the product. Demands that are inconsistent with reference groups probably can never be completely ruled out of experiments, especially vivid simulations. If experimental conditions are linked randomly with various reference groups, internal validity is not threatened. The implication is that the experimenter should assess whether a reference effect occurred, should examine manipulations to see if they make particular reference groups salient, and, in general, should look for uncertainty or ambivalence as competing explanations of experimental outcomes.

Summary

An apparent relationship among variables may actually reflect attempted solutions to maintenance problems, differential understanding of instructions and preferred behaviors, performance of unassigned tasks, or tenuous resolutions of contradictory demands. These threats to internal validity are common in organizational experiments, are difficult to randomize, and are sensitive to slight changes in an independent variable. They are also difficult to detect. Changes in realism reduce some problems but create other ones. That the recognition and solution of these problems is mandatory can be seen if one looks at the next source of problems, external validity. External validity is concerned with generalization, and one needs to worry about generalization only when there is something to generalize from, namely a stable and valid relationship.

PROBLEMS OF EXTERNAL VALIDITY

Once an experimenter knows something about his laboratory subjects, he wants to know what he has also learned about other populations. This is the problem of external validity. External validity is concerned with the representativeness or generalizability of experimental findings. The criterion is, "To what populations, settings, and variables can this effect be generalized?" (Campbell, 1957, p. 297). External validity is restricted when conditions in the experiment are hard to find in everyday life. If the features of an experiment are rare, it is reasonable to conclude that the incidence of the demonstrated relationship will also be rare.

The following discussion describes five characteristics of experiments that hinder generalization.

1. Task Prominence

Experimental tasks differ from everyday tasks in several ways, the most obvious being that they command undivided attention from the subject. Even if the task is boring and the subject embellishes or makes substitutions for it, a single task is still involved. This contrasts with everyday life where attention is diffuse, where several tasks compete for attention (Atkinson and Cartwright, 1964), and where the existence of alternative tasks affects present productivity (Feather, 1963). Performance in the laboratory seldom reflects these competing demands on effort. As a result, laboratory findings may not hold up when replicated in the field where competing demands exist.

In addition to being prominent, laboratory tasks are also bounded. The subjects know that laboratory events will last for only a short time. Furthermore, many tasks have discrete trials and this may disrupt continuity, concentration, or the feeling that one is accomplishing a significant piece of work. The laboratory exercise, like assembly-line activity, is repetitious and movements become stereotyped (Schachter et al., 1961). These characteristics of tasks are relevant to external validity because they suggest that laboratory findings may obtain if the subject has circumscribed experiences and small exposure to the independent variable but that, as experiences lengthen and exposure becomes more intense and prolonged, relationships will change.

Laboratory tasks are often chosen for their sensitivity to independent variables (Hovland, 1959) and their openness to observation, not their representativeness. Unfortunately, not enough is known about tasks to be certain whether properties that promote sensitivity are also properties that materially affect a relationship when they are absent. The question of sensitivity is not to be confused with the argument that a highly sensitive task is "rigged" so that it amplifies what is, in reality, a trivial relationship. A sensitive task may magnify an insignificant effect. But that is not our concern here. Instead, assuming that some common elements are necessary for generalization, if features that aid sensitivity are features that also have to be present in the actual event for generalization to occur, then it may be difficult to obtain external validity.

A final task variable that may affect external validity is that of error prominence. When organizational activities are scaled down to fit the laboratory, it is seldom possible also to scale down the impact on the system of human errors. As a consequence, errors that would have only a slight effect on a natural system are a major disruption in a contrived system. Bass (1964, p. 5) describes the possible effects in a laboratory exercise of a minor managerial blunder. "As in real-life, a manager may blurt out the wrong words resulting in a 'wildcat' strike, and production will close momentarily. In real-life, this real effect may reduce industry-wide production by, say, 2 percent. In our game, it may reduce it by 35 percent for a given firm. Or, it might easily bankrupt a company in our game; it seldom does in real life." Errors frequently are handled in natural organizations with little enduring effect on the system. Experimental findings may have limited generality because they obtain only when errors have a marked impact on outcomes.

The preceding examples suggest that experimental tasks differ from everyday tasks along dimensions that may affect external validity. Simplicity itself does not necessarily threaten external validity. It depends on what is simplified, the rarity with which experimental task properties exist in everyday tasks, and the centrality of the property for generalization.

2. Limited Alternatives

Just as it makes a difference in productivity whether a person is constrained to one task or several, so it also makes a difference whether a subject feels that he is a member of one group or several. The presence or absence of alternative tasks or groups often has a marked effect on a person's perception of his situation. Kiesler and Corbin (1965) report that conformity decreases linearly as group attractiveness decreases, *unless* the individual is committed to the group, i.e., has a high probability of continued future membership. When a commitment exists there is considerable discomfort if one learns that the group actually is unattractive. To resolve this discomfort, the subject could either devalue the group or enhance it by trying to conform to and be more like the other members. Since devaluation is not wholly satisfying given the prospect of continued membership, increased conformity should occur and Kiesler and Corbin (1965) found that it did.

The implication of these results is that perceived longevity of group membership and the feeling of volition in becoming a group member have a marked effect on subsequent behavior. Even when duration and commitment are not manipulated, the experimenter should assess the subject's conception of these features of group life since they may influence the results. The easiest solution to a discomforting situation is to disown one's acts, reject the group, or be indifferent. Furthermore, realignment of group ties is a common response in everyday life. When these alternatives are unavailable in the laboratory, relationships between variables may be affected. The implication is that it is important to know the extent to which a subject feels he must account for and resolve experimental occurrences. Less pressure for resolution should exist if the event or group is perceived to be fleeting, if alternatives are available, or if the problems are of minor importance. As pressures for resolution increase, the findings may be less applicable to situations where persons can choose among many alternatives, one of which is escape.

3. Recruitment

Procedures to enlist subjects for an experiment may broaden or narrow the populations to which experimental findings can be generalized. Campbell (1957, p. 308) describes two principles that are relevant to recruitment as a source of bias. "The greater the cooperation required, the more the respondent has to deviate from the normal course of daily events, the greater will be the possibility of nonrepresentative reactions. . . . The longer the experiment is extended in time the more respondents are lost and the less representative are the groups of the original universe." Whenever impositions are considerable and subjects can refuse to participate, experimental results may apply only to a highly select population. By the time the experimenter has assembled a group of persons who are able to meet procedural requirements of the experiment (e.g., be free for three hours every day for a week); he may have constituted a highly select group thereby reducing external validity.

Even within a specific population, recruitment biases may appear. In academic environments, students who decide to fulfill their subject obligations early in the school year differ from those who postpone their participation until the last minute. Some manipulations are sensitive to these differences in motivation, others are not. Monetary incentives in experiments probably are more effective near the end of the month than at the start of the month. Extra credit for course grades is probably a stronger inducement after examinations are returned than before.

It is important to realize that experiments impose unique demands. Not everyone can or is willing to meet these demands. The more effort the experimenter has to exert to obtain subjects, the less representative his subjects will be.

4. First-Day-at-Work Syndrome

It is possible that experiments tell us more about how a person will act on his first day at work than on his 400th day. A person who is in an experiment, like the newcomer on a job, often has low confidence in his judgments, is easily influenced, misunderstands instructions, is uniformed, finds the job novel and interesting, is cautious, and tolerates many demands that would anger him in more familiar settings. Many of these behaviors dissipate as he becomes more accustomed to the assignment. Thus data that are collected before a job becomes routinized and familiar may have limited generality. The implication is clear that subjects should be fully instructed about a task and should perform it long enough so that they are completely familiar with it. If it is not possible to produce this much familiarity, then the experimenter should assess the role that novelty and uncertainty play in the findings. If it appears that variations in uncertainty would not change the results, or that familiarity is unrelated to the outcomes, then external validity is not jeopardized.

5. Multi-determinants

Perhaps the most general problem of external validity concerns the fact that field events are affected by more variables than are present when laboratory events occur. These additional variables could increase the magnitude of a laboratory effect, or they could wash it out. The problem is essentially one of how to handle these additional variables in the laboratory so that both control and external validity are retained. For example, if an experimenter regards five dimensions to be important for characterizing an organization and he manipulates one of these five, what should be done with the other four? Should they be ignored for the moment and treated as potential variables that might affect a relationship? Should each of the four variables be set at a value greater than zero so that they are at least present when the relationship is studied?

Undoubtedly when a person becomes highly concerned with these problems he will go to the field rather than remain in the laboratory. However, it should be remembered that the many circumstances surrounding natural events are potential rather than actual influences. If a basic process is being studied, then the question of modifications from additional variables will change the appearance of the process but not its structure.

Summary

Organizational experiments are vulnerable to several threats to external validity. An organization experiment may be unrepresentative because experimental demands impose a high attrition rate on subjects, because tasks are excessively prominent or are performed when novelty and uncertainty are at their height, or because experimental settings provide few alternatives and only a limited number of influences. Simulations are not the complete solution to problems of external validity because they also have difficulties with recruitment, task familiarity, and task prominence. Since both organizational theory and research are in their early stages, it is reasonable to expect that more attention in the immediate future will be focused on internal validity rather than external validity.

CONCLUSION

Despite the recent interest in organizational behavior on the part of behavioral scientists and the large amount of empirical data that has been collected on this problem, there are surprisingly few well-supported causal propositions about the determinants of organizationl behavior. The data and methods have often been unsuited to stating propositions of this kind. Most of the investigators who have studied organizations have been concerned chiefly with problems of external validity. The point of the present chapter is that we are unlikely to learn much about organizations unless we give just as much attention to questions of internal validity.

Laboratories often seem insignificant as a means to learn about organizations because they are judged against criteria established for the more common field investigation. Laboratory experiments often are structured quite differently from natural organizations and, for this reason, questions of generalization can be sizeable, as has been noted throughout. But there are ways in which the investigator can cope with the problem of external validity and can, therefore, benefit from the strength of the laboratory to show unambiguous causal linkages between events.

External *and* internal validity can be achieved if the experimenter moves back and forth between the laboratory and field as in the example of emotional disruption, if he moves between abstract and simulated organizations in the laboratory, or if he structures a field study so that it contains more of the controls found in the laboratory. Instead of changing his setting, the investigator may change his activities. He may establish a stable relationship in a tightly controlled situation and then lessen these constraints to see what variables condition the relationship, or he may find an interesting phenomenon and then tighten the contraints to see why it occurred. *Either* strategy is pointed toward the same eventual conclusion.

Laboratory experiments also seem useful because they press investigators to be explicit. The most common objection to the laboratory is that it does not contain several "obviously" important features of organization, e.g., a complex environment. This objection is well founded. But, when the investigator thinks in terms of building an organization in the laboratory, he has to explicate these variables, and he usually has to state why these variables must be included. It often happens that he finds that a variable really makes no difference to his problem whether it is included or not.

A final problem in laboratory experiments is that it is difficult to tell what the referent reality is for an organizational study. It is unclear what dimensions of a natural organization should be modeled in the laboratory or even what the dimensions are. It is clear that laboratories and natural organizations differ, but it is unclear which of the differences may be crucial because they condition a causal relationship. Non-obvious differences may turn out to be crucial. The point is that, until these crucial differences become clearer, considerable trial and error approximation between the two settings must occur.

Experiments have numerous shortcomings but they are also somewhat more versatile than existing folklore would suggest. As more and more of the shortcomings of the laboratory are pinpointed, it should be possible to strengthen their role in organizational research. Furthermore, an increasing number of phenomena can now be created in the laboratory and it seems clear that imaginative investigators will be able to increase the phenomena that can be brought under laboratory control. Although there is little history of organizations in the laboratory, the promise seems considerable.

REFERENCES

ABBREVIATIONS

ASR   *American Sociological Review*
HR   *Human Relations*
JAP   *Journal of Applied Psychology*
JASP *Journal of Abnormal and Social Psychology*
MS   *Management Science*
SSR   *Sociology and Social Research*

Abelson, P. "Bigotry in Science." *Science*, 1964, *144*, 371.
Adams, J. S. "Toward an Understanding of Inequity." *JASP*, 1963, *67*, 422–436.
Adams, J. S. and Jacobsen, P. R. "Effects of Wage Inequities on Work Quality." *JASP*, 1964, *69*, 19–25.
Adams, J. S. and Rosenbaum, W. B. "The Relationship of Worker Productivity to Cognitive Dissonance About Wage Inequities." *JAP*, 1962, *46*, 161–164.
Ammons, R. B. and Ammons, C. H. "A Standard Anagram Task." *Psychological Reports*, 1959a, *5*, 654–656.
_____. "Rational Evaluation of the 'Standard Anagram Task' as a Laboratory Analogue of 'Real-Life' Problem Solving." *Psychological Reports*, 1959b, *5*, 718–720.
Aronson, E., Turner, J. A., and Carlsmith, J. M. "Communicator Credibility and Communication Discrepancy as Determinants of Attitude Change." *JASP*, 1963, *67*, 31–36.
Atkinson, J. W. and Cartwright, D. "Some Neglected Variables in Contemporary Conceptions of Decision and Performance." *Psychological Reports*, 1964, *14*, 575–590.
Back, K. W., Hood, T. C., and Brehm, Mary L. "The Subject Role in Small Group Experiments." *Social Forces*, 1964, *43*, 181–187.
Bartlett, F. C. *Remembering*. Cambridge: Cambridge U. Press, 1932.
Bass, B. M. "Experimenting With Simulated Manufacturing Organizations." In S. B. Sells, ed., *Stimulus Determinants of Behavior*. New York: Ronald, 1963, 117–196.
_____. "Some Methodological Issues in Experimenting with Human Simulations of Business Firms." Paper prepared for 3rd Seminar in Social Science of Organizations, U. of Pittsburgh, 1964.
Bass, B. M. and Leavitt, H. S. "Some Experiments in Planning and Operating." *MS*, 1963, *9*, 574–585.
Bass, B. M. and Vaughan, J. A. "Experimenting With the Man-in-the-Middle." Paper presented at 1st Seminar in Social Science of Organizations, U. of Pittsburgh, 1962.
_____. "Production Organization Exercise IV." Pittsburgh: U. of Pittsburgh, Graduate School of Business, 1963.
Becker, S. W. "Organizations in the Laboratory." Paper prepared for 3rd Seminar in Social Science of Organizations, U. of Pittsburgh, 1964.

Beveridge, W. I. B. *The Art of Scientific Investigation.* New York: Norton, 1950.

Blalock, H. M. "Some Important Methodological Problems for Sociology." *SSR,* 1963, *47,* 398–407.

Blau, P. M. "The Research Process in the Study of *The Dynamics of Bureaucracy."* In P. E. Hammond, ed., *Sociologists at Work.* New York: Basic Books, 1964, 16–49.

Boring, E. G. "Cognitive Dissonance: Its Use in Science." *Science,* 1964, *145,* 680–685.

Bruyn, S. "Rhetorical Devices in Sociological Analysis." *Sociological Qtly.,* 1964, *5,* 101–112.

Burns, T. "The Communication Exercise." Paper presented at 3rd Seminar in Social Science of Organizations, U. of Pittsburgh (Pa.), 1964.

Campbell, D. T. "Factors Relevant to the Validity of Experiments in Social Settings." *Psychological Bull.,* 1957, *54,* 297–312.

Campbell, D. T. and Stanley, J. C. "Experimental and Quasi-Experimental Designs for Research on Teaching." In N. L. Gage, ed., *Handbook of Research on Teaching.* Chicago: Rand McNally, 1963, 171–246.

Carlsmith, J. M. and Aronson, E. "Some Hedonic Consequences of the Confirmation and Disconfirmation of Expectancies." *JASP,* 1963, *66,* 151–156.

Cohen, A. R. "Upward Communication in Experimentally Created Hierarchies." *HR,* 1958, *11,* 41–53.

Cook, S. W. and Selltiz, C. "A Multiple-Indicator Approach to Attitude Measurement." *Psychological Bull.,* 1964, *62,* 36–55.

Cottrell, N. B. "Means-Interdependency, Prior Acquaintance, and Subsequent Competition." *HR,* 1963, *16,* 249–262.

Criswell, J. H. "The Psychologist as Perceiver." In R. Taguiri and L. Petrullo, eds., *Person Perception and Interpersonal Behavior.* Stanford: Stanford U. Press, 1958, 95–109.

Cyert, R. M., March, J. G., and Starbuck, W. H. "Two Experiments on Bias and Conflict in Organizational Estimation." *MS,* 1961, *7,* 254–264.

Dalton, M. "Preconceptions and Methods in *Men Who Manage."* In P. E. Hammond, ed., *Sociologists at Work.* New York: Basic Books, 1964, 50–95.

Delbecq, A. "Managerial Leadership Styles in Problem Solving Conferences, II." *J. Academy of Management,* 1965, 8, 32–43.

Dill, W. R. "Desegregation or Integration?: Comments About Contemporary Research on Organizations." In W. W. Cooper, H. J. Leavitt, and M. W. Shelly, eds., *New Perspectives in Organization Research.* New York: Wiley, 1964, 39–52.

Dittes, J. E. and Kelley, H. H. "Effects of Different Conditions of Acceptance Upon Conformity to Group Norms." *JASP,* 1956, *53,* 100–107.

DiVesta, F. J., Meyer, D. L., and Mills, J. "Confidence in an Expert as a Function of His Judgments." *HR,* 1964, *17,* 235–242.

Dubin, R. "Business Behavior Behaviorally Viewed." In C. Argyris et al., *Social Science Approaches to Business Behavior.* Homewood, Ill.: Dorsey, 1962, 11–55.

Efran, J. S. "Descriptive Account of Training Procedures." In P. Pepinsky, ed., *Studies of the Effects of Sponsorship and Strategy Upon the Actor's*

Independence and Upon the Social Assessment of His Productivity. Columbus, Ohio: Ohio State U. Research Foundation, 1961, C37–C46.

Enke, S. "On the Economic Management of Large Organizations: A Laboratory Study." *J. Business,* 1958, *31,* 280–292.

Evan, W. M. and Zelditch, M. "A Laboratory Experiment on Bureaucratic Authority." *ASR,* 1961, *26,* 883–893.

Feather, N. T. "Persistence at a Difficult Task With Alternative Task of Intermediate Difficulty." *JASP,* 1963, *66,* 231–238.

Festinger, L. "Laboratory Experiments." In L. Festinger and D. Katz, eds., *Research Methods in the Behavioral Sciences.* New York: Holt, Rinehart & Winston, 1953, 136–172.

Festinger, L. and Carlsmith, J. M. "Cognitive Consequences of Forced Compliance." *JASP,* 1959, *58,* 203–210.

Fiedler, F. E. "A Contingency Model of Leadership Effectiveness." In L. Berkowitz, ed., *Advances in Experimental Social Psychology,* New York: Academic, 1964, I, 149–190.

French, J. R. P., Jr. and Snyder, R. "Leadership and Interpersonal Power." In D. Cartwright, ed., *Studies in Social Power.* Ann Arbor: U. of Michigan Press, 1959, 118–149.

Friedell, M. F. "The Experimental Game as an Instrument for the Study of Social Behavior." Paper presented at Midwestern Psychological Assn., 1964.

Friedman, N. "The Psychological Experiment as a Social Interaction." Unpublished Doctoral Dissertation, Harvard U., 1964.

Garfinkel, E. "A Conception of, and Experiments With 'Trust' as a Condition of Stable Concerted Actions." In O. J. Harvey, ed., *Motivation and Social Interaction.* New York: Ronald, 1963, 187–238.

Guetzkow, H. "A Use of Simulation in the Study of Inter-Nation Relations." *Behavioral Science,* 1959, *4,* 183–191.

Guetzkow, H. "Organizational Leadership in Task-Oriented Groups." In L. Petrullo and B. M. Bass, eds., *Leadership and Interpersonal Behavior.* New York: Holt, Rinehart & Winston, 1961, 187–200.

Guetzkow, H. and Bowes, A. E. "The Development of Organizations in a Laboratory." *MS,* 1957, *3,* 380–402.

Gustav, A. "Students' Attitude Toward Compulsory Participation in Experiments. *J. Psychology,* 1962, *53,* 119–125.

Harvey, O. J., ed. *Motivation and Social Interaction.* New York: Ronald, 1963.

Heider, F. "Social Perception and Phenomenal Causality. *Psychological Rev.,* 1944, *51,* 358–374.

Hoffman, L. R., Harburg, E., and Maier, N. R. F. "Differences and Disagreement as Factors in Creative Group Problem Solving." *JASP,* 1962, *64,* 206–214.

Hoffman, P. J., Festinger, L., and Lawrence, D. H. "Tendencies Toward Group Comparability in Competitive Bargaining." *HR,* 1954, 7, 141–159.

Homans, G. C. "The Strategy of Industrial Sociology." In G. C. Homans, ed., *Sentiments and Activities.* New York: Free Press, 1962, 257–268.

Hood, T. "The Decision to Participate in Small Group Experiments: Patterns of Self Disclosure and the Volunteer." Technical Report 14, Durham, N.C.: Duke University, Dept. of Psychology, 1964.

Hovland, C. I. "Reconciling Conflicting Results Derived From Experimental and Survey Studies of Attitude Change." *American Psychologist*, 1959, *14*, 8–17.

Hovland, C. I. and Weiss, W. "The Influence of Source Credibility on Communication." *Public Opinion Qtly.*, 1952, *15*, 635–650.

Hutte, H. "Decision-Taking in a Management Game." *HR*, 1965, *18*, 5–20.

Jacobs, R. C. and Campbell, D. T. "The Perpetuation of an Arbitrary Tradition Through Several Generations of a Laboratory Microculture." *JASP*, 1961, *62*, 649–658.

Jensen, B. T. "Instructions for 'The Railroad Game.'" Technical Memorandum 608, Santa Monica, Calif.: System Development Corp., 1961.

Jensen, B. T. and Terebinski, S. J. "'The Railroad Game:' a Tool for Research in Social Sciences. *J. Social Psychology*, 1963, *60*, 85–87.

Jones, E. E. *Ingratiation*. New York: Appleton-Century, 1964.

Jones, E. E. and DeCharms, R. "Changes in Social Perception as a Function of the Personal Relevance of Behavior." *Sociometry*, 1957, *20*, 75–85.

Joyner, R. C. "SIN–Simulation of Interaction in Communication Networks, II: Experiments With the Common Target Game." Unpublished *MS*, Carnegie Institute of Technology, 1965.

Kaplan, A. *The Conduct of Inquiry*. San Francisco: Chandler, 1964.

Kelley, H. H. "Communication in Experimentally Created Hierarchies." *HR*, 1951, *4*, 39–56.

Kelley, H. H., Condry, J. C., Jr., Dahlke, A. E., and Hill, A. H. "Collective Behavior in a Simulated Panic Situation." *J. Experimental Social Psychology*, 1965, *1*, 20–54.

Kelley, H. H., Thibaut, J. W., Radloff, R., and Mundy, D. "The Development of Cooperation in the 'Minimal Social Situation.'" *Psychological Monographs*, 1962, *76*, (19, Whole No. 538).

Kennedy, J. L. "Experimenters Manual: Research and Development Game." Unpublished *MS*, Princeton University, 1963.

Kiesler, C. A. and Corbin, L. H. "Commitment, Attraction, and Conformity." *J. Personality and Social Psychology*, 1965, *2*, 890–895.

King, D. C. "Summary of Intergroup Exercise I." Unpublished MS, Purdue University, 1964.

Krugman, H. E. "The 'Draw a Supermarket' Technique." *Public Opinion Qtly*, 1960, *24*, 148–149.

Krupp, S. "Pattern in Organization Analysis." New York: Holt, Rinehart & Winston, 1961.

Kuethe, J. L. "Social Schemas." *JASP*, 1962, *64*, 31–38.

Latané, B. and Arrowood, A. J. "Emotional Arousal and Task Performance." *JAP*, 1963, *47*, 324–327.

Leavitt, H. J. "Task Ordering and Organizational Development in the Common Target Game." *Behavioral Science*, 1960, *5*, 233–239.

_____. "Applied Organization Change in Industry: Structural, Technical, and Human Approaches." In W. W. Cooper, H. J. Leavitt, and M. W. Shelly, eds., *New Perspectives in Organization Research*. New York: Wiley, 1964, II, 55–71.

Lewin, K. *Field Theory in Social Science*. New York: Harper, 1951.

Lorge, I., Fox, D., Davitz, J., and Brenner, M. "A Survey of Studies Contrasting the Quality of Group Performance and Individual Performance." *Psychological Bull.*, 1958, *55*, 337–370.

Lyle, J. "Communication, Group Atmosphere, Productivity, and Morale in Small Task Groups." *HR*, 1961, *14*, 369–379.

Maier, N. R. F. and Hoffman, L. R. "Organization and Creative Problem Solving." *JAP*, 1961, *45*, 277–280.

March, J. G. and Simon, H. A. *Organizations*. New York: Wiley, 1958.

Marx, M. H. "The General Nature of Theory Construction." In M. H. Marx, ed., *Theories in Contemporary Psychology*. New York: Macmillan, 1963, 4–46.

McGrath, J. E. "Toward a 'Theory of Method' for Research on Organizations." In W. W. Cooper, H. J. Leavitt, and M. W. Shelley, eds., *New Perspectives in Organization Research*. New York: Wiley, 1964, 533–556.

Mechanic, D. "Some Considerations in the Methodology of Organizational Studies." In H. Leavitt, ed., *The Social Science of Organizations*. Englewood Cliffs: Prentice-Hall, 1963, 139–182.

Meier, R. C. "Explorations in the Realm of Organization Theory IV: The Simulation of Social Organization. *Behavioral Science*, 1961, *6*, 232–248.

Milgram, S. "Behavioral Study of Obedience." *JASP*, 1963, *67*, 371–378.

Milgram, S. "Issues in the Study of Obedience: a Reply to Baumrind." *American Psychologist*, 1964, *19*, 848–852.

Miller, L. K. and Hamblin, R. L. "Interdependence, Differential Rewarding, and Productivity. *ASR*, 1963, *28*, 768–778.

Mills, T. M. A Sleeper Variable in Small Groups Research: The Experimenter. *Pacific Sociological Rev.*, 1962, 5 (1), 21–28.

Orne, M. T. "On the Social Psychology of the Psychological Experiment: With Particular Reference to Demand Characteristics and Their Implications." *American Psychologist*, 1962, *17*, 776–783.

Pepitone, A. *Attraction and Hostility*. New York: Atherton, 1964.

Pilisuk, M. "Cognitive Balance and Self-Relevant Attitudes." *JASP*, 1962, *65*, 95–103.

Proshansky, H. and Seidenberg, B., eds., *Basic Studies in Social Psychology*. New York: Holt, Rinehart & Winston, 1965.

Raven, B. H. and Eachus, H. T. "Cooperation and Competition in Means-Interdependent Triads." *JASP*, 1963, *67*, 307–316.

Riecken, H. W. "A Program for Research on Experiments in Social Psychology." In N. F. Washburne, ed., *Decisions, Values, and Groups*. New York: Macmillan, 1962, II, 25–41.

Ring, K. "Some Determinants of Interpersonal Attraction in Hierarchical Relationships: A Motivational Analysis. *J. Personality*, 1964, *32*, 651–665.

Roby, T. B. "Subtask Phasing in Small Groups." In J. H. Criswell, H. Solomon, and P. Suppes, eds., *Mathematical Methods in Small Group Processes*. Stanford: Stanford U. Press, 1962, 263–281.

Roby, T. B. and Lanzetta, J. T. "Considerations in the Analysis of Group Tasks. *Psychological Bull.*, 1958, *55*, 88–101.

Rosenberg, M. J. "When Dissonance Fails: On Eliminating Evaluation Apprehension from Attitude Measurement." *J. Personality and Social Psychology*, 1965, *1*, 28–42.

Rosenberg, M. J. and Abelson, R. P. "An Analysis of Cognitive Balancing." In M. J. Rosenberg et al., *Attitude Organization and Change*. New Haven: Yale U. Press, 1960, 112–163.

Rosenthal, R. "On the Social Psychology of the Psychological Experiment: The Experimenter's Hypothesis as Unintended Determinant of Experimental Results. *American Scientist*, 1963, *51*, 268–283.

Sampson, E. E. and Insko, C. A. "Cognitive Consistency and Performance in the Autokinetic Situation." *JASP*, 1964, *68*, 184–192.

Schachter, S. "Deviation, Rejection, and Communication." *JASP*, 1951, *46*, 190–207.

————. *The Psychology of Affiliation*. Stanford: Stanford U. Press, 1959.

Schachter, S. and Singer, J. E. "Cognitive, Social, and Physiological Determinants of Emotional State." *Psychological Rev.*, 1962, *69*, 379–399.

Schachter, S., Willerman, B., Festinger, L., and Hyman, R. "Emotional Disruption and Industrial Productivity." *JAP*, 1961, *45*, 201–213.

Schein, E. H. *Organizational Psychology*. Englewood Cliffs: Prentice-Hall, 1965.

Schein E. H. and King, D. C. "The House Building and Community Planning Intergroup Exercise." Unpublished MS, Massachusetts Institute of Technology, 1964.

Schultz, D. P. "Spontaneous Alternation Behavior in Humans: Implications for Psychological Research. *Psychological Bull.*, 1964, *62*, 394–400.

Selznick, P. "Foundations of the Theory of Organization." *ASR*, 1948, *13*, 25–35.

Sherif, M. and Harvey, O. J. "A Study in Ego Functioning: Elimination of Stable Anchorages in Individual and Group Situations. *Sociometry*, 1952, *15*, 272–305.

Sherif, M. and Sherif, C. W. *Reference Groups*. New York: Harper, 1964.

Shure, G. H., Rogers, M. S., Larsen, I. M., and Tassone, J. "Group Planning and Task Effectiveness." *Sociometry*, 1962, *25*, 263–282.

Simon, H. A. "Comments on the Theory of Organizations." In A. H. Rubenstein and C. J. Haberstroh, eds., *Some Theories of Organization*. Homewood, Ill.: Dorsey, 1960, 157–167.

Solem, A. R. "An Evaluation of Two Attitudinal Approaches to Delegation." *JAP*, 1958, *42*, 36–39.

Stogdill, R. "Leadership, Membership, and Organization." *Psychological Bull.*, 1950, *47*, 1–14.

Strickland, L. H. "Surveillance and Trust." *J. Personality*, 1958, *26*, 200–215.

Thibaut, J. "The Motivational Effects of Social Dependence on a Powerful Agency of Control." In W. W. Cooper, H. J. Leavitt, and M. W. Shelly, eds., *New Perspectives in Organization Research*. New York: Wiley, 1964, 87–96.

Thibaut, J. and Riecken, H. W. "Some Determinants and Consequences of the Perception of Social Causality." *J. Personality*, 1955, *24*, 113–134.

Toda, M. "The Design of a Fungus-Eater: A Model of Human Behavior in an Unsophisticated Environment." *Behavioral Science*, 1962, *7*, 164–183.

Tuckman, B. W. "Personality Structure, Group Composition, and Group Function." *Sociometry*, 1964, *27*, 469–487.

Underwood, B. J. *Psychological Research*. New York: Appleton-Century, 1957.

Vroom, V. H. "A Working Paper on Laboratory Experiments on Organization." Paper prepared for 3rd Seminar in the Social Science of Organizations, U. of Pittsburgh, 1964.

Wager, L. W. and Palola, E. G. "The Miniature Replica Model and Its Use in Laboratory Experiments of Complex Organizations." *Social Forces*, 1964, *42*, 418–429.

Weick, K. E. "Reduction of Cognitive Dissonance Through Task Enhancement and Effort Expenditure." *JASP*, 1964, *68*, 533–539.

————. "Laboratory Experimentation with Organizations." In J. G. March, ed., *Handbook of Organizations*. Chicago: Rand McNally, 1965a.

————. "When Prophecy Pales: The Fate of Dissonance Theory." *Psychological Reports*, 1965b, *16*, 1261–1275.

Weick, K. E. and Penner, D. D. "Triads: a Laboratory Analogue." *Organizational Behavior and Human Performance*, 1966, *1* (2).

Zajonc, R. B. "The Requirements and Design of a Standard Group Task." *J. Experimental Social Psychology*, 1965, *1*, 71–78.

Zand, D. E. and Costello, T. W. "Effect of Problem Variation on Group Problem Solving Efficiency Under Constrained Communication." *Psychological Reports*, 1963, *13*, 219–224.

Zelditch, M. "Some Methodological Problems of Field Studies." *American J. Sociology*, 1962, *67*, 566–576.

Zelditch, M. and Evan, W. M. "Simulated Bureaucracies: A Methodological Analysis." In H. Guetzkow, ed., *Simulation in Social Science: Readings*. Englewood Cliffs: Prentice-Hall, 1962, 48–60.

Zelditch, M. and Hopkins, T. K. "Laboratory Experiments with Organizations." In A. Etzioni, ed., *Complex Organizations*. New York: Holt, Rinehart & Winston, 1961, 464–478.

Zigler, E. "Metatheoretical Issues in Developmental Psychology." In M. Marx, ed., *Theories in Contemporary Psychology*. New York: Macmillan, 1963, 341–369.

2

Organizational Change and Field Experiment Methods

LOUIS B. BARNES

Harvard University

One group attending the 1964 Pittsburgh conference was asked to relate field experiment methodology to the issue of organizational change. In some ways the task seemed too ambitious. Each area encompassed vast amounts of thought and confusion. Each area also contained elements which became highly complicated when related to the other area. Any major organizational change involves complex approaches, relationships, and processes that have been only roughly identified and described in the literature on change. These complex variables also create problems for the designer of experiments. In conventional experimental designs, a *single* variable (approach, phase, or relationship) is usually manipulated so as to study its effects on other variables. In complex organizational changes, too many changes occur too fast to permit this isolation of strategic variables.

Organizational change and field experimentation is not an impossible subject for a group to discuss, but it is most certainly a difficult one. It involves identifying, categorizing, and relating multiple variables. It

Particular appreciation for comments on an earlier draft is given to Drs. Douglas R. Bunker, Dexter Dunphy, Larry E. Greiner, Edward Lawler, Preston LeBreton, D. Paul Leitch, Victor H. Vroom, Richard E. Walton. I also wish to thank Miss Margaret Hennig for help with the bibliography. Support for writing this chapter was furnished by the Division of Research, Harvard Graduate School of Business Administration.

means relating criteria and more complex experimental designs to "better" defined change efforts. Finally, it assumes that the field experiment is a truly useful way to study organizational change, an assumption not yet well supported by evidence.

These were some of the problems facing the group discussing Organizational Change and Field Experiment Methods during a two-week summer period in 1964. This chapter expands upon those discussions and is divided into two major parts. The first part describes organizational change in terms of its (a) approaches, (b) relationships, and (c) processes. With these change dimensions in mind, the second part examines issues surrounding social science experimentation in general and organizational field experiments in particular. We hope to show that the field experiment is one of the most promising, but inadequately-used methods now available for the study and measurement of organization change.

ORGANIZATIONAL CHANGE

APPROACHES TO ORGANIZATIONAL CHANGE

Industrial managers are fond of noting that change is the only thing that remains constant in their work. They live from one upset to the next. They encounter a steady stream of new machines, processes, procedures, structures, and management faces. As education and technical knowledge have increased, so has the pressure within even conventional organizations for the introduction of new people, practices, and procedures.

Yet despite the common occurrence of organizational change, its dynamics and underlying processes are understood in only rough, ill-defined ways. Managers and social scientists who create and study change situations find that organizational changes involve multiple sets of complex variables whose identity, interaction, and impact vary from situation to situation. Those involved in the serious study of organizational change face an even greater problem in describing change with a static language system when the very concept involves the shifting of dynamic variables in relation to each other. The situation can be illustrated by an example.

Before the orbiting of Russia's Sputnik I, most American aircraft manufacturers were in the airframe business. They designed, sold, and produced propeller or jet aircraft for military and commercial customers. Their interests were largely defined by the traditions of manned flight at subsonic speeds. The heroes of the industry were the men who designed and flew jets using knowledge of aerodynamics and engine performance. The great names of the industry were names that dominated it during and after World War II—Douglas, Martin, Lockheed, Grumman, Boeing, North American, Republic.

Since the advent of the Sputniks, the picture in and around these companies has changed considerably. Most of the airframe companies were subjected to severe internal shakeups and stresses as they tried to decide whether they were in the airframe, spacecraft, electronic systems, engine, or missile business. As technology and market possibilities expanded, so did the drain on financial resources and the entrance of new firms into the field.

As a project became not an aircraft but an entire space exploration system, new forms of coordination and cooperation developed. The single decision-maker found himself surrounded by a new breed of technical experts, hardware, problems, and problem-solving processes. He ignored these at his peril. Yet more than one aircraft company almost disappeared in an attempt to adapt to space technology requirements.

This rough sketch describes a series of changes that drastically affected one industry. The changes involved more than technology, fuels, engines, and electronic systems. Along with the changing technology came changes in manpower, training, production facilities, personnel, scheduling, organizational structure, performance criteria, marketing strategies. In some cases, a new management was needed to introduce the new technologies. In other cases, an old management was able to adjust itself and alter an existing organization. Most important, the airframe–space age example shows that organizational change involves variable causes and effects not easily isolated from each other. A change in technology may result in management changes which may lead to new procedures and policies which may again result in new technologies, and so on. Under the circumstances, oversimplification becomes desirable and almost inevitable. An analyst almost *has* to choose a limited number of variables which are recognized as dynamically interdependent and then try to work from there toward a more accurate understanding of reality.

In an effort to do this, Leavitt (1965) selected four interacting variables which he called Task, People, Technology, and Structure. Task refers to the organization's production of goods and services and, while these sometimes change independently, according to Leavitt, they change more often in response to People, Technology and/or Structural approaches which influence the Task variable and each other.

Leavitt also notes that the People, Technology, and Structural approaches represent potential strategies for organizational change. Each attracts specialists who develop expertise in changing the strategic variable and then use this change strategy as their lever for improving organizational Task performance. The People specialists tend to focus on personnel placement, management development programs, job counseling, and human relationships within organizations. Technology specialists approach change as production engineers, computer experts, or systems designers. Structural specialists work on organization planning, work flow procedures, and staff–line configurations, among other things.

Needless to say, each of the professional specialists may find himself overlapping into another's area from time to time. Despite these overlaps, each tends to develop strong biases for one variable being more "strategic" than another. The preferences probably reflect the skills and talents of the proponents more than they do any single "best" approach to change. Thus Chapple and Sayles (1961) argue for work flow and structural changes while attacking those People approaches that attempt to train and "convert." Golembiewski (1964) chooses Structure as the strategic approach whose dimensions either permit or frustrate human relationships. By contrast, industrial engineers introduce new work systems and Technology variables through the use of machine replacement, operations research, or simulation techniques. People strategists use training programs, placement procedures, and testing as their major tools.

All of these efforts have led to many large scale organizational changes but few systematic studies. In order to correct this shortage, social scientists have recently become heavily involved in the study of organizational change both as participants and observers. They have even begun to design, plan, and implement changes that seemed exclusively within the manager's realm a generation ago. Behavioral scientists can be said to work with the same four variables mentioned above: Task, People, Technology, and Structure. However, their major contributions are in the area of People approaches to organization change. These approaches have involved what Leavitt (1965) calls "power equalization" and what some behavioral scientists like to call "planned change." As Bennis (1966, p. 82) describes the planned change approach, it involves "a *change agent* who is typically a behavioral scientist brought in to help a *client system* which refers to the target of change. The change agent, *in collaboration* with the client system attempts to apply *valid knowledge* to the client's problem."

The "planned change" approach may or may not apply more "valid" knowledge to the Task-People-Technology-Structure variables. It does, however, specify an outside change agent *collaborating* with a client system. But collaboration obviously is only one way of distributing power in a People approach to change. There are other ways which involve shifting attention from *what* is being changed (the variables) to *how* the changes are being introduced and implemented.

In this second vein, Bennis (1966) constructs a typology of seven other change styles in addition to "planned change." The eight approaches differ according to power distribution, goal setting, and change implementation. Briefly, the other seven approaches can be described as:

1. *Indoctrination Change.* Mutual and deliberate goal setting but under unilateral power.

2. *Coercive Change.* Unilateral goal setting with deliberate intentions using unilateral power. Coercive change would be exemplified by Chinese "brainwashing" and thought control practices.

3. *Technocratic Change.* Unilateral goal setting but shared power. One party defines the goal; the other party helps to reach that goal without question as to the goal's value.

4. *Interactional Change.* Shared power under conditions where goals are not deliberately sought.

5. *Socialization Change.* Unilateral power but collaborative goal implementation; e.g., small children develop under the influence of parents who unilaterally define the goals.

6. *Emulative Change.* Unilateral power without deliberate goals. This is found in formal organizations where subordinates "emulate" their superiors.

7. *Natural Change.* A residual category. Shared power with nondeliberate goal setting; i.e., changes are due to accidents, unintended events, etc.

Bennis' typology, according to its author, is only a crude and overlapping approximation of approaches to change. But it does go one step beyond a consideration of the four change variables (Task, People, Technology, and Structure). It suggests that change can be initiated by using various power distributions which may be as important or more important than the variable itself in determining the outcomes.

In another study Greiner (1965) searched the literature on organizational change and identified the most commonly used approaches as:

1. *The Decree Approach.* A "one-way" announcement originating with a person with high formal authority and passed on to those in lower positions (e.g., Taylor, 1911; Gouldner, 1954).

2. *The Replacement Approach.* Individuals in one or more key organ-

izational positions are replaced by other individuals. The basic assumption is that organizational changes are a function of personnel changes (e.g., Gouldner, 1954; Guest, 1962).

3. *The Structural Approach.* Instead of decreeing or injecting new blood into work relationships, management changes the required relationships of subordinates working in the situation. By changing the structure of organizational relationships, organizational behavior is also presumably affected (e.g., Burns and Stalker, 1962; Chapple and Sayles, 1961; Woodward, 1958; Dalton, Barnes, and Zaleznik [in press]).

4. *The Group Decision Approach.* Participation by group members in implementing alternatives specified by others. This approach involves neither problem identification nor problem solving, but emphasizes the obtaining of group agreement on a predetermined course (e.g., Coch and French, 1948; Lewin, 1958).

5. *The Data Discussion Approach.* Presentation and feedback of relevant data to the client system by either a change catalyst or by change agents within the company. Organizational members are encouraged to develop their own analyses of the data which has been given to them in the form of case materials, survey findings or data reports (e.g., Mann, 1957; Andrews, 1953).

6. *The Group Problem Solving Approach.* Problem identification and problem solving through group discussion with the help of an outsider. This would be one type of "planned change" (e.g., Sofer, 1961).

7. *The T–Group Approach.* Training in sensitivity to the processes of individual and group behavior. Changes in work patterns and relationships are assumed to follow from changes in interpersonal relationships. T–Group approaches focus upon the interpersonal relationships first, then hope for, or work toward, improvements in work performance (e.g., Argyris, 1962; Foundation for Research on Human Behavior, 1960).

Not surprisingly, Greiner's seven approaches, like Bennis', tend to emphasize the power distribution style in each case. The approaches described above move in a roughly descending order from unilateral power to mutually-shared power; i.e., the Decree approach represents unilateral initiation by formal authority while the T-Group approach represents a highly collaborative attempt at shared influence. (At the same time, Greiner's Replacement and Structural approaches can be more generally classified as People and Structure approaches which can be implemented by any one of the other five power styles described by Greiner.) Without question, the Decree approach is more prevalent in industry than the other approaches. However, a survey of the literature shows increasing emphasis on Greiner's last four approaches and their greater uses of shared power. According to McGregor (1960) and Likert (1961) Problem Solving and T–Group approaches with most shared power) are even supplanting the earlier (and more manipulative) Group Decision approaches.

Leavitt (1965) attributes the increase in shared control to the fact that power distribution is more directly confronted in organizations than it once was. Whereas power historically accompanied formal status positions, it no longer does to the same extent. In a modern industrial society, power conflicts can arise when formal status differs from status depending upon knowledge, informal social control, or professional reputation. Formal status no longer overshadows other sources of power to the extent that it once did. When other sources of power became more evident, says Leavitt (1965, p. 1153): "It was to be expected then that the next moves . . . would be toward working out the power variable. And it was obvious too that the direction would be toward power equalization rather than toward power differentiation. The theoretical underpinnings, the prevalent values, and the initial research results all pointed that way."

The importance of Leavitt's observation is shown in some further work by Greiner (1965) who sought to identify the conditions that differentiated "successful" from "less successful" large-scale change efforts. Greiner found that *all* of the nine published accounts that qualified for inclusion (on the basis of large-scale change effort and data adequacy) involved attempts at what Leavitt has called "power equalization." In these cases, the change approaches differed but power equalization seemed a common feature.

Our review of organizational change has so far described *what* is being changed and *how* it is being changed. Leavitt's four variables, Task, People, Technology, and Structure emphasize *what* is being varied. The Bennis and Greiner descriptions show that differences in power distribution can affect how the changes will be initiated and implemented; change can be arbitrarily introduced by a single authority source, or the power can be more widely shared by the individuals concerned.

In addition to *what* approaches are used and *how* power is distributed, organizational change also involves the changing of human relationships —*who*. Some individuals assume key positions from which they try to influence others in an organizational change situation.

CHANGING RELATIONSHIPS

The folklore of change thrives on accounts of courageous individuals who unilaterally defied a complacent majority. These courageous (with hindsight) individuals usually advanced an idea they tried to demonstrate to society with little or no initial success. Under these circumstances, a David and Goliath syndrome developed. David, the courageous advocate of righteousness, progress, and a changed social order must slay the giants of resistance and tradition. The timid majority are pictured as unwilling to support the Davids, while those who support the Goliaths do so in order to maintain their vested interests. In the end, however, David slays the giant, Jack slays the beanstalk giant, and the prince slays the dragon. Virtue triumphs, and society (as represented by the next generation) sees the folly of its forebearers. The David's, Sophocles', Pasteur's, and Galileo's are elevated to positions of social reverence and respect. Individualistic courage is praised while conformity and resistance to change are eternally condemned.

Forgotten in these accounts of courage and individualism are the times some silly David clung to an idea that was intellectually and socially worthless. In these cases the forgotten resisters of change performed a service to society, for the initiators of change (again in retrospect) were rightly held in check.

These patterns of initiative and resistance are as familiar in organizations as in other social situations, except that the picture is more complex. Typically, the charisma of the change initiator sparks support among a sympathetic group of change advocates. The advocates challenge the change resisters. Either group may, with hindsight, turn out to have been rational and reasonable while the other was not. In either case, the process of change involved initiation, advocacy, and resistance.

For the moment, we shall ignore the creative initiators of change. They have received much attention in the writings on individualism, conformity, and courage. Their offspring range from the world's great religions and sciences to the fantasies of Don Quixote. They have overshadowed those we wish to focus upon briefly: their followers who advocate change and their adversaries who resist it.

Figure 1 describes a typology in which *either* advocacy or resistance may be accompanied by reasoned or emotional behavior. Rational Advocates may (and usually do) have to cope with change Radicals as well as with the resisters of change. Rational Resisters must cope with their own Traditionalists (who resist for the sake of resistance), as well as with the advocates of change. Both advocacy and resistance can be rational and realistic. Likewise, neither one may be. There is no guarantee that "change for its own sake" is any more rationally based than is "resistance to change."

Within organizational change situations, all four types probably operate, even though they are hard to isolate and identify at the time.

Nevertheless, some patterns and symptoms seem to characterize each type. In Figure 1, we describe the four types as Rational Advocates, Radicals, Rational Resisters, and Traditionalists.

FIGURE 1

Relationships of Persons
Within Organizational Change
Situations

	Advocates	Resisters
Rational Objective	Rational Advocates	Rational Resisters
Emotional Subjective	Radicals	Traditionalists

Rational Advocates

The Rational Advocates (R.A.'s) tend to create data-based pressures for change within the organization and respond favorably to pressures for change from outside. Though not the initiators of change, they are early to recognize change proposals and to support change initiators. The more the R.A.'s represent upper management, the easier it is for a change initiator to gain sponsorship. Once they personally test and observe the merit of new proposals, the R.A.'s begin to work changes into their own areas of responsibility. Because their understanding and advocacy of change is based upon data, their chances of success are also fairly strong. The importance of an R.A. group is indicated in a study of major organizational change by Barnes and Greiner (Blake and Mouton; Barnes and Greiner, 1964) in which the R.A.'s demonstrated a proposed change approach successfully to themselves first on a limited organizational scale, then began to move the approach systematically into other areas of the company.

Radicals

The Radicals become change advocates mostly in response to emotional influence and nonrational appeals. They continue change advocacy in this same vein. They may simply identify themselves with the change-for-its-own-sake initiators, or they may seek to identify themselves with prestigeous movements. Their advocacy of change, in any case, depends more upon subjective identification than upon objective analysis. This means that Radicals tend to support change movements almost regardless of a proposal's real merits. Such forms of influence and advocacy are described by Frank (1963) in a book called *Persuasion and Healing* describing various movements of psychotherapy, religious healing, and Communist brainwashing. Frank also describes studies in which an inert medicine hastened a healing process. The real "medicine" was the patient's psychological response to the inert placebo. The same placebo-type effects were found among psychiatric patients who improved simply because they *believed* (with no basis for this belief) that they would be helped. As Frank (1963, p. 24) notes: "Comparison of the effects of psychotherapy and placebos . . . suggests that certain symptoms may be relieved equally well by both . . . and raises the possibility that one of the features accounting for some of the success of all forms of psychotherapy is their ability to arouse the patient's expectation of help."

For the Radical who wants help, the placebo of an emotionally-based change proposal may be enough to draw his support. Not surprisingly, Frank reports that placebo successes occurred most often with patients who tended to be dependent, emotionally reactive, conventional, and more trusting than other patients.

Most likely, both types of change advocates (Rational Advocates and Radicals) respond partly to objective and partly to emotional appeals. Like any typology, the split is an oversimplification. Yet, it does serve to point out that change advocacy has its placebo enthusiasts as well as those who base their advocacy on realism. The same is true to those who resist change. For example:

Rational Resisters

The Rational Resisters represent reality-based resistance. They represent those who would lose status, prestige, or influence because of proposed changes. Rational Resisters are often found resisting political coups, company faceliftings, and threatening improvement programs. Their resistance can be useful unless their defensiveness becomes more habitual than their data-based appraisal of a situation. By constantly defending the status quo, they may also hasten the chances of their own defeat. The Rational Resister (R.R.) category suggests that resistance to change is as mature a response under some conditions as is change advocacy. Because of their rational tendencies, the R.R.'s may be valuable organizational members. They nevertheless pose a problem for change advocates who may feel obligated to repair or replace R.R. losses after a successful change introduction.

Traditionalists

The Traditionalists, like the R.R.'s, resist changes, but for less objective reasons. Their type of conservatism tends to respond negatively to almost any change other than changes "back" to the old ways. Just as the Radicals sponsor change for its own sake, the Traditionalists cling to conventional practice as an end in itself. They may suffer no actual deprivation as a result of proposed changes, but still take "prophet of doom" positions. When the doom prophesied fails to materialize or convince others, the Traditionalists tend to react with anger and envy toward the change advocates. Because they rely for defense upon emotional traditionalism, they tend to become isolated from reality as changes continue to develop. Furthermore, change advocates attempt to seal off the Traditionalists from change influences so as to accelerate change in the organization. They also tend to seek the removal of Traditionalists from the scene altogether.

Again, the four types, like categories in any typology, are less distinct in reality than on paper. Under the pressures of emotional strain, R.A.'s and R.R.'s may move toward less realistic positions. Nevertheless, the typology helps to define some of the change relationships found among organizational members. It also will help us to discuss the *processes* of change which lend a dynamic to change approaches and human relationships. This is done in the next section. After that, we shall examine field experiments as a methodology for studying these change phenomena.

CHANGE PROCESSES

Up to this point, our review of organizational change takes account of change variables, change approaches, and change relationships. The map is a simple one, but it helps to separate *what* is being changed (variables) and *how* it is being changed (approaches) from *who* the crucial parties are (relationships) in the change process.

At the same time, the organizational change process typically involves a passage of time. Starting with one complex of dynamic equilibria, the organization shifts to others during and after changes. This transition from one set of equilibria to another suggests that there may also be some identifiable phases of change which make up the whole process.

The most familiar of these change phase concepts was first suggested by Lewin in 1947 (Lewin, 1958). Three phases are involved: the unfreezing of an old pattern, the changing to a new one, and the refreezing of the new pattern. Lewin's model assumed that opposing forces create varying amounts of pressure on a situation. When the opposing pressures are equal, the situation does not change. However, when pressure is added to one force or subtracted from another, change begins to occur and the equilibria move to another level. This force-counterforce struggle keeps changing the equilibria while new pressures and the shifting weights of old pressures are constantly at work.

The Lewinian model furnishes a rough picture of the change process. However, it remains unclear on the subprocesses of change that occur within the three major phases. Our understanding of the subprocesses is rudimentary at best. Schein (1961) describes them as well as anyone in his paper on attitude changes. Referring to the "unfreeze" process, he notes:

> Some of the elements which all unfreezing situations have in common are the following: (1) the physical removal of the influence target from his accustomed routines, sources of information, and social relationships; (2) the undermining and destruction of all social supports; (3) demeaning and humiliating experiences to help the target see his old self as unworthy and thus to become motivated to change; (4) the consistent linking of reward with willingness to change and of punishment with unwillingness to change [p. 8].

With regard to the "change" process, Schein describes two components which may or may not be sequentially phased:

> The actual influence is most likely to occur by one of two processes. The target finds one or more models in his social environment and learns new attitudes by identifying with them and trying to become like them; or the target confronts new situations with an experimental attitude and develops for himself attitudes which are appropriate to the situation and which remove whatever problem he faces. These two processes—*identification* and *internalization*—probably tend to occur together in most concrete situations, but it is worthwhile, for analytical purposes, to keep them separate [p. 8].

Finally, Schein has a few comments on the subprocesses of "refreezing." He states:

> If the new attitude has been internalized while being learned, this has automatically facilitated refreezing because it has been fitted naturally into the individual's personality. If it has been learned through identification [with a role model] it will persist only so long as the target's relationship with the original influence model persists unless new surrogate models are found or social support and reinforcement is obtained for expressions of the new attitude [p. 10].

Although these comments by Schein help to clarify the workings of Lewin's concepts, they still leave the subprocesses largely unspecified. We need further clarification of the specific steps and subphases.

Greiner (1965) tried to do this in an effort to learn more about major organizational change efforts. He examined nine large scale studies. Four of these studies he labeled "successful" change efforts (Jaques, 1952; Rice, 1958; Guest, 1962; Seashore and Bowers, 1963). Organizational change in these situations seemed to be "growing in intensity, spreading throughout the organization, having a marked effect on actual behavior, and resulting in improved organization performance" (Greiner, 1965, p. 24). Several other studies appeared to report successful major change efforts but contained insufficient published data (e.g., Whyte, 1951; Mann, 1957; Lawrence, 1958; Dalton, Barnes, and Zaleznik, in press). A third set of reports and cases were labeled "less successful" by Greiner. This set of studies showed changes which "seemed to be fading, showing confinement to small parts of the organization, revealing little in the way of actual behavior change, and pointing to few signs of improved organization performance" (ibid., p. 24). In this set of studies were contributions by Gouldner (1954), Strauss (1954), Argyris (1962), and cases in Whyte (1955), and Lawrence et al. (1961).

In comparing the findings, Greiner reported ten conditions that seemed to differentiate the successful from the less successful. The "successful" major change efforts followed a sequence where:

1) The organization is under great pressures for improvement both from within and outside the organizational unit. These pressures precede the change attempts.

2) The organization and its management experience great difficulty in coping with the pressures.

3) A newcomer with experience and a reputation for improving organizations enters the picture.

4) The newcomer enters the organization at or near the top and begins to work with top-level managers.

5) An initial act of the newcomer is to clarify the working relationship he wishes to have with the organization.

6) The head man of the organization assumes a direct and highly involved role in implementing the changes.

7) The newcomer engages many parts of the organization in a collaborative, fact-finding, problem-solving diagnosis of organizational problems.

8) The newcomer provides new methods and recommendations for solving problems and taking action.

9) The newcomer's proposals are tested on a small scale and found useful for problem-solving before they are introduced to the rest of the organization.

10) The change effort is spread through a series of success experiences and absorbed into other parts of the organization.

The "less successful" change efforts showed uneven gaps in the above sequence. Some of the conditions seemed to be present while others were not, or else they appeared in highly distorted forms.

Greiner's ten phases shed some light on the subprocesses that occur in major organizational change. With some rephrasing, the ten points can be fitted to the Lewinian change model and to our earlier discussion of change, approaches, and relationships. For example, the "unfreeze" subprocesses become:

a) Pressures for improvement come from both inside (R.A.'s and Radicals) and outside (e.g., technology, economic, etc.) the organization. Management is unable to adequately meet the demands for improvement.

b) A change initiator appears with a record of success behind him. He sets forth the power distribution approach he wants to use in an effort to clarify his relationships with management.

c) The change initiator gains the initial support of the top-level manager (or else he *is* the top level manager) and the support of a few R.A.'s and Radicals as he sets up a diagnostic study of the organization's problems.

The "change" subprocesses are:

d) The change initiator suggests a series of new steps involving the Task, People, Technology, and/or Structure variables. These new steps are suggested in a way consistent with the power approach specified by the change initiator as necessary for his relationships with management.

e) The top-level manager agrees to try out the change initiator's proposals, at least on a limited basis. The proposals are initially tested and found workable by a small number of R.A.'s and Radicals.

f) Resistance begins to form among the R.R.'s and Traditionalists.

The "refreeze" subprocesses become:

g) Resistance strengthens among the R.R.'s and Traditionalists.

h) Change proposals are tested on a wider basis throughout the organization by R.A.'s and Radicals. Successes outnumber failures. Failures are explained by R.A.'s and Radicals as due to faulty approaches by R.R.'s and Traditionalists.

i) Change proposals become part of the organization's way of life. Exaggerated claims of success tend to come from Radicals.

During the transition, individual attitudes tend to change, goals become reshaped, new alliances are formed, and the R.A. and Radical proponents multiply in number so that the change program becomes internalized within the organization. Dalton, Barnes, and Zaleznik (in press) describe this internalization process as follows:

The model which we shall describe contemplates four subprocesses which proceed concurrently as part of the process of socially induced change: a) a movement from sense of negative self worth toward a heightened feeling of positive worth on the part of the individual or individuals who are the objects of influence, b) a move from generalized and global goals toward specific and concrete objectives, c) a movement away from prior social ties toward new relationships, and d) a movement from an external locus of motivation for change toward an internalization of the induced behavior.

Put another way, during the unfreeze, change, and refreeze phases (a) positive self worth increases, (b) goals become more specific and concrete, (c) new alliances and relationships are formed, and (d) motivation comes more from within and less from outside. At the same time, R.A.'s and Radicals use their power (either unilaterally or in some shared fashion to change Task, People, Technology, and/or Structure variables in a manner prescribed by a change initiator. Their efforts are resisted by the R.R.'s and Traditionalists, but with diminishing success as the change effort spreads within the organization.

Figure 2 presents a summary diagram of this organizational change process. An organizational equilibrium is unfrozen by internal and/or external pressures. The internal complaints and pressures are verbalized by those whom we have called R.A.'s and Radicals. They provide the early support for a change initiator who seems to have answers for some of the organization's unsolved problems. The change initiator communicates to management *how* he believes the problems should be solved by specifying a power distribution approach which involves both himself and others in the organization. This approach receives the support of the top-level manager as well as of R.A.'s and Radicals within top management. The change initiator also develops with management a plan for *what* approaches (Task, People, Technology, and/or Structure) should be emphasized. An initial trial change is attempted and found successful. Change efforts are expanded, although by this time .resistance has formed among the R.R.'s and the Traditionalists. As the resistance stiffens, change efforts intensify, successes mount, and the overclaiming of success begins. Under these conditions of refreezing, the organization reaches another equilibrium which remains only until further major change efforts unfreeze the situation again.

The major problem with Figure 2 is that it depicts a change process that occurs often but has been studied little in a systematic way. In addition, though major organizational change does occur often, much of the literature on change in organizations focuses upon the behavioral scientist and upon his interests in "planned change," (e.g., Argyris, 1962;

FIGURE 2

The Change Process in
Organizations

UNFREEZE

Pressures for improvement from both the inside (R.A.'s and Radicals) and outside (e.g., technology, economic, etc.) the organization. Management is unable to meet adequately the demands for improvement.

Change initiator appears with a record of success behind him. Sets forth the power distribution approach he wants to use in an effort to clarify his relationships with management.

Change initiator gains the initial support of the top-level manager and of a few R.A.'s and Radicals as he sets up a diagnostic study of the organization's problems.

CHANGE

The change initiator suggests a series of new steps involving the Task, People, Technology, and/or Structure variables. These new steps are suggested in a way that is consistent with the power approach specified by the change initiator as necessary for his relationships with management.

The top-level manager agrees to try out the change initiator's proposals, at least on a limited basis. The proposals are initially tested and found workable by a small number of R.A.'s and Radicals.

Resistance begins to form among R.R.'s and Traditionalists.

REFREEZE

Resistance strengthens among R.R.'s and Traditionalists.

Change proposals are tested on a wider basis throughout the organization by R.A.'s and Radicals. Successes outnumber failures. Failures are explained by R.A.'s and Radicals as due to the power approaches used by R.R.'s and Traditionalists.

Change proposals become part of the organization's way of life. Exaggerated claims of success tend to come from Radicals.

- - - - - - - - - → INCREASE IN SENSE OF POSITIVE SELF WORTH - - - - - - →

- - - - - - - - - → GROWING SPECIFICITY OF GOALS - - - - - - →

- - - - - - - - - → FORMATION OF NEW ALLIANCES AND RELATIONSHIPS

- - - - - - - - - → INTERNALLY RATHER THAN EXTERNALLY GENERATED MOTIVATION

Coch and French, 1948; Bennis, 1963; Foundation for Research on Human Behavior, 1960). This is unfortunate since behavioral scientists have really done more work with change in group settings than with organizational change. As Bennis (1966, p. 174) admits a bit ruefully toward the end of his paper on planned organizational change: "Up to this point, I have used the phrase organizational change rather loosely. In Argyris' case, for example, organizational change refers to a change in values of eleven top executives, a change which was not necessarily of an enduring kind and which apparently brought about some conflict with other interfaces. In most other cases of planned organizational change, the change induction was limited to a small, elite group."

This failure to either influence or study large-scale changes in organizations prompted Blake and Mouton (1964) to design a set of programmed learning exercises around a theoretical construction called the Managerial Grid. Blake and Mouton set up their laboratory seminars so that managers were the teachers, students, consultants, and researchers. In this way, the educational phase of the program was spread through an entire managerial system with little help from professional educators or change catalysts. As Bennis (1966, p. 174) points out: "Only in the work of Blake is organizational change discussed confidently in a systems way; his program includes the training of the entire management organization and at several locations he has carried this step to include wage earners."

Blake and Mouton claim that their approach has one major strength which relates to our earlier discussion of change "approaches"; they place great emphasis upon the fact that their Managerial Grid programs are based upon a theoretical framework involving five basic styles of management. Some behavioral scientists argue that Grid theory is not a theory but rather a description of power distribution approaches with one "best" approach. Blake and Mouton maintain that Grid theory furnishes not only a set of alternative power distribution approaches, but that it permits managers to compare these approaches with each other so that a manager can better evaluate and predict performance on problem-solving tasks. In addition, though they disclaim the "one best" approach, Blake and Mouton have definitely furnished a model which serves as an impersonal authority figure in an organizational change process. First reports on the Grid approach as it was tried in a large industrial plant and then researched in a field study by Barnes and Greiner (Blake and Mouton; Barnes and Greiner, 1964; Greiner, 1965) are impressive. In addition, the writer knows of three actual and five drawing board field experiments using the Managerial Grid approach and sponsored by the companies involved. All eight experiments involve large-scale change efforts.

With such a promising report of work in progress, it seems hard to understand why there should be any pessimism on the related topics of organizational change and field experiment methods. And yet there is. To begin with, Bennis (1966, p. 172) hedges his enthusiastic report of the behavioral scientists' "planned change" efforts when he notes that: "It is not at all obvious to me that the types of change induced by the change agents are: 1) compatible with 'human nature' or in accord with 'findings from the behavioral sciences' as some change agents assert, or 2) desirable even if they are in tune with man's need structure, or 3) functional." These cautious words partly open up a problem currently important to behavioral scientists themselves. In essence, the question being debated is whether or not their "science" permits active involvement and advocacy of preferred change approaches within organizations or anywhere else. The dispute is also found wherever behavioral scientists have voiced professional opinions or taken action on issues such as foreign policy, nuclear disarmament, civil rights, job retraining, executive development, or political elections.

This problem need not concern us if we are interested only in organizational change, but it becomes crucial as soon as we turn our thoughts to the *study of* change. Some behavioral scientists (e.g., Blake and Mouton, Argyris, Shepard, Bennis, Sofer, Rice, Jaques, Trist, F. Mann) seek and apparently achieve proficiency in both areas. But behavioral scientist critics decry these dual attempts to change organizations and also do research on the changes. The possible bias of social scientist involvement is of major concern in more than one academic setting these days. The dilemma posed by these bias problems cannot be avoided by anyone interested in field experiment methods. By exploring and taking a position on this underlying dilemma now, we can begin to clarify our later position on field experiment methods.

THE UNDERLYING DILEMMA

The underlying dilemma exists for a behavioral scientist when he feels forced to identify himself *either* with the values of scientific inquiry or with the values of change advocacy. Some behavioral scientists feel that the choice is necessary for the good of the profession. For them, the essence of professionalism is the impersonal detachment that goes with medicine, law, and, of course, science. They believe that professional inquiry becomes subjectively distorted as soon as a scientist finds himself emotionally involved in his data. They also point to the social sciences' struggle to gain respect from the "hard" natural sciences which have historically valued objectivity, detachment from personal interests, and the search for truth (Shepard, 1956; Merton, 1957; Barnes, 1960).

In their efforts to demonstrate objectivity and gain respect from the "hard" sciences, social scientists have tended to make a fetish out of detachment while creating an impressive array of research designs and methodological tools. These efforts, however, have not been entirely successful. Professional meetings continue to ring with sharp attacks on subjective analysis in study after study. The attacks are sharpest where the behavioral scientist–observer also tried to influence human behavior toward more "productive," "participative," "creative," "healthy," "reality centered," patterns. However, those attacked for subjective analysis have included not only changers of organizations, but also therapists, experimenters, psychoanalysts, and the architects and implementers of most educational changes within and beyond universities (e.g., Eysenck, 1960).

In essence, the critics of observer "involvement" want a science built upon the observation of human behavior rather than a science which involves attempts to practice as well as observe. Observers, so the reasoning goes, remain detached and relatively objective. Participants become involved and overly subjective; they begin to overvalue and push their own beliefs and "normative" theories.

In some cases, the distinction becomes rather fine. Although "observer" scientists would approve a study designed to compare certain variables (e.g., organizational structure "A" and organizational structure "B"), they would criticize observers who then became advocates and helped management to adopt one structure over another, even though the change efforts were based upon "scientific" evidence gained from the first study. In effect, the normative position of the "observer" scientist is that, since involvement corrupts, behavioral scientists should stick to the external observation of data; they should not be part of the data they wish to study.

Nevertheless, an increasing number of behavioral scientists have begun to work on the application of change knowledge as well as on the understanding of it. They subscribe to Kurt Lewin's statement that: "If you want to really understand how something works, try to change it." Instead of picturing themselves as studying unresponsive systems, they propose the physician-patient relationship where the physician tries to understand the patient's symptoms first, but then works to improve the patient's health as well. The behavioral scientist advocates see no real dichotomy between their own efforts and the "important" values of science (i.e., the overall search for knowledge and truth). They also see no real conflict between dedication to science and interest in practical application. Most would take the position of Kaplan (1964, p. 398–399) who writes that:

> Whether the behavioral scientist should concern himself at all with matters of policy, personal or social, is a question on which no concensus has been reached in the scientific community. On the one hand, many behavioral scientists are very much occupied with the problems that arise *in* human behavior (and not only in the attempt to describe or explain behavior), and are also professionally engaged with questions of what is to be done by people in quandries, in contexts ranging from marital to foreign affairs. On the other hand, there are those who regard such concerns as lying quite outside the scientific enterprise itself, and perhaps even as antithetical to that enterprise. Science, as they conceive it, is the search for truth, not usefulness. Whether the truth is useful is of no professional interest to the scientist, but only whether it is indeed true; how it is put to use is no business of his. . . . To engage in inquiry so as to achieve a utilitarian end is nothing other than a prostitution of the scientific intelligence.
>
> This second point strikes me as singularly lacking in perspective, especially on the history of science itself. Even the eighteenth century tradition of science as an occupation for gentlemen of leisure manifested a striking concern with the practical interests of war, commerce, industry, and agriculture, and even the purest of the sciences owe a not inconsiderable debt to such interests. The fact is that the distinction between "pure" and "applied" science, whatever its logical ground, is not of much help in understanding the actual growth of knowledge. . . . The irony is that the behavioral scientist, in his aspiration eventually to achieve the scientific standing of physics, is so often more royalist than the kings; the first two laws of thermodynamics, for example, were formulated long after the scientific data were available, "and they arose because of the social stimulation of steam power engineering," (R. S. Cohen in Frank, 1961). In its resolve to remain "pure," as in so many other respects, behavioral science is imitating physics, not as it is but as particular reconstructions have represented it to be.

This dilemma will not be settled easily. Some "observer" scientists will pursue an artificially pure ideal of science which stumbles against both history and reality. Other "participant" scientists will advocate personal theories without moving beyond their limited biases. However, the dilemma is not hopeless, e.g., different roles can be taken under different conditions. The change advocate in one study may be an observer in another. In the one case, he is observed as a participant in action, trying to change variables which will be studied by another researcher or team of researchers. In the other case, he is the observer of someone else's change efforts. Within the more tolerant traditions of science, he may take the role of the organizational change catalyst during one time or space period, the role of the painstaking observer during another.

Neither is necessarily incompatible with the reknowned "scientific method" which, as Kaplan (1964) has sagely noted, is as difficult to define as the "method" of baseball.

Into the confusion surrounding "observer" versus "participant" science enters the field experimenter. His interests, almost of necessity, encompass organizational practices as well as experimental methodology. His problem is to apply an experimental methodology to "real life" field situations. If he overcomplicates his research procedures, he may lose the cooperation of those who work in the organizations he is studying. If he oversimplifies research procedures, he may lose the respect of his professional peers who pass valued judgement on his work. Consequently, the field experimenter must consider the fine points of both organizational life and experimental design. In the following sections of this chapter, we shall examine the methodology and its possibilities.

FIELD EXPERIMENT METHODS

In theory, the field experiment provides the ideal vehicle for studying organizational change. It offers the possibility of controlled situations and before-after measurements of change. It can help trace causality, something that neither the single case study nor the comparative organizational study can do. It implies that the sophistication of the laboratory experiment can be transferred to the field situation, thus furnishing the field worker with a rigorous methodological approach.

In fact, however, the rigors of experimental design seldom reflect the realities of organizational life. The experimental laboratory must always oversimplify the variables found within a complex organization. Likewise, the complex organization cannot easily provide laboratory conditions. The laboratory involves a temporary system; the organization is a quasi-permanent system that exists beyond the lives of its members. The laboratory sets up temporary human relationships which all too often have a pretend-like quality. Organizations require relationships that are, so the slang expression goes, "for real." The laboratory builds an ambiguous hierarchy in which subjects report to an experimenter most often as volunteer or nonvolunteer enrollees taking his college course. An organization has several complex hierarchical systems which depend upon both formal authority and colleague influence over a period of time. To change and study a single variable in a laboratory may be relatively easy compared with isolating, changing, and studying the variable within an organization.

Organizational research also differs from laboratory experiments with regard to researcher status. The experimenter is typically master within the laboratory. He has defined the operating conditions and can call the tune. The organizational researcher, however, is typically a guest in someone else's establishment. The various organizational parts and persons may all choose to ignore him, or they may all demand attention simultaneously. When they demand attention, it may not be for purposes of cooperating. They may be only suspicious or curious about "what's going on?" At times, the organizational researcher will feel that he has absolutely no control over his "subjects." He can only cross his fingers and hope that natural events and some skill will permit him to carry out his work.

Under these conditions, it is not too surprising that large-scale field experiments have been relatively few and imperfect in design. As recently as 1964, Seashore (1964, p. 165) noted in one of the few papers written on field experimentation:

> A scanning of five recent major works on research design in the behavioral sciences uncovered not a single example of experimental work with formal human organizations, and no reference to the problems of conducting such research in field setting. . . . The total number of research ventures that might be reasonably considered to be field experiments with formal organizations is very small, perhaps from five to ten, depending upon how generous one chooses to be in tolerating deviations from ideal experimental conditions. None of these fulfills the canons of experimental design to the degree ordinarily expected in laboratory or field experiments in small groups. One must view these as rather primitive, pioneering ventures.

Seashore's pessimistic report is influenced somewhat by the stringent requirements he set for including a study as an organizational field experiment. He excluded those experiments conducted with organizational employees which were concerned with small groups rather than formal organizations. In addition, he included only those studies where there were: "a) a definable and measurable change in organization environment, structure, or process, b) some means for qualification of variables, c) the provision for testing of causal hypotheses through the method of difference." These criteria were set, says Seashore, "for no other reason than to narrow attention to the special problems that arise or become accentuated when one attempts field studies of relatively large and complex organizational units with methods that approach those of classical experimental design" (ibid., p. 164).

Another even more extensive paper on field experimentation was written by Seashore's Michigan colleague, John R. P. French, Jr., for a handbook on *Research Methods in the Behavioral Sciences,* edited by Festinger and Katz (1953). French's criteria for inclusion as a field experiment were slightly different from Seashore's in that French was less concerned with the size of the organizational units (i.e., small groups are included) and more concerned that the experimenter be the source of changes. To French (1953, p. 99):

> The essential feature which distinguishes the field experiment from the more common "field study" is the design of the research. The field experiment involves the actual manipulation of conditions *by the experimenter* [author's emphasis] in order to determine causal relations whereas in the field study the researcher uses the selection of subjects and the measurement of existing conditions in the field setting as a method of determining correlations. . . . In the field experiment (as opposed to the natural experiment where the researcher opportunistically capitalizes upon some ongoing changes and studies their effects in an experimental design) the manipulation of the independent variable is not left to nature, but is contrived, at least in part, by the experimenter . . . beforehand.

In the same chapter, French further emphasizes the experimenter's role and the classical experimental design when he presents his working definition of field experiments: "For the purposes of this chapter, then, we shall define a field experiment as a theoretically oriented research project in which the experimenter manipulates an independent variable in some real social setting in order to test some hypotheses" (ibid., p. 101).

Both French and Seashore use the classical experiment as practiced in the laboratory as a model for field experiments. Both writers also stress the importance of the experimenter's role in manipulating and controlling the relevant variables. At the same time, both writers recognize that they are placing an almost impossible demand upon the field researcher. Seashore talks about the problems of "scientific versus ethical and practical considerations" while French notes that there is a conflict between "research objectives and practical objectives." The underlying dilemma referred to earlier (science vs. application) is acknowledged but not resolved by Seashore or French. Both writers imply that the best resolution will come when researchers can do a better job of establishing laboratory conditions in field situations.

The field experimenter is thus left with an ideal (classical design), a prescribed role (manipulator and controller of variables), and little hope of achieving either in an organizational setting. The laboratory experimenters add further discouragement, if that is possible. Leon Festinger (1953, p. 137) writes that:

> It would seem clear that the experiments in industry such as have been described in [French's] chapter should not be called laboratory experiments. There is little or no attempt to set up special conditions. Typically, the situation is accepted as found and some manipulation is

imposed. The manipulation of the independent variable is usually a simultaneous manipulation of a set of factors. The degree of control obtained in these experiments is usually not sufficient to guarantee that the effects obtained are unequivocally related to the independent variable.

At this point, the would-be field experimenter must make a choice. He either must work toward an apparently hopeless ideal of classical design and experimenter influence, or else he must begin to revise his goals and procedures. We shall take the second path, but not until we have explored some of the problems which accompany the concepts of classical experimental design and experimenter influence. Our analysis will tend to suggest that the problems of field experimentation are not all in the field. Several issues plague laboratory experimenters as well. Some of these issues seem serious in the light of recent research findings.

THE PROBLEMS OF CLASSICAL DESIGN AND EXPERIMENTER INFLUENCE

The Classical Design Model

The classical model of experimental design includes what Campbell (1957) calls a "Pretest-Postest Control Group Design." This means that observations are made both before (pretest) and after (postest) a treatment is applied to one or more experimental groups. Similar observations are made in one or more control groups in which no treatment is applied. By using before-after measures and an experimental-control group structure, the researcher hopes to test specific hypotheses concerning the treatment's effects on one or more dependent variables. Such effects are reflected in different degrees or directions of change in experimental groups as compared with control groups.

As Campbell notes, the Pretest–Postest Control Group Design became the ideal of the social sciences in the 1900's because it seemed to overcome problems which tended to accompany simpler study designs. Campbell describes these earlier problems as: (a) History, (b) Maturation, (c) Testing, (d) Instrument Decay, (e) Statistical Regression, (f) Selection, and (g) Experimental Mortality. Each could contaminate or confound the data if not controlled or recognized. The confounding factors can be summarized as follows:

a) *History.* Some changes are due to external incidents which would influence the subjects, just as an experimental variable might. Though these extraneous stimuli may become part of the group's history, they are not intended as change variables.

b) *Maturation.* Changes take place in an experimental group which might be due to the passage of time alone. A control group would presumably show these same maturation tendencies over time. Hence the experimenter would not incorrectly attribute changes to the experimental inputs.

c) *Testing.* The process of testing itself can affect the attitudes and scores that subjects report in an experiment.

d) *Instrument Decay.* Measurements might be affected by the increasing fatigue, boredom, sophistication of those who are doing the observations in an experiment. In addition, different observers may have vastly different perceptions of similar incidents.

e) *Statistical Regression.* Changes can appear due to the fact that an experimental group began the experiment at one extreme or the other as reflected by the measuring instruments. Under these conditions and with "only one way to go," the experimenter could not know whether it was the change variable or just natural shifts toward the mean that accounted for the changes that took place according to his measuring instruments.

f) *Selection.* Members of an experimental group may be quite unrepresentative of the population. Without a strictly matched control group the experimenter can not tell whether it is his sample or the experimental variable which accounts for the changes.

g) *Experimental Mortality.* Changes may occur due to the dropping out of subjects who represent a crucial subset of biases, attitudes, etc.

Stouffer (1950) expressed the hopes of social scientists in general when he spoke of the classical model as an ideal. He pictured the model as a four-celled diagram shown in Figure 3 in which X_1, X_2, etc., refer to observed events.

FIGURE 3

Classical Experiment Design

	Before	After	
Experimental Group	X_1	X_2	Treatment Effect $=$ $(X_2 - X_1) - (X'_2 - X'_1)$
Control Group	X'_1	X'_2	

However, this classical-controlled model did not remain ideal for long. It had already become suspect in 1949 when Solomon (1949) showed that Before measurements tended to sensitize subjects to react to an experimental change differently than if there had been no prior measurement. As French (1953, p. 115) noted: "Solomon has shown that the conventional design with a single control group is inadequate where the pre-experimental measures interact with the experimental treatment and influence its effectiveness." Solomon's work also suggested that the experimental setting itself posed a problem for experimenters. It now appeared not only possible but highly likely that a subject would behave differently under experimental conditions than he might under more natural work conditions. Solomon tried to eliminate the effects of pre-measurement and the experimental setting by designing an elaborate Four Group Design which we shall examine later. But the important lesson his work teaches is that the classical design is but one of a number of imperfect alternatives from which an experimenter, either in the field or in the laboratory, can choose. Furthermore, while field settings create many problems for experimental work, laboratory conditions create their own problems of artificiality and subject self-consciousness.

The Influence of the Experimental Environment

Some of the problems posed by experimental settings are well illustrated in the work of Orne (1962), Orne and Evans (1965) and Milgram (1965). Their work shows that the relationship between subject and experimenter and other aspects of the laboratory setting may be more powerful determinants of subjects' behavior than the experimental manipulation of variables. For example, Orne (1962, p. 777) comments that: "A particularly striking aspect of the typical experimenter-subject relationship is the extent to which the subject will play his role [as a passive responder] and place himself under the control of the experimenter. . . . Just about any request which could conceivably be asked of the subject is legitimized by the quasi-magical phrase, 'This is an experiment,' and the shared assumption that a legitimate purpose will be served by the subject's behavior." Orne and Evans (1965) also provide a good example of how the experimental setting influences subject behavior. They conducted an experiment in which the experimenter tried to persuade hypnotized subjects to perform antisocial actions (e.g., throwing dangerous acid at another person, picking up a poisonous reptile). Ostensibly, the research was to determine whether or not hypnotized persons could be persuaded to perform antisocial acts. The subjects were actually in no danger from either the acid or the poisonous reptile. Some of the subjects, however, only pretended to be hypnotized during the experiment, though the experimenter did not know which subjects were hypnotized and which were not. A third group of "control" subjects were clearly not hypnotized during the experiment. The experimenter attempted to treat all subjects alike in persuading them to throw acid and handle the snake.

Orne and Evans report that the non-hypnotized subjects (both those who simulated hypnosis and those who did not) demonstrated antisocial behavior about as much as the hypnotized subjects did. They explain their findings as due to the fact that: "though they reported feeling rather uncertain about the tasks, and reported strong emotional reactions to the repugnant activities, the [non-hypnotized] subjects reported that they were quite convinced that they would not be harmed *because* the context was an experimental one, presumably being conducted by responsible experimenters" (1965, p. 199).

In another set of experiments, Milgram (1965) discovered that an experimenter obtained slightly greater (65%) obedience from subjects engaged in a sadistically unpleasant task when the setting was a university laboratory rather than an unimpressive office setting. However, even in the second "laboratory," almost half the subjects obeyed the experimenter's instructions. With regard to the authority of the experimental setting, Milgram (1965, p. 71) comments: "It would be valuable to study the subjects' performance in other contexts which go even further . . . in denying institutional support to the experimenter. It is possible that beyond a certain point, obedience disappears completely. But that point had not been reached in the Bridgeport office."

Quite clearly the experimental setting forms an important part of the relevant environment for subjects participating in a study. The Orne, Evans and Milgram studies indicate that this environment also can be a major determinant of subjects' behavior. If this is true, it poses a serious question as to the traditional role of the experimenter as a part of the subjects' environment. Laboratory experimenters in particular stress the importance of the experimenter's and his design's control of subjects and the relevant environment. Cronbach (1957) differentiates an experiment from a correlational study by noting that an experimenter is interested only in variations which he, himself, is responsible for introducing. Argyle (1957, p. 46) defines experiments on social behavior as: "investigations in which the investigator himself manipulates the conditions and makes observations in order to test an hypothesis." Festinger (1953, p. 137) writes that: "A laboratory experiment may be defined as one in which the investigator creates a situation with the exact conditions he wants to have and in which he controls some and manipulates other variables. He is then able to observe and measure the effect of the manipulation of the independent variables on the dependent variables in a situation in which the operation of other relevant factors is held to a minimum."

In these definitions it is the experimenter, not the subjects or environment, who creates, controls, manipulates, observes, tests, measures, and holds other factors to a minimal variation. However, one is tempted to wonder whether these are realistic expectations even under experimental conditions. Although the intended pattern of influence goes from experimenter to subjects and environment, studies cited above suggest that influence moves in other directions as well. It seems likely that not only the subjects and environment exert influence in a variety of unplanned ways, but also that experimenters exert "unintended" influence over the other two. Figure 4 shows these intended and potential influence patterns.

FIGURE 4

Intended Influence Patterns and
Potential Influence Patterns

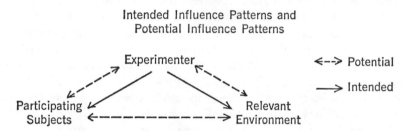

For the most part, behavioral science experimenters act as though the potential influence patterns either do not or should not exist in the laboratory. Meanwhile, the *intended* forms of experimenter influence are treated as an attainable goal. However, other writings, in addition to those already cited, suggest that subject and environmental influence may be *more* powerful and experimenter influence *less* predictable than once suspected. For example, a study by Brunswik (1956) attacked the assumption that one variable could be experimentally isolated from another when the two were related in the real world environment. Yet most laboratory experiments make at least several such assumptions. Even earlier, Tolman and Brunswik (1935) wrote of the "causal texture of the environment," a concept expanded upon recently by Emory and Trist (1965) in connection with organizational change. All four authors, though dealing with different settings, suggest that environmental influence may determine subject behavior more than the experimental treatment does and yet go disregarded as a major influence. Bronowski (1953, p. 89) makes essentially the same point in discussing the physical as well as the social sciences:

> It was assumed in the classical science of the last century that such a phenomenon as radioactivity, or the inheritance of a blood group, or

loss of nerve, or the rise of prices in a time of scarcity, is each the result of many influences, and that step by step these could be taken apart and the phenomenon traced to all its causes. In each case, what was happening could be treated as a laboratory experiment. It could be isolated from these events in the world which had no bearing upon it, and lay as it were beyond the box of the laboratory. And within this box, the causes could be studied one by one, much as we study how the volume of gas changes when the pressure is varied while we keep the temperature the same, and then when the temperature is varied while we keep the pressure the same.

But the picture of the phenomenon in isolation from the rest of the world and from the observer turns out to be false. There comes a time when it will not do any longer even as an approximation. Then it turns out that time and space, which Newton thought absolute, cannot be given physical meaning without the observer. The laboratory cannot exist in a void, and the experimenter cannot be put in a box. And as we refine our measurements, the limitations of the observer look larger and larger.

The Influence of the Experimenter

The "limitations of the observer" are further shown in a series of papers by Riecken (1962), Vikan-Kline (1962), McGuigan (1963), Rosenthal (1963a, 1963b, 1964, 1965) and Rosenthal et al. (1963). Riecken points up the complexity of the experimenter's influence by noting that subjects too can play the game of selective behavior. In describing the social situation formed by an experiment, Riecken (1962, p. 31) notes:

> In the light of these five features of the experiment—its invitational (to the subject) quality, the unspecified nature of the invitation's terms, the attributes of the relationship between the two principal personages (subject and experimenter), the temporal and spatial segregation of the experience, and the one-sidedness of the distribution of information—it is easy to see how the subject is impelled to "put his best foot forward." He attempts to appear in the best possible light within the constraints imposed by the situation, by concealing or exhibiting, exaggerating or belittling those qualities he believes will be positively and negatively evaluated in the particular experiment.

McGuigan (1963) goes on to show how different experimenters come up with different findings from the same experiment. He also attempts to point out that experimenters may influence subjects in ways that are quite different from their intended patterns of influence. In noting that the experimenter is a "neglected stimulus object," McGuigan (1963, p. 421) also observes that:

> While we have traditionally recognized that the [personality] characteristics of an experimenter may indeed influence behavior, it is important

to observe that we have not seriously attempted to study him as an independent variable.

In partial response to McGuigan's plea, Rosenthal et al. (1963) published a series of papers which showed the unintended impact of experimenters' expectations on subjects' behavior. Using both human and animal subjects in different experiments, Rosenthal et al. showed that the experimenter's own biases were partial determinants of the experimental results. In other words, the experimenter's expectations helped to determine subjects' responses even though experimenters did not consciously communicate these expectations before or during the experiment.

Still further evidence of varying experimenter influence is illustrated by Milgram's studies. Milgram (1965) studied the willingness of subjects to disobey the experimenter-authority figure who told them to administer powerful electrical shocks to another person. Subjects' obedience varied according to such things as the physical proximity of the experimenter to the subject and the extent to which colleagues supported subjects' disobedience. Milgram found that the experimenter exercised more control over the subject when (a) the two were in close proximity and when (b) the experimenter and subject worked alone without other subjects there to support disobedience. (See also Asch, 1952.)

The impact from these various studies has only begun to be felt in the social sciences. In a recent review on experimenter influence, Klintz et al. (1965) noted that personality, experience, sex, expectancy, modeling behavior, and early data returns have all been found possible determinants of *unintended* influence by experimenters. Klintz et al. (1965, p. 224) contend that:

> Wherever an experimenter-subject relationship exists, the possibility also exists for *E* [the experimenter] to complicate his data. . . . It appears that experimental psychology has too long neglected the experimenter as an independent variable. . . . It is hoped that experimental psychologists will no longer accept on faith that the experimenter is necessary but harmless.

An even sharper attack on experimenter "objectivity" and "observer" science experiments was written by Tooley and Pratt (1964) who argue that it is time for the experimenter to recognize himself as more than an objective outsider to the experimental situation. In a letter discussing the implications of Rosenthal's work on experimenter influence, Tooley and Pratt (1964, p. 254–255) comment:

> One popular approach to the problem [of experimenter influence over data] has been systematically to track down, and wherever possible

control (usually meaning "attempt to eradicate"), all sources of experimenter influence. This approach is based largely on the tired epistemology and inoperable value system of a passé "classical" physics paradigm which placed much value on so called "value free" inquiry and sanctioned ill-defined uses of the term "scientific objectivity"—both terms so fraught with surplus and often antithetical meaning as to be virtually meaningless. . . . Every inhuman attempt was made to "include the observer out" of the observed system.

An alternative approach entails a radical reconceptualization of the historic ideal of "scientific objectivity" and a radical revision of the role of investigator who has been structured and stereotyped as a detached, outside-looking-in observer. From our point of view, the investigator is inextricably involved in the system which he studies as a *participant-observer*, and is to be considered as *one* source of variation(s), among others to be accounted for in the experimental system. This can be as a source of within, between, or interaction variance (i.e., emergent or transaction variance). In some experimental systems, depending upon the purposes of the particular investigation, it might be desirable to minimize his participation (influence) in the system by programming his role in a highly structured, constricted, and stabilized manner. In other participant-observer situations (e.g., psychotherapy, education change induction, action research, etc.) the purpose might be to influence the system under investigation as much as possible, but still accounting for (though now exploiting) the variance within the system attributable to the several significant and relevant aspects of the investigator's participant-observation. From this perspective the quixotic attempt to eliminate the effects of participant-observation in the name of misplaced pseudo-objectivity is fruitless, not so much because it is impossible but because it is unproductive. Indeed if science succeeded in being totally "objective" in the erroneous sense of being value free and devoid of experimenter influence—then there could be no science, just a series of unrelated, uninterpreted, meaningless "facts" (which in themselves, as a matter of fact, constitute phenomenological inferences of varying degrees).

These different studies and comments have implications for field researchers in connection with the problem of unintended influence. They suggest that the field researcher may be both better and worse off than he has been accustomed to thinking. For many years, field researchers have lived with the stigma attached to the expression "Hawthorne effect" when laboratory purists discussed the pitfalls of field researcher influence. And the laboratory purists were right. The research in the Hawthorne plant's Relay Assembly Test Room showed that outside researchers and management had indeed created a new kind of environment for the workers (Roethlisberger and Dickson, 1939). Yet, the recent evidence suggests that it was partly *laboratory* conditions themselves that contributed to experimenter influence. The evidence also suggests that these conditions are not easily avoided through the use of more and tighter controls. Consequently, a tentative hypothesis might be that: *The more the experimental setting* (a) *deprives the subject of his customary controls* (*including self-control*) *and* (b) *places the subject under new controls imposed by the experimental design, then the more the subject becomes dependent upon the experimenter for cues on appropriate behavior.*

The experimental subject undoubtedly has some choice as to whether he will accept or reject the cues he receives from the experimenter or other subjects. Milgram's (1965) and Asch's (1952) research suggest that subject resistance to experimental authority will increase when the subject is supported by fellow subjects. But like Riesman's "other-directed man" who becomes more other-directed in times of uncertainty; uncertain subjects seem most sensitive to cues emitted by the experimenter. To the extent that the experimenter represents a non-threatening temporary authority, the subject probably tries to fulfill the experimenter's expectations (Binder, McConnell and Sjoholm, 1957; Spires, 1960). Because the conditions of non-threatening authority are probably more present under the usual laboratory conditions where the subject is a student volunteer, one might also suspect that experimenter influence would be greater here than where adult nonvolunteers are working in organizations (Rosenthal, 1965).

In this respect, the problem of unintended experimenter influence is probably less crucial in field experiments than in laboratory experiments. The field researcher typically poses less of an authority problem. Participants in a field study tend to be older than college student subjects and are already working within an established organizational hierarchy. The same lack of authority which prevents the experimenter from setting up exacting controls in an organization now becomes a mixed blessing. It also makes organizational members less dependent upon him than they might be under most laboratory conditions.

The Influence of the Subjects

At the same time, the field researcher faces the problem of "subject influence" upon him. He can become victimized by his own involvement and identification with people who work in the field situation. The researcher is, as Scott (1965, p. 278) says: "susceptible to the danger of becoming over-socialized with respect to the subject group so that he begins to see the world as his fellow participants see it . . . he finds less and less that requires explanation as he comes to share the premises and values of the group in which he is immersed." Scott proposes two antidotes for this problem of subject influence including (a) going back to early field notes in order to gain a more objective perspective, and

(b) discussions with more detached professional colleagues. Moreover, the problem possibly becomes reduced due to lower involvement when a team of researchers studies multiple organizational units (e.g., a comparative study or field experiment). However, it remains a source of unintended influence in field study observations just as experimenter bias may influence laboratory observations.

What is the proper attitude to take with regard to this wider influence network that varies from intended patterns and yet can contaminate supposedly "pure" experimental conditions? Unfortunately, as Klintz et al. (1965) suggest, many experimenters have tended to ignore or rationalize away the implications of these potential influence patterns, particularly those patterns resulting from their own involvement. There are reasons for this, some of them touched upon earlier: the experimental world is complicated enough without trying to take account of the experimenter's effects; the problem introduces another variable which is irrelevant for purposes of many experiments under study; scientists are supposed to remain detached from their data and be objective about it. Furthermore, by accepting experimenter involvement as a reality, social scientists acknowledge that they are still more social than scientist. For many, this is a bitter pill to swallow. They have struggled long and hard to gain membership within the fraternity of science while building their own foundation of detached objectivity. They fail to note that such foundations have flaws, even in the natural sciences as shown by recent developments in quantum theory. Percy Bridgman, a Nobel Prize winner in physics, wrote (1958, p. 88):

> The point of view of quantum theory has implications for us much wider than the technical details. It forces us to realize that we cannot have information without acquiring that information by some method, and the story is not complete until we have told both what we know and how we know it. In other words we have to remember that we always have an observer. Furthermore, the observer is ourselves, and therefore we cannot get away from him. But getting away from itself is what the human race has been trying to do ever since it started philosophizing or worshipping.

ALTERNATIVES AND ALTERATIONS

The above comments and the findings on environmental influence, experimenter influence and subject influence suggest that field experimenters need to search further for useful design alternatives and alterations. Even though, as Bridgman says, the experimenter cannot get away from himself, he can at least reformulate his role so as to take into account the problem of his own involvement. He must find ways to treat himself as a variable rather than eulogize his role as a detached controller of other variables. He also needs to explore further the possibilities for altering environmental and subject variables beyond the limits of those assumed by classical design requirements. In short, as McGuigan (1963), Tooley and Pratt (1964), and Klintz et al. (1965), suggest, it seems time to review and broaden our notions of experimental design.

We can do this in the final parts of this chapter by examining some procedures for altering experimental designs in terms of (a) environmental alterations, (b) subject involvement, and (c) experimenter involvement. To be sure, these various alternatives complicate the problem of experimental design. However, they also give the experimenter greater freedom of design and deserve more extensive use without accusations of scientific treason. The findings reported in the previous section indicate that experimental design is still in a rough and rudimentary stage of development. Rather than stifling further experimentation through such verbal constraints as "scientific method," "value-free objectivity," and "good experimental practice," it seems better to explore, innovate, reevaluate, and loosen up some of the unrealistically tight traditions of social science. This seems particularly possible now when data processing and computational procedures are themselves springing loose from the era of paper-and-pencil analysis. As Kaplan (1964, p. 162) has noted:

> The mathematics and statistics of the eighteenth and nineteenth centuries could conveniently manage only two changing variables at a time, and the ideal experiment was therefore conceived as an experiment in which all the variables but two were held constant. One, the "independent variable," was then manipulated, while observations were made on the other, the "dependent variable." This was the practical basis of the classical one-factor theory of experiment mentioned in the preceding section. But contemporary mathematics no longer imposes this constraint, and manipulation—whether to hold "everything else" constant, or to introduce changes in the one factor—is correspondingly no longer absolutely essential. Reconstructed logic is still occupied largely in catching up with the developments in statistical theory and technique of the early decades of this century. It has scarcely begun, it seems to me, to take account of the revolutionary changes in the logic-in-use by present-day scientists that have been brought about by the fantastic developments in the capacities of computers and of the whole data processing technology.

Environmental Alterations

A review of environmental alterations shows a series of procedures used by experimenters to help them control and understand what goes on within the experimental situation. Experimenters tend to treat these procedures as devices which help protect the experimental situation from outside interferences. They are referred to most often as experimental "controls" and they usually help to define the boundaries and limits of the experimental environment. French (1953) discusses some of these experimental-environmental controls in his chapter on field experiments in the Festinger and Katz (1953) book. Briefly paraphrased he mentions:

1. *Control Groups.* Matched with experimental groups on all variables which, if they differed, might confound the data. Control groups are usually established in laboratory experiments by placing a randomly drawn selection of subjects in both experimental and control groups. In field experiments, control groups are more often "matched" as closely as possible with the experimental groups.

2. *Measurement Controls.* Achieved through statistical manipulation of the data. For example, two similar but unequal sets of data may be equalized so as to permit direct comparison. In addition, the effects of one variable may be separated from the other variables through the use of multivariate techniques of analysis. Measurement controls and statistical records appear to have increasing promise as data processing methods improve.

3. *Replication.* Involves the repetition of an earlier experiment under as close to identical conditions as possible. French (1953) believes that field experiments should be replicated in the same setting as the first experiment. However, Selltiz et al. (1959) disagree and argue that the true test of replication comes from the repetition of studies under *different* unique conditions. In either case, the intent is to establish boundaries for the generalizations that can be drawn from the first experiment.

4. *Preliminary Experiments.* Designed to pretest procedures, instruments, and hypotheses and, as French says, "work the bugs out of the experimental manipulations."

5. *Standardization.* The uniformity of conditions as well as the uniformity of procedures. An effort is made to keep "all other things equal" for both experimental and control situations by standardizing all but the crucial experimental variable(s). This involves not only matched control group(s) but the standardizing of environmental influences and experimenter behavior.

6. *Insulation.* Eliminating some conditions that might otherwise influence the experimental or control situation. The experimental laboratory itself is one form of insulation, designed to prevent contaminating outside influences.

7. *Safety Factors.* Provide a form of data collecting "insurance" by urging the experimenter to collect enough data to make a good field study out of an unsuccessful field experiment.

8. *Size of Units.* A crucial criterion for organizational field experiments for Seashore (1964). But, as French (1953) points out, the smaller the unit, the greater the possibility of control. Consequently, French leans toward small-group field experiments as scientifically more feasible.

9. *Length-of-time Controls.* Subject to the same logic as the unit-size control mentioned above. The shorter the length of time, the less chance for contaminating variables to creep into the experiment. By shortening the time of the experiment, the experimenter also probably restricts the scope of changes that can be introduced.

The fact that these devices are thought of as "controls" tends to highlight their restrictive qualities and undervalue their potential as substitutes for each other and as design alternatives. Too often a potential experiment founders for lack of one of these devices when another might have taken its place. By altering the environmental structure of the experiment slightly, the same experimental variables might be tested in a different way.

Several such environmental alterations are suggested by Selltiz, Jahoda, Deutsch, and Cook (1959) and French's (1953) list of control devices suggests others. For example:

1. Measurement controls or different types of "control" groups can substitute for the direct manipulation of the experimental variables. Measurement controls can be used by establishing data collection procedures which show that certain events consistently occur prior to certain other events. The risk is that this relationship will demonstrate correlation but not causality. The researcher must then search for and study examples of each set of variables which were unaccompanied by the other set. He may also wish to set up a comparative study (instead of an experimental-control group study) in which he introduces the first set of variables into one group and the second set into the other group.

2. Control groups which cannot be matched well with experimental groups can be turned instead into comparative study units. In reality, most field experiments take the form of comparative studies in that the control groups or organizational units are not deprived of the experimental variable but simply experience a substitute in a different degree or form. A well-known example where potential control groups were intentionally turned into comparative groups would be the Morse and Reimer (1956) "field experiment" involving four clerical divisions of a large organization. Two of the divisions were coached toward more participative decision-making procedures. The other two divisions were coached toward more hierarchical decision making. There were no "control" divisions in the classical design sense. Campbell (1957, p. 306)

touches upon the artificiality of the "control" group concept in social research when he notes that:

> In presenting the above designs, X (symbolizing the exposure of a group to an experimental variable) has been opposed to No-X as is traditional in discussions of experimental design in psychology. But while this may be a legitimate description of a stimulus isolated physical science laboratory, it can only be a convenient shorthand in the social sciences, for any No-X period will not be empty of potentially change inducing material. The experience of the control group might better be categorized as another type of X, a control experience, an X_c instead of No-X.

3. Measurement controls can substitute for other forms of standardization. In many cases, it is possible to equalize data from two situations so as to make them directly comparable. In other cases, where randomized control groups cannot be established, a matched sample of both experimental and control populations can be drawn using certain basic criteria (e.g., age, organizational status, experience, test scores). These matched samples can be compared with each other and with the rest of the population in both experimental and control situations. In still other cases, an analysis of variance will permit the researcher to separate out for himself the variables he wants to compare in two or more groups. Thus the standardizing of situations can be replaced somewhat by a statistical isolation of variables.

The greatest possibilities for environmental alterations seem to come from control group or measurement variations. We noted earlier that the classical design involved one or more experimental groups and one or more control groups measured both before and after experimental treatment. But it is important to consider other experimental-control group configurations just as it is important to consider other measurement strategies.

For example, the reader will recall that Solomon (1949) indicated that "before" measures could influence behavior by sensitizing subjects to behave during the experiment differently than if the measurement of behavior, attitudes or relationships had not been made. As a partial remedy for the problem he posed, Solomon proposed altering both the group structure and the timing of measurements. He added two new groups to the experimental design; one was to be experimental, the other control. Neither group was to be measured before the experimental treatment. Using an extension of Stouffer's (1950) diagram, Solomon's Four Group Design would appear as shown in Figure 5. Campbell (1957) has referred to it as the "new ideal design for social scientists."

In effect, Solomon's (1949) model can be tested both for the effects of

FIGURE 5

Solomon Four-Group Design

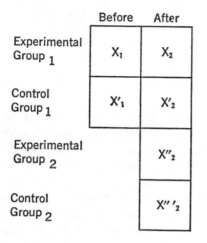

Experimental Group 1 — Before X_1, After X_2

Control Group 1 — Before X'_1, After X'_2

Experimental Group 2 — After X''_2

Control Group 2 — After X'''_2

Treatment Effect $= X''_2 - \dfrac{X_1 + X'_1}{2}$

Measurement Effect $= (X'_2 - X'_1) - (X'''_2 - \dfrac{X_1 + X'_1}{2})$

experimental treatment and for the effects of "before" measurements on "after" responses. However, the "new" ideal model poses major problems of implementation for field experimenters. It requires at least four matched groups or organizations, a difficult task if done with any precision. In addition, if the experimenter wishes to study the effects of experimental variable No. 2 over and above the effects of variable No. 1, he needs two more experimental groups, one measured before the experiment, the other not measured. If he wants two "after" measures (e.g., short-term and long-term effects of experimental treatment) he needs four more groups. Finally, given the problems of poorly matched organizational units, experimenter influence, and subject involvement, it may be too much to hope that any "before" measure of the X''_2 experimental group would equal the average of X_1 and X'_1, the two groups which were measured before the experimental treatment. However, the researcher is required to make this assumption when using the Solomon design.

Once exposed to the complexities of the Four Group Design, the field experimenter is strongly tempted to look for simpler alternatives. One of these can be called the "One-Group Before-After Design." It is diagrammed in Figure 6. Argyle (1957) refers to this design as the "Simple Successive Conditions" design where the "before" condition is either the first of two or more experimental conditions or a pre-experimental situation. The big advantage of this design is that it requires no matching control groups. In addition, with before and after (or successive experimental conditions) measures, both change and no-change subjects can be studied. Argyle describes a more complicated version of this design and its conditions for success in discussing the Lewin, Lippitt, and White (1939) experiments. These experiments tested different styles of leadership among boys' groups using a counterbalanced treatment of different conditions. Several groups were used. Each received each treatment in a successively counterbalanced order. Argyle (1957, pp. 48–49) writes that: "Lippit (1940) . . . used successive conditions in his experiment . . . and furthermore was able to observe interesting transfer effects at the change-over. The boys were unaware that an experiment was in progress and it may be that the successive conditions design is practicable only when this is the case."

Like Argyle (1957), Selltiz, Jahoda, Deutsch, and Cook (1959) believe the One-Group Before-After Design is most useful when (a) the "before" measure will affect neither subsequent behavior nor responses to the "after" measure, and (b) "other" influences (e.g., history, maturation, etc.) which might affect the experimental treatment are absent. However, they view this design as being adequate only in fields where much experimental work is underway (e.g., learning and sensory preception) and as vulnerable in fields such as organizational behavior. Campbell (1957) takes somewhat the same attitude and refers unenthusiastically to the One-Group Before-After Design as "pre-experimental." Campbell notes that there are too many opportunities for unmeasureable contamination of results. Without control group comparisons, a single group may be influenced by unknown extraneous variables.

The problem with this position is that it places more faith in control groups than they deserve in field situations. Control groups are theoretically identical with experimental groups in every respect but experi-

FIGURE 6

One-Group Before-After Design

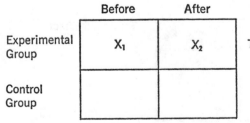

Treatment Effect $= X_2 - X_1$

mental treatment. In most field situations, however, such matched organizational units are difficult to arrange and almost impossible to maintain over any period of time. Under some conditions, the statistical control of a "before" measure would be superior to control group structures. It seems that experimental designers have been more puritanical than practical in their early dismissal of this design. Under conditions where the researcher knows his organization and its available statistics, he may be able to determine the importance of "other" influences to some extent. He may also be able to gather much of his "before" data from these same statistical sources or disguise "before" measures so that they interfere minimally with subjects' later responses and behavior. Minimal interference of "before" measures seems likely when there is a long period of time (e.g., a year or more) between successive measures, and such intervals are often required in organizational change efforts. As we noted earlier, however, long-time intervals also increase the possibility of extraneous influences due to maturation effects.

Still another design alternative is the "After-Only" Design, considered useful when assignments to experimental and control groups can be made according to randomization or matching procedures. Again, however, the problem of achieving randomized or truly matched organizational units limits this design. As a substitute, some field researchers compare individuals rather than organizational units as when randomly picking a sample of salesmen rather than a single district to test-market a new product. In other cases, researchers will fall back upon a design which Campbell (1957) critically labels the "Static-Group" comparison (i.e., the control group has not been equated with the experimental group on a randomized basis before the study). Figure 7 pictures the After-Only Design using both experimental and control groups. Despite its limitations, Argyle (1957) notes that the After-Only Design has been

FIGURE 7

After-Only Design

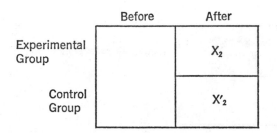

$$\text{Treatment Effect} = X_2 - X'_2$$

preferable in the majority of social experiments because it avoids (a) the problems of unknown changes occurring over time, and (b) the problems of "before" measurements affecting later measurements.

A good example of an After-Only experiment is found in the studies of longwall coal mining done in England by the Tavistock Institute. Trist and Bamforth (1951) describe how a mechanized longwall mining procedure was compared on an After-Only basis with a composite method which contained work practices of both the old hand-got methods and the mechanized longwall methods. By using measurement controls to help equalize the data, the researchers convincingly compare the two work methods in terms of productivity, absenteeism, down time, and satisfaction.

The above environmental alterations can be introduced without altering experimenter-subject relationships. However, there is nothing in environmental alterations that prevents either subject involvement or experimenter involvement from being changed. These two variables often affect each other more than either responds to environmental alterations. Thus, the extent and ways in which an experimenter behaves will affect subjects' involvement and vice versa. Although few subjects are encouraged to be more than subjects, there are a few exceptions. These we shall examine under the heading of Subject Involvement Alterations.

Subject Involvement Alterations

An experimental design *can* be varied so as to encourage different kinds of subject involvement. This is typically the least varied of the three dimensions discussed in this section (i.e., environment, subject, and experimenter), although laboratory experiments tend to treat the subject according to one model while field studies use another. The prevailing laboratory assumption holds that the subject should be kept unaware of the experimenter's intentions so as not to contaminate the data with false reports, adjusted behavior, etc. The same assumption would "ideally" hold in field studies but field conditions usually force compromises in the direction of disclosure. To the extent that each of these practices prevails, they need serious revaluation.

For example, some laboratory experimenters go to great lengths to disguise the true nature of the experiment. Abstract tasks, confederates with false reports, misleading instructions or incorrect data feedback are used, among other devices. At the same time, as Orne (1962) and Orne and Evans (1965) have reported, the typical laboratory experiment is surrounded by enough mystique so that the subject is both second guessing the experimenter and willing to go along with the game. There is further evidence from the reports of McGuigan (1963) and Rosenthal

(1963 a and b, 1964) that subjects do a pretty good job of second guessing the experimenter's hypotheses while Orne and Evans' (1965) work suggests that subjects comply with an experiment's instructions to an extent that they would not consider under more normal conditions.

One of the interesting things about some of Orne and Evans' work, however, was the use of an "aware" control group. As we noted earlier, some of the "hypnotized" subjects pretended to be hypnotized but were actually not. Orne and Evans wanted to learn whether these "aware" subjects would comply with experimenters' instructions as fully as hypnotized subjects did. The aware subjects did follow instructions, but their compliance was apparently due largely to their desire to "go along" with the experiment. By using this "aware" control group, Orne and Evans showed that an "unaware" experimenter can induce compliance among non-hypnotized as well as hypnotized subjects. More important for our purposes right now, they also showed that varying degrees of subject involvement can help to show an experiment's impact upon "unaware" subjects and upon "unaware" experimenters. This experiment-within-an-experiment made some experimenters into subjects and some subjects into experimental assistants. In this case, however, the experimental assistants were not deceiving their own colleagues (e.g., fellow students); they were simply asked to take a role (hypnotized students) and then follow their own dictates.

The problem of subject involvement in field situations is both similar to and different from laboratory settings. It is similar in that organizational members typically "go along with" management and the experimenter without any clear-cut benefits for themselves. It is different in that subjects are less under the control of either the experimenter or the experimental situation. As a result, they can usually demand (and get) a fuller explanation of the study's purposes and design. For example, in an organizational field experiment now underway with eight widely dispersed districts of a large government agency, we found it useful and necessary to take elaborate steps to make sure that the study "made sense" to the 2,800 people participating. Once the study with its eventual feedback of data did make sense to agency personnel, questionnaire responses were quite high. Returns were over 90 percent on a two-hour questionnaire the first time and over 80 percent a year later when the questionnaire was readministered.

Under these conditions, subjects in a field experiment can be *too* aware of the experimental variables. However, as we have already seen, the same is true in almost any experimental situation involving subjects who "know" that a study is underway. The important requirement would seem to be not the withholding of information, but the *equalized distribution of information.* When one field setting receives a certain message, questionnaire, or visit from the experimenters, it is important that the other field settings receive the same treatment. The assumption here is that subjects in field settings should not necessarily be isolated from experimenter involvement, but that the involvement should be made as identical as possible.

These comments suggest that subject isolation and unawareness may be less important than attempting to identify the impact of each variable upon subjects, some of whom may be highly aware of the experimental design. The above comments also suggest that keeping all other things "equal" in experimental situations is more important than keeping all other things "constant." Moreover, input variables *can* be more and more easily identified and equalized through measurement controls and statistical manipulation. Consequently, the day may still come when multiple variables acting upon a field situation may be seen as a useful path for varying subject involvement rather than as a serious block to field experimentation.

Experimenter Involvement Alterations

The most challenging and potentially productive alterations in field experiments will come from alterations the experimenter makes in his own involvement. Although traditional experimental design combines the "observer-scientist" and "detached-controller" roles (Bernard, 1957), this makes little sense in light of the complexity of field experiments and the findings on experimenter involvement-influence.

The complexity of field experiments suggests a dividing of responsibility into experimental treatment and data collection and analysis. The individuals who plan and implement a new organizational approach through Task, Technology, People and/or Structure changes may lack adequate knowledge of field research, statistics, psychometrics, or interviewing procedures. The opposite is also true. Both designer and observer tasks require manpower and talents that increase with knowledge of experimental design and analysis. As in almost any other field, expertise and specialized skills are increasingly useful in such subareas. It is difficult at best for one man or group to work on all facets of a field experiment and keep abreast of methodological developments.

The findings on experimenter involvement and influence suggest that dividing the traditional designer and observer roles may lead to more "objective" studies. The irony is that some experimenters value the traditionally combined roles of detached-manipulator and observer-scientist while they avoid the research which tells them that the detached-manipulator may be what they respect least of all—an involved participant who influences subjects despite his best intentions (Klintz et al., 1965). Laboratory experimenters who defend their science are in the uneasy position of being found to be involved participants. One way of resolving the dilemma is for them to evaluate anew those times and places where a division of the designer and observer roles might prove useful. There is nothing inherent in the rules of "good" experimental design (only in its traditions) that prevents the observer from being a different person or group than the designer of the experiment. In fact, accurate observation, regardless of who does it, should receive a higher priority than the overlapping of designer-observer roles, particularly when the overlapping jeopardizes the truly "scientific" nature of an experiment.

The possibility of splitting as well as combining the roles of designer and observer suggests a series of alternative designs based upon alterations in experimenter involvement. These alternatives appear in Figure 8 which shows how the designer of an experiment may or may not be the same person(s) as the observer. In addition, the diagram suggests that these different roles may be taken by either members of the organizational system or by one or more outside researchers. In Figure 8, two outside research units are shown (Outside Researcher $_1$ and Outside Researcher $_2$).

The diagram suggests that by arranging the designer-observer roles in different ways, a number of experimental alternatives become explicit. The first is the familiar Classical Design Field Experiment. As shown in Figure 8, the same outside researcher designs and observes the experiment. Thus when Outside Researcher $_1$ both designs and observes the study, it is, in a sense, controlled by him from beginning to end. The same would be true if Outside Researcher $_2$ fulfilled both functions.

However, the other four alternatives shown in Figure 8 are less familiar than the classical design model. They include the Internal Experiment, the Natural Experiment, the Split-Role Experiment, and the Operational Experiment.

An *Internal Experiment* uses members from within an organizational system as both designers and observers of experimental efforts. Though probably the least impressive to behavioral scientists, variations of this design are probably the most common within organizational situations. At the same time, accounts of internal experiments rarely get published in behavioral science journals. Most of the time, the accounts are anecdotal in nature or else restricted to After-Only case descriptions of a single organizational unit. The method is further hampered by the fact that many managers are awed by the terminology and research barriers put up by the behavioral scientists themselves. These language and re-

FIGURE 8

Experimental Designs Influenced by
Allocation of Designer-Observer Roles

OBSERVER

DESIGNER	Organizational System Members	Outside Researcher₁	Outside Researcher₂
Organizational System Members	Internal Experiment	Natural Field Experiment	Natural Field Experiment
Outside Researcher₁	Operational Experiment	Classical Design Field Experiment	Split-Role Field Experiment
Outside Researcher₂	Operational Experiment	Split-Role Field Experiment	Classical Design Field Experiment

search technology barriers hide the fact that ample data often exist in the form of company records, reports, and observations. If these data were collected and ordered by organizational personnel, the chances are that some fairly sophisticated experimental studies could emerge.

An example of an internal experiment was one by Carron (1964) who studied the attitude changes resulting from a Human Relations Training program given to selected managers within his company. As a corporate staff member, Carron set up both an experimental and a matched control group and took attitude measurements before training, after training, and seventeen months later. Using vector geometry to help analyze his data, Carron found significant attitude changes among the experimental group which persisted over time.

The *Natural Field Experiment* was referred to earlier in this chapter as a situation in which the researcher "opportunistically capitalizes upon some ongoing changes" (French, 1953). In a natural field experiment, members of the organizational system initiate and implement changes, while an outside researcher assumes the task of observing, measuring and analyzing the changes.

An example of a natural field experiment is a study of attitude changes done by Lieberman (1956) while a member of the Survey Research Center at Mighigan. Lieberman was engaged in a larger research study in a company and took advantage of promotions and role changes among union members. Some of the union members were promoted to foremen. Others were elected to be union stewards. Still later, some of the foremen and stewards were forced to return to the worker ranks; the foremen because of an economic recession and the stewards because they either resigned or were not reelected.

Lieberman thus had (a) an experimental group of workers who became foremen, (b) another experimental group of workers who became union stewards, and (c) a control group of workers who could be individually matched with members of the two experimental groups. In addition, Lieberman could compare the "demoted" foremen or stewards with those who stayed in the higher-status positions.

The hypothesis being tested was "People who are placed in a role will tend to take on or develop attitudes that are congruent with the expectations associated with that role." Attitude measures were taken before and after the promotions. They were taken once again after the demotions. The results showed that attitude changes tended to follow role changes; new foremen tended to become more pro-management than they had been as workers, while new union stewards become slightly more pro-union. Following demotion, those who had been foremen reverted to their old attitudes; those who had been stewards retained more of their steward attitudes, but these were fairly close to their old attitudes as workers.

Lieberman's study, together with the author's own experience with natural field experiments (Dalton, Barnes, and Zaleznik, in press), suggests that ample opportunities exist for field experimentation if the researcher has already established field relationships and has some awareness of the changes being planned by or imposed upon the organization. One problem is that contacts between behavioral scientists and managers are typically limited to specific consulting activities and/or to the researcher's own specified research projects. However, observation opportunities still exist for researchers who maintain their field contacts over time.

Not surprisingly, the criticism of natural experiments centers largely on the fact that the experimenter loses some control over the design. For this reason, most experimenters would consider the natural experiment a lower form of design than the classical design field experiment. For example, Selltiz, Jahoda, Deutsch, and Cook (1959, p. 93) quote Greenwood in support of their contention that:

> Natural situations are complicated and do not permit the investigator to assume, with any confidence that the groups to be compared differ only by chance. As Greenwood (1945) has stated: ". . . the created situation gives us better control power over our phenomenon. We can determine at our own discretion the circumstances which shall be present, and thus arrive at more conclusive evidence of causality. . . . The ability to produce the necessary changes permits the test of hypotheses otherwise not amenable to vertification."

However, a more positive view of natural experiments is reported by Daniel Katz (1953, p. 78) who writes:

> The best opportunity for the use of hypothesis testing is on the occasion of the "natural experiment." The difficulty with the use of hypotheses in field studies is the inability to determine causal relationships with any definiteness, since most of our measures are not taken with respect to systematic changes in some ascertained independent variable. Now, a natural experiment is a change of major importance engineered by policy-makers and practitioners and not by social scientists. It is experimental from the point of view of the scientist rather than of the social engineer.

An argument can be made that, aside from experimenter control, the natural field experiment has several advantages over the classical design experiment. The natural experiment divides research roles by leaving the design and implementation of the experiment with management and the data collection and analysis with outside researchers. Although both parties might check on the timing of experimental treatments so as to match these best with observation-measurement opportunities, each deliberately avoids influencing the other's work. For some managers, this has the advantage of keeping behavioral scientists out of the day-to-day operations of the organization. Likewise, for some researchers, it has the advantage of leaving the power and the headaches of implementing changes up to management. Furthermore, the loss of experimenter control in natural field experiments seems exaggerated. Almost all the relatively few controls available to an outside researcher are available under natural experiment conditions as well.

A *Split-Role Field Experiment* involves not only the organization, but also two separate researchers or research teams from outside the organization. In this case the experiment is designed and partly implemented by one of the two outside researchers (e.g., Outside Researcher$_1$). The other researcher (e.g., Outside Researcher $_2$) serves as the observer and collector of data. The Split-Role design has the advantage of separating the designer and his vested interests or hypotheses from the observer-evaluator function.

An example of the Split-Role field experiment is found in the Seashore and Bowers (1963) study of five departments in an industrial plant. In this experiment, the change advocate (Outside Researcher $_1$) was a colleague of Seashore's and Bowers' from the Survey Research Center. The changes were implemented by management with considerable coaching from Outside Researcher $_1$. The observation and evaluation of the changes were handled by Seashore and Bowers in their Outside Researcher $_2$ roles. Four independent change variables were introduced by Outside Researcher $_1$. These experimental variables were derived from Likert's (1961) modified theory of management and involved the introducing of purposeful change into three of the five departments. The independent variables were:

1) Increase in emphasis on the work group as a functioning unit of organization.
2) Increase in the amount of supportive behavior on the part of supervisors.
3) Increase in participation by employees in decision-making processes within their area of responsibility
4) Increase in amount of interaction and influence among work group members.

Seashore and Bowers (1963) report that the introduction of these variables by Outside Researcher $_1$ appeared to be relatively successful in the three experimental departments. Survey results after the changes also showed greater increases in employee satisfaction within the experimental departments. Company records showed somewhat more ambiguous findings in the areas of production, machine efficiency, waste, and absence rates. In their analysis of the results, Seashore and Bowers (1963, p. 101) note that:

> On the face of it, the experiment appears to be a success, and the theoretical propositions embodied in the experiment appear to have considerable support. However, the evidence is not conclusive and there is room for difference of opinion about the significance of these results.

With regard to the Split-Role Design, Seashore (1964, p. 169) comments:

> To accommodate the requirements of both experimental change and practical application ventures, there is likely to arise a new professional group devoted to change agentry, different in important respects from their professional colleagues in the fields of training and management consulting. The researcher himself is not likely to have the qualifications or time to perform this essential research function, and in the interests of objectivity, he probably should not be involved in it. For such practical reasons, the research plans in field experiments should in many cases provide for some kind of division of labor between those who do the theoretical, analytic, and interpretative work, on the one hand, and those who engage in active and personal interventions in the subject organizations.

The *Operational Field Experiment* is the final alternative shown in Figure 8 involving different patterns of experimenter involvement. The Operational Experiment places an outside researcher in the role of designer with members of the organizational system filling the observer-evaluator roles. A similar relationship often exists in many consultant-client relationships. In addition, however, Outside Researcher $_1$ makes an explicit attempt to base the suggested change variables upon previous research and social science hypotheses. Then, as in the case of the Split-Role Design, Outside Researcher $_1$ becomes highly involved in the implementation of the change variables in key areas of the organizational system (e.g., LeBreton, 1965). Meanwhile, the organization sets up (or already has available) controls by which to measure the success of the changes in the experimental units.

Among the field researchers who most strongly advocate Operational Experiments are members of the Tavistock Institute in England. Because they tend to treat organizations as "open systems" responding to environmental influences, the Tavistock representatives (e.g., Trist, Higgin, Murray, and Pollock, 1963) also treat the outside researcher as a source of potential influence. Rather than trying to eliminate his influence, they consider him a change advocate who works closely with members of the organizational system in implementing change in crucial areas of the organization. In this sense, the experimental design becomes a collaborative endeavor during its implementation stages, even though the original design may have been formulated by Outside Researcher $_1$. In discussing operational experiments, Trist et al. (1963) have written:

> In all [our] projects described, it is the intention to take them through to the point where the research findings have been built into working models of system change which have been thoroughly tested out (validated) under real life conditions. We usually refer to these as operational experiments. . . . A main responsibility of the research team is to work out general principles on the basis of which working models or operational experiments may be constructed.

In this experimental relationship, organization members served as observers and used both conventional and special measures of efficient performance. In the Operational Experiments reported by Trist et al. (1963) on methods of coal mining, the measures most used were those collected in the daily course of mining operations (e.g., tonnage produced, labor efficiency, output per man shift). The outside researchers did most of their data collecting during the early stages of the research while they were trying to formulate their hypotheses on the important change variables.

One major problem of Operational Experiments is the one it poses for those who conceptually think in terms of more traditional models of experimentation. For them, the Operational Experiment appears to be a gross distortion of experimental method. It intermingles experimenter and subjects, neglects the "control" of environmental variables and typically pays more attention to change than to experimental design. With all these objections, the Operational Experimentalists would probably agree. They would argue back, however, that, in field experiment situations, the experimenter tends to influence his subjects whether he wishes to or not; that the environmental variables will influence the setting regardless of the controls attempted by the experimenter and that the problems of changing an organization are more challenging and realistic than the problems of observing one while using a conventional experimental design. Again, as we saw before, a dilemma confronts the would-be field researcher. Does he identify himself with the values of scientific objectivity or with the values of applied change induction? The Operational Experimentalists would argue that such a forced choice is not necessary. Others would see it as imperative. Our own opinion is that the state of current field experiment design leaves room for all of these alternatives as long as the researcher has thought carefully about the alternative he is choosing and the reasons for his choice.

CONCLUSION

I have attempted to conceptualize and describe organizational change in terms of *approaches, human relationships,* and *change processes.* The *approaches* to change are grossly identified as Task, Technology, People, and Structure. Their design and implementation hinge largely on aspects of power distribution among managers, employees, and outsiders. *Human relationships* during organizational change are viewed as relationships among subgroups of change initiators and organizational members who either advocate or resist the changes in data-based rational or emotional ways. *Change processes* are divided into a sequence of subprocesses moving toward changes in attitude, reshaped goals, new alliances, and internalized motivation.

In the second part of the chapter, field experiment methodologies are analyzed as ways of studying the above components and subcomponents. In general, the discussion group in Pittsburgh felt dissatisfaction with the restrictiveness of classical experiment designs. At first glance, such designs seemed suited for laboratory experiments but constraining on field experimenters; at second glance, classical designs seemed restrictive even in laboratory settings. In an attempt to broaden thinking on an experimenter's range of design possibilities, I have examined experimental designs that could be worked out around *environmental alterations, subject involvement alterations,* and *experimenter involvement alterations.* Taken together with the components of organizational change, these alternative design possibilities suggest a massive amount of work for the behavioral science fraternity. This in itself, of course, is healthy. What did not seem healthy to the discussion group in Pittsburgh was the inclination of some behavioral scientists (ourselves included at times) to prematurely formalize the experimental process in field research. With the "search" taken out of research design, organizational field experimentation has become bogged down in the intricacies of design detail and is left partly paralyzed. Our hope was that through our discussions, some of the excitement of organizational research might henceforth be redirected toward large-scale field experiments in organizational settings.

REFERENCES

ABBREVIATIONS

ASR   *American Sociological Review*
RH   *Human Relations*
JAP   *Journal of Applied Psychology*
JASP   *Journal of Abnormal and Social Psychology*
MS   *Management Science*
SSR   *Sociology and Social Research*

Andrews, K. "Executive Training by the Case Method." In K. Andrews, ed., *Human Relations and Administration; The Case Method of Training,* Cambridge: Harvard U. Press, 1953.
Argyle, M. *The Scientific Study of Social Behavior.* London: Methuen, 1957.
Argyris, C. *Interpersonal Competence and Organizational Effectiveness.* Homewood, Ill.: I–Dorsey, 1962.
Asch, S. E. *Social Psychology.* New York: Prentice-Hall, 1952.
Barnes, L. B. *Organizational Systems and Engineering Groups.* Boston: Harvard Graduate School of Business Administration, Division of Research, 1960.
Bennis, W. G. "A New Role for the Behavioral Sciences: Effecting Organizational Change." *Administrative Science Qtly.*, 1963, 8 (2), 126–165.
_____. *Changing Organizations.* New York: McGraw-Hill, 1966.
Bernard, C. *An Introduction to the Study of Experimental Medicine.* Trans. by H. C. Greene. New York: Dover Publications, 1957 (first published in the French edition in 1865).
Binder, A., McConnell, D., and Sjoholm, N. A. "Verbal Conditioning as a Function of Experimenter Characteristics." *JASP*, 1957, 55, 309–314.
Blake, R. R. and Mouton, J. S. *The Managerial Grid.* Houston: Gulf Publishing Co., 1964.
Blake, R. R. and Mouton, J. S.; Barnes, L. B. and Greiner, L. E. "Breakthrough in Organization Development." *Harvard Business Rev.*, November–December 1964, 133–155.
Bridgman, P. W. "Quo Vadis." *Daedalus* 1958, 87 (1), 85–93.
Bronowski, J. *The Common Sense of Science.* Cambridge: Harvard University Press, 1953.
Brunswik, E. *Perception and the Representative Design of Psychological Experiments.* Berkeley: U. of California Press, 1956.
Burns, T. and Stalker, G. M. *The Management of Innovation,* London: Tavistock Publications, 1961.
Campbell, D. T. "Factors Relevant to the Validity of Experiments in Social Settings." *Psychological Bull.*, 1957, 54 (4), 297–312.
Carron, T. J. "Human Relations Training and Attitude Change: A Vector Analysis." *Personnel Psychology*, 1964, 17 (4), 403–424.
Chapple, E. D. and Sayles, L. R. *The Measure of Management.* New York: Macmillan, 1961.
Coch, L. and French, J. R. P., Jr. "Overcoming Resistance to Change." *HR*, 1948, 1, 512–532.
Cronbach, L. J. "The Two Disciplines of Scientific Psychology." *American Psychologist*, 1957, 12, 671–684.

Dalton, G. W., Barnes, L. B. and Zaleznik, A. *The Authority Structure as a Change Variable* (in press).

Emory, F. E. and Trist, E. L. "The Causal Texture of Organizational Environments." *HR*, 1965, *18* (1), 21–32.

Eysenck, H. J. "The Effects of Psychotherapy." In H. J. Eysenck, ed., *Handbook of Abnormal Psychology*. New York: Basic Books, 1960, 697–725.

Festinger, L. "Laboratory Experiments." In L. Festinger and D. Katz, eds., *Research Methods in the Behavioral Sciences*. New York: Dryden Press, 1953, 136–172.

Festinger, L. and Katz, D., eds., *Research Methods in the Behavioral Sciences*. New York: Dryden Press, 1953.

Foundation for Research on Human Behavior. *An Action Research Program for Organizational Improvement* (*in Esso Standard Oil Co.*). Ann Arbor, Mich., 1960.

Frank, J. D. *Persuasion and Healing*. New York: Schocken Books, 1963.

French, J. R. P., Jr. "Experiments in Field Settings." In L. Festinger and D. Katz, eds., *Research Methods in the Behavioral Sciences*. New York: Dryden Press, 1953.

Golembiewski, R. "Authority as a Problem in Overlays." *Administrative Science Qtly.*, 9 (1) June 1964, 22–49.

Gouldner, A. *Patterns of Industrial Bureaucracy*. Glencoe, Ill.: Free Press, 1954.

Greenwood, E. *Experimental Sociology; A Study in Method*. New York: King's Crown, 1945.

Greiner, L. E. "Organization Change and Development." Unpublished Ph.D. dissertation, Harvard U., 1965.

Guest, R. *Organizational Change, The Effect of Successful Leadership*. Homewood, Ill.: Dorsey, 1962.

Jaques, E. *The Changing Culture of a Factory*. New York: Dryden Press, 1952.

Kaplan, A. *The Conduct of Inquiry*. San Francisco: Chandler, 1964.

Katz, D. "Field Studies." In L. Festinger and D. Katz, eds., *Research Methods in the Behavioral Sciences*. New York: Dryden Press, 1953, 56–97.

Klintz, B. L., Delprato, D. J., Mettee, D. R., Persons, C. E., and Schappe, R. H. "The Experimenter Effect." *Psychological Bull.*, 1965, *63* (4), 223–232.

Lawrence, P. R. *Changing of Organizational Behavior Patterns: A Case Study of Decentralization*. Boston: Harvard Graduate School of Business Administration, Division of Research, 1958.

Lawrence, P. R., Bailey, J. C., Katz, R. L., Seiler, J. A., Orth, C. D., Clark, J. V., Barnes, L. B., and Turner, A. N. *Organizational Behavior and Administration*. Homewood, Ill.: I. Dorsey, 1961.

Leavitt, H. J. "Applied Organizational Change in Industry: Structural Technological, and Humanistic Approaches." In James G. March, ed., *Handbook of Organizations*. Chicago: Rand McNally, 1965, 1144–1170.

LeBreton, P. *General Administration: Planning and Implementation*. New York: Holt, Rinehart & Winston, 1965.

Lewin, K. "Group Decision and Social Change." In E. E. Maccoby, T. M. Newcomb, and E. L. Hartley, eds., *Readings in Social Psychology*. 3d ed. New York: Holt, 1958, 197–211.

Lewin, K., Lippit, R., and White, R. K. "Patterns of Aggressive Behavior in

Experimentally Created 'Social Climates.' " *J. Social Psychology,* 1939, *10,* 271–299.

Lieberman, S. "The Effects of Changes in Roles on the Attitudes of Role Occupants." *HR,* 1956, *9,* 385–402.

Likert, R. L. *New Patterns of Management.* New York: McGraw-Hill, 1961.

Mann, F. C. "Studying and Creating Change: A Means to Social Organization." In C. M. Arensberg, et al., eds., *Research in Industrial Human Relations.* New York: Harper, 1957.

McGregor, D. *The Human Side of Enterprise.* New York: McGraw-Hill, 1960.

McGuigan, F. J. "The Experimenter: A Neglected Stimulus Object." *Psychological Bull.,* 1963, *60* (4), 421–428.

Merton, R. K. *Social Theory and Social Structure,* Glencoe, Ill.: Free Press, 1957.

Milgram, S. "Some Conditions of Obedience and Disobedience to Authority." *HR,* 1965, *18* (1), 57–76.

Morse, N. C. and Reimer, E. "The Experimental Change of a Major Organizational Variable." *JASP,* 1956, *52,* 120–129.

Orne, M. T. "On the Social Psychology of the Psychological Experiment." *American Psychologist,* 1962, *19,* 776–783.

Orne, M. T. and Evans, F. J. "Social Control in the Psychological Experiment: Anti-Social Behavior and Hypnosis." *J. Personality and Social Psychology.* March 1965, *1* (3), 189–200.

Rice, A. K. *Productivity and Social Organization, The Ahmedabad Experiment.* London: Tavistock Publications, 1958.

Riecken, H. W. "A Program for Research on Experiments in Social Psychology." In N. F. Washburne, ed., *Decisions, Values, and Groups.* New York: Pergamon Press, 1962, II, 25–41.

Riesman, D., Glazer, N., and Denney, R. *The Lonely Crowd.* New Haven: Yale U. Press, 1950.

Roethlisberger, F. J. and Dickson, W. J. *Management and the Worker.* Cambridge: Harvard U. Press, 1939.

Rosenthal, R. "The Volunteer Subject." *HR,* 1965, *18* (4), 389–406.

————. "The Effect of the Experimenter on the Results of Psychological Research." In B. Maher, ed., *Progress in Experimental Personality Research.* New York: Academic Press, 1964.

————. "Experimenter Modeling Effects as Determinants of Subjects' Responses." *J. Projective Techniques and Personality Assessment,* 1963a, *27* (4).

————. "On the Social Psychology of the Psychological Experiment." *American Scientist,* 1963b, *51* (2), 268–283.

Rosenthal, R., Persinger, G. W., Vikan-Kline, L., and Fode, K. L. "The Effect of Early Data Returns on Data Subsequently Obtained by Outcome Biased Experimenters." *Sociometry,* 1963, *26* (4).

Schein, E. "Management Development as a Process of Influence." *Industrial Management Rev.* (School of Industrial Management, M.I.T.), 1961, *2* (11), 1–19 (Reprint).

Scott, W. R. "Field Methods in the Study of Organizations." In James G. March, ed., *Handbook of Organizations.* Chicago: Rand McNally, 1965.

Seashore, S. E. "Field Experiments with Formal Organizations." *Human Organization,* 1964, *23,* 164–170.

Seashore, S. E. and Bowers, D. G. *Changing the Structure and Functioning of an Organization; Report of a Field Experiment.* Monograph No. 33. Ann Arbor: Survey Research Center, Institute for Social Research, 1963.

Selltiz, C., Jahoda, M., Deutsch, M., and Cook, S. W. *Research Methods in Social Relations.* Rev. ed. New York: Holt, 1959.

Shepard, H. A. "Basic Research and the Value System of Pure Science." *Philosophy of Science,* January 1956, 48–57.

Sofer, C. *Organization from Within.* London: Tavistock Publications, 1961.

Solomon, R. L. "An Extension of Control Group Design." *Psychological Bull.,* 1949, *46,* 137–150.

Spires, A. M. "Subject–Experimenter Interaction in Verbal Conditioning." Unpublished Ph.D. dissertation, New York U., 1960.

Stouffer, S. A. "Some Observations on Study Design." *American J. Sociology,* January, 1950, *40,* 353–361.

Strauss, G. "The Set-up Man: A Case Study of Organizational Change." *Human Organization,* 1954, *13,* 17–25.

Taylor, F. W. *The Principles and Methods of Scientific Management.* New York: Harper, 1911.

Tolman, E. C. and Brunswik, E. "The Organism and the Causal Texture of the Environment." *Psychological Rev.,* 1935, *42,* 43–77.

Tooley, J. and Pratt, S. "Who Will Watch the Brain Watchers?" "Letters to the Editor," *Behavioral Science,* 1964, *9,* (3).

Trist, E. L. *Wider Organizational Networks and Their Environments* (Mimeo).

Trist, E. L., Higgin, G. W., Murray, H., and Pollock, A. B. *Organizational Choice.* London: Tavistock Publications, 1963.

Trist, E. L. and Bamforth, K. "Some Social and Psychological Consequences of the Longwall Method of Coal Getting." *HR,* 1951, *4* (1) 3–30.

Vikan–Kline, L. "The Effect of an Experimenter's Perceived Status on the Mediation of Experimenter Bias." Unpublished Master's Thesis, U. of North Dakota, 1962.

Whyte, W. F. *Money and Motivation.* New York: Harper, 1955.

Whyte, W. F. *Pattern for Industrial Peace.* New York: Harper, 1951.

Woodward, J. *Management and Technology.* London: Her Majesty's Stationery Office, 1958.

3

The Comparative Study of Organizations

TOM BURNS

University of Edinburgh

THE PURPOSE OF COMPARATIVE STUDIES

For a sociologist the use of the adjective "comparative" to qualify the "study of organizations" is something of a pleonasm. Comparative study is the fundamental sociological method and has been since Montesquieu. This is true even for research which has a single community, tribe, or organization as its object. In such studies the social anthropologist (as against the ethnographer) or the sociologist (as against the historian or the reporter) is faced from the outset with the need to eliminate or reduce the uniqueness of the actual people, actions, relationships, and settings he observes. To do this, as S. F. Nadel (1951) has pointed out in the case of social anthropology, the social scientist must reduce his essentially narrative record to terms which are applicable to a wide range of quite different collectivities; he must then go on to reconstruct what he has observed in a way which will reflect both his own actual research experience and the similarly analyzed and reconstructed experience of other students. In all this, comparison is fundamental, if implicit. More particularly, in case studies of all kinds, one relies on the initial novelty of the situations observed, one's unfamiliarity with what is routine behavior for the actors, the apparent idiosyncracy of the criteria by which certain individuals or acts are labeled deviant, to alert one's critical understanding.

At the most elementary methodological level—that of the early Chicago school, say, where R. E. Park's injunction to aim at being a good journalist seems to have served as a governing principle—the distinction between sociological researchers and reporters lies in the self-conscious attempts in the former to relate their research observations to common experience and to other observers' findings in an explicit rather than implicit way.[1] The difference is all-important. It reflects the obligation to explain.

Comparative studies fall clearly on the *diagnostic* side of the dichotomy proposed by Zetterberg (1962) for social research—the other side consisting of *model-construction*. In other words, comparative studies are concerned with the answer to the question "what is it?" rather than to "how does it work?" For scientific inquiry, the second question is the operational point of departure for field and laboratory experiment, with which may now be associated simulation. These are the topics dealt with in other chapters of this book. This chapter is concerned with ways in which the first question, "what is it?" may be answered. Of course, the social scientist is dealing with matters of general knowledge and common observation. This means that the social scientist is necessarily concerned with the assumptions which prevail among the people he studies—and which, as a "citizen," he shares. But he is concerned with these assumptions only in pursuit of a higher order explanation. To paraphrase a previous statement (Burns, 1962), the purpose of comparative studies of organizations is to achieve an understanding of organizations which is different from that current among the people through whose conduct the institutions exist: different, new, and better.

The *praxis* of comparative studies is therefore to criticize: to criticize or question assumptions about the meaning of behavior, and claims about the value of achievements. It is the business of social scientists to conduct a critical debate, in this sense, with society at large about its equipment of social institutions. In so far as sociology, at least, is effective, it has been effective in this way from Marx and de Tocqueville, and from Booth and Giddings, on. And not only in sociology. It is Paul Lazarsfeld who has underlined the critical, assumption-questioning purposes of so much social science, and his classic illustration is still worth repeating. In his "exposi-

---

1. The distinction is very fine even in the best of the studies—e.g., Zorbaugh's *The Gold Coast and the Slum* and Donovan's *Saleslady*—but is none the less there and, I think, valid. Reporting must direct itself to a public that possesses a very specific and strictly contemporary accumulation of experience and a degree of insight and understanding; the reporter levels with his reader. The social scientist must, however crudely, relate his report to an accumulating, organized body of knowledge independent of him and his reader. In order to learn about one institution, as Goffman remarks, "we would be well advised to look at others" (Goffman, 1961, p. 3).

tory review" of *The American Soldier* (Lazarsfeld, 1949, pp. 177–178), he lists a number of conclusions which most people would probably dismiss as obvious:

> 1. Better educated men showed more psycho-neurotic symptoms than those with less education. (The mental instability of the intellectual as compared to the more impassive psychology of the-man-in-the-street has often been commented on.)
> 2. Men from rural backgrounds were usually in better spirits during their Army life than soldiers from city backgrounds. (After all, they are more accustomed to hardships.)
> 3. Southern soldiers were better able to stand the climate in the hot South Sea Islands than Northern soldiers (Of course, Southerners are more accustomed to hot weather.)
> 4. White privates were more eager to become noncoms than Negroes. (The lack of ambition among Negroes is almost proverbial.)
> 5. Southern Negroes preferred Southern to Northern white officers. (Isn't it well known that Southern whites have a more fatherly attitude toward their "darkies"?)
> 6. As long as the fighting continued, men were more eager to be returned to the States than they were after the German surrender. (You cannot blame people for not wanting to be killed.) B, 561.
>
> We have in these examples a sample list of the simplest ways of interrelationships which provide the "bricks" from which our empirical social science is being built. But why, since they are so obvious, is so much money and energy given to establish such findings? Would it not be wiser to take them for granted and proceed directly to a more sophisticated type of analysis? This might be so except for one interesting point about the list. *Every one of these statements is the direct opposite of what was actually found.* Poorly-educated soldiers were more neurotic than those with high education; Southerners showed no greater ability than Northerners to adjust to a tropical climate; Negroes were more eager for promotion than whites; and so on.

The central position occupied by the comparative method in social psychology and sociology and the way in which this is related to the essentially critical (assumption-testing) nature of the science are part of the continuing experience of social research. My own experience in organizational studies is, I believe, characteristic, and may serve as a paradigm of the learning process which such research essentially is.

Most studies of organization depend a good deal on interviews with managers; and one begins these interviews traditionally with questions about the particular job one's respondent does and how it fits in with other people's. The next step is to examine the discrepancies between the picture one gets from different respondents of the organization in which they all participate. There are always discrepancies; but, of course, the question presented by such internal inconsistencies is not "Which version is right?" but "How do these differences arise?" "How is it that these different versions of the same set of social circumstances have arisen in the minds of persons who have to cooperate with each other in the very circumstances they view so differently?" The need to account for these differences marks the first stage beyond description.

Some years ago, at the outset of one such inquiry (Burns and Stalker, 1961), I encountered a major difficulty even before this first comparative stage had been reached. A whole series of interviews with managers followed a rather disconcerting pattern. In answer to my first question, they would say, "Well, to make all this clear, I'd better start from the beginning," and then proceed to give me an account of their careers in the firm. This account would be lucid, well organized, and informative, but would stop short at some months beforehand. I would then ask again what they were, in fact, doing now. After a pause, they would go on to explain, equally lucidly, what they would be doing when the present reorganization was over and their department could settle down to work as it was now planned. After a succession of such occasions, I was fairly certain that I had encountered the sociologist's poor substitute for the natural scientist's "discovery"—the feeling that what had looked like solid, commonsense ground was turning into rather liquid assumptions. Had other managers, in more stable concerns, been recounting history too, without my being aware of it? If it came to that, what did those not supervised by a foreman or by a manager "do"—on what activities did they spend the hours of the working day?

These questions, taken a little further and looked at in the light of previous research, formed the starting point of a study of a hundred top executives in ten British companies (Burns, 1954, 1957). In the context of the present discussion, one particular aspect of the study is worth mentioning in detail.

It will be apparent that the "comparative method" as we have hitherto considered it, is a method of generating questions (e.g., "hypotheses"). R. K. Merton (1959) in his prefatory essay to *Sociology Today* quoted Aubrey, Darwin and Agnes Arber to remind us that, as the last of these has said, "the difficulty of most scientific work lies in framing the questions rather than in finding the answers." What is not so often insisted upon is that questions do not suggest themselves. They arise from doubt. Doubt, in turn, arises from the existence of an alternative where none was previously suspected; it arises from a discrepancy between facts, or between proferred interpretations, or between facts and assumptions. The studies of ten companies were founded on the discrepancy between the assumption that managers know what their job is and the evident inability of a number of managers to describe their jobs. At the end of each of the ten studies (which resulted from the confrontation of the managers in the first firm with this discrepancy, and their decision to cooperate in a study to "ascertain the facts"), there was an accumulation of data consisting of their own minute-to-minute records, on standard time-sheets, of all they had done which could be described as "work for the firm," or even as "time spent on the firm's behalf." The concluding task was, first, for each to give an estimate of how he had distributed his time among the subjects which, by agreement, made up the total management function; and, secondly, to give a similar estimate for the top-management group (self-defined and numbering eight people on an average, managing director included).

Taking the estimates made by individuals of the whole group's activities, and comparing them with the actual figures, the most noticeable effect was the wildly different conceptions offered by different members of top management groups of how the efforts of the group were directed.

Accuracy can hardly be expected from estimates by one person of how a whole group, even one in which he works, spends its time. The point of these estimates was that they represented, in crude terms, the assumptions each person had about the context of organized activity in which his own work was being done; they showed the kind of weight he thought was being given to each subject by the rest of the management group.

Even among heads of concerns, there was a widespread tendency to overestimate attention to production, to underestimate the claims of outside interests on time; but the discrepancies were far fewer than those encountered among their subordinates. One technical manager and his deputy thought that their colleagues must be spending 70 percent of their time on current production problems as against an actual 12 percent. A production manager thought of sales and attention to customers' needs as claiming 5 percent of the whole group's time as against 23 percent.

By far the greater number of individual recorders overestimated grossly the proportion of all management time spent on current production. This was true, for example, even of works managers and works supervisors; three of them thought that production matters bulked twice as large as they in fact did.

Comparison of individual recorders' estimates of their own time with the actual figures reinforces the conclusion that there is a general tendency to overestimate the proportion of time spent on clearly defined or "important" subjects of production, costs, accounts, and to underestimate time taken up by personal matters, general management policy discussions, and the like. This may indicate either the deflection of managers from the central tasks of management by the emergencies of problems concerning people and by time-consuming discussions of future uncertainties, or it may reveal genuine misconceptions of the direction of management effort.

To ascertain that there is a sizable difference between the pattern of behavior which is conceived as normal, and which even acts normatively, and that which is actually followed is, of course, only the beginning. There are varieties of difference, qualitative and quantitative, and the interpretation eventually focuses on the variation. But the point I wish to establish here is that explanation, which is the object of comparative studies, is here arrived at by the critical comparison of the actual and the assumed patterns of action.

THE DILEMMAS OF TAXONOMY

The object of comparative study is to provide answers to the question "What is it?"—answers that are more comprehensive, more meaningful, and, eventually, more useful than those in common currency. The procedure of comparative study is to analyze the object of study—an organization—into components, and then to translate the question "what is it?" into two others: "What is it like?" and "What is it not like?" The reasoning process is essentially analogical.

Analogical reasoning has for some time been regarded as scientifically rather disreputable; the traditional view—now largely exploded—of the process of scientific discovery as being founded on inference, and the confusion between proof and methods of study has relegated analogy to the status of "spurious explanation" (Reichenbach, 1951, pp. 5–26). It is only recently that renewed interest in the empirical study of scientific investigation of the roles of metaphor and analogy in it (Pepper, 1942; Schon, 1964) has suggested that there is more than one mental process involved, that there is a sequence of stages, and that each stage has its attendant and appropriate form of intellectual operation. In fact, the model we now have seems remarkably close to the picture Whitehead (1929, p. 5) gives in his famous aperçu:

> The Baconian method of induction . . . if consistently pursued, would have left science where it found it. What Bacon omitted was the play of a free imagination, controlled by the requirements of coherence and logic. The time method of discovery is like the flight of an aeroplane. It starts from the ground of particular observation; it makes a flight in the thin air of imaginative generalization; and it lands again for renewed observation rendered acute by rational interpretation.

Still bound by the traditional dismissal of analogical reasoning as unscientific, social scientists have tended to regard comparative studies as taxonomic and as justified only insofar as they lend themselves to the creation of a classification system. And this in spite of the fact that the history of sociology, from Montesquieu through Spencer, Marx, and up to Weber himself, is littered with the debris of ruined typologies that serve now only as the battleground for that academic street-fighting that so often passes for theoretical discussion. Most of the discussions of the group concerned with comparative studies at the Ford Foundation Seminar turned (somewhat centrifugally, however) on the problem of taxonomy. At the outset, it was argued that preoccupation with problems of classification was central to the group's concern (which was assumed to be the feasibility of making statements about organizations in general). And, although it was claimed that taxonomy (which was an appropriate end product of comparative studies) differed from typology (which was not), the distinction, if it exists,[2] was not particularly evident most of the time.

The existence of powerful support for the notion that comparative studies of organizations have the construction of some system of classification as their end product, and the way in which the notion constantly reappears in various guises in the discussion of organizational analysis require some examination of the taxonomic procedures that seem to be available. We can begin with two major attempts, made almost simultaneously, to elucidate a single major taxonomic principle for the classification of organizations of all kinds.

TYPOLOGIES BASED ON A SINGLE TAXONOMIC PRINCIPLE

In some ways, at least, social scientists, and especially sociologists, are nothing if not open-minded. Any consideration of the subject of this section has to deal with two books published some years ago within a few months of each other: Amitai Etzioni's *A Comparative Analysis of Complex Organizations* (1961) and P. Blau and W. R. Scott's *Formal Organizations: A Comparative Approach* (1962). Read separately, each is useful, illuminating and compendious. Taken together, they sow doubt and confusion from their opening paragraphs on. The first sentence of Etzioni's book reads, "The comparative study of organizations is a much neglected field." Blau and Scott prefer the alternative gambit. Introducing the bibliography appended to their book they remark, "The more

2. We may well obliterate the suggestion that there is any real difference between these two terms as merely adding to confusion by introducing a false dilemma. The *Shorter Oxford Dictionary* gives a variety of meanings for the two words, of which the following are clearly appropriate to the present matter: *taxonomy:* Classification, esp. in relation to its general laws or principles; that department of science, or of a particular science or subject, which consists in or relates to classification. *typology:* Archaeol. The classification of remains and specimens according to the type they exhibit and its evolution, etc.

than 800 items in the bibliography which follows represent a third of the bibliography which we have compiled."

Scott (1965, p. 485), in his contribution to R. E. L. Faris' *Handbook of Modern Sociology*, rubs in the same point of difference: "Organizations being ubiquitous, sociological explorations in virtually every substantive area have been compelled to take account of their presence. While the analysis of organizations is the stock in trade of the industrial and military sociologist, the last two decades have seen the investigation of organizations or organizational phenomena in such diverse areas as criminology, mental health, medicine, secondary and higher education, religion and social welfare." It could be argued that the comparative study of organization is not necessarily identical with the study of organizations on a comparative basis, but it is clear that both Etzioni and Blau and Scott aim at, first, a taxonomy of organizations in general (i.e., at the elucidation of elements or characteristics of organizations which are clear, distinct and qualitatively invariant), and, second, a typology of organizations in terms of these elements or characteristics.

The spectacle of two formidably elaborate and almost concurrent attempts to arrive at reasonably watertight classifications, which nevertheless employ utterly different criteria and result in irreconcilably disparate typologies, raises a number of questions. For our present purposes, it is enough to consider whether the construction of such classificatory schemes is, in fact, the central object of comparative studies, however wide ranging.

To resolve this question, and to consider the consequential matter of the status of organizational studies by comparative methods, it is necessary to make a rather closer examination of methodological foundations than is afforded by the customary deferential nod in the direction of Cohen and Nagel, etc., for classificatory systems which this kind of study turns up are clearly much more than the cognitive maps they pretend to be. They are Darwinian rather than Linnaean, seeking to explain rather than merely to identify. But to explain by subsuming particular instances of relationships, or of social norms or routines, under more general headings involves discriminating between different modes of variables. And it is here that language itself proves so deceptive.

To explore the studies of Etzioni and Blau and Scott a little further: each makes use of a single principle according to which the major species of the class—"organizations"—are defined. For Etzioni this major principle is compliance, the other half, so to speak, of the notion of authority; since Simmel pointed out that the logic of the social relationship of power and authority, from coercion to persuasion, involves submission and compliance as necessary complements, it is permissible, though perhaps a little perverse, to treat varieties of authority and influence in terms of their mirror images, i.e., as varieties of compliance. But Etzioni goes on to compose an orthogonal series of variants out of three "degrees of involvement"—moral, calculatory and alienatory. Only too clearly, these stand for the kinds of sentiment relevant to the degrees of compliance corresponding to three modes of exercising power—persuasion, reward, and coercion.

The outcome of this exercise in higher tautology is, not surprisingly, a three-by-three scheme of nine organizational types which resolves itself into three "congruent" types, with the other six "incongruent" types representing various degrees and directions of abnormality. And, further, we have a "dynamic hypothesis" postulating that "congruent types are more effective then incongruent types. Organizations are under pressure to be effective. Hence, to the degree that the environment of the organization allows, *organizations tend to shift their compliance structure from incongruent to congruent types and organizations which have congruent compliance structure tend to resist factors pushing them towards incongruent compliance structures*" (Etzioni, 1961, p. 14).

All of which prompts three questions: First, if there is so much pressure towards congruence, how do organizations get to be "incongruent" in the first place? Second, what is the "environment" doing in there if it is not to afford blanket cover for all contingencies which might weaken or wreck the hypothesis? And, third, for whom and for what are organizations to be reckoned "effective"?

This last question provides one connection of substance with the typology devised by Blau and Scott. The taxonomic principle in their case is to determine the kind of prime beneficiary served by an organization—owners, members, "public-in-contact" (clients), or public-at-large. In this, they are following Talcott Parsons (1956) fairly closely; the difference between their "prime beneficiary" and Parsons' "type of goal or function" is largely a matter of a variant reading of Parsons' basic concept of "output." In addition, they halt the Parsonian analysis at the societal level and consider the instrumental function of organizations only, rather than follow him and classify organizations in terms of the ways in which these functions are construed internally.

Blau and Scott see in their *cui bono* principle a way of introducing meaningful distinctions between types of organization and also of explaining something of the nature of organizations as a class. Their criterion sorts organizations into four subclasses: "(1) 'mutual-benefit associations,' where the prime beneficiary is the membership; (2) 'business concerns,' where the owners are prime beneficiary; (3) 'service organizations,' where the client group is prime beneficiary; and (4) 'commonweal organizations,' where the prime beneficiary is the public-at-large" (1962, p. 43).

Thus we seem to have a satisfactory way of distinguishing business concerns, trade unions, hospitals, and police forces. But do we? As the authors go on to remark, following Berle and Means (1932, p. 14), "public corporations transform owners into mere stockholders and vest controlling power in the hands of top-level employees, enabling them to govern the enterprise in their own interests." And does such a shift "constitute fundamental transformations of business concerns into distinctly different types of organization" (Blau and Scott, 1962, p. 44)? In what sense was General Electric in the 1930's distinctly different as an organizational type from, say, the Ford Motor Company, in which the stock was still largely in the hands of persons who saw themselves, and were regarded, as owning the business? For that matter, how justified is it to regard a hospital operated as a business enterprise by a consortium of medical practitioners as an organization fundamentally different from a hospital publicly maintained or privately endowed? Different, yes, but surely not in the sense in which Blau and Scott have devised their scheme of organizational types.

Cui bono? is in fact not a simple question to answer. Quite apart from the different replies the question can elicit for organizations that are palpably similar in type, a simplistic assumption lies behind the question itself. This assumption is that the goals of an organization—e.g., the purposes it serves or, again, the individuals or groups for whom it exists to "do good"—are explicit, stable, and coherent. But, as Howard Becker (1963, p. 7) has pointed out in a very different context: "The question of what the purpose or goal of a group is, and, consequently, what things will help or hinder the achievement of that purpose, is very often a political question. Factions within the group disagree, and maneuver to have their own definition of the group's functions accepted. The function of the group or organization, then, is decided in political conflict, not given in the nature of the organization."

More precisely (and with none of the ambiguity arising from Becker's indiscriminate equation of "group" and "organization," or of "goal," "purpose," and "function"), Cyert and March (1963, p. 28) have found it necessary to discard the common sense notion that organizations have clear, fixed, and characteristic goals: "Agreement on objectives is usually agreement on highly ambiguous goals; . . . behind this agreement on rather vague objectives there is considerable disagreement about sub-goals, [and] organizations appear to be pursuing different goals at the same time. . . . Since the existence of unresolved conflict is a conspicuous feature of organizations, it is exceedingly difficult to construct a useful, positive theory of organizational decision-making if we insist on internal goal consistency."

The trouble with the attempt to devise a taxonomy of organizations from first principles, as political theorists discovered long since with that more limited, more specific, but equally elusive notion—the State, is that, as Bavelas (1959–60, p. 498) has remarked, "Human organizations are not biological organisms; they are social inventions."

In lapsing into the fallacy of misplaced concreteness, social science follows common usage, as it usually does (Burns, 1958), and seeks to justify it. The justification lies in the definition of organizations as "social units oriented to the realization of certain goals" as Etzioni's definition runs (1961, p. 79). Yet the definition, as we have seen, is spurious; it defines—i.e., limits the kinds of things the words refer to—only if we conveniently forget that organizational goals are often, indeed usually, in dispute.

COMPREHENSIVE CLASSIFICATORY SYSTEMS

Granted that organizations are social inventions and not organisms or real objects, yet, it might be agreed, they seem credited by everybody, social scientists included, with a fair number of the attributes of reality and independent existence. If prisons, factories, government departments, labor unions, ships, air transport companies, and hospitals are organizations, then a good deal of hard material is incorporated in them, and they represent substantial facts of life for those in them and for those who have to deal with them.

Taking this straightforward, pragmatic line, it should be clearly feasible to list a number of attributes of organizations which will vary quantitatively or qualitatively between different organizations, and which would, when ordered, correlated, and contrasted, yield a simple classification of organizations that might of itself contribute to an understanding of them, and that would certainly provide extremely useful basic data for intensive studies within restricted fields or samples. Industrial and business organizations arc, in fact, classified for many administrative purposes by a limited range of variables, such as number of employees, issued capital, turnover, project turnover, rate of growth, type of product, rate of investment in research and design (R & D). Such classification has, moreover, been exploited and supplemented to good effect by economists for generations.

It was with this in mind, although it was not explicitly stated, that the attempt was made, at the Ford Foundation Seminar, to construct a list of variables that would characterize organizations and that might be used to develop a classificatory system. Reconstructed, and amplified a little, the list reads:

Economic Dimension
1. Number of employees
2. Capital investment
3. Number of clients, customers, subscribers (i.e., nonemployed members)
4. Horse-power ratio (or some other measure of proportion of inanimate power to manual labor force)
5. Direct labor costs in proportion to total costs.

Administrative Dimension
6. Proportion of managers and supervisors to total personnel
7. Number of administrative levels
8. Number of different job titles and distribution of personnel between them
9. Line-staff ratio
10. Degree of geographical concentration or dispersal of resources, personnel, and destination of output
11. Method, frequency, and direction of communication within the organization
12. Form of control exercised over staff or members
13. Span of control (number of subordinates per supervisor)
14. Responsibility (relative frequency of monitoring by superiors)

Institutional Dimension
15. Degree of specificity, in quantifiable terms, of goals and output, e.g., profit, remuneration, hours of work, in the case of businesses, as against effectiveness of hospitals as judged by patients, professional press, staff, sponsoring body
16. Extent (number, comprehensiveness, particularity) of formal rules
17. Degree of specification of jobs (or some other measure of extent to which performance is programmed by central or higher administration)
18. Specialized training requirements, educational qualifications, etc.
19. Complexity and duration of job cycle
20. Degree of segmentation (i.e., extent to which persons with different job titles work in the same unit) or segregation
21. Frequency and nature of interaction with people and places outside the organization

22. Visibility of individual's performance in comparison to that of others in organizations
23. Variation (e.g., ambiguity, conflict) in requirements and assessment of individuals.

The list does not, of course, pretend to be complete. More seriously, once one is outside the category of economic variables in familar use, the items become increasingly difficult to render into operational terms; questions of the units and instruments of measurement are posed that are inherently difficult to answer and one is almost bound to find different answers in different situations. Some of the variables, again, are operational and others conceptual. But the basic difficulty is that the individual items appear to be specific to different kinds of organization. Capital investment, for example, is not particularly relevant (or easily discernible) to government departments or labor unions, although it is of prime importance for business concerns.

The list, in fact, represents a selection of the kinds of data that are available to investigation or that might be obtained in different organizations. The question arises, whether, instead of attempting to compile an exhaustive catalogue of such variables (which would certainly be extremely unwieldy and of dubious value), it might not be more profitable to turn to research studies themselves, examine the variables adduced in them, and devise a means whereby the data might be standardized or rendered comparable for purposes of secondary analysis.

This possibility is not so much modeled on, as suggested by, the Yale Human Relations Area File and the Yale Technology Project. The Human Relations Area File consists of a very large compendium of abstracted and original monographs and reports by social anthropologists on primitive communities. It was created during the 1930's and exists as a body of data that can be used by social scientists as comparative data for secondary analysis. The Yale Technology Project was set up to study the implication of modern technological development for industrial organizations, individuals, and society at large (although this last stage was not fully realized). What eventuated was about thirty case studies of firms and plants of varying size. The studies were reported in a good many books and papers, many of which achieved a substantial reputation. The original data remain, however, rich sources of information and insight, comprising for each concern:

a) Background material: newspaper clippings, house journals, etc.
b) Information from respondents: open-ended interviews, but following a common patter—"Tell me about your job. . . ." "What kinds of headaches. . . ?" "What do you like about it. . . ?" "What do

you think an ideal company would be like. . . ?" Some questionnaire material is also deposited.

c) Official company and documentary material: (1) on organization
structure and regulations (organization charts, personnel rosters,
organization manuals); (2) technology (formal descriptions of
technical resources)

d) Observations: time diaries and other raw data; interoffice communications; records of meetings

e) Research findings, conclusions, descriptions of research methods.

The general problem of ordering such data, as against the Human
Relations Area File, is that, by a generation ago, social anthropologists
were satisfied that they had developed an adequate and coherent theory
of social structure; this is not true of social scientists for organizations.
The purposes of an attempt to create a large repository of research data
on lines such as the Yale projects [3] indicated would be:

1) To provide more adequate empirical reference or support for statements in the field of organizational theory

2) To widen the range of statements which it is possible to offer about
specific objects of study

3) To provide a data archive facility

4) To provide data for secondary analysis, on the same lines as those
developed in the field of political sociology, possibly, like the latter,
on the cross-cultural as well as national basis.

The merits of any such archives are entirely dependent on the effectiveness with which retrieval procedures yield data of the kind the
original researchers used and relied upon. It is, in some ways, a concrete
or symbolic representation of the general problem of using secondary
data (i.e., other people's research) for comparative studies.

At the present stage of development in the social science of organizations, it does not seem feasible to contemplate developing a matrix of
organizations into which original data could be separated out according
to their empirical attributes (such as those listed on pp. 124–125). There
are, then, two methodological problems. The first is the design of a
system (actual or notional) of storage and retrieval for research data on
organizations comparable to those already devised for space technology
and the like, and, more generally, for new library systems, and for
language translation. The second, is the elucidation of the criteria
relevant to ordering data for such a system.

We are, it will be noted, back to problems of classification, but with a

---

3. Udy, who put forward the general proposal under discussion, is engaged on the
further exploration of the material of the Yale Human Relations Area File and the
Yale Technology Project for comparative purposes.

difference. The objects for classification are not organizations or parts or attributes of organizations but analytical concepts and frames of reference within which methodological procedures can be designed and comparative studies usefully made. The classificatory scheme that is now envisaged points in the direction, not of typologies—of a natural history of organizations—but of the effective extension of studies of organizations by providing ready access to comparative data.

AN ANALYTICAL SCHEMA FOR COMPARATIVE STUDIES

The valid guides for comparative studies, it is suggested, are analytical rather than empirical or methodological. What is necessary is the composition of a system of categories by which research data, the analytical methods applied to the data, and findings can be identified; such a system has to be reasonably logical, but the criteria of adequacy (serviceability) is its comprehensiveness. The appropriate paradigm, in fact, is a thesaurus. One of the objections to the catalogue of empirical (methodologically determined) data listed in the previous section is that it is admittedly incomplete and would almost certainly remain so however determinedly residual and potential types of data were hunted down. At the other extreme, the listing of social forms—structural, institutional, or collective—can be equally open-ended; unless one accepts the boundaries imposed by a particular theoretical system, the ordering of data for comparative study under such headings as status system, peer group, reference group, and managment style has to be regarded as subject to revision in terms of the theoretical (and methodological) requirements of individual researchers and is, as a series, constantly liable to prove incomplete.

If one begins afresh, as the Ford Foundation Seminar group did, by considering the practical realities of organizational research, it looks as if a useful distinction could be made between the kind of observations, records, and statements applying clearly to individuals, those applying to categories or groups, and those applying to an organization as a whole. Unfortunately, as soon as one considers these divisions as other than sources of data, the division breaks down. It is a basic assumption of social science that social structure influences the behavior of individuals; but this influence can only be inferred from the behavior of individuals; but this influence can only be inferred from the behavior of individuals. At first sight, indeed, survey research, which is always concerned with individuals, would seem to follow exactly the classic model of induction. Characteristics of groups, sections and categories, and probabilistic "laws" applying to a population or collectivity are inferred from the study of individuals and used as principles to explain individual behavior. It is certainly difficult and almost certainly impossible, therefore, to distinguish sociologically relevant data about individuals from data that apply to groups or larger collectivities. In the last resort, all social research data apply to individuals.

As soon as one moves into analytical categories anything in the nature of a schema of categories in terms of a quantitative order becomes impracticable. If the object of study is individuals and individual behavior, it will almost always be necessary to obtain information about work groups and sections and about the organization as a whole, since these at least impose constraints on the possible range of behavior in which individuals can engage; similar qualifications apply if the object of study is work groups or the organization as a whole.

Beyond this, there are extra-organizational factors which limit the possibilities open to the organization as a whole and, consequently, the groups and individuals within it: economic factors, the educational system, cultural values, the level of technology, and the like. Ultimately, "economic factors," "educational system," "level of technology" and similar terms are also reducible to the attributes of individual people and their behavior; but explanatory propositions about any particular set of individuals ordinarily require the treatment of aspects of the behavior of other individuals in terms of such abstract entities. It is necessary, that is, to "close the system" one is studying in a more or less arbitrary manner (Gluckman and Devons, 1964), substituting abstractions for the individuals external to the system, abstractions which may be treated as variables in the extent to which they impinge on the individuals within the system defined for study.

In doing this, the student of organizations adopts, in a more or less articulate way, the mode of thought and the assumptions which prevail among individuals in any collectivity. In so far as one individual's actions are dependent on those of others, he has to regard them as institutionalized and therefore predictable. Each individual works within a framework of the institutionalized activity of others and contributes to the framework of institutionalized activity within which others work. The degree to which institutionalization "governs" behavior (in the sense of its following presumptive laws and, therefore, being predictable) is related not only to the uniformity or nonconformity of the behavior of individuals themselves but also to the social distance from the closed system of action which is the object of attention at the time. So "the government" is habitually treated as virtually a constant if one is studying the behavior of a school board, "technology," as a constant if one is occupied with the behavior of shoe-salesmen. Similarly, in the reverse direction, the *variation* in the behavior of school boards may, for most purposes, be ignored in a study of the behavior of government officials concerned with education, and of shoe salesmen, in a study of a research laboratory in a footwear plant.

Institutionalized complexes like "the formal organization," "the market," "labor union policy" are treated as abstractions, therefore, when they lie outside any closed system of action that is the object of study, and the variance within the closed system that is ascribed to their influence is a function both of the degree to which the action they represent is institutionalized, and of their remoteness.

These elementary and ineluctable features of the study of social behavior have to be rehearsed because we are searching for a system of categories that will not alter as we shift attention from one closed system of study to another. With this in mind, we can attempt to list a number of elements of social action relevant to organizational studies that, taken together, both characterize organizations and provide analytical categories for comparative purposes. The condition set out in the preceding paragraph acts as a general constraint and as a principle by which analytical categories may be generated. For, to begin with, it is clearly necessary to examine, analyze and account for the *interchanges of all kinds which take place between the largest "closed system" among the possible objects of study*—be it industry or defense system, single plant, branch of an organization, work group or class of individuals—*and relevant institutional elements on the outside.*

At this point, a second analytical dimension makes itself apparent. There are, in fact, three models of analysis which have been applied to precisely the functional relationship between an organization, regarded as a closed system, and its environment. Two of these are becoming fairly fully articulated and are often contrasted with each other as dichotomous; the usual labels are "system theories" and "factor theories." Both, however, allow the notion of interaction and mutual influence between organization and environment which the third, "response theories," does not.

These three models are also relevant to what is topically the next level of analytical categories: those which apply to the *events and the actions within the closed system which derive immediately from the nature and variety of its interaction with the environment.* A system theory model tends to represent these major events in terms of the primary and secondary tasks generated within the closed system, and the distribution of these tasks among groups and individuals, as a more or less unstable equilibrium requiring constant surveillance (i.e., management). Factor theory models represent major events in terms of goals, subgoals, and the system of expectations and performances that between them contribute to the operation of the closed system. Response theory models are appropriate to accounts which are couched in terms of the division of labor, management systems, role systems, and the like.

The closed system (i.e., the field of investigation) is now visible as a complex array of human and technical action. The coordination of these activities in terms of a socio-technical system serving the tasks of the total organization is effected by a *network of communication* conveying information and instructions.

The communication network operates effectively in the service of the closed system insofar as the information and instructions are attended to because (a) they are "authoritative" and (b) responses called for are appropriate in terms of the commitment of the individual. Logically sequential to the analysis of communication structure, therefore, are sets of analytical categories relevant, first, to the *authority structure* and the varieties of authority and, second, to the commitments of individuals to relationships which involve compliance with authority.

For the most part, commitment to membership of a closed system in which authority relationships obtain is resolvable into two kinds: a contractual or quasi-contractual *engagement* of effort in return for rewards, material and immaterial; and *involvement,* dedication to effort over and above engagement, separate from it, or directed to other kinds of objective. There are, then, three types of analysis following and dependent upon that which applies to the communication network. They are concerned with: authority; engagement (and rewards); involvement (and responsibility).

This series of analytical categories applies to a set of relationships and to attributes of action that, together, may be regarded as the institutional apparatus within which *individual behavior* occurs. This apparatus may be formulated according to three different theoretical models. It can, according to a response theory model, be seen as a prescription of behavior—in the sense in which social structures, situations and the evaluative definitions applied to certain social positions may be said to prescribe roles and role behavior. Or, in terms of factor theory, it may be regarded as a set of constraints within which the individual operates in a sufficiently institutionalized (and therefore dependable) way. Or, in terms of a system theory, it may be seen as a set of conventions in continual interplay with the ways in which individuals define their occupational and other kinds of behavior. The choice of theoretical model is available at the last as at the previous levels.

The list of analytical categories themselves is, or should be, exhaustive. Taken together, that is, they serve to distinguish organizations from other institutions. They are:

1) Relationships between the organizations and its environment
2) Definitions of tasks and division of labor
3) Communication system
4) Authority structure
5) Systems of engagement and rewards
6) Involvement (responsibility)
7) Definition of individual social identities in organizational settings.

ORGANIZATIONS IN SOCIETY

Although the analytical schema we have outlined begins by studying the categories relevant to examining the relationship between the organization and its social, economic, technical, and political context, it treats the relationships from the point of view of the organization itself. This is orthodox enough, and unexceptionable, if one adopts the orientation to the subject that prevails almost universally among social scientists concerned with the study of organizations. Yet the point of view is widely questioned among European social scientists, who have in recent years shown a growing disquiet at the way in which social science, and especially sociological theory, has become more and more enclosed within a set of analytical concepts pertaining exclusively to the internal structure and dynamics of social, psychological, political, or economic systems. For sociology and social psychology, this is explicable perhaps in terms of the metaphysical climate prevailing among older, more influential and better-known disciplines; economics, social anthropology, and psychoanalysis, for example, showed similar proclivities during the second quarter of the century. They tended to work increasingly within the boundaries of equilibrium theory, structural functionalism, and libidinal organization. But these are all now showing clear breaks with their past.

This inward-looking direction of social science [4] is most clearly evident when one considers Gouldner's (1959a, p. 404) contrast of "natural systems" models with "rational" models as representing the "two distinct approaches to the study of complex organizations." Gouldner cites Selznick's work as the best contemporary exemplar of the first; for the second, in which the organization is treated "as a rationally conceived means to the realization of expressly announced group goals" (ibid.), he clearly points towards the work of Simon and the Carnegie Institute of Technology school of organizational analysis. Yet how large or important is the distance between them? Selznick moved from his early treat-

---

4. For a critical examination of this tendency in sociological theory, see G. Poggi, "A Main Theme of Contemporary Sociology: Its Achievements and Limitations," *British J. Sociology*, 1965, *16*, 283–294.

ment of the organization as one kind of environment for interaction to a consideration of organizations themselves as adaptive systems; common to both kinds of study is a latent analytical distinction between system and circumstance and a preoccupation with the conditions under which the system can persist as a viable entity; in short, the mode of thinking is as biologistic as that of nineteenth-century social philosophers was "geologistic," and is determinedly *introspective* throughout. Simon (1958) is no less concerned throughout his work with the optimum conditions for goal-attainment, which is implicity equated with survival. If one contrasts his rendering of the role of innovation with, say, Schumpeter's, the identification of Simon's analytical methods and approach with the interests of the individual organization is strikingly evident. Gouldner's two models are, in fact, variations on the same dominant theme.

What is needed, not to replace this approach but to supplement it, is a conceptual scheme relating the organization to society in a way that will not relegate the latter to the position of "environment" or of biological "culture." This involves the development of analytical categories that (a) identify organizations as functioning elements of society and (b) apply to the positive and negative consequences for society of the nature and operation of organizations.

Thus, the set of analytical categories suggested in the previous section needs to be supplemented (for many research purposes), by two further categories, one logically anterior and the other logically posterior. The implication is, of course, that the two sets are connected, although not necessarily in a one-to-one relationship. The organization itself, in the present theoretical setting, is seen as acting as a transducer between the two sets of factors and, in itself, as a pattern of institutional forms organized by entrepreneurs or by administrators (i.e., "organizers") out of the first set of factors, called here "institutional generators" and in conformity with their perception of the second set, the "action consequences."

The logical initial presumption is that organizations are started and kept in being because of some demand arising either (a) in society at large (for goods or services of specific kinds, such as are provided by productive industry, merchants, business, welfare agencies; or by government departments and agencies, police forces, armed forces), or (b) in a set of individuals (for activities in which they can engage only if they are planned ahead and engage other appropriate persons; churches and recreational and sports groups fall into this category, though perhaps not exclusively, and another subgroup would include political parties, labor unions, criminal gangs, and dramatic societies). Demand, to be an effective "institutional generator," must clearly exist above a particular threshold in the preference ordering of the variety of wants existing among the members of large and complex societies.

Labor force and capital resources are obvious constituent elements in the process of forming and maintaining an organization. The point of view adopted here, however, presents them as active "generators." Since the Keynesian revolution, the maintenance of "full employment" has been an explicit policy of Western states and was before then axiomatic for socialist societies. And almost any period of history can show instances of organizations set up only and merely to provide work. These are, however, the extreme cases of the requirement in organized society that livelihoods be provided. Capital, as representing the continually accumulating value produced by labor and technical progress, acts also as a generator insofar as it "requires" profitable investment or useful application. The material resources available to society, in particular localities or sectors of activity, serve as generators in the same way.

Demand and resources are formed and articulated to the point at which particular organizations and kinds of organization may be generated in accordance with three sets of institutional elements in society: "value system," "educational system" and "technological system." The last two may be taken as self-explanatory, but the first, it should be said, relates to the conventional system of norms, upheld by beliefs, which enters into the institutional forms that can be utilized in generatory organizations. Marcuse (1956, 1964), for instance, has written at length about not only the universality of alienated work in both Freudian and Marxian terms, but of the even more striking phenomenon of the virtually universal acceptance of alienated work as a normal condition of life in Western society. H. A. Simon, in discussion, has made much the same point of the "extraordinariness" of workers actually performing tasks demanding a high degree of skill and involvement that are utterly remote from their personal interests and the rest of their cognitive field.

Variation and developmental change in the value system of society, as in the educational system and the technological system, manifestly affect profoundly not only the institutional pattern and structure of organizations, not only the capacity of society to meet demand and use resources, but the *kinds* of organization which may be brought into being and the social characteristics of the entrepreneurs and administrators who try to start organizations and run them.

Action consequences are of the same conceptual order as institutional generators and may be more briefly indicated. The two sets of elements are:

Institutional Generators	*Action Consequences*
Demand	Payoff to members, supporters, users, public
Labor force	Capital formation or depletion
Capital	Formulation or reformulation of demand
Material resources	Bearing of rigid or elastic strategies on value systems and educational systems
Value system	Technological contribution
Educational system	Growth, stability, or decline in the number and variety of inputs and outputs
Technological system	

There is no special symmetry to be imputed to the two sets of categories, but it will be noticed that the final item (concerning variation in the flow and nature of inputs and outputs) directly affects demand, which is the first. It is feasible therefore, within limits, to regard outputs as a category which is both specific to organizations and also most indicative of the relationship between organization and society.

Stanton Wheeler, in discussion, and independently of the conceptual apparatus outlined above, suggested that organizations were brought into being in order to operate certain "processes" on behalf of society in an effective—i.e., organized—way. Organizations were, in short, divisible largely into those which processed *things* (manufacturing industry) and those which processed people (that is, which existed so as to effect changes in people who pass through them). There seemed to be an uncomfortably large residual category of organizations like churches, political parties, and sports teams that clearly belong to neither division, but, if the schema is elaborated, it is unexpectedly fertile in developing categories of relationship between organizations meaningful for comparative purposes. One possible formulation is given in Figure 1 with examples inserted in each cell.

ORGANIZATION AND CHANGE PROCESSES

The previous section began by drawing attention to the preoccupation with the internal structure and processes of organizations, and pointing out that in this regard sociologists and social psychologists were working within walls knocked down some time since by other social scientists.

There is one other set of limits to theoretical perspectives, however, which the sociologists and social psychologists have apparently been able to break out of as soon as their colleagues or, at least, to see the need for so doing. These have to do with the incapacity of structural equilibrium theories to deal adequately with the dynamics of human behavior. The presumption has been that we have to begin analysis of the complexities of behavior by analyzing "the state of the system at a given moment" and then move on to accounting for changes in the system through time. It is, fortunately, unnecessary to rehearse arguments I have given at length elsewhere (Burns, 1958), since it is now fairly generally accepted that to work from concepts which assume, first, that behavior, relationships, purposes, functions, and causal sequences are frozen into immobility at a given moment and, secondly, that this paralyzed anatomy is then open to inspection by researchers is to desert the ground of empirical reality too abruptly and to forgo any real chance of relating theoretical explanations to even common experiences of social change. As Scott, in discussion, remarked, the study of behavior over time in terms of process was almost entirely neglected because of the lack of conceptual apparatus. "Functional role," "work group," "administrative system," he suggested, were, at best, partial concepts. What was needed were concepts which incorporated the notion of process—learning, socialization, influence, reward processes, for example. These and other ideas related to generic social processes to which the terms used in social

FIGURE 1

Organizations and Outputs

	Organizations Concerned With Change Processes		Organizations Concerned With Maintenance Processes	
	Things	People	Things	People
Internal to Organization	Manufacturing Industry	Hospitals Schools	Public Utilities	Established Churches Health Services
External to Organization	Research and Development	Evangelical Churches Political Parties	Distribution	Police

FIGURE 2

Types of Comparative Study

A complete analytical schema for the comparative study of organizations along the lines we have discussed would have to be realized in terms of three sets of variables. In tabular form, it can be represented in this fashion:

Analytical Categories	Diachronic Studies			Synchronic Studies		
	System Theory Models	Factor Theory Models	Response System Models	System Theory Models	Factor Theory Models	Response System Models
Organizations in Society	1	2	3	4	5	6
Relationships between the Organization and its Environment	7	8	9	10	11	12
Definitions of Tasks and Division of Labor	13	14	15	16	17	18
Communication System	19	20	21	22	23	24
Authority Structure	25	26	27	28	29	30
Systems of Engagement and Reward	31	32	33	34	35	36
Involvement (Responsibility)	37	38	39	40	41	42
Definition of Individual Social Identities in Organizational Setting	43	44	45	46	47	48

topography—administrative system, work group—were irrelevant. This involves, moreover, going beyond the methodological procedure of examining structural changes over time. What counts is not the measurement of changes in structure and scale (important as these may be), but the identification and analysis of the effect of intervening variables which work out in sequential, tree-like processes. Gouldner (1954) in his study of the different forms of bureaucratic organization, in fact studied changes in the nature and structure of organization as a process occurring via management succession. At a different level of comprehensiveness the present writer has recently been engaged in the study of the personality changes consequent upon engagement and involvement in occupational roles (Burns, 1965).

The claim that the system outlined in the previous section is exhaustive is easy enough to make. But this property may easily exist because of the elasticity of some of the categories (notably the last: "definition of individual social identities") and the dubious durability of the threefold classification of theoretical models actually in use. Its utility doubtless rests, first, on the extent to which individual students can resolve ambiguities—a problem faced by all cataloguers and index-makers—and introduce refinements to suit their needs, secondly, on the degree of consensus prevailing among users, and, thirdly, on the logical necessity, and therefore degree of universality, attaching to refinements. What is immediately obvious is that certain of the cells in the table are extremely well populated and others practically empty, and that, roughly speaking, the density of research data would increase as one moved from the top left-hand to the bottom right-hand corner.

The second half of this chapter is devoted to a review of instances of comparative studies. Necessarily, they are characteristic of the way in which different approaches have developed and become exploited rather than characteristic of this or any other formal schematization of the comparative method applied to organizations. What any review of actual studies reveals is that, far from falling into logically coherent patterns, they seem to be continually and almost obstinately departing from them. Like any other kind of inquiry which has a history and an establishment, organizational studies seem at the time to be pursuing not so much the right kind of knowledge as the right kind of questions; not definitive information but fresh hypotheses; not exploring and mapping new territory but staking claims and prospecting.

Given that the purpose of comparative study is properly analytical explanation (or critical understanding), the schema is aimed at producing categories of relevance for using material for comparative purposes rather than a classificatory system of comparative studies. Comparative studies themselves, of course, are a different matter, since they tend to restrict themselves to a single, or a few, comparative categories and to develop these in refined and complicated ways. In what follows, therefore, both comparative studies and studies of particular relevance to the comparative method are arranged only tentatively according to the sequence of analytical categories; and no attempt has been made to find specimens to fit every box. The review also concentrates on the variety of approaches applicable to the first two analytical categories, which relate especially to the study of organizations as a whole.

DIACHRONIC STUDIES OF ORGANIZATIONS IN SOCIETY

Historical contrast is the classic method of comparative studies, indeed of sociology. There is therefore a special appropriateness in starting with long-term comparative studies. It was used systematically, almost exclusively, by Marx. In effect, the purpose of using historical comparison in this way is to arrive at an understanding of the contemporary social situation by examining its origins.

The understanding thus arrived at is twofold. First, and most important, the common perception of the contemporary situation, however systematized and uniform that appreciation may be, is seen for what it is: a snapshot of a process. This revelation, though, has its limitations, and Carl Becker's (1932, p. 19) remark on historical explanation carries both implications: "We can identify a particular thing only by pointing to the various things it successively was before it became that particular thing it will presently cease to be."

Secondly, the terms and concepts applied indiscriminately to each and every stage of the existence of an institution may be shown to conceal changes of a fundamental kind. A classic example of this is Marx's statement on the effects of the factory system and the new technology on the organization of labor:

> Along with the development of the factory system and of the revolution in agriculture that accompanies it, production in all the other branches of industry not only extends, but alters its character. The principle, carried out in the factory system, of analysing the process of production into its constituent phases, and of solving the problems thus proposed by the application of mechanics, of chemistry, and of the whole range of the natural sciences, becomes the determining principle everywhere. Hence, machinery squeezes itself into the manufacturing industries first for one detail process, then for another. Thus the solid crystal of their organisation, based on the old division of labour, becomes dissolved, and makes way for constant changes. Independently of this, a radical change takes place in the composition of the collective labourer, a change of the persons working in combination. In contrast with the manufacturing [i.e., handicraft] period, the division of labour is thenceforth based, wherever possible, on the employment of women, of children of all ages, and of unskilled labourers, in one word, on cheap

labour, as it is characteristically called in England. This is the case not only with all production on a large scale, whether employing machinery or not, but also with the so-called domestic industry, whether carried on in the houses of the workpeople or in small workshops. This modern so-called domestic industry has nothing, except the name, in common with the old-fashioned domestic industry, the existence of which presupposes independent urban handicrafts, independent peasant farming, and above all, a dwelling-house for the labourer and his family. That old-fashioned industry has now been converted into an outside department of the factory [Marx, 1906, Chap. 15, Sec. 8b].

The transformation undergone in the division of labor, work roles, productive organization, and the relationship of home and family to occupation to which Marx points, all lies concealed under an unchanging terminology. In the same way terms like "bureaucracy," "organization chart," "technology," "R & D" tend to conceal fundamental changes that have occurred during the last twenty years in the perception and operation of the practical activities and social institutions to which they refer.

For any writer on social institutions in the nineteenth century, explanation seems to have been conceivable only in terms of historical contrast. Even Tocqueville's *Democracy in America* contains implications of a basically historical contrast, the method he employed elsewhere. It is difficult, now, to appreciate how revolutionary was Durkheim's development of comparative analysis on a contemporary, cross-cultural basis.

The Durkheimian revolution was possibly too successful. In terms of organizational studies, the analytical possibilities offered by the change in institutional forms, roles, and beliefs from one generation to another (which is what Marx was concerned with) have remained curiously unexploited. This is true despite the notable achievement of the one major study in this field, Berle and Mean's *The Modern Corporation and Private Property*. Widely quoted as their findings have been by students of industrial and business organizations, the neglect of longitudinal comparative studies, especially those involving historical research, seems to have led to a failure to incorporate their insights into the body of writings that makes up contemporary organization theory. There is no reference to the book, for example, in what is probably the most widely-used text of all—March and Simon's *Organizations*. Yet no work bears so closely on the topic which so many writers have made of central importance—i.e., goals, and the way in which they are formulated by and for organizations.

Their thesis is that, during this century, there has developed a separation between ownership and control, between the holding of shares and the control of the policies and activities of a company by a management that may or may not hold a minority of shares. This tendency is held to be as inherent in the structure of large-scale enterprise as is the tendency towards monopoly, arising as it does out of the division between ownership and the use of property. Power has been passing into the hands of the managers of enterprises and out of those of the multitudes of small shareholders, among whom ownership is now usually dispersed and whose joint influence cannot, in practice, match that of the single compact minority interest of the board. Further, and more generally, the technical, financial, and administrative complexities of a modern large-scale enterprise have transformed the relationship between the shareholding owner and the manager of productive capacity.

Elton Mayo (1949, p. 32) remarked upon—but nobody has examined—one of the implications of the emergence of the large-scale enterprise: "Instead of the life of a business coming to an end in two or three generations, we have, by improving industrial organisation, conferred upon such business a 'species of immortal life' which must be maintained by the community at its peril." Again, the implications that this has for the relationships between the corporation and specific environmental fields (labor supply, governmental agencies, labor unions) have been remarked upon (for example, by Celier, 1959 and by A. T. M. Wilson, 1961) but not investigated—at least by sociologists or social psychologists.

The most general examination of historical contrasts can bring to light new and revelatory perspectives of social change. It is years since Galbraith (1959) produced his now celebrated historical aperçu concerning the new and insecure relationship between production and market which has appeared as production in America and elsewhere has caught up and overtaken spontaneous consumer demand. This provided a theoretical rationale for the stimulation of the propensity to consume by advertising, styling, and consumer research. It also suggested a causal basis for the development of industrial research and development as a permanent entrepreneurial activity. Since this explanation is at least reasoned, it is to be preferred to the current acceptance of this quite fundamental change in the ideology and operation of productive and other organizations as a function of scientific progress itself or, to sound the depths of tautology, of "social change." It has received very little attention from students of organizations.

Keirstead (1948), again, used his explorations of economic history to point to the fact that when one introduces time into the discussion of the profit-maximizing assumption, it is obvious that for the modern corporation almost every consideration, including maximizing profit, becomes subordinate to survival. This has obvious connections with the Berle and Means' thesis:

> Directly, that is, the realities of industrial enterprise are organised in terms of the firm rather than of the entrepreneur, then almost any profit terms upon which the firm can survive become preferable to grosser

profits on which it might possibly not survive. There is, in fact, no change in the logical basis, but merely in the way in which it works: (a) through individual mortals, (b) through corporations which are relatively potentially longer-lived. For an individual entrepreneur, profit-taking can be maximized for any period of time however short, since the rewards will certainly be a substantial help towards his own survival. Moreover, for the individual the random sector of circumstances affecting his strategies increases enormously with time. And he makes hay, therefore, when the sun shines, and a bird in the hand is worth two in the bush. For the Corporation, randomness does not increase at anything like the same rate. And survival means only survival of the firm. The birds in the bush, which are tomorrow's or the next ten years' production, are just as important as that in the hand [Burns and Stalker, 1961, p. 35]

While it is American lawyers and economists who have made most effective use of historical comparison in analyzing the current relationships between organizations and their social and economic environment, and have thereby pointed to the major influences on the internal structure and on the formulation of the policy-aims of organizations, what little exploitation of historical comparison as a research method has occurred in other social sciences has been done in Europe. Alain Touraine's (1955) study of automobile workers, to take one instance, has been considerably enriched by the comparison he has drawn between the situation of workers in modern, large-scale, technologically advanced plants and that which prevailed earlier. The erosion or rejection of supervisory relationships based on direct subordination, for example, is seen as a consequence of the development of specialized management systems, in which the individual's work behavior is governed by a variety of functional specialists, all exercising impersonal kinds of authority.

Almost identical conclusions were reached by Janowitz (1960) in his study of U.S. Army and Navy officers. Apart from the historical sample of 760 generals and admirals "developed for the purpose of analyzing trends in social background and professional careers," extensive use is made of the writings of professional soldiers in the past and present to illustrate the change in forms of authority from those based on domination to those involving manipulation. My own studies of industrial organizations have depended increasingly on the enlightenment which a historical perspective not only brings of itself, but forces one to search for. At its simplest, it becomes impossible to regard the bureaucratic form that is now conventionally accepted as the ideal type of rationalistic organization as something towards which past ages have been struggling, or as a perfect model that stands as a Platonic idea behind all the imperfect representations actually present as working organizations.

The notion of organizations as developing and changing in time is critically important, especially in any attempt to perceive the relationships between them and the historical situation of society in, by and for which they are created. The fact that organizations change so profoundly in institutional character and structure from one generation to another while still serving virtually the same ends both for their members and for society calls for a more thorough-going explanation of the structure and function of the organization as it is now; it provides comparative material to aid that explanation; and it enforces considerations of the general societal forces and conditions which are at work. Crozier's (1963) study of the postal check clearing section of the French post office and of a number of plants in the tobacco monopoly was comparative not only in the obvious sense but in that the general findings were related to the historical circumstances of administration, governmental and industrial, in France.

SYNCHRONIC STUDIES OF ORGANIZATIONS IN SOCIETY (CROSS-CULTURAL)

It seems reasonable to draw a parallel between long-term historical and large-scale cross-cultural studies. The parallel is meaningful in more than one sense; just as historical comparison requires a wide-ranging historical competence, so does the cross-cultural study demand more than the application of identical research procedures in different societies. We are in danger, as Hans-Paul Bahrdt (1961) has suggested, of creating a "sociological man" out of the measurable variables yielded by studies of voting behavior, industrial morale, wage-payment system, bureaucratic organizations, and leisure, a sociological man just as unreal and, eventually, just as big an obstruction to theoretical development as "economic man" proved to be.

It is in this respect that Weber presents so eminently laudable and dangerous a methodological model. The placing of his work within the context of cross-cultural studies rather than comparative historical studies is justifiable on the grounds that historical material is used as often to point contrasts between the institutional apparatus of very different forms of social organization prevailing in different historical epochs as to trace the processes which changed value systems, structures, and organizational forms. What gives his work [5] its character is the alliance between outstanding intellectual powers and immense scholarship.

Weber was concerned with the way in which social values and normative images of social organization develop as a kind of mental

5. In particular, *Wirtschaft und Gesellschaft* which traces the relationship between various forms of economy and the dominant types of authority, of religious beliefs, of organization and legal systems; and *The Protestant Ethic and the Spirit of Capitalism* (Weber 1964; 1930).

equipment with which men fashion an acceptable or workable framework of institutions. He is constantly reiterating his purpose of establishing the subjective, cognitive, structures with which men impart meaning to their social actions. Indeed, the force of the concept of ideal types lies not in its analytical applications, but in the way in which it reflects this normative rendering of the structures the individual reads into and attaches to the social circumstances of his life, and to which, eventually, he strives to make these circumstances conform.

Ideal types, in fact, represent a normative extreme of system theorizing, in that the shared value elements which inhere in the parts and maintain the system are, so to speak, maximized. It is, therefore, inappropriate to convert the elements Weber itemizes in his description of bureaucracy as an ideal type into autonomous factors which it is reasonable to convert into variables and then to seek for correlations between them as though they were independent.

The difference may be sufficiently displayed by citing two widely different excursions into cross-cultural analysis: the comparative studies made by Bendix (1956) of management ideologies in the course of industrialization in Europe and America and Udy's taxonomical analysis of data on the organization of work drawn from the Human Relations Area Files at Yale.

Bendix's book is a carefully documented account of the value systems of entrepreneurs and managers, and the counter-systems of workers' beliefs in England during the primary and secondary phases of industrialization, in Russia during the development of its industrial system under capitalism, in the United States during this century, and in East Germany since 1945. He pays consistent attention to the contextual system of values and beliefs in the polity and in the organs of society related to the industrial enterprise. In this he is, of course, immensely aided by the circumstances of his own career that make him free of primary and secondary sources in German and English. The section on Russia, significantly, relies very heavily on secondary material, notably Vasili Klyuchevski's *History* and a German history of Russian manufacturing industry published in 1900. He makes the Weberian principles followed throughout quite clear in a preliminary statement:

> Studies of ideologies imply a neglect of persons and private beliefs. I shall treat entrepreneurs and managers as "members" of a social group by virtue of their position in economic enterprises and by virtue of the common problems and experiences to which such positions expose them. And I shall attribute to this group ideologies of management which have been articulated in response to the logic of authority relationships in economic enterprises. While the publicly expressed ideas of a social

group frequently reflect a range of views rather than a single, fully developed ideological position, even this range of views will *not* do justice to the diversity of personal beliefs or attitudes of the group members. As I see it, this is not a serious defect, dictated though it is by the questions I have asked and by the nature of the materials available for study. For the attitudes of individuals do not become the public opinion of a group merely by the process of addition. Instead, public opinion is formed through a constant process of formulation and reformulation by which spokesmen identified with a social group seek to articulate what they sense to be its shared understandings. A study of ideologies deals with these formulations and reformulations and hence with those attitudes which have proved strong enough to gain adherents [Bendix, 1956, pp. xxi–xxii].

Udy (1959a and b) drew on data in the Human Relations Area Files relating to the organization of manufacture and production generally (i.e., including hunting and collecting food) in 150 different nonindustrial societies. In his paper, Udy took seven characteristics of bureaucratic organization from Weber's description of bureaucracy as an ideal type and found that, whereas there was a positive correlation within each two clusters of three and four characteristics, there was no association between the clusters themselves. The first cluster comprised (1) a hierarchy of at least three levels of authority, (2) functional specialists in the organization not engaged in manual work, and (3) differential allocation of rewards. The second cluster consisted of (1) specification of goals as the production of goods, (2) rewards differentiated by performance, (3) participation by a form of contractual relationship, and (4) distribution of rewards by those in higher authority to subordinates.

The first cluster of characteristics, Udy claims, refers to the hierarchic ordering of authority, and the second to principles of rationality—the two major components of Weber's ideal type; the conclusion is that, empirically, and outside the special circumstances of Western industrial societies, there is no necessary connection between the two. But, as Scott (1965, p. 499) rightly comments, "The absence of any association between the hierarchical and rational elements is possibly due to an inclusion within Udy's sample of a considerable number of organizations in which a previously existing political hierarchy had been imposed on a production situation (through 'custodial recruitment'). In these situations, role assignment was based on ascribed political status, rewards were not likely to be distributed according to performance, and organizational objectives were more often diffuse than specific." Leach (1960) has drawn sufficient attention to the dubiousness of the basic data, and to the risks of this kind of analysis of them; the point of Scott's remarks in the present connection is to reinforce the prescription mandatory for cross-cultural analysis or organization (at least in the contemporary situation): that, in comparing social institutions, it is essential to insure, not only that the units are equivalent, but that the context of the cultural situation and of the social system at large does not contain factors which render comparison of the institutions under study invalid. This prescription is, of course, additional to the general considerations affecting the treatment of system theory models as if they were complexes of independent variable factors.

Bendix used comparative analysis to establish a general thesis concerning the necessary relationships between managerial ideology and the organization of industrial production, that is, variations in the substantive and systemic properties of the one were shown to be reflected in changes in the substantive and systemic qualities of the other. Udy's work is, in essence, an attempt to test the necessary coherence of the elements said by Weber and his followers to compose the mode of rational organization towards which industrialization tends. A quite distinct purpose and methodological approach is visible in the attempt to elucidate the components of a system by changing the cultural context— an attempt that may be generated, as in the case of French's Norwegian study (French, Israel, and Ås, 1960) by an initial failure of research findings established in one cultural situation to replicate themselves in another. This kind of check can lead the investigator either to abandon the second project, or the whole series, as invalid or methodologically unsound, or it may give rise to the kind of questioning suggested earlier as the critical stage in research: the questioning that must preface research design and the collection and analysis of data that are to supply the answer, but that can arise only from doubt.

Cross-cultural studies provide opportunities for this kind of fertile difficulty in generous measure; they have, however, to be matched by research opportunism and imagination. French's Norwegian study supplies an instance of the way in which the "failure to replicate" in a different cultural setting may be used to reconstruct the hypothesis and reinterpret the finding of the original research so as to strengthen their validity and widen their application. While he was at the Oslo Research Centre, French undertook a replication of the well-known "resistance to change" experiment (Coch and French, 1948) in an entirely different cultural setting. It will be remembered that, in the original field experiment, three groups of workers were constituted to follow different procedures, labeled "no participation," "participation through representation," and "total participation" in accomplishing a technical and product change. In the event, the third group demonstrated higher-level job satisfaction, lower turnover, and, most important, higher productivity. The Norwegian plant manufactured rubber footwear instead of pyjamas, but "the factory there was similar to the American factory. . . . The work was also on piece-rate. In this particular Norwegian factory, there was an additional point of similarity to many American companies: the company president talked a good game of participation but he obviously did not practice it" (French, 1964, p. 36). There was also a basic similarity between the ideology and form of government characteristics of both countries.

Yet the experiment did not replicate the original findings. Labor-management relationships improved (or rather, mutual understanding and the perception of management-labor relationships as cooperatively rather than competitively based was greater) more in the "total participation" groups than in the "control" groups and there was a tendency for more participation to produce satisfaction, but both these dimensions were less susceptible to measurement (and, in the original study, were the subject of "incidental observations" rather than measurement). In the critical variable related to productivity, "there was essentially no difference between the experimental and control groups in the level of production following the experiment" (ibid., p. 41).

This negative result led to a review of the assumptions concealed within the original formulation. "We are," says French "trying to become more refined in our thinking and participation." He makes a distinction between psychological participation ("the extent of influence on a jointly made decision which the participant *thinks* he has") and objective participation ("the amount of influence on the decision he *actually* has"). But, more important, an entirely new variable (new, that is, in the context of this particular study) is introduced to take care of the discrepancy: "We said to ourselves 'if the experiment comes out differently here in Norway than it did in the United States, what might account for the differences?' Our answer to this question is contained in the following hypothesis: To the extent that participation is considered legitimate, it will have favourable effects on the dependent variables of satisfaction, labour-management relations, and productivity . . ." (ibid., pp. 37, 38).

Legitimacy, in fact, turns out to be the normative controls on output, familiar since the Hawthorne bank-wiring room studies, and not unknown to F. W. Taylor. But to point this out is not to criticize the experiment or the experimenters; the context of social norms governing commitment to work methods improvement, cooperation with bosses, value placed on high earnings, their plans or groups of plans, and so on was clearly constant for the first experiment. The procedure appropriate to science is to observe complete conceptual parsimony in framing hypotheses and to introduce factors only under compulsion.

This procedure is implicit in the fourth variety of cross-cultural comparison, which is properly termed "exploratory." It is a procedure increasingly practiced in pragmatic terms among economists concerned with the conditions under which economic institutions, certain specific entrepreneurial activities, or large-scale construction or development schemes may expect to succeed in the emergent countries. The procedure, simple enough in methodological terms, is to examine the structure, constitutent parts, functions of comparable institutions or processes in similar countries, where they exist, and the social, economic, and cultural conditions that appear to make for success or failure. Naturally, in most cases, true parallels are rare, and it is usual to have to resort to a search for the constituent elements and functions and for the relevant contextual conditions as they exist in partial or embryonic form. This is the procedure adopted by Thorsrud and Emery (1965) in their examination of the institutional forms and conditions essential for the success of a new social apparatus of industrial democracy in Norway.

There is one final development in the use of cross-cultural comparison that deserves mention here, although it is concerned with organization as a methodological instrument rather than as a field of study. It is evident that since the war the lines of theoretical development, methodological practice, and research interest of the social sciences in different countries (previously so different as to often amount virtually to different disciplines though sharing the same name) have tended to converge. Just as the social sciences themselves, from economics on, have emerged and developed as part of the response system of individual societies to the process of industrialization and the social, economic, political, and psychological change processes associated with industrialization, so the increasing *community* of experience among advanced industrial societies in the present third phase of industrialization has conditioned the approximation of sociology, social psychology, and behavioral science in general. The approximation has meant largely a convergence on American models, but this has been due as much to the common belief that social pressures and social changes follow the American pattern as to the academic hegemony of American behavioral science during the past twenty years.

During the 1960's, however, as European societies have emerged from the traumatic experience of the 1940's, the variety of interaction between what is common in international experience and national cultures has made itself apparent. The assumption of the convergence of advanced industrial societies is now very much in question. The growth of interest in Europe and America in cross-cultural studies during the 1960's is, therefore, no historical accident.

It is the special circumstances that surround the contemporary interest in cross-cultural studies that renders the comparative study of organizations in this context of special importance and interest. International organizations, political and economic, operate for the most part in the context of different national societies according to organizational models and practices that are, in principle, uniform for all their national subsidiaries or branches. Where this is the intention, it may be assumed that the differences in structure and in practice, where they exist, reflect national differences in the institutional forms appropriate to the task, in industrial and organizational ideology, and in norms of achievement and competence—differences, that is, going beyond manifest economic, technical and other variations, and underlying assumed uniformities. This, at all events, is the strategy underlying the current research of Willener into the role of middle management in identical functional positions in steel plants in the Coal, Iron, and Steel Community countries, and the studies being mounted by Burns and Trist into the problems specific to large international corporations.

RELATIONS BETWEEN ORGANZATION AND ENVIRONMENT

At this next level of analysis, the observation post of study is stationed within the individual organization, looking outward, so to speak. The shift of position and orientation is already expressed in the identification of society at large and institutional elements in society as "environment."

Emery and Trist (1965) have produced a preliminary analysis of the interrelationship between system and environment in terms of four basic types of environment. The suggestion is that organizational systems are formulated largely by their competent (i.e., appropriate) modes of behavior in different types of setting. They state "the following general proposition":

> that a comprehensive understanding of organisational behaviour requires some knowledge of each member of the following set, where L indicates some potentially lawful connection, and the suffix 1 refers to the organisation and the suffix 2 to the environment:

$$L_{11}, L_{12}$$
$$L_{21}, L_{22}$$

> L_{11} here refers to the processes within the organisation—the area of internal interdependencies; L_{12} and L_{21} to exchanges between the organisation and its environment—the area of transactional interdependencies from either direction; and L_{22} to processes through which parts of the environment became related to each other—i.e., its causal texture —the area of interdependencies that belong within the environment itself [p. 22].

The authors go on to postulate four states that the environment can assume and to note the appropriate character of organizational response.

1. "Placid, randomised environment," corresponding to Simon's (1957) idea of a surface over which an organism can locomote, and which is mostly bare but has in it widely spaced, randomly deposited heaps of food. This would represent the market situation of classic economic theory, and best tactics are continual trial and error.

2. "Placid, clustered environment," corresponding to the economists' state of imperfect competition in which learning can take place—i.e., "the clustering enables some parts to take on roles as signs of other parts." The appropriate organizational response is a rudimentary strategy based on discerning some locations as potentially richer.

3. "Disturbed-reactive environment," a type 2 environment in which a number of other similar organizations coexist. "One has now not only to make sequential choices but to choose actions that will draw off the other organizations."

4. "Turbulent fields," in which dynamic processes (e.g., increasing pace of technological development as a response to competition) arise within the environment to create significant variances for the organizations.

The four types, and the behavior of organizations in response to them, are illustrated by synopses of case studies.

The general thesis bears some resemblance to that developed in connection with studies of the electronics industry (Burns and Stalker, 1961, Chap. 5). Here, four types of systemic response to states of market and technical environment were distinguished and labeled "organization within a stable program," "organization for change," "organization for a constant or predictable rate of novelty," and "organization in the least predictable conditions." These four levels of response were reduced to two ideal types, mechanistic and organic, which represent appropriate responses to a relatively stable or relatively changing market and technical environments. Crozier arrives at much the same differentiation of ideal types of environmental-organizational relationship (Crozier, 1963, pp. 370–371). Woodward (1958) in a study of over 200 industrial concerns related organizational system to technology or, more generally, to varieties of "situational demand." The theoretical model is explicitly of the response system kind:

> Organisation appeared to grow in response to a number of stimuli. The "organisation conscious" firms tended to draw on the concepts of management theory, irrespective of how appropriate they were to the technical situation. Fashion was another important factor. Materials

controllers and industrial engineers were becoming popular at the time of the research, and it was interesting to see how they spread from one firm to another. Moreover, organisation had been modified to some extent in every firm to accommodate individuals—"empire builders" who distorted the pattern in their search for status, and misfits for whom sinecure had to be found. These distortions often continued long after the people concerned had died or left the firm.

But although "situational demands" did not determine formal organisation, they appeared to have considerable influence on spontaneous or informal development. In a number of firms formal organisation did not satisfy "situational demands" adequately, while informal organisation did [p. 38].

She concludes: "The systematic analysis of 'situational demands' might well be used to predict the effects of technical changes on management structure" (p. 39).

Goffman (1961) eliminated the interactive processes that obtain between all organizations and their social environment to establish a category of total institution which included prison, hospital, homes for the incapable, barracks, boarding schools, and monasteries. The interesting feature of this celebrated essay in the present context is that, although the separation of "staff" and "inmates" is stressed, the specifically boundary-maintaining function of the directors of such institutes is deliberately left out of the account. In addition, of course, the differing instrumental prescriptions of these institutions by society are also omitted. Despite—or rather because of—this, it is a brilliant instance of the establishment of an analytical category that cuts across common usage classifications. It gains not only from the critical undertones implicit throughout in the matching of characteristics between hospitals and prisons, but from the explanatory force of the comparative method when used to demonstrate similarities and even identities in social systems, social controls, and role-performances in what are ordinarily regarded as utterly different physical, social, and moral situations.

DEFINITION OF TASK AND DIVISION OF LABOR

This section composes the very large body of work concerned with the way in which the purposes of our organization are defined within it and the consequent distribution of the total tasks among groups and individuals. It is at this point, not surprisingly, that a sharp distinction occurs between the theoretical models which different students have developed and exploited.

There is a sense in which the development of the social sciences depends on the constant conversion of the substantively qualitative into the substantively quantitative. Apart from this, in the case of the most recalcitrant qualitative material, Barton and Lazarsfeld (1955) have argued (and it is a theme to which Lazarsfeld frequently recurs), codification is necessary to point out dangers, indicate neglected possibilities, and support improvements. Even at this level, one of the major contributions of factor theories makes itself felt—that which comes from the obligation to order concepts, to distinguish them to insure that they maintain the definition given to them in the first place throughout the analysis and that the set of terms is adequate to the task of analysis. It is at this stage that concepts may be, and often have to be, reformulated after consideration (Goode and Hatt, 1952, pp. 49–50) of the meaningful elements of the concepts actually employed, of the variety of usages of the terms in the literature and of the variety of other terms used for the same phenomena. "Respecification of the concept," claim the authors, "always leads to more fruitful hypothesis." Reordering the concepts, according to analytical procedures such as representation of material in matrix form, can also lead to more fruitful analysis. At the very least, it can lead to the consideration of material with "a fresh eye," lending a kind of binocular vision to the theoretical insights the researcher has developed. This is, indeed, the great merit of mathematical models, fruitless though they may have been so far in advancing the substantive content of the social sciences.

Since the Barton and Lazarsfeld paper appeared there has been an immense change of front even among the most qualitative-minded schools of research to quantitative analytical methods, which must be considered separately from the mathematical developments proper that have affected and occurred with the social sciences. The last ditches defended by such slogans as "those who count, don't" have all been surrendered—almost all, that is; there are still memorable engagements being fought (Schlesinger, 1962). Research orthodoxy now requires the translation of impressionistic or case study procedures, still the necessary prelude to most empirical research projects, into survey procedures, for validation if for nothing else.

Few statistical procedures are specific to the study of organizations, and the development of quantitative techniques in the comparative analysis of organizations as a whole has lain mostly with economists. If once the processes of interaction between the environment and the organization can be satisfactorily itemized, the construction of a matrix of quantitatively expressed variables from which component analysis ("latent structure" analysis) can be made becomes possible, as Barton's (1961) pioneer attempt has shown. R. R. Blake has developed a simple matrix formulation out of two variables—"concern for people" and "concern for production." The resulting grid allows for the positioning of any individual concern (relative to others previously studied) and for recording

progress through the change process which the research team or consultant is involved in promoting (Blake and Mouton, 1964). Chapple and
Sayles (1961) employ task, structure, and technology as variables in an
approach, fundamentally different in ideology, and much more sophisticated analytically, but not dissimilar in conception.

There is a sizeable and familiar difficulty, however, standing in the way
of a wholesale move into quantitative procedures. Once one deserts the
accepted common ground of "administrative sociology" and economic statistics in which one is either dealing with units which are the accepted
currency of analysis at any level of study—registered companies, money
values, production quantities, number employed, capital value of equipment, turnover, labor costs, and change rates in them; or occupational
status, earnings, educational qualifications, labor turnover, age of employees, number of skills, and functional specialties—it becomes extremely
difficult to define variables and units of measurement in any but an entirely ad hoc manner, and this largely destroys the value of quantitative
procedures. This, it should be added, is a failing attributable to social
theory, not to formal analysis. Power (or its converse, compliance), for
example, which features so large in the theoretical analysis of organizations, is an extremely refractory term to render into useful quantitative
formulations (for an example, the curiously naive reduction by Fromm
cited in Barton's standard paper on "Property-Space" (Barton, 1955,
pp. 52–53). The concept of power is, in fact, extremely complex and
various; Emmet (1954), in an illuminating paper, lists five major types,
each containing two or three subtypes—and all excluding coercion. The
observations made by two contributors in a discussion at the Operational
Research Conference in Cambridge in 1964 express the general difficulty
in succinct terms:

> The scientist's problem, said Stansfield, was to describe what he
> observed in nature, and relationships between the phenomena, in terms
> which were as precise as possible while remaining understandable to
> others. A great deal of information in any situation has to be condensed
> through the use of symbols. The symbols used are words, as used in
> definition, and mathematical symbols. He did not see that Rapoport's
> paper, at least in its earlier section, said anything more than that the
> most precise and economical way of describing nature was in terms of
> mathematical relations. If this was so, it was something which was
> assumed at the outset of any scientific career; he personally had done
> this during his first year at this university, but had had to spend his next
> five years contending with the difficulties of definition. One began by
> thinking one knew what an atom was, and then spent several years in
> discovering how much experience and consensus had built up over
> several generations in such a way that other people knew what one
> was talking about, a way, moreover, that would take several volumes

to spell out at length. The difficulty in social science was that this common experience and consensus did not exist. He himself was uneasy about the devotion of so much attention to the development of a mathematics for the social sciences, in the absence of a common understanding of what the mathematics could possibly stand for. . . . Gayner reinforced the doubt raised by Stansfield by pointing to the history of the natural sciences. It was true that mathematics served as the common language of sciences, but the progress in any individual natural science had been dependent on theoretical formulations related to the specific content of these sciences. Mathematics could hardly have served as the language of chemistry without the prior existence of such terms as element, atom, molecule, valency, atomic weight. These were verbal terms with a firm and virtually universal definition without which one would not know what the mathematics was about [Burns, 1964].

METHODOLOGICAL APPROACHES IN DIACHRONIC CASE STUDIES

In principle, there should be no difference between long-term diachronic studies and short-term ones. Obviously, studies which make use of historical data require the investigator to do more than explore the part of the institutions to which his special interest attaches. To treat history as a rummage box that will surely produce (and it unfailingly does) evidence to support theories with ambitions beyond anything which the available contemporary evidence or research material will support is reckless amateurism, which draws its just retribution from the professional. Nevertheless, apart from adding this extra academic dimension to himself, the student of organizations comparing institutional differences over generations (as with Boulding, 1953), or centuries (as with Bendix, 1956), is treating time as a major, independent variable in much the same way as the student of organizational change compares system states over a period of months, or a year or two. The object is to use the contrast between two conditions of the same system separated by time as a basis for comparative study, or to study the process aspect itself of institutional activity.

In Gouldner's (1954) study of a gypsum mine, the different forms taken by the organization at the beginning and end of the period were the result of the predominance of first one and then another distinct bureaucratic pattern. These forms took their shape from the intentions, cognitions, and aspirations of the chief manager, on the one hand, and, on the other, from the counter-system devised by subordinates by way of response. The two forms of "representative bureaucracy" and "punishment-centered bureaucracy" were suggested by the opportunity of actually watching the transition from one to the other over the "succession crisis," when an outsider took over the chief executive position.

This is something, therefore, akin to field experiment—the difference being, of course, that the change is generated within the system under observation, not imposed or introduced. There is no sense in which changes in the system are controlled, and no sense in which they can be checked and measured by comparison with the course of events in a "control" group unaffected by the induced change. Short-term longitudinal studies are, therefore, methodologically more primitive than field experiments. This is revealed, incidentally, in the remarks which Gouldner (1954, p. 259) offers in defense of his "violating the canons of good interviewing": "Before a miner was going to tell us anything about *his* feelings, he wanted to know about *ours*." Nevertheless, he adds, "we were all convinced that our best data was [sic] obtained during such moments of real interaction."

Much the same point is made, rather more elaborately, in the remarks on interviewing in *The Management of Innovation* (Burns and Stalker, 1961). The interviews were lengthy, lasting anywhere from one hour to a whole working day, developing along "fairly free lines" after the opening, which was usually conducted on formal, routine lines. During the later stages,

> it proved possible to create a more productive relationship than can be constructed on the basis of one person's seeking information from another. The conventions governing such interviews and the limits of the information regarded as admissible or relevant are nowadays prescribed fairly strictly. To go beyond these limits, it is not enough to demonstrate interest or even sympathy; in the writers' experience, an informant will get to the point of formulating and presenting his experience, beliefs, opinions, anxieties, and criticisms only when there has been established a relationship which is reciprocal in some genuine sense; when there is some point for the informant in going further than the needs of courtesy, and compliance with an undertaking by the firm to co-operate with the researcher, seem to require of him. Thus the researcher has to make the relationship "real"; one in which he is prepared to behave on his side as what he declares himself to be. This can only be done by showing how he is making use of the information he is receiving; by the occasional interpretation of a situation in terms which are both derived from his perception of the situation as an outsider and as a sociologist or psychologist, and which are also appropriate to his informant's ability or preparedness to comprehend. From then on, whether the interpretation is accepted or not, there is a freer, more satisfactory quality about the interview, a stronger desire to recruit and present facts, examples, views. There are no interpretations and appraisals contained in any part of this report which have not been communicated at some time or other to persons involved in the situations at issue. Invariably, also, we have found our own ideas being amended, extended, or corrected by such traffic [pp. 13–14].

I am now inclined to be less defensive about this kind of interviewing procedure ("All this," I wrote, "is very far removed from any method of investigation which could possibly be called scientific!"). This particular study involved not merely examining a technically and socially complex system in process of change from one situation, undefined and possibly obscure or misrepresented, to another. The new state of the system (the emergence of which, the study had been designed to observe) was not in some cases realized at all or in anything like the terms envisaged by those involved. The process of change, moreover, occurred according to a complex of variables that could only be identified as (or after) they produced their effects. All this requires—to use an old-fashioned word—a "cybernetic" relationship between researcher and subject. Research becomes, in fact, a true search process among the experience of individual members of the social system, in which hypothesis and deduction become a serial process. There is a sense in which, in their eagerness to achieve "scientific detachment," social scientists have cut themselves off from their main resource—the ability of human beings to memorize and report their own experiences.

The need for this fairly highly sensitized interaction was, in fact, particularly acute during the principal phases of this study. The purpose of the study was, as originally conceived, simple and straightforward. Earlier studies has suggested that there were two distinct systems of management practice: one "mechanistic," appearing to be appropriate to an enterprise operating under relatively stable technological and market conditions; the other, "organic," appearing to be required for condition of change. The main phase of the research began when it appeared possible to study the experiences of a number of engineering firms interested in entering new fields of electronics research and development and thus moving from relatively stable conditions to a situation of fairly rapid technical and market change. The presumption was that it would be possible to observe the processes of organizational adaption from a mechanistic to an organic system in a variety of contexts. In the event, hardly any firm succeeded in accomplishing the change, or, indeed, in realizing its intentions. In half the cases, laboratory groups were disbanded by management or were disrupted by resignations. Others were converted into test departments, "troubleshooting" teams, or production departments. The research project as originally conceived, therefore, was a disappointing failure. On the other hand, seen in terms of the quite unexpected problem of why the working organization of the firms did not change as their circumstances changed, the project become immediately far more interesting theoretically.

A third procedure that may be subsumed under this heading of short-term diachronic studies is the "tracer" method developed by Woodward. In essence this is similar to the illuminating pursuit of the "stages through which an actual problem proceeded in an actual company" observed and recorded in the classic "Observation of a Business Decision" study by Cyert, Simon, and Trow (1956). Marples' (1960) tracing of a design from inception at a management committee to finished production is reported in more detail than the Cyert, Simon, and Trow study, but follows essentially the same pattern. These two latter examples are necessarily diachronic, but are concerned specifically with the delineation of decision-making paths; the comparison is between actual patterns of decision-making and presumed or traditional patterns. The Carnegie Institute group's distinction between "programmed" and "non-programmed" decision-making provided the foundation for much of the behavioral and simulated behavioral studies issued from the same school since (see Newell and Simon, 1961). Marples' elucidation of the tree-like development of decisions which constitutes the formal structure of events as conceived by traditional management thinking reveals multifarious loops, false leads, and restarts; this study, too, shows a close kinship with the development of models of the development process on which Critical Path Analysis techniques are founded.

Woodward's use of tracer methods is directed more specifically to institutional analysis. It is "based on the assumption that when the management of a firm makes a decision to manufacture a product, or series of products, a control system is brought into existence." The research comprised three case studies of production orders in three firms: for an analogue computer; for a batch of receivers forming part of a comprehensive aircraft communication, navigation, and direction finding system; and for a four-week production program for a brand of soap. "The 'tracer' approach implies a very detailed study of part of a firm's total activities over a period of time: the methods used were based on social anthropology, the direct and prolonged observation of the daily behaviour of people towards each other until patterns of interaction were 'identified' " (Woodward and Eilon, 1964, p. 4).

As in the earlier tracer studies, comparative analysis is directed towards the contrast between the formal system of control designed or intended by management and the actual behavior of the organization. Thus, the more formalized a control system, the less possible it is to measure achievement standards by anything other than the relative degree of failure; the study follows the implications of this observation for information flow, for internal political activity, and for the individual management role—and career. Researchers in each firm were given "guide lines to indicate the ground they were expected to cover," (ibid., p. 5) but, beyond this, were free to develop their case studies as they wished.

Woodward and Eilon's remarks on the utility of their fully articulated exploitation of the tracer method are worth quoting in full:

> All three research workers felt that the use of a "tracer" was helpful in finding out what happened inside a factory. Its disadvantage, particularly relevant to Case II, where the main control problem was to fit a number of different orders into an overall production programme, was that the concentration of one order meant losing some of the significance of the different orders on each other. This was outweighed by its advantages, however. The first of these was that it was possible to compare objectives and attitudes at all levels of the hierarchy and between line and staff departments in relations to the same task, and to see how the same task created different problems for and offered different satisfactions to the various individuals and groups concerned with it. Secondly, the "tracer" provided a valuable reference or "homing" point for the research workers themselves during a long and complex investigation. It would have been impossible to make such a detailed study and to ask the same questions of the same people so many times without having this reference point to which the answers could be related.
>
> Thirdly, following the "tracer" through the firm at the pace at which it was being made enabled the research workers to see the envolvement of the control system and the relationships associated with it in a "real" time context. The fact that an individual, asked at a progress meeting to follow up a certain component, did so on the morning before the next progress meeting, could have significant implications not only for the control system itself, but also for the human relations associated with it. It was also possible to see how time ebbed away in the politics of decision-making, and how and when a sense of urgency was introduced into the control-system. In this respect, the "tracer" method has advantages over the more generalised organisation study and gets round the difficulty so often encountered in attitude surveys of relating what is said to the events taking place in the factory at the time the survey is being carried out [1964, p. 9].

COMMUNICATION SYSTEM

Probably greater advances have been made methodologically and theoretically in this area of study than in any other directly concerned with organizations and organizational behavior. This is largely due to the work of H. A. Simon and his colleagues, work that has been directed more and more towards the articulation of mathematical models of organizations themselves, but that has, so far, had its greatest impact on the way in which organizations and organizational behavior are perceived and conceptualized.

Of fundamental importance is the distinction established early in the work of the group between programmed and non-programmed decision-making (Cyert, Simon and Trow, 1956; Simon, 1958; March and Simon, 1958). Work within an organization takes place—and can only take place —on the assumption that other work processes are taking place around it. This is not a matter of simple routines: in programmed decisions the choice made is to some extent a forgone conclusion, although it may be necessary to perform a complicated series of calculations before a single choice is actually made. Simon (1958) instances driving a car to a destination, which involves almost exclusively programmed decision-making, although a good deal of computation (most of which is done "unthinkingly") takes place based on information obtained through the eyes. Experience in driving counts, but the more experienced the driver, the nearer the approach to a fully programmed series of decisions—i.e., he knows what to do "automatically" on every occasion of choice. There is no substantial dissimilarity, says Simon, between this and what happens in practice when a monthly schedule is planned in a factory.

Programmed decision-making is what it is because of the existence of an institutional framework around the individual. "The pattern of behavior in a business firm in which this particular decision [the choice of an aggregate production rate for a factory] represents one small detail, may be regarded as a mosaic of such decision-making programs. . . . So far as any of the programmed decision-making processes is concerned, all the other programs that surround it are a part of its environment" (p. 53). In non-programmed decisions the alternatives of choice are not given in advance, but must be discovered by a rational process of searching. Not that in non-programmed decisions the chooser is compelled to calculate in terms of expectations and his degree of belief in them; Simon suggests that such searches for alternatives are conditional upon a higher level of aspiration, when satisfaction will have to be sought outside the routine, habitual, programmed courses of decision-making.

To a very large extent, the processes which we have in mind as specific to work organizations are reducible to cognitive apparatuses of these two kinds; moreover, the organization processes referred to as specifically managerial are reducible to non-programmed decision-making and especially to the design of new or amended programs, which will, of course, include the provision of subroutines for monitoring and controlling the output of programs or parts of programs. Conversely, it could be said that the social scientist, in studying organizations, and therefore in elucidating the patterns of communications and of behavior, is concerned to determine the programs—the institutional mosaic—within which work and other role-behavior takes place, and, further, to find out who, among managers, peer-groups, former generations, reference groups, powerful or influential groups or individuals or trade unions, write the programs.

Less methodologically exotic, but fairly closely related to behavioral studies in general orientation is a series of what might be termed "behavioral recording studies." Walker, Guest, and Turner's study (1956) based on observations of foremen's activities and communications and their very detailed recording is familiar, but self-recording studies have been comparatively little exploited until very recently, when a number of researches using this technique appears to have started concurrently in England and America.

Self-recording techniques merely exploit a little more thoroughly and a good deal more ruthlessly the more familiar of all elements in social research methodology—the fact that people can be asked to report all kinds of information about themselves and will frequently oblige by answering. This amounts to social scientists having the inestimable advantage of turning the very subjects they wish to study into observational and recording posts.

In 1948 Sune Carlson was conducting a small seminar composed of the presidents of a number of Swedish business and manufacturing companies. At one point it became clear that it would be interesting, and perhaps profitable, for them to study how they spent their time. The ensuing study lasted four weeks for each member who participated (a number dropped out, and complete records were eventually obtained from five). Records were made by the subject and his secretary of all communications and worktime contacts with other people, by correspondence, notes and memoranda; by telephone, conference, and meeting; by conversation; the information content of the communication was classified under a number of headings; the names and organizational locations of the others involved in communication were recorded; and action was classified in terms of purpose—obtaining information, making decisions, giving orders.

My own study used a similar recording method, but was applied to the top executive group in each of a number of firms. All of them recorded during the same period (four or five weeks in most cases). The project was designed as a comparative study. Ten concerns and ninety-eight executives, members of self-defined "top management groups" were included in the study.

The method, as then established (Burns, 1954), has been followed subsequently with few variations (Burns, 1957; Horne and Lupton, 1965; Burns and Sinclair, 1963; Butler, 1960). The method is to arrange for records of how they are spending their time to be kept simultaneously by a number of people over a period of some weeks.

The standard recording form has six divisions showing:

Time   (taken for the episode)
Persons (communicated with or present, if any)
Mode   (of activity—e.g., conversation, reading or writing or dictating letters)
Place   (i.e., in which part of the workplace the episode took place— own office, office block, assembly department, home, outside factory, traveling)
Subject (the functional category of task or problem which formed the subject of the episode)
Purpose (giving or receiving information or advice, both or neither; giving or receiving instructions or decisions, both or neither)

The results bear on many other matters than the distribution of individual and group managerial time or the substantive content of their functional roles—which, indeed, is the least interesting part of the results. More important is the picture—the moving picture—such studies give of the management system, seen as a communication network. And the production of this information itself yields comparative data of considerable interest. For seven manufacturing concerns, to take one instance, the proportion of all management time spent in spoken communication (all forms, from conferences to telephone conversations) ran as follows:

$$80–71–68–56–55–44–42 \text{ (percent)}$$

The order is significant. The firms are arranged from left to right also in terms of their investment in R & D—i.e., their susceptibility to environmental (technological and market) change. Moreover, the direction of communication changes. In the first firm, slightly more than half of all communication was lateral—i.e., with colleagues—this proportion dropped until, in the seventh firm, virtually all communication was vertical in direction.

AUTHORITY STRUCTURE

Study of the nature and legitimacy of authority and social controls has been familiar since the Hawthorne experiments (Roethlisberger and Dickson, 1939). The Bank-Wiring Room Study still remains the most strikingly successful attempt to elucidate the rationale (i.e., the cognitive structure) of the complex system of guides and rules governing work behavior. The Hawthorne study has been, in fact, the starting point of all organizational studies of work behavior in terms of either conformity or nonconformity with managerial direction and supervision.

There is a large number of comparative studies that regard the structure, form and behavior of the work groups as dependent on the single variable of management or supervisory "style." The best known is the series of studies by the Survey Research Center of work groups relating variations in productivity to differences in supervisory behavior. Supervisors of high production groups were men likely to show concern for their subordinates, to spend time in planning and other facilitating activities, and less likely to supervise closely (Kahn and Katz, 1953). These conclusions, nevertheless, have been challenged by studies mounted as replications by Argyle in England (Argyle et al., 1959), a circumstance which is connected with French's "discovery" of the operation of legitimacy and the discussion of Blau and Scott of the development of a normative framework within which supervisory control operates (Blau and Scott, 1962, pp. 141–143; Gouldner, 1954).

It will be remembered that the establishment of the behavior patterns in the Bank-Wiring Room was rendered possible through the perception by the research team of differences not only between the rules imposed by and expectations of management and the rules and norms of the work groups, but differences within the work group itself. A study of the institutional structure and characteristic behavior of management cliques and cabals in a factory began with casual observation of minor behavioral differences (Burns, 1955).

The identification and analysis of the normative controls developed within groups by explicit and implicit comparison with those imposed by organizational requirements as interpreted by senior executive authority has, for many years, been a major theme of organizational studies, ranging through medical students (Becker et al., 1961), post office workers in Holland (Van Beinum, 1963) and France (Crozier, 1965), textile workers in Norway (French, Israel and As, 1960), engineering operatives in England (Baldamus, 1961), industrial scientists in the United States (Kornhauser, 1962) and in Britain (Burns and Stalker, 1961), prisoners (Sykes and Messinger, 1960), and social workers (Blau, 1955).

SYSTEMS OF ENGAGEMENT AND REWARD AND INVOLVEMENT

Comparative studies at this level are at present in a rather more dynamic phase than appears to be the case with the analysis of authority structure. Comparative studies by Behrend (1959), by de Bal (1964), and by Lutz and Willener (1960) of wage and incentive schemes, based on wide-ranging surveys have all pointed to the complex interaction between (a) the perception of earnings as a return for work, appraised in terms of normative standards developed by individuals and categories of workers by comparison with others (reference groups) and (b) the perception of wage and bonus payment systems (used by individuals as well as by organized groups as the outcome of a bargaining procedure between workers and managers.

More generally, there are three directions in which studies of the individual within the organization have developed. One is sufficiently illustrated by the analysis of the varieties of role structure prescribed by different work situations. Adapting the "system theory" concept of role-set (Merton, 1957) to operational use in analytical procedures, Kahn et al. (1964) collected data on the different demands made within the organization, on supervisors by immediate and other superiors, peers, and subordinates, and construed them in terms of the possibilities of the integrated role, role-dilemma, or role-conflict that they presented to the individual. In rather different terms, I have studied the commitments of individuals to the organization, to their departmental colleagues, to their age-grade, to their own careers, and to a professional ethos within the contexts of a broadcasting organization and a large hospital. Out of these commitments, it is argued, are constructed the variety of social systems that coexist within the social milieu of work—the most important being the working organization itself, the system of internal politics, and the career system (Burns, 1965).

More interesting methodologically is the development of the theory of human decision-making (Newell, Shaw, and Simon, 1958) to the point at which it is possible to identify the operationally relevant information, the kind of information processing, and the rule for combining the kinds of information processing involved in the decision-making of individuals in specific circumstances and for specific ends.

> Within this framework the problem of constructing a model of some specific decision behavior becomes a problem of uncovering the basic rules of operations employed by the decision maker to lead him to the particular decisions under consideration. If the decision process is one which is frequently employed by the individual, questions about the procedure followed, the records consulted, the information that is processed and the output can provide a rough picture of the more important parts of the decision process. These interviews are frequently more rewarding if there is one person to ask the questions while another takes notes. It must be noted, however, that this approach asks an individual to describe and in some sense justify why he behaves as he does. To the extent that many people are unable to describe how they reached a particular decision the information gathered in this manner must be regarded with some caution.
>
> A more reliable guide to decision processes is a protocol of an individual's decision behavior. A protocol is a tape recorded transcript of the verbalized thoughts and actions of a subject who has been

instructed to think or problem solve aloud. Since a protocol is a description of what a person does, it avoids some of the problems inherent in the interviews and questionnaire techniques.

A variant on the interview approach is to ask the individual to write out a decision routine which he thinks will accomplish the task at hand. By questioning him to construct routines of this type and then asking relevant questions, e.g., "But what happens if . . . ?" he may be led to expand and alter what he has written before [Clarkson and Pounds, 1963, p. 22].

The consequential development of the procedure in terms of a model appropriate for writing a computer program to simulate the decision processes of a given individual belongs to the discussion of the development of simulation as a research tool, but the opportunities the procedure promises for analysis in just those situations which have been studied through survey methods and open interview by the Michigan group and by Burns are obvious.

SOCIAL IDENTITIES

Payment and incentive schemes relating to individual workers clearly involve consideration of groups, norms, and organizational settings. Even F. W. Taylor, who, as Friedmann (1955) has insisted, was bent on treating the individual worker as far as possible as an isolated individual and maximizing productive efficiency in terms of each separate worker, observes that there exists what he called "systematic soldiering," or shirking; he remarks on a kind of tacit agreement among workers in a firm, perhaps in a whole neighbourhood, about the amount of work they should do (Taylor, 1911). A number of comparative studies have concentrated on this "outer framework" of normative principles within which the individual's *occupational identity* (involving all the roles into which a person enters and role-behavior he manifests in his capacity as member of the productive system of society) forms itself. Popitz identifies six "images of society" which enter into the varieties of the worker's attitudes to the enterprise as a system to which he is expected to become committed as a participant member as well as engaged as resource: static order, progressive order, structural dichotomy (of class and power) as collective fate, dichotomy as individual conflict, progressive or reforming social order, and class struggle.

Conversely, the specific nature of the occupational role of the chief executive enters into the analysis of the boundary-maintaining processes, which are his operational province. Selznick (1957) posits a categorical difference between the leadership and the executive role. "A new 'logic' emerges" (p. 3). Drawing on comparisons and analogies between leaders in business, governmental and military organizations, he suggests that the institutional role of the leader is defined by his key tasks of: defining the goals in the light of the commitments of the organization; building policy into the social structure of the organization; maintaining values, distinctive identity and integrity; and ordering internal conflict. From a different point of departure, similar prescriptions are reached from an analysis of the situation and behavior of the chief executives in sixteen companies (Burns and Stalker, 1961, Chap. 10). Here the role is initially defined in terms of its major characteristics of social isolation. There are, in principle, it is suggested, four ways of dealing with this social isolation: exploiting it, escaping from it, and, in either case, resorting to means which are either organizationally legitimized or not. This, in turn, gives four kinds of relationship with the members of the concern, each of which promotes a specific array of responses and thus acts as a determinant of the organizational structure (or at least of the way in which that structure behaves).

Crozier (1965) has followed the line of Chinoy (1955) and of Andrieux and Lignon (1960) in relating the occupational and leisure identities of white collar workers.[9] In the discussion of his results, he suggests that individual office workers themselves confront a problem of boundary maintenance between the occupational world and its environment (i.e., in this case, other social milieux of which they are members). It is at this point that studies of organizations and the individuals in them go into reverse, so to speak. The selves which are partitioned into social identities so as to accord with the specifications written out by the varieties of social organizations they take part in are, in these studies, recomposed in an attempt to identify and describe the total social situation and behavior pattern of the individual.

COMPARATIVE RESEARCH AS A RESEARCH STRATEGY

The tools, conceptual and methodological, that social scientists work with are extremely crude and easily blunted. Statistical procedures afford the most precise and rigorous methods generally available, and statistics are a way of oversimplifying; if the procedures and results are probabilistic, statistics often distort as well.

There is, therefore, a good deal to be gained from applying the concept of comparative study to methodology as well as to subject matter. The very useful exercise which Goode and Hatt (1952) called re-conceptualization is, in fact, no more and no less than an attempt to take a fresh look at material and methods, a deliberate escape from the limitations any particular method among those available to social scientists imposes.

The self-recording technique described above, for example, was de-

9. This is also the theme of Zweig's (1962) study of workers.

vised as a rather desperate resort to obtain entirely fresh data and an entirely different formulation of a research problem which was then new to me and appeared utterly intractable; the adequate description and analysis of a concern which was to all appearances flourishing and expanding, but which was rife with conflict and frustration and broke all the most elementary rules of orthodox management practice, down to the refusal—as a matter of management policy—to define managerial roles or to have an organization chart drawn.

Major developments in research techniques and methods have emerged, in fact, from endeavors to mount an assault on a research problem from an entirely different angle of approach. Bavelas' creative experimental work with small groups stemmed from his effort to recompose the early Lewinian interpretation of the dynamics of interaction within groups in entirely different conceptual terms, with entirely different kinds of observational data, analyzed with entirely different instruments. Survey research itself involves, or should involve, a reformulation of the aperçus which develop in the impressionistic observations and open-ended interviews of the pilot phase into the quite different conceptual framework of an experimental design.

It is something of a tragedy that the "binocular" vision the dualistic strategies thus developed can bring to research is so often lost because of the tendency of each new departure to become a specialized field of study, autonomous and academically segregated. The great merit and strength of simulation is that it enforces a reconsideration of data and processes and analysis in totally different terms from those in which problems are presented; yet such merit and strength as the method has brought to the social sciences are being dissipated by its exploitation in terms of business games and of a new specialism.

It may be worthwhile for social scientists to address themselves to the problem of developing research expertise in more than one branch of methodology and of combining them in research strategies that will not merely offset disadvantages inherent in one branch but, of themselves, develop more penetrating and more reliable methods than can be hoped for from each pursued in isolation.

REFERENCES

ABBREVIATIONS

ASR   *American Sociological Review*
HR   *Human Relations*
JAP   *Journal of Applied Psychology*
JASP *Journal of Abnormal and Social Psychology*
MS   *Management Science*
SSR   *Sociology and Social Research*

Andrieux, A. and Lignon, J. *L'ouvrier d'aujourd'hui.* Paris: Riviere, 1960.

Argyle, M., Gardner, G., and Cioffi, F. *The Measurement of Supervisory Methods.* London: Oxford U., Institute of Experimental Psychology, 1957 (Mimeo).

Bahrdt, H.–P. "Zur Frage des Menschenbildes in der Soziologie." *European J. Sociology,* 1961, 2, 1–17.

de Bal, M. B. "Crise, mutation et depassement de la rememeration au rendement." *Sociologie du Travail.* April–June 1964, 6, 113–134.

Baldamus, W. *Efficiency and Effort.* London: Tavistock Publications, 1961.

Barton, A. H. "The Concept of Property-Space in Social Research." In P. F. Lazarsfeld and M. J. Rosenberg, eds., *The Language of Social Research.* Glencoe, Ill.: Free Press, 1955.

Barton, A. H. *Organizational Measurement and Its Bearing on the Study of College Environments.* New York: College Entrance Examination Board, 1961.

Barton, A. H. and Lazarsfeld, P. F. "Some Functions of Qualitative Analysis in Social Research." *Frankfurter Beitraege zur Soziologie,* 1955, 1, 321–361.

Bavelas, A. "Leadership: Man and Function." *Administrative Science Qtly.,* 1959–60, 4, 491–498.

Becker, Carl. *The Heavenly City of the Eighteenth Century Philosophers.* New Haven: Yale U. Press, 1932.

Becker, H. *Outsiders.* New York: Collier–Macmillan, 1963.

Becker, H., et al. *Boys in White.* Chicago: Chicago U. Press, 1961.

Behrend, H. "Financial Incentives as the Expression of a System of Beliefs." *British J. Sociology,* 1959, 10, 137–147.

Bendix, R. *Work and Authority in Industry.* London: Chapman and Hall, 1956.

Bendix, R. *Max Weber, An Intellectual Portrait.* Glencoe, Ill.: Free Press, 1960.

Berle, A. A., Jr. and Means, G. C. *The Modern Corporation and Private Property.* New York: Macmillan, 1932.

Blake, R. R. and Mouton, J. *The Managerial Grid.* Houston: Gulf Publishing Co., 1964.

Blau, P. *The Dynamics of Bureaucracy.* Chicago: U. of Chicago Press, 1955.

Blau, P. and Scott, W. R. *Formal Organizations: A Comparative Approach.* San Francisco: Chandler, 1962.

Boulding, K. E. *The Organizational Revolution.* New York: Harper, 1953.

Burns, T. "The Directions of Activity and Communications in a Departmental Executive Group." *HR,* 1954, 7, 73–97.

_____. "The Reference of Conduct in Small Groups: Cliques and Cabals in Occupational Milieux." *HR,* 1955, 8, 467–486.

————. "Management in Action." *Operational Research Qtly.*, 1957, 8 (2).

————. "The Idea of Structure in Sociology." *HR*, 1958, 217–228.

————. "The Sociology of Industry." In A. T. Welferd, *Society*. London: Routledge and Kegan Paul, 1962.

————. "The Systems Concept as a Common Frame of Reference." In *Operational Research and the Social Sciences*, Proceedings of Operational Research Society Conference. Cambridge, England, 1964; London: Tavistock Publications, 1966.

————. "Ambiguity and Identity." Department of Sociology, U. of Edinburgh, 1965 (Mimeo).

Burns, T. and Sinclair, S. *The Child Care Service at Work*. Edinburgh: H.M.S.O., 1963.

Burns, T. and Stalker, G. M. *The Management of Innovation*. London: Tavistock Publications, 1961.

Butler, W. P. "A Study of Communication." *Personnel Practice Bull.*, 1960, 16 (3).

Celier, C. "The Social Sciences and the Changing Role of Management." Paris: OEEC, 1959, 31–40.

Centers, R. *The Psychology of Social Classes*. Princeton: Princeton U. Press, 1947.

Chapple, E. D. and Sayles, L. R. *The Measurement of Management*. New York: Macmillan, 1961.

Chinoy, E. *Automobile Workers and the American Dream*. Garden City: Doubleday, 1955.

Clarkson, G. P. E. and Pounds, W. F. "Theory and Method in the Exploration of Human Decision Behaviour." *Industrial Management Rev.*, 1963, 5 (1), 17–27.

Coch, L. and French, J. R. P., Jr. "Overcoming Resistance to Change." *HR*, 1, 1948. Also in D. Cartwright and A. Zander, eds., *Group Dynamics*. 2d ed., New York: Row, Peterson, 1960, 319–341.

Crozier, M. *Le phenomène bureaucratique: Essai sur les tendences bureaucratiques des systemes d'organisations modernes et sur leurs relations en France avec le systeme et culturel*. Paris: Editions du Seuil, 1963.

Crozier, M. *Le monde des employés de bureau*. Paris: Editions du Seuil, 1965.

Cyert, R. M. and March, J. G. *The Behavioural Theory of the Firm*. Englewood Cliffs: Prentice Hall, 1963.

Cyert, R. M., Simon, H. A., and Trow, D. B. "Observation of a Business Decision." *J. Business* (University of Chicago), 1956, 29, 237–248.

Donovan, F. R. *The Saleslady*. Chicago: U. of Chicago Press, 1929.

Eisenstadt, S. N. "Bureaucracy and Bureaucratization." *Current Sociology*, (Blackwell), 1958, 8 (2).

Emery, F. E. and Trist, E. L. "The Causal Texture of Organisational Environments." *HR*, 1965, 18, 21–32.

Emmet, D. "The Concept of Power." *Proceedings of the Aristotelian Society New Series*, 1954, 54, 1–26.

Etzioni, A. *A Comparative Analysis of Complex Organizations*. Glencoe, Ill.: Free Press, 1961.

Everett, E. H. *On the Theory of Social Change*. Homewood, Ill.: Dorsey, 1962.

French, J. R. P. "Laboratory and Field Studies of Power." In R. L. Kahn and E. Boulding, eds., *Power and Conflict in Organisations*. London: Tavistock Publications, 1964, 33–51.

French, J. R. P. and Coch, L. "Overcoming Resistance to Change." *HR*, 1948, *1*, 512–532.

French, J. R. P., Israel, J., and As, D. "An Experiment in Participation in a Norwegian Factory: Interpersonal Dimension of Decision-Making." *HR*, 1960, *13*, 3–19.

Friedmann, G. *Industrial Society*. Glencoe, Ill.: Free Press, 1955.

Galbraith, J. K. *The Affluent Society*. London: H. Hamilton, 1958.

Gluckman, M. and Devons, E. *Closed Systems and Open Minds*. Manchester, England: Manchester U. Press, 1964.

Goffman, E. "On the Characteristics of Total Institutions." In *Asylums*. New York: Doubleday (Anchor Books), 1961.

Goode, W. J. and Hatt, P. K. *Methods in Social Research*. New York: McGraw-Hill, 1952.

Gouldner, A. W. *Patterns of Industrial Bureaucracy*. Glencoe, Ill.: Free Press, 1954.

————. "Organization Analysis." In R. K. Merton, L. Broom, and L. S. Cottrell, eds., *Sociology Today*. New York: Basic Books, 1959a.

————. "Reciprocity and Autocracy." In L. Gross, ed., *Symposium on Sociological Theory*. New York: Row, Peterson, 1959b, 241–270.

Hoggart, R. *The Uses of Literacy*. London: Chatto and Windus, 1957.

Horne, K. and Lupton, T. "The Work Activities of 'Middle' Managers: An Exploratory Study." *J. Management Studies*, 1965, *2*, 14–35.

Janowitz, M. *The Professional Soldier*. Glencoe, Ill.: Free Press, 1960.

Kahn, R. L. and Katz, D. "Leadership Practices in Relation to Productivity and Morale." In D. Cartwright and A. Zander, eds., *Group Dynamics*. New York: Row, Peterson, 1953, 612–628.

Kahn, R. L., et al. *Organizational Stress: Studies in Role Conflict and Ambiguity*. New York: Wiley, 1964.

Keirstead, B. S. *The Theory of Economic Change*. London: Macmillan, 1948.

Kornhauser. *Scientists in Industry*. Berkeley: U. of California Press, 1962.

Lazarsfeld, P. F. "The American Soldier: An Expository Review." *Public Opinion Qtly.*, 1949, *13*, 380.

Leach, E. R. Review of S. H. Udy's *Organization of Work*. ASR, 1960, 25, 136–138.

Lefebvre, H. "Perspectives de sociologie rurale." *Cahiers Internationaux de Sociologie*, 1953.

Lockwood, D. "Social Integration and System Integration." In Zollschau and Hirsch, eds., *Explorations in Social Change*. London: Routledge and Kegan Paul, 1965, 244–257.

Lutz, B. and Willener, A. *Neveau de mecanisation et mode de remuneration*. Luxemburg: (Mimeo) C.E.C.A., 1960.

March, J. G. and Simon, H. A. *Organizations*. New York: Wiley, 1958.

Marcuse, H. *Eros and Civilisation*. London: Routledge and Kegan Paul, 1956.

————. *One Dimensional Man*. London: Routledge and Kegan Paul, 1964.

Marples, D. *The Decisions of Engineering Design*. London: Institute of Engineering Design, 1960.

Marx, K., *Capital*. Trans. by E. and C. Paul. London: Swan, Sonnenschein, 1906.

Mayo, E. *The Social Problems of an Industrial Civilisation*. London: Routledge and Kegan Paul, 1949.

Merton, R. K. "The Role-Set: Problems in Sociological Theory." *British J. Sociology*, 1957, *8*, 106–120.

————. "Problem Finding in Sociology." In R. K. Merton, L. Broom, and L. S. Cottrell, eds., *Sociology Today*. New York: Basic Books, 1959.

Michels, R. *Political Parties*. Trans. by E. and C. Paul. London: Allen and Unwin, 1914.

Nadel, S. F. *Foundations of Social Anthropology*. London: Cohen and West, 1951.

Newell, A. and Simon, H. A. "The Simulation of Human Thought." In W. Dennis et al., *Current Trends in Psychological Theory*, Pittsburgh: U. of Pittsburgh Press, 1961.

Newell, A., Shaw, J. C., and Simon, H. A. "Elements of a Theory of Human Problem-Solving." *Psychological Rev.*, 1958, *65*, 151–166.

Parsons, T. "Suggestions for a Sociological Approach to the Theory of Organisations." *Administrative Science Qtly.*, 1956, *1*, 63–85 and 225–239.

Pepper, S. C. *World Hypotheses*. Berkeley: U. of California Press, 1942.

Poggi, G. "A Main Theme of Contemporary Sociology; Its Achievements and Limitations." *British J. Sociology*, 1965, *16*, 283–294.

Popitz, H., Bahrdt, H. P., Jueres, E. A., and Kesting, A. *Das Gesellschaftsbild des Arbeiters*. Tübingen: Mohr, 1957.

Reichenbach, H. *The Rise of Scientific Philosophy*. London: Cambridge U. Press, 1951.

Roethlisberger, F. J. and Dickson, W. J. *Management and the Worker*. New Haven: Harvard U. Press, 1939.

Schlesinger, A. "The Humanist Looks at Empirical Social Research." *ASR*, 1962, *27* (6), 768–771.

Schon, D. *The Displacement of Concepts*. London: Tavistock Publications, 1964.

Scott, R. E. "Theory of Organizations." In R. E. L. Faris, ed., *Handbook of Modern Sociology*. Chicago: Rand McNally, 1965.

Selznick, P. *Leadership in Administration*. New York: Row, Peterson, 1957.

Shaw, C. R. *The Jack Roller*. Chicago: U. of Chicago Press, 1930.

Simon, H. A. *Models of Man*. New York: Wiley, 1957.

Simon, H. A. "The Role of Expectations in an Adaptive or Behaviouristic Model." In M. J. Bowman, ed., *Expectations, Uncertainty and Business Behaviour*. New York: Social Science Research Council, 1958.

Sykes, R. and Messinger, S. "The Intimate Social System." In *Theoretical Studies in Social Organizations*. New York: S. S. R. C., 1960.

Taylor, F. W. *The Principles of Scientific Management*. 1911. Reprinted in *Scientific Management*. New York: Harper, 1947.

Thorsrud, E. and Emery, F. E. *Industrial Democracy*. London: Tavistock Publications, 1965.

Tocqueville, A. de. *Democracy in America*. Ed. by P. Bradley. New York: Vintage Books, 1954.

Touraine, A. *L'Evolution du travail ouvrier aux Usines Renault*. Paris: C.N.R.S., 1955.

Udy, S. *Organization of Work*. New Haven: HRAF Press, 1959a.

————. "'Bureaucracy' and 'Rationality' in Weber's Organization Theory." *ASR*, 1959b, *24*, 791–795.

Van Beinum, H. J. J. *Summary of "Een Organisatie in Bewegung."* Privately published by author, 1963.

Walker, G. and Turner. *The Foreman on the Assembly Line.* New Haven: Harvard U. Press, 1956.

Weber, M. *The Protestant Ethic and the Spirit of Capitalism.* Trans by T. Parsons. New York: Scribners, 1930.

————. *Wirtschaft und Gesellschaft.* Ed. by J. Winchelmann. Kiepenheuer und Witsch, 1964.

Whitehead, A. N. *Process and Reality.* Cambridge: Cambridge U. Press, 1929.

Willener, A. *Images de la société et classes sociales.* Berne, 1957.

Wilson, A. T. M. "The Manager and his World." *Industrial Management Rev.,* (M.I.T.), 1961, 3 (1), 1–26.

Woodward, J. *Management and Technology.* London: H.M.S.O., 1958.

Woodward, J. and Eilon, S. "A Field Study of Management Control in Manufacturing Industry." Paper contributed to Operational Research Society Internation Conference, *Operational Research and the Social Sciences,* Cambridge, England: 1964.

Zetterberg, H. L. "Theorie, Forschung und Praxis in der Soziologie." In R. Konig, ed., *Handbuch der Empirischen Sozialforschung.* Stuttgart: Ferdinand Enke V., 1962, I, 65–104.

Zorbaugh, H. W. *The Gold Coast and the Slum.* Chicago: U. of Chicago Press, 1929.

Zweig, F. *The Worker in an Affluent Society.* New York: Heinemann, 1962.

4

Computer Simulation Models for Organization Theory

THORNTON B. ROBY

Tufts University

This chapter is concerned with potential uses of the computer simulation model as a conceptual tool in the development of organization theory. The objective of the chapter will be to highlight methodological issues and, whenever possible, suggest lines along which these problems might be resolved. No attempt will be made to survey the current state of computer simulation except insofar as existing models are used for illustrative purposes; moreover the discussion does not enter into the details of computer programing.

One reason for this treatment of the topic is that there are already a number of very competent expositions of existing simulation efforts and of programming procedures (for example, Orcutt et al. (1961); Borko (1962); Green (1962); and Feigenbaum and Feldman (1963). These are not all directly relevant to organizational applications but they do repre-

Partial support for the completion of this chapter was obtained under Contract NONR 494 (15) with the Office of Naval Research and under Contract AF19(628)2450 with the Decision Sciences Laboratory (Electronic Systems Division), Air Force Systems Command, United States Air Force.

The general outline of this chapter was formulated and developed in discussions with Professors Geoffrey Clarkson, Robert Joyner, Kenneth Knight, Frederick Munson, and Anthony Obershall at the 1964 Pittsburgh Conference on Organization Theory. The suggestions offered by that group during the conference and in subsequent correspondence are greatly appreciated. Remaining errors of omission or commission are the exclusive responsibility of the author.

sent an impressive fund of ingenious and effective techniques that may be adapted to the latter area. Thus there does not, at the present time, seem to be a pressing need either for a survey or for a how-to-do-it manual. Instead, it is attempted to assess the probable impact of computer simulation on the construction of organizational theory and to consider how computer simulation might be used with other techniques now at hand.

Computer development has occurred at a pace unprecedented in previous technological innovations. During this growth period of not more than ten years or so, most of us have been either too engrossed or too aloof to develop a useful perspective on what has happened. It may still be too soon to assess with confidence the influence computers ultimately may have on the development of organizational theory; it is clear that computer techniques represent a distinctly new approach and, although they should not alter the ground rules of scientific procedure, they may profoundly change the tactics. Perhaps it is not too soon to speculate on some of the implied tactical changes.

The emphasis of this chapter then is programmatic: beginning with a general consideration of the purpose of computer application in organizational theory, we single out as the special focus of this chapter the use of the computer simulation model as a novel and unique theoretical tool. The next section is concerned with the basic ingredients of a computer simulation model. Three aspects of this problem are considered: the initial nucleus from which the model is refined and elaborated; the substantive elements or building blocks of which the model is constructed; and the language in which the model is couched. The next topic examined is the process of testing and revising the computer model, and of relating it to empirical data. A rather Utopian four-stage testing process is outlined: internal testing, initial testing of ad hoc validity, generalization to new substantive areas, and, finally, process evaluation. A final section goes on to venture possible applications of computer simulation in the future, recognizing that these applications are not presently feasible.

VARIETIES OF COMPUTER APPLICATION

Although this chapter is directly concerned with the application of the computer in developing simulation models it will be useful to begin with an examination of possible computer uses that lie outside the strict definition of computer simulation. This survey will help to establish by exclusion exactly what is intended by the term "simulation model," but in addition it will be pointed out that many of these not-quite-simulation studies may be closely related to, or ancillary to, simulation studies proper. It is of course hoped that with obvious changes many of the methodological remarks that follow will apply to these related uses of the computer.

AS AN AID IN DATA REDUCTION OR STATISTICAL ANALYSIS

Here the function of the computer is largely to help interpret or digest empirical data obtained through other means, such as field studies or laboratory experiments. Typically the computer programs employed for such investigations do not contain any special features that mark them as applying to the organizational problem as opposed to, say, problems in agriculture or medicine. The emphasis is on the statistical technique itself and the syntax of the program is derived from the statistical procedure employed. Although this is clearly a non-simulation use of the computer, even this application may impinge on true simulation in one direction not explored extensively to date: generation of distributions for determining the significance of certain results that may occur in an empirical set of observations—that is, the establishment of purely statistical bench marks without intrinsic substantive interest. Thus if the investigation concerned the incidence of communication between individuals in a group or the distribution of sociometric scores in a group, the computer could be used to determine what the chance distribution should be, given the obtained marginal score distributions. Any observed set of scores could then be evaluated against this base line and a precise probability could be placed on any interesting deviations that occurred in the empirical data.

More generally, if the means and variances are available for a number of performance measures that have been obtained in an observational situation, the statistical base line model may be used without substantive hypotheses to obtain distributions for expected profiles of the dependent variables and to determine with what frequency such profiles could be expected to occur if the variables are essentially unrelated.

DERIVING THE CONSEQUENCES OF AN ACCEPTED THEORY

Here the emphasis is not on theory construction as such but on the application of theory which has already been at least tentatively accepted. The theory may be scientifically or logically well founded, as it is in much of operations research, but it could as well be based on folklore or common sense. In this sort of application the computer is an associate consultant, a consultant with the unique advantages of being able to reckon with many variables and a comparative freedom from bias as to what answers the vice-president may wish to hear. This may, therefore, be an extremely effective use of computers but it is not a scientific enterprise. The objective is to provide well-considered answers to specific problems or optimal decisions on policies, rather than to generate or to test hypotheses.

PROVIDING SOLUTIONS FOR A MATHEMATICAL MODEL

Often it is possible to describe a system in great detail and subtlety with a mathematical model, but the eduction of numerical or precise qualitative consequences may be very difficult indeed. Richardson's (1948) War Moods model, although it leads to some almost testable propositions, obviously contains many more implications than can be developed by ordinary analytical techniques. The computer can be employed to derive numerical estimates suitable for empirical tests from such a model but this is a rather different application from a true computer simulation program. The principal difference is that the structure of the indicated process is here dictated by the standard procedures of numerical computation (such as iterative solutions of differential equations) rather than by dynamics hypothesized for the system under investigation.

The boundary may be very fuzzy. In fact it is easy to imagine mixed models in which certain processes are represented by mathematical functions and others, by a more literal attempt to simulate actual organizational dynamics; however, it will be emphasized below that the latter objective is always the ultimate goal of a simulation model in the strict sense.

AS AN ADJUNCT TO THE LIVE STUDY OF ORGANIZATIONS

In this application the simulation program is designed to provide an environment for organizational behavior. The simulated environment may involve only the external world within which the investigated organization is assumed to operate or it may include part of the organization itself. In the latter case one would be studying individual or subgroup reactions to organizational conditions.

There are impressive advantages in the use of the computer for this purpose. It offers the possibility of control over a virtually unlimited number of exogenous variables and conditions. It makes it possible to build response-contingent relationships into the environment so that rapid and realistic feedback can be provided to the live subjects whose behavior is being tested. And finally the data can be recorded and processed directly and in great volume. This application requires on-line access to a computer, but the costs of such access are no longer prohibitive.

The chief reason for distinguishing between this application and the pure simulation objective again lies in the criteria that are most relevant. In the present use, one is primarily interested in realism as it affects the live participant in the organization study. The question is not so much whether the simulated component is anatomically similar to its real world counterpart as whether it is similar enough to elicit and sustain the illusion of reality and to elicit representative behavior on the part of live subjects.[1]

PROGRAMMING EXERCISE

The primary objective here is to show what a computer can do when used with a little ingenuity. The emphasis is on verisimilitude of performance rather than on producing results that can be compared rigorously with empirical data; and the customary canons of scientific parsimony tend to be put aside for a sort of kitchen sink approach that rivals the prodigality of nature itself. In spite of the slightly derogatory flavor of the title given this application, it may have real didactic and propaedeutic value. It permits the exploration of computer capabilities in a somewhat freer way than do more restrained procedures, and in a way possibly congenial to persons with an intimate knowledge of substantive processes but a distaste for the rigors of more austere theory construction. Thus it is possible that this application may, at last, provide a bridge between the rich intuitions of psychological practitioners and the hallowed methods of scientific theory construction.

As a tool of preliminary theoretical formulation, the above procedure seems to be a rather good form of the well-known *Gedankenexperiment*. As compared with the customary practice of following through a set of postulations in one's imagination, the computer offers several benefits: first, it has led to a language—in simplest form, the flow diagram—which is particularly useful for elaborating complex interrelations and processes. In addition, the prospect of obtaining a volume of palpable, though fictitious, results may counteract the sense of futility that tends to be associated with a purely hypothetical formulation of conditions.

REAL SIMULATION MODELS

The aim of real simulation models is to use computers to derive testable and generalizable consequences from a set of constructs that are internally consistent, have explanatory power, and are themselves susceptible to further analysis and test. Thus the objectives and criteria are

1. According to "Turing's Test" (Turing, 1950), the latter criterion should be valid for either application. Our position in this matter is developed in a later section on process correspondence.

essentially the same as those of the familiar hypothetico-deductive method. From this point of view, the computer simulation model is a candidate for membership in the powerful team already including the more abstract mathematical or logical model, on the one hand, and laboratory or field research, on the other. The principal concern of the following discussion is to examine ways in which computer simulation models may be integrated most effectively into this team.

FORM, CONTENT, AND LANGUAGE

This section will examine three interrelated topics. The first concerns the general structure of simulation models; the second concerns the building blocks or terms that are used; and the third topic is the symbolic expression of this content. Emphasis throughout will be placed on the initial choices made by the theorist in formulating the model. It is assumed that the ensuing processes of testing and revision may modify or reverse many of these initial choices.

OVERALL ARCHITECTURE

In the initial attack upon any significant problem in organization theory, it is clear that some type of simplifying assumptions must be appealed to. These assumptions are best made quite explicitly so that the theorist will be alerted to the probable kinds of error threatening his findings. Thus the most important typology of first approximation models seems to be in terms of the guiding fictions introduced at their launching.

The first of three types of guiding fictions to be described will be labeled *organismic*. Models of this type attempt to incorporate the entire system under consideration and to represent all of the important interactions between components of the system, but in gross aggregative or statistical form. The model achieves *prima facie* descriptiveness at the level of overall system behavior, then adjusts and refines the definition of constituent processes to satisfy the requirements of fine structure descriptiveness. Although none of the approaches to be described is the monopoly of any scientific discipline, the organismic approach has been followed typically by sociologists.

The *idealized* model may also attempt to deal with the total system with respect to substantive components, but it deliberately simplifies the assumed functional relations among the components. Examples are the assumption of strict rationality of decision processes or perfect community of interests and objectives among organizational members. Here descriptiveness is sacrificed for sharpness of functional implications much as in the analogous ideal laws of physics. Further development of models of this type must entail enrichment of their dynamics with auxiliary influences—for example, social prejudices and partially conflicting goals. This initial approach has been associated with economists.

A third angle of attack will be labeled *segmental,* and it deals with the substantive components of an organizational system singly and in isolation. Ordinarily the components examined in this way will be individuals, but subgroups, roles, or other organizational building blocks might be used. The assumption is that a thorough explication of the behavior of such units within an organization will indicate clearly how they fit together: refinement must then consist in making amends for this assumption which is, in practice, simplistic. Social psychologists are perhaps the most prominent advocates of this approach.

It is easy enough to characterize these approaches in terms that establish any one of them as the path of righteousness and set the others beyond the pale. The first approach is bold and holistic; the second is incisive and elegant; and the third is sound and methodical. Alternatively, the first approach is pretentious; the second is perversely formalistic; and the third approach is pedestrian and niggling. As a matter of record, however, comparatively successful theories have been developed starting from each of these approximations and none of them is inherently self-defeating. The optimal approach for a particular problem depends both on the ultimate objectives and upon the state of knowledge at the time of theorizing. Undoubtedly it depends too on the particular tastes and skills of the modeler.

Still at the level of overall architecture, a second distinction may be based on the objective of study in the model. Here again a three-way classification is suggested. The first type of problem is the so-called developmental system, concerned with the changes in the organization itself as a result of its interaction with the task environment. A second object of study concerns the performance of an organization at a given level of development, typically at maturity. The third object of study is the effect of the organization on the behavior of constituent individuals.

Although this distinction differs from the earlier one, it is not entirely unrelated. The organismic model may lend itself most naturally to the study of group development, to the overall transformation of organizational characteristics. The idealized or normative model is not usually concerned with development except to specify the asymptote towards which the development may proceed; on the other hand, the normative model is perhaps the approach of choice for the study of group performance. Finally, the segmental model, which focuses on the individual participant in the group, is perhaps best suited for the investigation of effects of organizational participation on the behavior of individuals.

ILLUSTRATION

In order to provide a concrete reference for the distinctions made above and a framework for later illustrative material, we shall consider a problem in the theory of organization permitting various approaches. The problem concerns the nexus of relations between the external activity of an organization and its internal communication processes. It has attracted both theoretical and experimental attention.

An approach to this problem beginning at the organizational level and using the organismic approximation may be based on the Homans' (1950) model. This model is built around four variables: friendliness, interaction, activity, and imposed "task load." In the present case, the task load describes the environmental input, interaction is an observable process variable, friendliness is a measurable but not directly observable system-state variable, and activity is the output variable. These distinctions among variables will be described in more detail below.

Simon (1957) has translated this model into a system of differential equations and has based a number of interesting analyses on a "phase space" treatment of the model. Most of his conclusions, however, relate to the asymptotic behavior of the system and to shifts in asymptotic behavior as a function of changes in the basic parameters. Translation of Simon's differential equations into a Monte Carlo simulation model might permit an investigation of several aspects of the problem that would be impractical to study analytically, for example, a more detailed investigation of nonlinear cases and functional relationships involving three or more parameters. Even more beneficial would be the derivation of quantitative results that could be compared with field or laboratory data.

Proceeding from these investigations at the aggregative level, the model can be articulated further to yield a more detailed picture of group behavior, as Simon (1957, p. 113) has indeed suggested. In fact, the same parameters used to describe organizational characteristics can be indexed more specifically to refer to the activity, interaction, and sentiments of subgroups within the group or, finally, to the individuals in the group. Thus, without essentially changing the model, and beginning with an organismic approximation, it is, in principle, possible to simulate organizational behavior in any degree of detail.

Representative of the idealized approach to this problem would be the paradigm suggested by Roby and Lanzetta (1956) for investigating the information exchange in work groups in which individual group members have comparatively stable and distinct task responsibilities. Briefly this formulation assumes that task responsibilities can be defined in terms of the classes of information which they generate or which they require for successful execution of instrumental responses. The normative communications between various persons in the group can be estimated by matrix multiplication.

Here again, although some progress can be made using conventional mathematical techniques, a much greater range of problems might be treated by expressing the functional relations in probabilistic terms and studying the resulting Monte Carlo simulation. Refinement of this model would obviously take a different course than the foregoing organismic one. In this case, the factor of interpersonal attitudes has been omitted deliberately in the first approximation, and it must somehow be introduced in later phases to achieve any degree of realism. Possible procedures for successively modifying simulation models are discussed in detail in a later section. For the present it will be noted that the modification may, in this case, take the form of a correction for attitudinal factors in the basic functions of a normative model or, alternatively, of direct superimposition of a secondary system of socially oriented communications on those predicted by the task-defined normative system.

To illustrate the segmental approach to a model of organizational communication, one might begin with a program of individual interaction behavior such as that developed by the Gullahorns (1964). This model (also based on formulations of Homans [1950]) investigates the probability of specific types of communications to specific persons as a function of current needs and of past reinforcement for communication; thus, the task inputs would be treated as generating current needs for information and the behavior of individuals in seeking out sources of information might be simulated by some streamlined version of the Homunculus model.

For any of these approaches, the focus of interest may be on the way in which a group changes over time, on the productivity or effectiveness of the group as a social unit, or on the effect of participation in the organization on the behavior and attitudes of individual group members. It is apparent that these three processes interact and that none of them can be thoroughly understood without taking the others into account. But it is equally evident that there are differences in time scale and emphasis among the three problems that justify looking at them in comparative isolation.

INGREDIENTS

This section will attempt to make a set of terminological distinctions concerning the substance of a simulation model and will later illustrate these distinctions using the message problem discussed above. Some of these distinctions may seem painfully copybook and most of them are not new. However, it seems important to reexamine the terminology which is used in more conventional scientific approaches. One reason for this is that a new layer is added to the investigative process. In conventional behavioral research the experimenter is clearly part of the environment. He may modify the organization in specific ways, but some part of the organization is always inaccessible to direct manipulation. In simulation studies, however, the experimenter pulls all the strings even if they are so tangled that he does not know in advance what they will do. From this standpoint the variation in a simulation model is wholly exogenous to the system under investigation.

The distinctions made below attempt to capture this point and also to indicate the kinds of decisions the theorist or experimenter makes, to what extent these decisions are arbitrary, and to what extent they are constrained by the logic of the problem. An attempt is made to put all this in a reasonably tidy framework, but the framework is less important than the aim to make explicit the issues involved.

Figure 1 provides a rough schematization of the total program specification as here considered. This specification describes both the system model itself, and the steps taken to test the model. For the present, chief attention is focused on the latter aspect of the program.

Summarizing the sequence briefly, a particular initial configuration, consisting of initial states and an event schedule, is entered, either explicitly or as part of an imbedding program. The configuration interacts with the system dynamics—defined by the system syntax statement —to produce certain intervening states and events. The process continues until it is terminated by instructions which may or may not be contingent upon outcomes. In either case, the interval covered is a simulation cycle. Even though a vast number of different measures may be taken, the recorded results of a simulation cycle constitute a single "observation" of the model because the entire process is dependent on the particular initial configuration.

Sampling instructions then indicates the next initial configuration to be investigated. The new initial configuration may be determined in advance or may be in part contingent upon the outcome of the preceding simulation cycle. The program run concludes when all relevant initial configurations have been sampled.

FIGURE 1

Schematic Description of Program Specifications for
a Computer Simulation Model

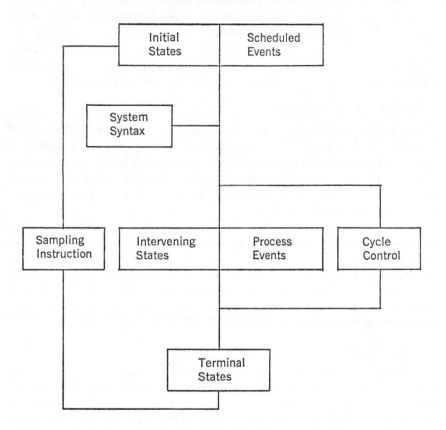

Printout (or other display) will ordinarily consist of terminal states, process events, or a summary of these results. In addition, it may include initial states in order to identify simulation cycles and intervening states to aid in interpretation.

Three types of decision are highlighted by this cursory account. One class of decisions concerns the length of a given simulation cycle and the conditions for terminating it. The cycle may be permitted to run until a certain terminal state is reached or, alternatively, it may be run through a certain fixed set of scheduled events (for example, a given budget of problems that a committee is to solve). A second class of decisions concerns the "sampling" process: the density of observations in the vicinity of a given initial configuration and the range of initial configurations that is covered during the entire program run. A final decision concerns the volume and type of data preserved and recorded.

These decisions are considered again within the context of specific tests for the model. Before reaching that point, however, it will be necessary to examine in more detail the ingredients of the model itself. Some of the distinctions made here are assumed to be inherent in the situation or in the conceptualization of the process. Others are of a more arbitrary character. Generally speaking the distinctions listed first are more essential ones and distinctions made later are more elective.

1. Explicit Entry–Computed Result

As already noted, everything that happens in a simulation model happens at the dictate of the simulation-theorist and the results are, strictly speaking, tautological. There is, however, a useful psychological distinction to be made between the terms and values explicitly entered into the model and those which ensue after a sequence of computations and which motivate the simulation study.

This distinction is one of degree and it is useful to specify four stages: first, those terms entered explicitly by the simulation-theorist; second, terms generated as a direct function of explicit entries (for example, the expression of event probabilities in actual event occurrences); third, intervening variables or processes obtained primarily to fractionate and simplify the problem of programming; and, finally, system performance measures and states presumably comparable with empirical data.

2. Functional Status

A second distinction concerns the causal or variational properties of terms in the system: three broad classes of terms may be defined. *Syntactic* statements incorporate the assumed mechanisms that are operative—all relationships among substantive terms. It is assumed that these statements are an inherent part of the description of a model and are modified only by express intention. *Parametric* terms are constant for a data cycle; they may affect other terms of the system or govern functional relationships but are not themselves modified. However, they may be modified in successive simulation cycles as part of a systematic "sampling" process designed to test the model under a variety of conditions. *Variable* terms are those subject to modification as determined by syntactic statements in the model and the values assumed by system parameters or other variables.

3. Environmental-Organizational (Exogenous-Endogenous)

The distinction here is between those aspects of the model referring to the task environment within which the organization is operating and those aspects referring directly to the human component of the system—that is, the organization itself. As a number of theorists have noted (Simon, 1957, Chap. 1) when the interaction between the environment and the organism is closely reciprocal, the cause-effect relationships between exogenous and endogenous elements may be obscure. Even so, the distinction has sufficient descriptive and heuristic value to be worth maintaining.

The three distinctions introduced above refer to the functional status of terms in the model. The next three distinctions are concerned with the substantive properties or referents of the model. They all revolve around the concept of "aggregation" as it has been used in social theory. From the present standpoint aggregation is itself an aggregative term, is a matter of degree, and refers to several aspects of possible compression or elaboration of descriptive terms.

Any variable term referring to an organization may be adequately tagged by three indices—one specifying the substantive referent, a second specifying the persons involved, and a third specifying the time of description in relation to other events. These three indices, and the related axes of extension or elaboration, will be referred to as *hyletic, locative,* and *temporal* respectively. Aggregation then takes the form of lumping along any of these axes and elaboration is the degree of specification along one or more of the axes.

4. Hyletic Aggregation-Elaboration

This index might describe the environmental referent of a certain message, the affect reflected in a specific interpersonal attitude or the ostensible purpose of a certain act. Clearly the qualitative breakdown of these substantive categories may be carried as far as measurement permits and as theoretical precision requires. A crucial consideration here is that the category systems for the various terms should be defined in such a way as to simplify the expression of functional relations among the terms. For example, action categories should, if possible, bear a clear relationship to specific classes of environmental states or events, as should communication category systems. Even interpersonal attitudes should ideally be developed with reference to the other hyletic specifications in the model. Thus the appropriate degree of extension along this axis depends in large part on the definition of the task logic and of the functions which represent the organizational operating procedures.

5. Locative Aggregation-Elaboration

Variables or events may be tagged in various ways with respect to the individuals concerned. In the case of messages (or attitudes), an ordered pair of persons is involved; for actions, only the responsible agent need be named. Although the index is in this case discrete, it does not follow that locative aggregation is an all-or-none matter. To illustrate, the representation of interpersonal attitudes in a group may specify the persons bearing the attitudes or the persons toward whom those attitudes are directed or it may contain no individual identification. In the latter case, the mean or other statistics describing the distribution of attitudes may be given.

6. Temporal Aggregation-Elaboration

The temporal specification of variable states or events may be given on an absolute time axis or with reference to other events or states. A temporally aggregative description of a given set of events might consist of a simple frequency count or of a more detailed statement of the temporal distribution. An aggregative description of state variables can be given in terms of mean level over time or it may include specification of the range of variation, trends, or periodicities.

A third set of distinctions among the terms of the model similarly concerns the mode of representation. However, where the above distinctions bear on the amount of system information retained, this last set of distinctions is more a matter of the most efficient or perspicuous way of representing a particular aspect of the system.

7. State-Event

In principle there are state descriptions of a system such that, if the initial state is given, any subsequent state description will summarize adequately the incidence of intervening system events. Conversely, if the initial state is given together with the exact chronology of system events, the new system state is determinable. Thus, in principle, state and event descriptions may be informationally equivalent.[2] In practice, though, any attempt to express physical reality in uniform state or event terms is at best awkward and may greatly increase the difficulty of conceptualization.

Some types of variables lend themselves more naturally to description as states or conditions while other terms are described naturally as events or processes. There seem to be no methodological drawbacks to basing this decision on convenience and custom for each term of a system individually as long as it does not complicate functional relations between terms.

2. An able and provocative discussion of the philosophical background and the current status of this distinction is contained in Whitrow (1961). The picture that emerges is one of a dichotomy of thought originating with Parmenides and Archimides (states or existents) on the one hand, and Heraclitus and Aristotle (process or flux) on the other.

8. Determinate-Stochastic

This distinction is again a familiar one and the choice is one of conceptual convenience. Philosophical questions aside, any stochastic system may be thought of as based on an underlying set of determinate laws, and any determinate system may be regarded as the limiting case of a stochastic system.

9. Scale Units

This distinction concerns the scale assumptions that are incorporated in a model. At one extreme there may be only nominal classifications with no order relationships among terms. Intermediate scale levels incorporate counting and ordering operations. The strongest scale assumptions are of continuous measurement with interval or ratio scale properties.

It may be debated whether this distinction is arbitrary in quite the same way as the two preceding ones. Very briefly, the pro argument would be that the gain in quantitative information obtained by expressing measures on a continuum is in general offset by the loss in qualitative information entailed in specifying the continuum.

AN ILLUSTRATIVE MODEL

In order to illustrate the distinction introduced above, a model will be described that treats the relation between communication and performance in an organization. For the sake of concreteness it will be supposed that the problem under investigation is the relation between the degree of specialization or departmentalization in small retail establishments and resulting productivity, morale, and interpersonal attitudes.[3]

The assumed functional relations are schematized crudely in Figure 2. Directed lines indicate causal influences and the small circles indicate confluence or interaction of causal effects. The meaning of the various terms is explained in greater detail in the following paragraphs. A glance at the figure suffices to show that the approach is organismic. It should be emphasized that this formulation is designed to provide instances of the distinctions suggested above; it is not offered as a contribution to organization theory. The intention is to show the range of choice that is possible, possible bases for making a choice one way or the other and the effect of choices made at one point on other terms of the model. The discussion is summarized in Figure 3.

The first term, *task logic,* concerns the entire set of functional rules

3. Compare Rome and Rome (1962) or Siegel et al. (1964) for models at approximately this level of comprehensiveness.

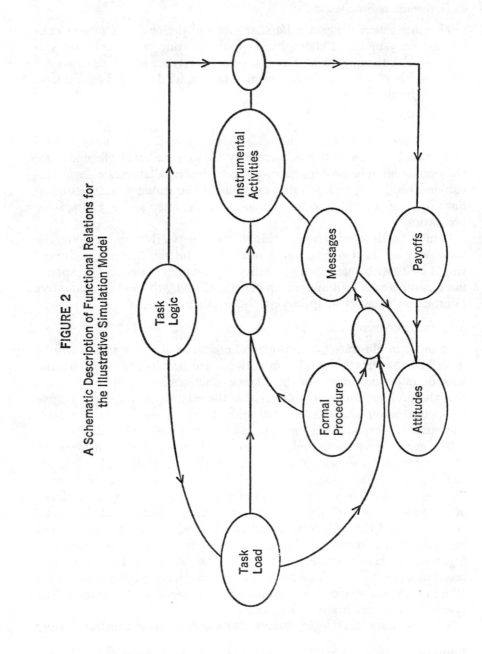

FIGURE 2

A Schematic Description of Functional Relations for
the Illustrative Simulation Model

FIGURE 3

Terminological Classification for an Illustrative Simulation Model

	A. Task Logic	B. Task Load	C. Formal Procedures	D. Attitudes	E. Messages	F. Instrumental Activities
1. Entry-Result	Static entry	Generated entry	Manipulated entry	Static entry and result	Intervening variable	Result
2. Causal Role	Syntatic	Parametric	Syntatic	Variable	Variable	Variable
3. Reference	Environment	Environment	Organization	Organization	Organization	Organization and environment
4. Hyletic Elaboration	Economic	Customer demands	Positions	Affect	Personal or task	Task function
5. Locative Elaboration	—	Point of Input	Task assignment, channels, jurisdiction	Attitude bearers	Who to whom	Agent
6. Temporal Elaboration	Imposed priorities	Diurnal fluctuation	Priorities, phasing	—	—	Lag
7. State-Event	—	Event	—	State	Event	Event
8. Determinacy	Mixed	Stochastic	Determinate	Determinate	Stochastic	Determinate
9. Scale	—	Category	—	Interval	Category	Category

that are postulated for the effective environment within which the organization operates. In the present case these rules could presumably be derived from the study of marketing economics. Task logic is an explicit entry and is concerned with a syntactic description of the environment. The specific causal role of task logic in this model has two aspects. First, it determines the task load imposed on the group. In life, the load would be affected by group activity also, but this feedback loop is omitted in the model. A second capacity in which the task logic acts is in setting a utility score on various instrumental activities, depending on the time of their execution. These contingencies are reflected in the hyletic and temporal elaboration of the task logic.

Task load in the illustrative model is not entered explicitly in detail but is instead generated from certain parameters of the task logic. It is therefore considered as a parametric term and is of course descriptive of the environment. Task load may be elaborated in all three modes. Here the hyletic elaboration consists in the specification of customer demands. The locative elaboration indicates the physical points (for example, service counters) at which inputs occur. Temporal elaboration specifies the fluctuations in task input rate during a given day, week, or year. Strictly speaking, these elaborations are built into the task logic itself, but it is rather more natural to identify them with the substantive term. In relationship to the final three distinctions, task load is expressed as a succession of discrete random events. An alternative expression would suggest the continuous rates that are a determinate function of task logic parameters.

Formal procedure is the organizational counterpart of the task logic and, like the latter, is a syntactic term. Unlike task logic, the formal procedure is manipulated systematically in order to study the effects of specialization. Formal procedure is quite extensively elaborated in the illustrative model. There is a specification for the particular task units clustered together and the standard reaction to particular task load items. The allocation of tasks to persons or departments is stipulated, and formal channels of communication and lines of authority are indicated. Temporal elaboration includes a statement about the priorities of task load items in case of conflict, and the normal succession of informational and instrumental processes. Formal procedure is described here as determinate since all prescriptions are given in categorical form. As with task logic, the state-event and scale distinctions are not directly applicable to this syntactic statement.

Attitude covers the social climate of the organization and the job-related morale of participants. At the beginning of each simulation cycle a certain value is entered as part of the initial configuration, and the final value is printed out as one of the dependent variables of interest. Attitudes are identified by their affective content such as job satisfaction and liking for other members of the organization, and the bearer of the attitude is specified. There is no special need for temporal specification except to indicate the terminal value. In terms of the final three distinctions, attitudes are represented as part of a state description of the organizational members and they are assumed to be measurable on an interval scale; thus conceptual operations such as superimposition of attitude modifiers and averaging are presumably justified. Attitudes are hypothesized to vary as a determinate function of the number of messages from other team members and of the payoff from instrumental activities. An alternative would be to represent attitudes as categorical states governed by certain transition matrices (cf. Cohen, 1958).

Messages are wholly dependent on other existing state variables of the system and on the task load. In the model we suppose they are not of direct interest and are not recorded, hence occur only as ephemera in the simulation process, for use only by the theorist in conceptualizing the model. Messages may be specified in terms of content to any extent required; here it is assumed sufficient to identify them as task or social messages. Locative elaboration specifies the source and receiver, and temporal elaboration describes their time of occurrence.

In this model social messages are considered as occurring with a certain probability determined by the existing friendship attitudes between persons, and task messages as governed by task load and by organizational procedures. To illustrate the latter, suppose person A receives a certain customer order; he then contracts persons B, C, etc., in a certain priority specified in organizational procedure. Since task load is a stochastic variable, it is natural to consider messages as stochastic. Alternative treatments of messages are possible; for example, the mean rates of message transmission between persons can be regarded as state variables varying continuously and rigidly determined by interpersonal attitudes and task load inputs.

The *instrumental activities* of the organization, or some criterion measure thereof, constitute the basic results of the simulation study. They are organizational variables insofar as they describe the activity of the system, but in some cases—for example, sales—they are also assumed to have a direct environmental effect. The elaboration of instrumental activities entails a substantive account of their economic function and identification of the responsible agents. A form of temporal elaboration would be to measure the lag between occurrence of a task load element —for example, a customer demand—and execution of the corresponding instrumental activity. These detailed elaborations would not ordinarily be preserved in the printout, but would be represented by summary indices.

Instrumental activities in the illustrative model occur as a determinate function of task load or associated messages, and are expressed as discrete events in category form. Like the other event-type variables in the model, instrumental activity might be alternatively expressed as continuously varying profiles, specifying the momentary expenditure of effort on each task-relevant dimension.

This synopsis is based on a tentative framework for describing terms of a simulation model. Undoubtedly the distinctions illustrated here will require further revision when they are put to use. They will have served their present purpose if they suggest, first, the kinds of options open to the theorist in formulating a model and, second, the potential advantage of placing the required decisions within the context of an explicit, systematic framework.

SIMULATION LANGUAGE

The foregoing paragraphs have placed a heavy emphasis on the latitude which the theorist has in formulating a model. It should be observed that, in the present era of computer simulation, the actual choices made seem to be based as often on the affinity between certain programming languages and the respective poles of description as they are on purely conceptual or scientific grounds. Such affinities undoubtedly exist; as an obvious example, the list-processing languages lend themselves well to categorical description while algebraic languages are more convenient for continuous or graded formulations.

Of course the choice of a programming language may itself have been based on a judgment as to its scientific suitability for the problem at hand, but such judgments are also susceptible to historical accident and to convenience. Moreover the programming languages most used at present in simulation models are not well suited to mixed formulations even though such hybridization may be strongly indicated. To illustrate, observations of groups suggest that their learning is often characterized by relatively gradual adjustment and consolidation, interspersed with dramatic modifications in procedure. The former aspect of group development may be very conveniently characterized by continuous functions, but the latter aspect suggests that this continuity should be taken with a grain of saltation. Existing computer languages seem to nudge the theorist in one direction or another and to discourage these mixed formulations.

Perhaps the most important thing to stress at this point is that the terminological choices that are made—for whatever reason—are not inconsequential from a psychological standpoint, even in those cases where two phrasings are equivalent in the informational or logical sense. First, there is the question of how rapidly and smoothly the model will mature as a function of the initial formulation. Even if the ultimate description of a real world process is not seriously affected, the initial formulation certainly influences the rate at which errors are detected and corrected. For example, it seems likely that minor logical flaws or small substantive discrepancies may find lurking-places more easily in stochastic models than they do in deterministic models, other things being equal. In another area of investigation, there must presently be several dozen rival stochastic learning theories that connot be dislodged by existing empirical evidence (Galanter and Miller, 1959). This does not, of course, detract from the usefulness of stochastic models but it suggests that processes should not be assumed aleatory if they can be formulated as well in deterministic fashion.

A more serious danger is that the initial formulation may in some way lead to a cumulative Whorfian distortion of the picture that emerges of the underlying dynamics of the system. As remarked above, the symbolic language employed affects the sort of intervening variables and explanatory constructs that are likely to be posited. To the extent that these are hypostatized, they may become very difficult to eradicate from later versions of the model. In this connection a particular risk is imposed by the process of aggregation. The familiar pitfall here is the assumption of organizational characteristics having no well-defined basis in the behavior of individual organization members (e.g., "group mind," "group cohesiveness").

The most secure safeguard against conceptual errors that may creep in through the choice of a programming language, or of specific terminological alternatives, is a systematic testing procedure; an attempt to specify such a procedure is offered below. In addition, however, it would seem that some very worthwhile methodological research might be conducted in the translation of existing models from one terminological framework to another one as different as possible. As examples, it would be interesting to see whether the General Problem Solver (now couched in IPL V) or the WANG algorithm model (now in Lisp) could be expressed, however clumsily, in a Fortrantype programming language.

As a final cautionary note on this topic, it should not be forgotten that, quite apart from the choices open to the theorist in selecting a simulation terminology, the basic nature of the digital computer may impose certain ineluctable constraints on the kinds of hypotheses that are examined and on the ways in which variables are expressed. Even with loops and parallel processing capabilities, computer programs imply a sequential ordering of processes that to some extent violates nature. It would be most unfortunate if a generation of theorists were, themselves, being subtly programmed by this seemingly compliant *factotum*.

TESTING THE COMPUTER MODEL

This section will describe a multistage testing procedure and discuss the modifications which may result from such tests. Four stages of testing are suggested: internal tests; preliminary empirical tests, secondary validation, and process comparison. For each stage of testing several questions are considered: the breadth of sampling of the explicitly introduced independent variables; the intensity of sampling, that is, the number of data runs that are obtained at particular points; the sort of output which should be examined; and the nature of tests and criteria to be applied. It should be understood that the rather pedantic ordering of the tests here given is for expository purposes only; in practice the tests described might be combined in various ways, might be finessed entirely, or might occur in a different order from the one here followed.

INTERNAL ANALYSIS

As here understood, internal analysis concerns not only logical properties of the model but also the general behavior of the model independent of its correspondence with any specific set of data. Many of the discrepancies in this respect will ordinarily be disposed of during the initial formulation and programming of the model. However, even this automatic culling should be more effective if there is a specific check-list to keep in mind.

Important tests are as follows: (1) Are the postulated functional relationships mutually consistent? (2) Are processes unambiguously defined over the relevant domain of independent variables? (3) Do the functional relationships conform to the general pattern intended? and (4) Are substantive invariances and boundary conditions preserved? The first two questions are essentially logical, and the second two are quasi-substantive, although they can be investigated without any direct comparison with data.

Each of the suggested tests points to certain critical sampling regions, that is, distinct configurations of explicit input variables that should be studied. For example, in order to examine mutual compatibility of the assumptions, as well as the degree to which boundary conditions and invariances are preserved, the critical point of test would seem to be at extreme values of the independent variables. Any tendency for a model to come apart at the seams or to exhibit runaway growth processes is most apt to be revealed at these extreme points. A second consideration, however, is that something should happen over the normal operating range of the model; a model is unlikely to be fruitful or suggestive if it makes differential performance predictions only for extreme values of the input variables. From this standpoint, then, it is desirable to investigate the interior of the domain; an additional reason for exploring intermediate values is to determine whether functional relationships observed for extreme values tend to be monotonic. Still a third consideration is that the model should be scrutinized with particular care at those points for which the results can most easily be evaluated by common sense reasonings or with the aid of analytical mathematical models. If the simulation model behaves appropriately in these more comprehensible regions, there is some cause for confidence in its behavior under more complex conditions. The net implication of these remarks may appear to be that one should test the model everywhere. Fortunately this is almost literally possible with computers, the limiting factor being the willingness of the theorist to examine and digest the results once obtained. In any particular case, however, one or the other of the foregoing considerations should take precedence and guide the selection of independent conditions.

Having established an appropriate sampling range, it remains to specify the intensity of sampling, that is, the number of simulation cycles obtained in the vicinity of a particular initial configuration. Here the question of interest might be the standard error of estimate of dependent variables or, in some cases, the continuity of functional relationships at certain points. Under special conditions it may not be necessary to obtain more than one estimate of each independent configuration. For example, if there is a known linear relation between some independent variable and the output, then the standard error of estimate can be obtained in the form of deviations from linear regression. In general, if functional relationships are continuous, the error of estimation may be judged by deviations from best-fitting curves.

The variability of estimates enters into an evaluation of the model in several ways. If the computed output varies inordinately relative to the degree of jitter explicitly introduced in the input variables, the model is unlikely to be stable enough for useful prediction. In addition, some foreknowledge of the variance is important in a test of the model's validity. This is particularly true if the variance is not uniform over the range of input configurations—that is, if there is inherently greater variability in the output data at certain regions of operation.

For the sake of concreteness a few representative internal tests may be suggested for the communication-performance problem discussed above:

1. The model presumably contains functional relationships describing frequency of communication in terms of task input and also relating

frequency of communication to interpersonal attitudes. One obvious test is whether the predictions from these functional relationships are in conflict at any point—that is, whether there is "play" enough for both factors to operate.

2. There are natural limits on the maximum message rates for individuals and the maximum message rates possible for the organization as a whole. For example, no one person may be talking more than 100 percent of the time and no channel may be used more than 100 percent of the time. There must be provisions in the model to insure that these limits are not violated.

3. The model should guarantee that the number of people in the group, the number of messages transmitted and other discrete items will remain equal to, or greater than, zero.

4. If the relationship between communication and task load is assumed to be positive over all levels of the latter, it should be determined whether this, and similar relationships, do obtain in the simulated data.

PRELIMINARY EMPIRICAL TESTS

The tests suggested here compare the simulation with a set of empirical target data which has been available during the construction of the model. It should be accepted in advance that, insofar as any postulates built in the model are ad hoc with respect to these data, this cannot be taken as a confirming test of the model. It is a necessary rather than a sufficient test of its validity.

It is in keeping with this objective that the statistical test selected should not measure gross "goodness of fit" but should instead be designed to examine those specific aspects of the model in which it seems to follow the target data and the points at which there are appreciable discrepancies. Visual inspection may be sufficient to determine relative agreement: if not, it would seem that some multivariate analysis technique could be devised that explicitly indicates the strengths and weaknesses of the simulation (Grant, 1962).

The tests that are relevant to this stage of testing include (1) the general functional parallelism of the computed output and the empirical data —whether the same variables tend to be related in both and whether they are related in the same direction, (2) whether the dependent data are descriptively similar to the available empirical data, and (3) whether there is fine structure reproduction; that is, whether the variability and other details of the simulated data incorporate or capture corresponding features in the empirical data.

The range of independent variables examined for this test stage should obviously match as closely as possible the corresponding independent variables in the empirical data. However this matching may not be automatic, particularly where there is an indirect measure of such variables as friendship. For this reason it often will be necessary to adjust the sampling range of the computer model in order to obtain order-of-magnitude alignment with empirical data; more detailed comparison would follow this gross adjustment. Finally the intensity of sampling should be such as to place the simulation data on at least as solid a basis as are the target data at corresponding points. If fine structure simulation is intended, it will also be necessary to compare the corresponding data not only for mean values but also for variability and other distributional features.

SECONDARY VALIDATION

As soon as the model provides a reasonable fit to a set of target data, the objective becomes one of showing that the model can be predictive for an essentially new situation. The problem of what is new is, however, a difficult one. Generalization to new data within the same domain of independent variation merely demonstrates the reliability of the empirical target data. On the other hand, it is too much to expect absolutely fresh flowers from a field as well trodden as that of organization theory, and the requirement that a model should generate surprising results may be over-stringent.

Thus it seems advisable to separate out several criteria for this secondary validation process. One criterion is the predictive scope of the model, and the other is its heuristic value. These are, in general, related but there is no strict logical dependence. It is quite possible for a model to be highly predictive over a wide range of phenomena but to give only humdrum predictions simply because the phenomena are familiar and well understood. On the other hand the model may give surprising and correct predictions within a narrow range yet still be quite wrong when used more broadly.

Although the surprise value of the model may carry more weight as far as its acceptability is concerned, scope is probably the more fundamental consideration. However if scope is to be elevated to primary importance as a criterion, it should be understood to include the degree to which the model articulates with other models and theories concerning related phenomena. Certainly the "environment" in which a model must prove its continued usefulness is characterized as distinctively by the presence of other theoretical postulations as it is by the body of established facts.

With these criteria in mind, it is clear that the sampling process should ideally be such that the model is interrogated for the whereabouts of its own "crucial" experiments. That is, it should be possible to program simulation runs in such a way as to test the limits over which the special dependent relationships characterizing the model will hold, and to suggest points of inflection or inversion of those relationships that can then be investigated in the laboratory.

PROCESS CORRESPONDENCE

If the computer simulation model is to be used as a conceptual or explanatory tool, process correspondence is absolutely essential; that is, the model will have explanatory value only to the extent that it reduces the overall operation of organizations to an articulated set of comprehensible and, presumable, testable mechanisms.

What is meant by "process correspondence" is roughly that the same things go on inside the black box, or the transfer function relating environmental inputs to subsequent outputs, in the simulation model and in its real-world counterpart. This is a highly ambiguous definition, however, and it is worth some space to try to develop a more useful picture of process correspondence. We begin by noting two tempting but, as we believe, narrow positions that may be taken in this matter.

One position is that process correspondence entails nothing more than the similarity of the interim output variables for the simulated and empirical systems. That is, does the simulated model, beginning with certain environmental conditions, transform them to a similar terminal set of environmental conditions through a set of steps similar to those of the observed empirical counterpart? Granting this test to be valid (in fact, trivially valid at the level of molecular disturbances), it is not directly helpful for several reasons. First, there may be real difficulties in measuring the interim products in many organizational processes (what, for example, is the instantaneous status of a certain piece of information?). Second, we are not, in general, interested in simulating just a single process but in studying the behavior of an organization over a variety of processes and of input conditions. Mere identity of interim products on each of these individually provides a criterion of correspondence but, in itself, gives little insight into the physiology of the organism.

A second position adopts the other extreme of descriptive verisimilitude: does the simulation model seem to engage in the same activities as are observed in the organization when faced with the same circumstances? To underscore the danger of this position it is not entirely unfair to cite the checkered history of television. There we used to see wrestlers displaying all the signs of rage and agony, and quiz contestants all the signs of deep cerebration; yet we now know that those life-like processes had little bearing on the final outcomes.

In order to examine the question more closely, a rather detailed notational scheme is required: Let X_i^0 denote the initial state of an environmental variable (perhaps multidimensional or vector-valued) of substantive type i, and X_i^T denote its terminal state after processing by the real or simulated organization over a period, T. Further, let G^T represent the total effect of the real group considered as an operator, and C^T represent the total effect of the simulation model considered as an operator. Then the minimal requirement for the validity of the model is established by the identity of the terminal products; symbolically:

$$G^T X_1^0 = X_1^T \qquad\qquad C^T X_1^0 = X_1^T$$
$$G^T X_2^0 = X_2^T \qquad\qquad C^T X_2^0 = X_2^T$$
$$\cdots\cdots\cdots \qquad\qquad \cdots\cdots\cdots$$
$$G^T X_n^0 = X_n^T \qquad\qquad C^T X_n^0 = X_n^T$$

(It is here assumed that a satisfactory way has been discovered for relating the X variables in the simulated environment to those in the real environment.) This result might be called *black box* correspondence, and it is the primary concern of the test phases described above. Although the parallelism of initial input, or abutting environmental states, and terminal outputs suggests strongly that there are similar mechanisms at work, it does not demonstrate it conclusively.

Proceeding from any specific instance of initial and terminal state agreement, it may be possible to discover interim coincidence, symbolically:

$$G X_i^0 \; /= X_i^1 \qquad\qquad C X_i^0 \;\; = X_i^1$$
$$G X_i^1 \;\; = X_i^2 \qquad\qquad C X_i^1 \;\; = X_i^2$$
$$\cdots\cdots\cdots \qquad\qquad \cdots\cdots\cdots$$
$$G X_i^{T-1} = X_i^T \qquad\qquad C X_i^{T-1} = X_i^T$$

Each input variable or state X_i, for which this parallel holds, and each temporal point, $0 \ldots T$, for which there is coincidence, constitutes a case of *transfer correspondence*. Thus the overall degree of transfer correspondence may be partially ordered in terms of the range of input variables and of the density of interim values for which there is coincidence.

Left in this form, however, this is a rather tricky criterion. If the environmental variables, X_i, refer to complex, multidimensional conditions, then the incidence of strict agreement between processes may become vanishingly small, even if the systems are essentially identical. On the other hand, if the variables are compared one dimension at a time, then agreement is non-diagnostic; assuming a continuous monotonic progression in each dimension, there will be an infinity of coincidences between the two systems.

The measurement problem posed by this is the one of defining a "distance" between the paths followed by comparable environmental variables and intergrating this distance over the entire time of traversal. The most obvious measure of this kind, a Euclidean distance function, may entail assumptions—such as interval scaling of the separate variables and isometry between varibles—that cannot ordinarily be justified. An alternative is to compare the times at which the two systems pass through corresponding state values. An example will illustrate the two measures.

Figure 4 schematizes a process comparison between a real organization and a simulation model in which a certain two-dimensional variable is transformed from an initial state $X_i^0 = (0,0)$ to a terminal state $X_i^{10} = (5,5)$. It is supposed that the simulation program procedes by successive advances along the x and y axes whereas the live organization follows a more irregular path. Referring to an earlier remark, notice that exact coincidence of the two paths occurs at only five points. Presumably there would be even less coincidence in a problem of realistic dimensionality.

As a first step (already incorporated in Figure 4), intervals of measurement for both paths are made proportional to the total time of traversal. The suggested measures of path difference then are the discrepancy in the state values reached at particular times or in the intervals at which the two processes first touch each level of the component dimensions of X_i. Numerical values for this example are given in parallel columns at the bottom of the figure. Comparisons between state values or traversal times on each dimension might consist of correlations, mean-squared differences, or summed absolute differences.

This procedure is directly applicable only if there is terminal coincidence of environmental variables or "products." This condition has however already been assumed a necessary one for the further investigation of process correspondence. Given terminal coincidence, the spatial distance measure between paths depends on the metric properties of the environmental variables, but the temporal measure does not. Either comparison procedure may indicate not only the overall degree of transfer correspondence but also the particular aspects of the process in which the real and simulated systems are most at variance.

The other major aspect of the question of process correspondence concerns the similarity of activities by means of which the simulation model and the organization accomplish a given transformation. Determination of any such similarity depends on the availability of measures describing the real or simulated organization, but cannot, in the present view, be based directly on such measures. It requires a more conclusive test of homeomorphism which has to take into account both use and consequences of various operators.

FIGURE 4

A Schematic Comparison of Path Difference in the
State and Temporal Domains

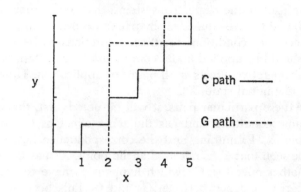

	Position					Traversal Time			
	x axis		y axis			x axis		y axis	
	C	G	C	G		C	G	C	G
0	0	0	0	0	0	0	0	0	0
1	1	1	0	0	1	1	1	2	3
2	1	2	1	0	2	3	2	4	4
Time 3	2	2	1	1	Scale 3	5	7	6	5
Units 4	2	2	2	2	Units 4	7	8	8	6
5	3	2	2	3	5	9	10	10	9
6	3	2	3	4					
7	4	3	3	4	$\Sigma\,d^2$	7		7	
8	4	4	4	4					
9	5	4	4	5					
10	5	5	5	5					
$\Sigma\,d^2$	5		5						

In order to illustrate the required test, consider the following paired
sets of measured sequences:

$$G_a X_i^0 = X_i^1 \qquad C_u X_i^0 = X_i^1 \qquad G_a X_j^0 = X_j^1 \qquad C_u X_j^0 = X_j^1$$
$$G_b X_i^1 = X_i^2 \qquad C_v X_i^1 = X_i^2 \qquad G_b X_j^1 = X_j^2 \qquad C_z X_j^1 = X_j^2$$
$$G_c X_i^2 = X_i^3 \qquad C_w X_i^2 = X_i^3 \qquad G_c X_j^2 = X_j^3 \qquad C_w X_j^2 = X_j^4$$

Here it is assumed that certain transfer correspondences have been determined between G and C for the initial environmental state X_i^0. It is also assumed that the important state variables describing G and C themselves have been recorded at the time these transformations are occurring. The question is, whether we are justified in equating the actions used in the respective systems, that is, whether G_a and C_u, G_b and C_v, G_c and C_w are equivalent by pairs? According to the present position, the necessary conditions for these operations to be equivalent are that they should be applied under comparable circumstances and should have similar operative effects at all points of application. This must be checked for a new initial state, X^0.

For these particular pairs, it will be noted, first, that C_u is used under the same conditions and has the same effect as G_a for a second state variable, X_j. Examining next the correspondence between G_b and C_v, it will be seen that C_v is not used at the point, X_j^1, as G_b is, but is replaced by another operator, C_z, which happens to have the same effect as G_b. The correspondence between G_b and C_v fails because the two systems react in different ways to the same environmental state, X_j. The associated form of correspondence (in this case lacking) may be referred to as *activity* correspondence.

Finally, C_w cannot be equated with G_c because it has a different effect when both are applied at X_j^2. This aspect of correspondence, present in the pair G_a and C_u but lacking in the pair G_c and C_w, will be referred to as *operator* correspondence. It might be noted that the distinction between activity and operator correspondence has somewhat the same implications as the distinction made in comparative physiology between "homology" and "analogy." In the former case, the emphasis is on the locus of involvement and, in the latter case, on functional effects.

In summary, the question of process correspondence has two major aspects; one relating to the results achieved by two systems under comparison and the other relating to direct measures on the organization system or its presumptive model. These two aspects are themselves compound, and any final measure of correspondence will likely be one of degree. In this discussion, we have been able only to hint at the necessary measurement procedures.

REVISION

Typically, necessary modifications and expansions of a model will be indicated by the nature of the diagnostic tests which the model has failed to satisfy. There are, however, certain general considerations on revision which will be the concern of this section. A principal objective is to present an ordered typology of revision procedures.

Computer simulation models permit, and indeed invite, more extensive tinkering than do analytical mathematical models. It is comparatively easy to add and make changes in a computer model and to investigate consequences. However, there are several reasons for introducing the changes both gradually and systematically. One reason is that this may be the best advised tactic for developing the model in question: that is, if small changes are unsuccessful, to introduce gradually greater changes until the model satisfies the criteria that are set for it. Second, the effects of a particular change may give useful insight into the working of the model only if the changes are introduced gradually enough so that their consequences can be traced. And, finally, any modification is likely to increase the complexity of the model; hence, generally speaking, the more gingerly modifications are introduced, the less complex will be the final product.

The proposed typology of revisions will be presented in an assumed order of increasing gravity. That is, the earlier presented revisions will be those which presumably have the least effect on the basic structure and substantive implications of the model; later revisions may entail more radical effects.

Calibrational revisions, first, are those which do not modify either the universe of discourse or the explicit form of assumed functional relations. Such revisions are aimed at increasing the descriptive correspondence between the model and empirical data. They do not necessarily imply any second thoughts about the basic mechanisms which are incorporated in the model or in the domain of relevance of the system being described.

Within this general category there is a secondary ordering, again becoming increasingly radical. The conservative extreme in this ordering consists of multiplying the variables in the model by a constant factor or adding a constant to algebraic variables. This will not at all affect linear functions hypothesized in the model, nor will it affect the general form of more complex relationships. A slightly more radical change is to impose a nonlinear transformation on a variable—for example, to transform it by a log or square-root function. Although this may have a more far-reaching effect on the mechanics of a model, it will not alter relations which depend only on ordinal properties; nor will it affect the general pattern of dependence between variables.[4] Lastly, the most profound changes of a calibrational nature are those in which the terms are reidentified in such a way as to alter their functional relationships.

To give these gradations concreteness, suppose one aspect of a com-

---

4. This statement requires some qualification since, for example, correlations between the mean and variance of a measure may be reduced to zero by transforming the measure. The statement then applies to "real" rather than artifactual relationships.

munication model is an assumed linear function relating social liking to the rate of communication between pairs of group members and that the model is to be compared with a set of data in which measured socio-metric ratings are related to observed frequency of communication. A first revision might be made in order to equate the mean and variance of the liking and communication terms in the model with those in the tar-get data. If this did not produce a satisfactory agreement of simulated and empirical results, it might then be attempted to relate the sociometric rating (still measured in the same fashion) to the probability of com-munication within a given time interval, thus setting an upper limit on the magnitude of the effect. Finally, it might be concluded that the sociometric measure as estimated was actually one of status equivalence, implying that the frequency of communication would be a function of the similarity of total sociometric scores obtained by two individuals rather than of their mutual sociometric ratings for each other. This third form of revision, without actually changing the universe of discourse, puts the terms in a new light and suggests new dynamics.

Functional revisions are those in which there is an explicit modi-fication of the relationships among variables. The qualifier, "explicit," is emphasized because there may be equivalent changes induced by cali-brational revision of the variables themselves (as illustrated above). Functional revision is not assumed to enlarge or essentially alter the uni-verse of discourse of the model. The simplest form of functional revision entails only a change in the assumed relation between two variables—for example, a linear relation is changed to an exponential one. A more far-reaching sort of functional revision would be the decision that two independent variables originally assumed to have an additive effect are perhaps compensatory or facilitative.

Several special types of functional revision should be noted, as they are of wide applicability. The first is the gradual refinement of a relation in such a way as to take account of specific contingencies. To illustrate, a first approximation model might contain, as terms, the probabilities that any person, A, will communicate with any other person in the group. The refined model, then, might introduce the conditional probabilities that A communicates with anyone in the group given conditions X, Y, Z, . . . or, again, it might specify the probabilities that A will communicate with specific persons B, C, D, . . . given certain conditions. Such revision would typify the refinement of models which are initially aggregative in the hyletic and locative domains. Corresponding refinement is possible for the temporal domain, but it requires somewhat more discussion.

Suppose that two persons or other system components, A and B, jointly control some state variable, X. Using a terminology introduced earlier, this operative control may be represented by sequences of the type:

$$AX^0 = X^1$$
$$BX^1 = X^2$$
$$AX^2 = X^3$$
$$BX^3 = X^4$$
$$\cdots \cdots$$

That is, the output of either agent is treated as the input for the other agent in a continued alternation sequence.

The difficulty with this formulation is that most social interaction processes do not follow such a punctilious schedule. Typically the operators act simultaneously or else the several agents may act over varying time intervals. This is most troublesome if the operators, A and B, do not commute, that is, if the compound effect, A B, differs from the compound effect, B A.

This problem may be handled by requiring the operators A and B to take smaller bites—that is, by finding "roots" of the operators, say $A^{1/k}$, such that $A^{1/k}$ applied k times has the same effect as the original A. Then the simultaneous operation over an interval of length, l, by both operators may be represented by $(A^{1/k}B^{1/k})^l$ and successive operation over intervals of length l and m respectively may be represented by the term $(A^{1/k})^l \ (B^{1/k})^m$. The indicated revision then is to find an order of magnitude for the operator effect for which such representations give descriptive results.[5]

Substantive revision involves an enrichment of the system, an expansion of the universe of discourse. This raises two kinds of questions: first, of the intimacy of interaction between the original and supplementary systems; and, second, of the degree of comparability of the old and new variables. These are presented most readily by example. Suppose a first ap-

---

5. The following indication of proof is not intended to be rigorous:
Suppose there are two operators, A and B, which are noncommutative and for which, say:
$$AB - BA - D.$$
Next, suppose that, for both A and B, it is possible to find "roots", $A^{1/k}$, $B^{1/k}$, such that $(A^{1/k})^k = A$; $(B^{1/k})^k = B$.
Then consider the difference:
$$(A^{1/k}B^{1/k})^k - (B^{1/k}A^{1/k})^k = D_k.$$
It must be shown that D_k approaches O as k increases. Premultiplying through by $A^{1/k}$ one obtains:
$$A^{1/k}(A^{1/k}B^{1/k})^k - (A^{1/k}B^{1/k})^k A^{1/k} = A^{1/k}D_k.$$
As k increases, $A^{1/k}$ approaches the identity operator $A^0 = I$, hence the left-hand member of the equation goes to 0, and D_k must also vanish. Validity of the proof depends on the assumption that the roots do indeed exist and that the exponentiated products remain bounded.

proximation model of organizational communication is based entirely on normative considerations, that is, on how much communication is required by the task messages. It is almost certain that a model thus begun will require padding out in terms of social (non-task) communication. One question, then, is whether the latter can be treated as a separate system conforming to its own laws and not affecting or affected by task processes, or whether the non-task communications interact directly with task communications. A second question is whether the non-task communications have the same properties with respect to the other terms of the system as do the task communications, for example, whether liking is similarly increased by a given number of task of non-task communications.

The process of revision and the resulting modified model will tend to be simpler if new terms act in functional parallelism. It will also be simplified if there is a valid convertibility between the separate terms. If both conditions hold, a model may be augmented by simple superposition of the two processes. In the illustrative case the frequency of task and social communication, respectively, may be predicted from their separate functional rules and the total communication obtained by adding the two. Justification for these simplifying conditions must come from the correspondence between the model and the observed organizational behavior. It appears, though, that a more penetrating investigation could be made of theoretical aspects of the amalgamation of subsystem components. In particular, what is required is a "dimensional analysis" of organizational variables, that is, an investigation into what constitutes apples and oranges and the way in which apple systems and orange systems may interact (Langhaar, 1951; Ipsen, 1960).

Before leaving the topic of revision, it might be noted that, while many of the modifications discussed—and particularly the more complicated ones—must be based on fairly close auscultation of the model, it appears quite possible that certain revisions may be pre-programmed. As a first step in this direction, the computer might be programmed to compare simulation results with empirical results and to follow a systematic calibration process which minimizes the discrepancy. As has been noted, however, (see Minsky, 1963) this may be an extremely inefficient process unless some of the characteristics of the model are known in advance.

SUMMARY OF CRITERIA

Five general classes of criteria underly the foregoing discussion: coherence, validity (or predictiveness), scope (or generalizability), transparency, and parsimony. The ordering given is intended to convey a roughly defined priority in which the criteria should be met.

The coherence criterion concerns whether the assumptions on which the simulation model is based are sufficiently well defined to generate clear implications for some set of external data, whether the implications turn out to be right or wrong. The criterion includes the requirement that the terms of the model should retain the status that is intended for them; that is, parameters should remain constant, state variables should describe possible states, and independent variables should determine functionally the dependent variables in the system.

The second criterion is that of validity. The question is how well the computed outputs of the simulation model match the available empirical data under similar conditions. There are several facets of this matching: whether there is general duplication of phenomena—for example, whether a monotonic functional relationship is reflected in the simulation data; whether the same points of inflection occur; and whether there are comparable interaction effects between the independent variables. A second level of agreement concerns whether the simulation results are qualitatively and quantitatively similar to those of the empirical system. A third question concerns the variability of the system; ideally, both the between-organizations and within-organizations variability of behavior should compare with empirical results in the same task environment. It has been emphasized that the validity requirement entails both descriptive and functional fidelity. A successful model is one that continues to yield a descriptive picture of the organization under transformations by the assumed independent manipulations. It was suggested, moreover, that statistical tests should not be limited to gross "goodness-of-fit" but should indicate particular aspects of the simulated data which are most or least in agreement with empirical data.

The third criterion invoked was that of scope: over how wide a range of application does the model remain valid? To this consideration may be added the question of how well the model articulates with other hypotheses relating to the same domain of organizational processes.

The fourth criterion is that of transparency; that is, the degree to which a model is explanatory, the extent to which it reduces to meaningful and, presumably, testable components. A good model in this sense is one that suggests the points at which the predictions will be of an especially interesting or fruitful nature. It is also one which suggests its own limitations.[6]

6. Toulmin (1961, pp. 100 and 203) gives the example of finding a scientific explanation of the death on their birthdays of three children in one family.

The fifth criterion is that of parsimony. This is probably a secondary criterion but an extremely important one. It has at least three bases. The first basis is the well-known aesthetic appeal of an economic model. It is not a frivolous consideration; it has been identified time and again as a decisive factor in directing the thoughts of prominent theorists and in tipping the scales of general acceptance when competing theories could not otherwise be evaluated differentially.

The other two bases are perhaps more down to earth. One is the greater transparency of a parsimonious model (other things being equal) and the consequently greater suggestiveness and sharpness of implication. A final argument for parsimony is that it probably increases the viability of a model. In the present view, the special postulations tacked onto a model in disregard of parsimony have much the same long-run effect as the furbelows developed by trilobites and dinosaurs: immediate adaptability is obtained at the expense of total unsuitedness to new problems.

RECAPITULATION

A number of uses for computers in conjunction with organization research and theory were discussed and the simulation model was singled out as the special focus of interest. It was observed, however, that other applications are useful and not incompatible with the more puristic objective of this discussion.

Recognizing that the simulation model as here defined lies in the mainstream of the hypothetico-deductive scientific tradition, there are two strong implications for its further treatment; first, that it must be closely integrated with more conventional methods of scientific research —that is, analytical mathematical models and laboratory investigations— and, second, that there is no such thing as a "good enough" model. Testing and revision as here described is not a terminable process.

It was suggested that simulation models could be approached from several rather distinct initial assumptions labeled Organismic, Idealized, and Segmental. Each of these achieves a workable first approximation at the cost of certain explicit oversimplifications that are presumably repaired as the model is developed. The model may be aimed at an explanation of the development of organizations through time, of the asymptotic performance of organizations, or of the influence of the organization on the participant individuals. These processes interact very closely, but their separate investigation is warranted by differences in time scale and in the salience of certain functional relationships.

Because computer simulation affords complete control and a wide range of options, it is important to examine the status of terms in such a model as compared with more conventional scientific approaches. Three sets of classificatory distinctions were offered. The first set concerned the functional status of variables vis-à-vis the theorist and the hypothesized organization. A second set of distinctions concerned aggregation or extension along three axes: the locative (personal), the hyletic (substantive or referential), and the temporal. A final set of distinctions concerned the language in which the model is couched.

Although these distinctions represent a wide range of options, it was noted that there may be hidden constraints associated with terminological choices made by the experimenter and perhaps also resulting from the very structure of the simulation process. Methodological study is required to determine the severity of such constraints.

A four-part regimen was suggested for evaluating a model at a given level of development. The first part consists of internal testing and is aimed at both logical properties in the ordinary sense and also at the general conformity of the model to an intuitive or analytic picture of how it should behave in important respects. The second testing phase relates the computed output of the model to a set of target data that have been accessible during formulation. Here it was emphasized that the question is not just gross "goodness-of-fit," but a more detailed statement of where the model departs from observed data. Given such *prima facie* validity, the model may next be extended to "new" regions. It was emphasized that "surprisingness" or novelty of implications is a rather different criterion from scope and may be overstringent. The latter criterion is more fundamental, although it may not be as compelling. The concept of scope as here employed also includes compatibility with the existing body of theory concerning related aspects of the organization.

The last stage of testing covered process correspondence. It was shown that, in addition to "black box" correspondence, defined by comparable input-output relations over a wide range of inputs, at least three other forms of correspondence may be defined. Transfer correspondence refers to the similarity of interim outputs, or, more abstractly, to the temporal path of the process. Activity correspondence relates the internal state of the simulated organization to that of its real-life counterpart. Operator correspondence implies that equivalent internal states have equivalent transfer effects on the environment. It was stressed that the implied equivalence relations cannot be based on the literal similarity of variables, but must be analyzed through a bootstrap process.

Turning to the process of generalizing and revamping a model, the point was made that this should be as gradual and systematic as possible. Several broad types of revision were indicated. Calibrational revision changes the variables and the parameters explicitly. For convenience, one can think of these as successively modifying ratio and interval properties, ordinal properties, and nominal properties of the variables entering into the model. Functional revision involves an explicit alteration in the mechanics of the model or in the arguments of particular functional relations. Several special types of functional revisions were described which are aimed at refinement of the model. The third and generally most far-reaching form of revision entails an extension of the universe of discourse, bringing in new terms and new mechanisms. It was noted that the effects of this type of revision depend upon interconvertibility of the effects and upon whether they are additive or interactional.

Finally, a set of five general classes of criteria were suggested by which a model may be evaluated. These are: coherence, validity, scope, transparency, and economy. The latter two criteria were given particular emphasis because of the suspicion that the relative ease of spawning computer simulation models may weaken extrinsic arguments for these criteria.

A GLANCE AHEAD

Having opened the discussion by noting computer applications that are current but fall short of the simulation model as here defined, it might be appropriate to close with some conceivable applications that seem to transcend current practices. These are suggested in full cognizance of the fact that they are not presently feasible. In compensation for this, there is the now trite observation that to state an apparent impossibility in the computer age is often a useful first step toward bringing it to realization.

The first suggested extension is the conduct of real experiments on the computer. By this, we mean building in the same error components as have been obtained in performance measures of the real organization and imposing experimental conditions as in a laboratory study. While few scientists would accept the findings of such an "experiment" without empirical verification, it might be possible to limit the latter to a spot check of sample results.

There are several types of investigation for which such experimentation seems especially suitable. One is to obtain a volume of parametric data for which the results would be essentially interpolative and not controversial. Here the use of the computer as opposed to live organizations is largely a matter of economy. However, computers might also be used to explore conditions precluded for humanitarian or ethical reasons from empirical investigation—for example, the behavior of an organization under disaster conditions. Such an application is not so much a search for new findings as an extrapolation of results obtained under more attainable conditions. Still, the computer study might pinpoint interactive effects which could then be more closely studied under infrequent natural conditions.

A second extension would be the use of the computer as a construct-generator. One of the great difficulties in theory in the biological and behavioral sciences has been to span levels of analysis, to apply results at one level to problems at another. As is well known, the communication between organic chemistry, biology, neurophysiology, psychology, and sociology has been extremely slow and uncertain. Even where the relevant principles are known at one level, it is extremely difficult to project them to a higher level and, conversely, to reduce the established phenomena at a higher level to those of the lower level. Perhaps the most striking example of this has been in evolutionary theory; the relevant factors here have been known for fifty to a hundred years, yet the task of translating them into a predictive ecology is still very far from complete.

What is suggested then is the possibility of a systematic programmed process akin to the forms of aggregation that the theorist has used in the past in order to make sense of extremely complicated systems, a procedure by means of which one learns not only what an immense number of infinitesimal processes will accomplish, but also obtains a conceptually manageable macrostructure. This becomes an especially important need if theory construction takes the segmental point of departure described earlier. Even supposing that it is possible to predict organizational behavior by entering a sufficiently detailed statement of individual actions and reactions, it is not clear that one can thereby obtain any idea of what is really going on. Granting the primacy of the predictive criterion, it is certain that scientists will not rest content until they can relate their predictions to a set of verbalizable mechanisms.

A kindred extension is the use of the computer as an instrument of genuine induction. In a way, it is odd that there has not been as concerted an attempt in this direction as there has been to develop programs for deductive theorizing. Certainly the special advantages of computers over humans seem as pronounced with respect to inductive as with respect to deductive reasoning. The drawback cannot be a dearth of raw material either; although there are, in the case of organization theory, many types of data for which no adequate measures exist, there are certainly enough solid statistical facts for a good beginning.

Of course the most probable explanation for the failure to develop computer programs for induction is the rather unsatisfactory philosophical and methodological state of the topic. Yet this difficulty itself may be a function of the fact that induction has never been systematically used. The major criticisms of Mills' system of canons, for example, is that they do not sound like what scientists do. It is at least possible that, if the computer were forced to this drudgery, it might lead to the development of an adequate and workable inductive theory. It was Darwin's regret in later years that he had to turn himself into a machine for digesting facts, but this is almost exactly what computers are designed for to begin with.

A final extended use of the computer would be in inter-theory translation. We mean by this more than just a comparative study of the performance of two models on similar data. Rather what is intended is an investigation into the equivalences of terms and syntax of two related theories and, of course, an analysis of their points of divergence. A typical, and familiar, problem to be examined would be whether the difference between two theories is substantive or "merely semantic."

REFERENCES

AFIPS Conference Proceedings, Vol. 25. Spring Joint Computer Conference. Baltimore: Spartan Books, 1964.

Bales, R. F. "Small Group Theory and Research." In R. K. Merton, L. Broom, and L. F. Cottrell, eds., *Sociology Today*. New York: Basic Books, 1959.

Borko, H., ed. *Computer Applications in the Behavioral Sciences*. Englewood Cliffs: Prentice Hall, 1962.

Cohen, B. P. "A Probability Model for Conformity." *Sociometry*, 1958, *21*, 69–81.

Galanter, E. and Miller, G. A. "Some Comments on Stochastic Models and Psychological Theories." In K. Arrow, J. Karlin, P. Suppes, eds., *Mathematical Methods in the Social Sciences*. Stanford: Stanford U. Press, 1959.

Grant, D. A. "Testing the Null Hypothesis and the Strategy and Tactics of Investigating Theoretical Models. *Psychological Rev.*, 1962, 69, 54–61.

Green, B. *Digital Computers in Research: An Introduction for Behavioral and Social Scientists*. New York: McGraw-Hill, 1963.

Guetzgow, H., ed., *Simulation in Social Science: Readings*. Englewood Cliffs: Prentice Hall, 1962.

Gullahorn, J. T. and Gullahorn, J. E. "Computer Simulation of Human Interaction in Small Groups." In *AFIPS Conference Proceedings*. Spring Joint Computer Conference. Baltimore: Spartan Books, 1964.

Homans, G. C. *The Human Group*. New York: Harper, 1950.

Ipsen, D. C. *Units, Dimensions, and Dimensionless Numbers*. New York: McGraw-Hill, 1960.

Langhaar, H. L. *Dimension Analysis and Theory of Models*. New York: J. Wiley, 1951.

Minsky, M. "Steps Toward Artificial Intelligence." In E. Feigenbaum and J. Feldman, eds., *Computers and Thought*. New York: McGraw-Hill, 1963.

Orcutt, G. H., Greenberger, M., Korbel, J., and Ruilin, A. M. *Micro-analysis of Socio-economic Systems: A Simulation Study.* New York: Harper, 1961.

Richardson, L. F. "War Moods." *Psychometrika,* 1948, *13,* 147–174 and 197–232.

Roby, T. B. and Lanzetta, J. T. "Work Group Structure, Communications, and Group Performance." *Sociometry,* 1956, *19,* 105–113.

Rome, S. C. and Rome, B. K. "Computer Simulation Toward a Theory of Large Organizations. In H. Borko, ed., *Computer Applications in the Behavioral Sciences.* Englewood Cliffs: Prentice Hall, 1962.

Siegel, A. I., Wolf, J. J., Borcik, J. D., and Mieble, W. *Digital Simulation of a Submarine Crew Performance, I, Logic of a Psychosocial "Model" for Digitally Simulating Crew Performance.* Report done under Contract NONR–4021(00), FBM, 1964.

Simon, H. A. *Models of Man: Social and Rational.* New York: Wiley, 1957.

Toulmin, S. E. *The Place of Reason in Ethics.* Cambridge: Cambridge U. Press, 1961.

Turing, A. M. "Computing Machinery and Intelligence." *Mind,* 1950, *59,* 433–460.

Whitrow, G. J. *The Natural Philosophy of Time.* London: Thomas Nelson, 1961.